PREFACE

This book lists families who have Texas roots. Most of the approximately 2500 books are in the Library of Congress; The Daughters of the American Revolution Library in Washington, D. C.; or the National Genealogical Society Library in Arlington, Virginia. Those books not available in the Washington, D. C. area are indicated by code in other locations.

No book of this kind can be complete. Many family histories are privately printed and are not in libraries. There may be Texas genealogies published after this book was written. However, the authors have tried to give as complete a list of books about Texas families as possible.

When the authors first planned this book, they believed there would be more genealogies of Texas families than they uncovered. It is interesting to note that very few histories of Texas families were written prior to 1910, although many were written before that time in the New England and Mid-western states. For this reason the authors have added about 60 pages of other books, including county histories and other references to Texas families that will be helpful to any genealogist researching a Texas family.

The authors have also included a list of the major Texas libraries with genealogical collections. We hope and believe that this book will be of substantial assistance to anyone doing research on Texas families.

Donald O. Virdin
October, 1998

Texas Family Histories and Genealogies

Lu Verne V. Hall and *Donald O. Virdin*

HERITAGE BOOKS
2009

HERITAGE BOOKS
AN IMPRINT OF HERITAGE BOOKS, INC.

Books, CDs, and more—Worldwide

For our listing of thousands of titles see our website
at
www.HeritageBooks.com

Published 2009 by
HERITAGE BOOKS, INC.
Publishing Division
100 Railroad Ave. #104
Westminster, Maryland 21157

Copyright © 1999 Lu Verne V. Hall and Donald O. Virdin

All rights reserved. No part of this book may be reproduced or transmitted in any form or by any means, electronic or mechanical, including photocopying, recording or by any information storage and retrieval system without written permission from the author, except for the inclusion of brief quotations in a review.

International Standard Book Numbers
Paperbound: 978-0-7884-1193-9
Clothbound: 978-0-7884-8153-6

CONTENTS

Texas Family Histories and Genealogies	1 – 197
Major Texas Libraries with Genealogical Books	198
Codes to Library Abbreviations & Glossary	199
Texas County Histories and Other Texas Books Useful to Genealogists	200-263
Bibliography	264-265
All Name Index	266-376

A —

ABBOTT – Abbott, Suzanne Wilson
An unfinished tale: the genealogy of Kenneth Dale Abbott, Jr. By Suzanne Wilson Abbott. Lubbock, Tex. S. W. Abbott. c1982-c1984. (LC)

ABERNATHY – Abernathy, Arvord Milner, 1906-
Into the setting sun went the Abernethys, the Bolton, the Davises, the Talbots. Hamilton, Tex. A. M. Abernethy. 1986. (LC)

ABLES – Kleiber, Linda Ables
The Ables and related families. Calvert, Tex. Kleiber. 1976. (DAR)

ABSHIER – Cessna, Thelma Abshier
Footprints of the Abshier family in America. Devers, Tex. Cessna. 1981. (DAR)

ABSTON – Abston, Verna Ann Dolan, 1937-
Eight generations & plus. By Verna Ann (Dolan) Abston. Houston, Tex. V. A. Abston. c1984. (LC)

ADAMS – Baldwin, Emma G.
An Adams-Goolsby genealogy, some descendants of Robert Adams of Virginia, Georgia, and Texas, 1624-1982, and a Shirley generation, some descendants of Thomas Shirley of Virginia, South Carolina, Georgia, and Texas, 1612-1982. Compiled by Emma G. Baldwin. Tenaha, Tex. E. G. Baldwin. c1983. (LC)

ADAMS – Stambaugh, Jack L.
The Adamsons as we see them. Compiled by Jack L. Stambaugh, John E. Robinson. Dallas, Tex. J. L. Stambaugh. 1981. (LC)

ADAMS – Trippet, Pattie Rose
A man called Adam. By Pattie Rose Trippet. Waco, Tex. P. R. Trippet. c1983. (LC)

ADAMS – Vicars, Valeska Bucholz
Adams family: Lorenzo Dow Adams, Joshua Adams and their descendants: collateral lines of Lewellen, Bills, Mohundro, Hardin, Ballenger, and Gaither. Seabrook, Tex. V. B. Vicars. 1980? (LC)

ADAMS – Wood, Eugene Leroy
Some descendants of the Adams, Floyd, and Wood families of Pulaski and Casey Counties of Kentucky. Albuquerque, N. M. Wood. 1967. (DAR)

ADAMS – Woods, Gary Doyle
The Hicks, Adams, Bass, Floyd, Pattilo, and collateral lines, together with family letters, 1840-1868. By Gary Doyle Woods. Salado, Tex. A. Jones Press. 1963. (LC)

ADAMSON – Barnes, Alma Nettie Wilson
Wilson Esther Adamson (1800-1875) and William (1798-1841). Houston, Tex. Barnes. 1979. (DAR)

ADCOCK – O'Kelley, Harold Ernest, 1925-
Four families through Georgia: a southern history of the Adcock, Blackwell, O'Kelley, Yates and related families. By Harold Ernest O'Kelley. San Antonio, Tex. Ninety Seven Twenty Five, Inc. c1985. (LC)

ALDERMAN – Trube, Mattie E. B.
Your family and mine. By Mattie E. B. Trube. Houston, Tex. 1973. (LA)

ALDRIDGE – Aldrich, Arnold Deane
A genealogical survey of the descendants of Moses Aldrich and Arnold Aldrich of Inverness Township, Quebec, Canada. By Arnold Deane Aldrich. Houston, Tex. D. Armstrong Co. c1985. (LC)

ALDRIDGE – Bryson, Deby Alldredge, 1921-
Alldredge, Aldridge roots and branches. By Deby Alldredge Bryson and Mary Neel Trammell. Wyandotte, Okla. Gregath Co. 1990. (LC)

ALDRIDGE – Chambers, Mildred Aldrich
Our Aldrich family. Mildred Aldrich Chambers. Midland, Tex. M. A. Chambers. 1986. (LC)

ALEXANDER – Sanders, R. S., 1921-
The Alexanders of Plum Creek: a genealogical history of ancestors and descendants of Joseph Alexander. By R. S. and Betty Sanders. Abilene, Tex. JL Press. Weinert, Tex. 1989. (LC)

ALLFORD – Alford, Eileen
Alford-Kennedy family history. By Eileen Alford. San Antonio, Tex. 1971. (FW)

ALLEE – Allee, Jonathan
The Allee family. Phoenix, Ariz. Allee. 1973? (DAR)\

ALLEN –
John Edwin Allen, born December 17, 1867, Ector, Texas, and his wife, Delilah Catherine Nelms Allen, born August 23, 1872, Ector, Texas. Bonham? Tex. 1971 (i.e. 1973). (LC)

ALLEN – Allen, Juanita
Allen and their descendants: Ector, Fannin County, Texas, 1867. By Juanita Allen. Houston, Tex. J. Allen. c1982. (LC)

ALLEN – Allen, Juanita Catherine, 1908-
Mrs. Lucia Butler Ford, descendant of a duke of England, pioneer settler of Ector, Texas, Fannin County, 1828. By Juanita Allen. Houston, Tex. Allen.c1960. (LC)

ALLEN – Allen, J. D.
History of George L. Allen and their descendants, 1745-1960. By J. D. Allen. Fort Worth, Tex. 1960. (FW)

Allen's landing: the authentic story of the founding of Houston. By Ralph E. Dittman. Houston, Tex. A.C. & J.K. Allen Pub. c1986. (LC)

ALLEN – Eckhardt, Ura L.
Allen family, no. 1-11, 1960-1970. By Ura L. Eckhardt. Houston, Tex. 1970. (FW)

ALLEN – Macomber, Edward Milton, 1930-
Connections: a pedigree record of the direct ancestors of Edward Milton Macomber, with partial lineage of 112 related surnames... By Edward Milton Macomber. Rev. Austin, Tex. E. M. Macomber. 1987, c1985. (LC)

ALLEN –
Our ancestors and their descendants who were among the first settlers at Ector and Bonham, Fannin County, Texas. By Vivian and Brenda Newingham. Bonham, Tex. 1968. (LC)

ALLEN – Newingham, Vivian (H.)
Our ancestors and their descendants of our grand parents, Ed and Kate Nelms Allen of Ector, Fannin County, Texas. By Vivian (H.) Newingham. Bonham, Tex. 1968. (FW)

ALLEN –
Ancestors and descendants of Moses Allen, born Virginia, 1815; pioneer settler of Bonham and Ector, Fannin County, Texas, 1827. Bonham? Tex. 1971. (LC)

ALLEN – Sone, Fayth
Generation unto generation. By Fayth Sone. San Antonio, Tex. Naylor Company. 1940. (LC)

ALLERTON – Allerton, Walter S.
A history of the Allerton family in the United States, 1585 to 1885. Chicago, Ill. By Samuel Waters Allerton. 1900. (DAR)

ALLRED – Allred, James V.
Allred, 1553-1961. By James V. Allred. Bowie, Tex. 1961. (LC)

ALTMAN – Parsons, Nahum Vincent
Altman and Knowles families of Texas. El Paso, Tex. Parsons. 1969 (DAR)

ALTMAN – Parsons, Nahum Vincent
Altman and Knowles families of Texas, with related lines of Austin, Chadwick, Henderson, Lilley, Palmer, Steele (and) Thompson. Also Margaret P. Parsons. El Paso, Tex. 1969. (NGS)

AMES – Ames, Merlin M
Homelands; America's old-world background. By Merlin M. Ames... and Jessie H. Ames. St. Louis, Dallas (etc.). Webster Publishing Co. c1939. (LC)

AMIS – Amis, Kathleen Wright
A family tree. Compiled by Kathleen Wright Amis. Dallas, Tex. 1942. (LC)

AMSLER – Amsler, Amanda Howze
    Amslers of Austin's colony. Houston, Tex. Amsler. c1976. (DAR)

AMSLER – Amsler, Amanda Howze
    Amslers of Austin's colony. Compiled by Amanda (Howze) Amsler. Houston, Tex. Amsler. c1976. (LC)

ANDERSON – Anderson, John Q.
    Anderson, Grant (and others). By John Q. Anderson. College Station, Tex. 1959. (LC)

ANDERSON – Cuilar, Willie C. A.
    The Andersons of Rowletts Creek, 1973. Dallas, 1973. (FW)

ANDERSON – Cullar, W. Clytes
    The Andersons of Rowlett's Creek. Also by Jerry M. Flook. Dallas, Tex. 1973. (NGS)

ANDERSON – Cullar, W. Clytes Anderson
    The Andersons of Rowlett's Creek. Dallas, Tex. Cullar. c1973. (DAR)

ANDERSON – Igo, June Jones, 1928-
    The Thomas Wesley Anderson family from Alabama to Texas. Compiled by June Jones Igo. Austin, Tex. J. J. Igo. 1982. (LC)

ANDERSON – Manz, Mabel Ann Anderson, 1914-
    The Andersons of Candacraig, 1581-1985: following the lines of the 12th Laird Alexander Anderson, his sister Jean Anderson Davie, his brother Arthur Anderson and his brother Adam Gordon Anderson. By Mabel Anderson Manz. Austin, Tex. M. A. Manz. 1985. (LC)

ANDERSON – Woodbury, Harry, 1918-
    The John Benton Anderson family, 1850-1980, of West Tennessee and East Texas. Compiled and written by Harry Woodbury. Gulfport, Miss. H. Woodbury. 1980. (LC)

ANDREWS – Andrews, James Ray
    The Andrews family. Dallas, Tex. Andrews. 1961. (DAR)

ANDREWS – Andrews, James Ray
    The Andrews family: descendants of Varney Andrews, Virginia soldier of the American Revolution. By James Ray Andrews. Rev. Dallas? 1963. (LC)

ANDREWS – Adrews, James Ray, Sr.
    Genealogy of the Andrews, Maxey and related families of Henrico County in Colonial Virginia; Bondurant, Ford (Faure), Salle, Sampson. By James Ray Andrews, Sr. Dallas, Tex. 1965. (LC)

ANDREWS – Andrews, Ella Smith (Johns)
    The families of John Andrews, 1764-1842, George Andrews, 1765-1842, Ephraim Andrews, 1769-1834, with allied lines. By Ella Smith (Johns) Andrews.. [S.l.]: E. S. Andrews. 1984. (LC)

ANGLIN – Williams, Evelyn West, 1933-
    In search of Anglins. By Evelyn West Williams. Boyd, Tex. E. W. Williams. 1982.
    (LC)

APPLING – Deviney, Esther G.
    The Applings, the Mooneys, through the years, 1685-1976: a genealogical and pictorial treasury. By Esther G. Deviney. Austin, Aus-Tex Duplicators. 1976. (FW)

ARCHER – Archer, Coleman J. (Coleman John), 1926-
    The legacy of John McQuatty Archer. By Coleman J. Archer. Arlington, Tex. Century Print. c1987. (LC)

ARCHER – Peacock, Ruby Leona Henderson, 1925-
    Twigs and branches from the Archer-Harper-Henderson-Reeves family tree. By Ruby Leona Henderson Peacock. Roaring Springs, Tex. R.L.H. Peacock. 1984? (LC)

ARMISTEAD – Eckkhardt, Ura L.
    Armistead family, no. 1-2, 1965-1970. By Ura L. Eckhardt. Houston, Tex. 1970. (FW)

ARMSTRONG – Cansler, Norma Todd
    Armstrongs of the Catawba; a genealogical history. Compiled by Norma Todd Cansler. Dallas. B & W Print. and Letter Service. 1969. (LC)

ARMSTRONG – Updike, Ethel S.
    Armstrong, Branyon, Bryson, and allied families of the South. By Ethel S. Updike. Salt Lake City. Hoby Press. c1967. (LC)

ARNING – Wolf, Leonora Stoll, 1928-
    Christian Arning, Wilhelmine Bosse, and their descendants, 1844-1987. By Leonora Stoll Wolf. New Braunfels, Tex? L. S. Wolf. c1988. (LC)

ARNOLD – Bliss, Nancy Hamilton
    Of Eagles and old islands: the Arnolds and the Oldhams and their descendants. By Nancy Hamilton Bliss, Ann Hamilton Pippin. Kirkwood, Mo. N. H. Bliss; Greenville, Tex. A. H. Pippin. c1988. (LC)

ARNOLD – Spiller, Lorena Martin
    The Arnold-Martin family history. Tulsa, Okla. Spillers. 1960. (DAR)

ASKEW – Glover, Earl Scott, 1932-
    Some Askew family history. By Earl Scott Glover. Houston, Tex. E. S. Glover. 1987. (LC)

ATHEY – Athy, Lawrence F.
    Captain George Athy (of Galway and Maryland) and his descendants: a guide to the first six generations of the Athy, Athey, Atha, Athon family in America. By Lawrence F. Athy, Jr. Houston, Tex. L. F. Athy. 1987. (LC)

ATKINS -- Atkin, Timothy W. (Timothy William), 1948-
A genealogy of the family of William H. Atkin and Mary Ann Turner in the United States of America. By Timothy W. Atkin. San Antonio, Tex. T. W. Atkin. 1985. (LC)

ATKINSON – Boddie, Mary Atkinson Delaney
Edward Spear Atkinson (1845-1916), ancestors and descendants (1297-1970). Lake Jackson, Tex. 1973. (NGS)

ATKINSON – Renfro, Roy E. (Roy Edward), 1945-
Renfro revelations & relations. Dr. & Mrs. Roy E. Renfro, Jr. Sherman, Tex. R. E. Renfro. 1980. (LC)

ATTERBURY – Lemons, Nova A.
Through the orchard. Supplement: Arterberry, Hillsberry, Lemons, Ragsdale. By Nova A. Lemons. Dallas, Tex. N. A. Lemons. c1990. (LC)

ATTERIDGE – Atteridge, Paul T.
The Atteridges of Canada and their descendants. By Paul T. Atteridge. Houston, Tex. 1976. (LA)

ATWOOD – Denny, Alma Atwood
The genealogy of the Thomas Atwood family. Comanche, Tex. Denny. c1972. (DAR)

ATWOOD – Denny, Alma Atwood
The genealogy of the Thomas Atwood family. ?Comanche, Tex. 1972. (NGS)

AUSTIN – Jones, Marie Beth
Peach Point Plantation: the first 150 years. By Marie Beth Jones; photos by Kathy Jones. [S.l.:s.n.]. c1982. [Waco, Tex: Texian Press]. (LC)

AUTRY – Autry, James L.
Autry genealogy. By James L. Autry. Houston, Tex. 1915. (NY)

AUTRY – Autry, Mahan Blair
The family and descendants of Captain John Autry. Corsicana, Tex. Autry. 1964. (DAR)

AVERY – Roberts, Eloise M.
Some colonial families. Avard, Okla. Roberts. 1926. (DAR)

AVERYT – Tucker, Elsie Perry, 1923-
Averyt and other kin. Compiled by Elsie Perry Tucker, Magnolia, Tex. Stagecoach Library. 1981? (LC)

AYCOCK – Aycock, Jane Everline
James and Richard Aycock, their descendants, earliest settlers of Wilkes County, Georgia, Jane Everline Aycock, Bill Winston Aycock, Frances Aycock Bednar. 1987 Rev. Richardson, Tex. J. E. Aycock. 1987. (LC)

AYLOR – Eckhardt, Ura L.
    Aylor family, no. 1-2, 1961-65. By Ura L. Eckhardt. Houston, Tex. 1965. (FW)

B –

BABCOCK – Krueger, Ruth Whiting, 1922-
    Babcock genealogy. By Ruth Whiting Krueger. Little Rock, Ark? R. W. Krueger. 1988? (LC)

BADER – Boehme, Gerald Ferdinand
    Joseph Bader, co-founder of Castroville, Texas: family history. By Gerald Ferdinand Boehme. Castroville, Texas Family Research. c1963. (LC)

BAGGARLY – Sutherland, Frank
    The de Baggerley, Baggiley, Baguley, Baggerly, Baggarly family of England and America: England 1066, America 1748; the letters and papers of Miss Sadie J. Baggarly, 1925-1931. Compiled by Frank Sutherland. Dallas, Tex. F. Sutherland. 1983. (LC)

BAGLEY – Perry, Kaaren M. (Karen Michel), 1942-
    Bagley family tales. By Kaaren M. Perry. Rockwall, Tex. K. M. Perry. 1985? (LC)

BAILEY – Seymour, Geneva Bailey
    Bailey-Bouret. By Geneva Bailey Seymour. Lubbock, Tex. Seymour. c1980. (LC)

BAIN – Bain, Ethel M., 1907-
    The Bain family; ancestors and descendants of Peter Bain of Tennessee, 1775-1980. By Ethel M. Bain. San Angelo, Tex. E. M. Bain. c1980. (LC)

BAIRD –
    A Baird family in America and allied lines. Collected and compiled by Josie Baird and Delila Baird. Rotan, Tex. 1071. (LC)

BAKER – Baker, Albert C.
    The William Thatcher Baker family, 1830-1971; biography of William Thatcher Baker and genealogical records compiled 1971 by Kathryn Baker Witty and Alma Baker Rea. Coat of arms from the genealogy of the Baker family. By Albert C. Baker, Decorah, Iowa, 1920. Lubbock? Tex., 1971? (LC)

BAKER – Baker, J. M., 1909-
    Baker families along the Gaartx trail. By J. M. and Velma Baker. Temple, Tex. Baker. c1980-c1984. (LC)

BAKER – Baker, Mary Lou, 1946-
    Pedigree pride of Bakers, Kathcarts, and Helms of Crawford, Washington , and Dent Counties, Missouri. Mary Lou (Baker) Baker, compiler. Jacksonville? Tex. M. L. Baker. c1981. (LC)

BAKER – Burton, Angela M.
Nellie B.-tales of a Texan. By Angela M. Burton. Prairie Village, Kan. Squire Pub., 1970. (FW)

BAKER – Eckhardt, Ura L.
Baker family, no. 1-5, 1965-1970. By Ura L. Eckhardt. Houston, Tex. 1970. (FW)

BAKER – Parks, Stan
Missouri Bakers book. Burkburnett, Tex. A and J Parks. 1979 (1985 printing). (LC)

BAKER – Witty, Kathryne Baker
The William Thatcher Baker family, 1830-1971. Hamilton, Tex. Witty, 1971. (DAR)

BALDWIN – Baldwin, Emma
A Baldwin genealogy, 1503-1986. By Emma G. Baldwin. Tenaha, Tex. E. G. Baldwin. 1985, c1986. (LC)

BALL – Martin, George Castor
Ancestry of Nellie Castor Ball Oldham of Wissinoming, Philadelphia, Pennsylvania; Ball family memorial. By George Castor Martin. San Antonio, 1949. (LC)

BALLARD – Ballard, C. R., Mrs., 1909-
They came to Texas: the family history and genealogy of Cecil Raymond Ballard and Maurice (Bradford) Ballard, 1734-1975. Compiled by Mrs. C. R. Ballard. Sequin, Tex. Mrs. C. R. Ballard. 1979? (LC)

BALLINGER – Reeves, Emma Barrett
Three centuries of Ballingers in America. Nacogdoches? Tex. Reeves, c1977. (DAR)

BARBEE – Barbee, James Edward
A brief history of the early Barbee families of Smith County, Texas. By James Edward Barbee. (Houston? 1995-). (LC)

BARBER – Bernard, Ted Butler, 1899-
Barber "grandparents"; 125 kings, 143 generations. By Ted B. Bernard and Gertrude Barber Bernard. McKinney, Tex. T. B. Bernard. 1978. (LC)

BARBER – Hoover, Barber Nell
The Barton-Barber family of Hays Co., Texas. By Barber Nell Hoover. Doylestown? Pa. 1960? (LC)

BARBER – See also: Anderson, Barbour, Beebe, Davis, Faxon, Lake, McConnell, Merrill, Potter, Throckmorton.

BARBER – Willingham, Willie Cleone White, 1915-
Family reference book of the lineage of Jim Williams – Barber, Buie, Crawford, White, Williams, Woodward, Hugh Williams, - Jones, Rogers, Williams; Enoch A. White – Brannans, Gartmans, Marshalls, McWilliams, Pearson, Whites, Youngs; Dallas P. Willingham – Baker, Brummett, Willingham; J. M. Livingston – Cornelius, Livingston, Mason, Moore, Myers. Willingham. By Willie White Willingham. Gustine, Tex. W. C. W. Willingham. c1986. (LC)

BARCUS – Barcus, George W.
Genealogy and family history of Rev. Edward Rosmon Barcus and wife Mary Frances Smith Barcus. By George W. Barcus. Waco, Tex. 1930. (FW)

BARE – Trimble, David B.
American origins. San Antonio, Tex. Trimble. 1974. (DAR)

BAREFOOT – Daugherty, Anne
Barefoot – Withrow families. S.1.: Daugherty, c1966. Dallas, Tex. Ray L. Stanphill. (DAR)

BAREFOOT –
Barefoot-Withrow families; with Choate and Mobley lines. By Anne and Vivian Dougherty. Dallas. Litho by R. L. Stanphill. 1966. (LC)

BARKER – Barker, L. M. B.
Genealogy of Barker family. By L. M. B. Barker. Waco, Tex? 1961. (FW)

BARNES – Comstock, Ernest Bernard
The Barnes lineage. Dallas, Tex. Comstock, 1937. (DAR)

BARNES – Comstock, Ernest B.
Barnes lineage, line of descent from Thomas Barnes of Hartford, Conn., the first immigrant. By Ernest B. Comstock. Dallas, Tex., 1937. (FW)

BARNES – Leonard, Alice Vinson
History of the Barnes-Vinson families. By Alice Vinson Leonard. Laredo, Tex. 1973. (LC)

BARNES –Veatch, Nellie Barnes
A history of the Barnes-McDowall families. By Nellie Barnes Veatch. Wolfe City, Tex. Henington Pub. Co., 1968. (LC)

BARNETT –
The Barnetts of Smith County, Tennessee; some ancestors and descendants. Lubbock, Tex., 1963. (LC)

BARNETT. See also: Barfield, Johnson, Marks, Matthews.

BARNETT – Reynolds, Harriet Dickson
Barnetts of Georgia. Houston, Tex. Reynolds. 1973. (DAR)

BARRERA – Garza, Lionel, 1921-
Brief history of both banks of the Rio Grande and the San Antonio rivers: 450 years of history and genealogy of the ascendants and descendants of Mucio Garza and Romana Barrera. By Lionel Garza. Kingsville, Tex. B. Torres Print Co. 1986. (LC)

BARRETT – Reeves, Emma B.
A few Barrett kin. By Emma B. Reeves. Waco, Tex. Texian Press. 1971. (FW)

BARRON –
Our Barron tree. By Twyla G. McMillan and Anecia F. Dutton. Marshall? Tex., 1973. (LC)

BARRON – Barron, Mildred D.
Soles and Barron families of Alabama and Texas. By Mildred D. Barron. Bryan, Tex. Wallace Print. 1969. (FW)

BARRON – McMillan, Twyla G.
Our Barron tree. Marshall, Tex. McMillan; Odessa, Tex. Dutton.. c1973. (DAR)

BARTHOLOMEW – Bartholomew, George Wells, Jr.
Record of the Bartholomew family. Historical, genealogical and biographical. By George Wells Bartholomew, Jr. Austin, Tex. The Compiler. 1885. (LC)

BARTON – Bode, Caroline Latham, 1947-
The Franklin and Malinda Barton family. Compiled by Caroline Latham Bode. Burnet, Tex. Nortex Press. c1981. (LC)

BASHAM – Ledford, Mary Ellen
The Ledford-Basham-Bryant book. By Mary Ellen Ledford. Irving, Tex. M. E. Ledford. 1989. (LC)

BASKERVILLE – Brown, Reba Holmes
American shoots from the Baskerville family. Port Arthur, Tex. Brown. 1975. (DAR)

BASS – Bell, Albert D.
Bass families of the South. Rocky Mount, N.S. Bell. 1961. (DAR)

BASS – Wood, Christine (K.)
Kaleidoscopic family Bass, 1769-1971; descendants of two brothers, Peter and Lawrence Bass. By Christine (K.) Wood. Lubbock, Tex. 1971. (FW)

BASS – Wood, Christine Knox
Kaleidoscopic Family – Bass, 1769-1971, Descendants of Two Brothers, Peter & Lawrence Bass. Lubbock, Tex. 1971. (NGS)

BASSETT – Eckhardt, Ura L.
Bassett family, no. 1-2, 1966-70. By Ura L. Eckhardt. Houston, Tex. 1970. (FW)

BATCHELDER – Williams, Lyle Keith, 1915-
The Batchelor—Williams families and related lines. By Lyle Keith Williams. Fort Worth, Tex. Williams. 1976, c1977. (LC)

BATCHELOR – Williams, Lyle Keith
The Batchelor-Williams families and related lines. Fort Worth, Tex. Williams. 1976. (DAR)

BATEMAN – Bateman, Harris
Bateman family genealogy. Tulsa, Okla. Bateman. 1970. (DAR)

BAYEMAN – Bateman, Harris
Bateman Family Genealogy and related lines Ball, Cayce, Ewell. Tulsa, Okla. 1970. (NGS)

BATEMAN – Batteman, Harris
Bateman family genealogy, and related lines:Bertrand, Cayce, Drake, etc. Tulsa, Okla. 1979. (NGS)

BATES -- Bates, Edmond F.
"Bates." Tradition and history of the Bates family of Virginia. Compiled and pub. by Edmond F. Bates. Denton, Tex. News Print. 1911. (FW)

BATSON – Bornemann, Vivian (Davis)
The Batson family in Virginia, North Carolina, and Georgia, Mississippi, Louisiana, and Texas. Related families: Dale, Hatten, Culpepper, Price, Smith, Lott, Longino, Daughdrill, Davis, Terrell. New Orleans, La. 1959. (NGS)

BATTLE – Battle, Herbert Bemerton
The Battle book, a genealogy of the Battle family in America. Austin, Tex. Battle, 1930. (DAR)

BATTLES – (Author unknown)
History of the Battles family. S.l.: s.n., 195? (DAR)

BAYLIES – Bayles, Howard Green
The Bayles famililes of Long Island and New Jersey and their descendants, also the ancestors of James Bayles and Julia Halsey Day. Compiled by Howard Green Bayles, with the cooperation of Frederick Phinney who did much of the research work. Houston, Tex. H. G. Bayles. 1944. (LC)

BEALL – Cummins, Bertie B.
The Georgia Bealls and their kinfolks. By Bertie B. Cummins. Abilene? Tex. The Author. 1964. (FW)

BEAL – McLean, William Hunter
Alexander Beall, 1649-1744, of Maryland: one line of descent in America: one of the initial "five Beall families of Maryland" identified by ancestry and biographies from 1649 to 1976. By William Hunter McLean. 1st. Ed. Fort Worth, Tex. Fort Worth Genealogical [sic] Society. c1977. (LC)

BEAN – Crabb, Martha L., 1928-
Over the mountains: a narrative of the Bean, Selman, and Germany families. By Martha L. Crabb. Baltimore: Gateway Press. Dumas, Tex. M. L. Crabb. 1990. (LC)

BEAN – MacBean, Bernie, 1906-
The Clan MacBean in North America. By Bernie and Carol Bean. Cut and Shoot, Tex. Clan MacBean, c1976-c1987. (LC)

BEARD – Fairbrother, H. W.
Genealogy: Richard Beard of Maryland to Miriam Partlow of Texas. By H. W. Fairbrother. Baltimore, 1972. (FW)

BEARD – Cooney, Pauline Beard, 1900-
History of the Beard, Bedichek, Craven, and allied families: including Trundle, Hough, McDowell, Sinclair, Veache, Crispin, Holme, Hart, Rush, Van Horn, Minge, Savage, Yoder, Cooney, Jeviden, Skeen, Brown, Dorn, and Clem. Researched and compiled by Pauline Beard Cooney. Austin, Tex. P. B. Cooney, 1979. (LC)

BEARDEN – Haack, Robert D. (Robert David), 1961-
A genealogy and kinology of the paternal history, Jerri Gayle Roden. By Robert D. Haack. Corpus Christi, Tex. R. D. Haack. c1983. (LC)

BEAUMONT – Randolph, George Alice (M.)
Slaughter-Cook-Beaumont history and genealogy. By George Alice (M.) Randolph. Plainview? Tex. 1962. (FW)

BECERRA – Rubio, Abel, 1929-
Land grab: the last Becerra grant in Texas. By Abel Rubio. Austin, Tex. Eakin Press. 1986. (LC)

BECERRA – Rubio, Abel, 1929-
Stolen heritage: a Mexican-American's triumphant quest for the lost Becerra grant in Texas. By Abel Rubio. Austin, Tex. Eakin Press. c1986. (LC)

BECERRA – Rubio, Abel G., 1929-
Stolen heritage: a Mexican-American's rediscovery of his family's lost land grant. By Abel G. Rubio; edited and with foreward by Thomas H. Kreneck.
1st Ed. Austin, Tex. Eakin Press. c1986. (LC)

BECK – Wasserman, Lillie, 1915-
The Anton and Rosina Koenig Beck family and their descendants, 1844-1979. By Lillie Beck Wasserman. Brenham? Tex. Wasserman. c1979. (LC)

BECKHAM – Beckham, Annie L. (L.)
Beckham family, Virginia, North Carolina, Georgia and Texas. By Annie L. (L.) Beckham. Dallas, Tex. 1957. (FW)

BECKHAM –
Bible records and manuscripts: Pt. I Beckman family and allied line. Pt. II Cowgill family and allied lines. Dallas, Tex. General Levi Casey Chap. DAR. 1965. (FW)

BECKHAM – Texas DAR
Bible records and manuscripts. 1965. (DAR)

BEDDOE –
A history of the Beddoe family, with addenda... comprising an account, in part, both traditional and written, from the eleventh century to the sixteenth century, and... to the present... Dallas. (n.d.). (NY)

BEDWELL – Ericson, Caroline R.
Bedwell beaux and belles; a brief history of the Bedwell family. By Caroline R. Ericson. Nacogdoches, Tex. 1972-3. (FW)

BEESON – Beeson, Henry Hart
A genealogy of the Beeson-Beason family. By Henry Hart Beeson. Houston, Tex. 1968. (FW)

BELL – Bell, Cassie W.
Elzora Bell and Alex Watson and all related families. By Cassie W. Bell. Fort Worth, Tex. Cook. 1967. (PH)

BELL – Cook, Cassie W.
Corrections, additions, and deletions to Elzora Bell and Alex Watson... the Bells, Kennedys, Pages, DeWeeses, Magnesses, Cooks. Comp. By Cassie W. Cook, Fort Worth, Tex. Cook. 1971. (PH)

BELL – Bell, Frank F.
Bell-Sharpe, Dallas, Tex. Bell. 1960. (DAR)

BELL – Smith, Lois Eudora (Bell)
The descendants of W. C. and E. A. Bell, Fort Worth, Tex. Smith. 1976. (DAR)

BELL – Stewart, James, writer to the signet-
The Bell family in Dumfriesshire. By James Stewart. Huffman, Tex. M. B. Reigard. 1984. (LC)

BENNETT – Bennett, Carmen Taylor
The Bennetts: Italy, France, England, Virginia, Georgia, Texas, 1501-1982. By Carmen Taylor Bennett. Lubbock, Tex. Duncan Press. 1982. (LC)

BENNETT – Bennett, Inez Moore
The descendants of Hiram Bennett, pioneer settler of Dallas County, Texas. By Inez Moore Bennett. Dallas, Tex. B & W Print. and Letter Service. 1973. (LC)

BENNETT. See also: Covington, Holt, Richardson, Sabin.

BENSON – Freeman, Corrie Lee Benson, 1901-
The Bensons: a story of a family of eight. By Corrie Lee Benson Freeman. Dallas, Tex. [s.n., 1979?]. (LC)

BERGSTRESSER – Jones, Wyne V.
The Bergstresser family in America. By Wyne V. Jones. Houston, Tex. Author. 1959. (NY)

BERGSTRESSER – Jones, Wayne V.
The Bergstresser family in America. By Wayne V. Jones. Houston, Tex. W. V. Jones. c1988. (LC)

BERKSTRESSER – Jones, Wayne V.
Descendants of William Wilhelm Berkstresser of Versailles, Mo. By Wayne V. Jones. Houston, Tex. 1960. (FW)

BERNARD – Bernard, Ted Butler
Bernard 'grandparents' back to 300 B.C. McKinney, Tex. Bernard. 1976. (DAR)

BERNARD – Bernard, Ted B.
Bernard "grandparents" back to 300 B. C.: 106 kings, 82 generations. By Ted B. Bernard. McKinney, Tex. Bernard. 1976. (FW)

BERNARD – Thomsen, Alice Bernard, 1912-
A Bernard genealogy and history: with Samuel, Ebenezer, and Timothy being the founding fathers of the family. Researched and compiled by Alice Bernard Thomsen. Houston, Tex. A. B. Thomsen. 1979. (LC)

BERRY – Anderson, Gertrude
John Berry and his children. Jack Pope, editor; authors Gertrude Anderson... [et al.]. Austin, Tex. J. Pope. Georgetown, Tex. Dist. By John Berry Association. c1988. (LC)

BERRY – Berry, Brian Joe Lobley, 1934-
Westward the American Shapleys: the family and descendants of David Shapley, a seventeenth century Marblehead fisherman, with pedigrees of the spouses (Atwater, Berry, Chapman, Coleman, French, Parks, Talmage, Utter, and connecting lines): English ancestry and American descent of five additional Shapley immigrants, Alexander, John, Nicholas, Philip, and Reuben. By Brian J. L. Berry. Baltimore: Gateway Press. Richardson, Tex. B. J. L. Berry. 1987. (LC)

BERRY – Bills, Ann Raby, 1944-
The Berrys of Byers: a history of Henry and Della Benson Berry of Byers, Texas: their ancestors and descendants. By Ann Raby Bills and W. Ross Berry. Holliday, Tex. A. R. Bills. c1987. (LC)

BERRY – Hamilton, Lynn Berry
Berry-Berrey family, the family of Elija Berry, Va., Ga., Ala., Tex. Harlingen, Tex. Hamilton. c1980. (DAR)

BERRY – Hamilton, Lynn Berry, 1921-
Berry-Berrey family; the family of Elijah Berry, Va., Ga., Ala., Tex., 1700-1980. By Lynn Berry Hamilton. Harlingen, Tex. Mrs. C. H. Hamilton, Jr., 1980. (LC)

BERRY – Renfro, Roy E. (Roy Edward), 1945-
Renfro revelations and relations. Dr. & Mrs. Roy E. Renfro, Jr. Sherman, Tex. R. E. Renfro. 1980. (LC)

BERRY – Spear-Wilson, Iowa Leona, 1898-
Spear family memorial, 1620-1986: some Spear men, their ladies, and some affiliated families: a branch of the Vermont-England Spears: census records showing English roots. By Iowa Leona Spear-Wilson. Abilene, Tex. I. L. Spear-Wilson. c1985. (LC)

BERRYHILL – Brittain, Virginia (T.)
The Berryhill family in America. 1st Ed. By Virginia (T.) Brittain. Pasadena, Tex. McDowell Print. and Secretarial Service, 1968. (FW)

BERTHE – Sheffield, E. J. B.
Tree of time. By E. J. B. Sheffield. Baytown, Tex. 1967. (FW)

BETTS – Brantley, Mary E.
Some Betts Family Records, De., Ga., Al., Ms., Tex. Records. Atmore, Ala. ?1983. (NGS)

BETTS – Brantley, Mary E.
Some Betts family records: Delaware, Georgia, Alabama, Mississippi, and Texas records. By Mary E. Brantley. 1st Ed. Atmore, Al. I. Brantley. 1982. (LC)

BEVERLEY – Eckhardt, Ura L.
Beverley family, assorted notes, book 2. By Ura L. Eckhardt. Houston, Tex. 1970. (FW)

BEVILL – Morris, Mildred Elizabeth Solley
Bevill-Burton family history. Austin, Tex. Morris. Duplicated by Aus-Tex Duplicators, 1967. (DAR)

BIARD – Smith, Maud Biard
The Biard family. Paris, Tex. Smith. 1954. (DAR)

BIARD – Smith, Maud (B.)
The Biard. By Maud (B.) Smith. Paris, Tex. 1954? (NY)

BIBO – Fierman, Floyd S.
Impact of the frontier on a Jewish family. By Floyd S. Fierman. El Paso? Tex. Western College Press. 1961. (LA)

BIGGERS – Biggers, Hal
Eugene Morris Biggers and allied families. Houston, Tex. Biggers Printing Co. 1976. (DAR)

BIGGERS – Jeter, Margaret McDonald, 1926-
History of the Mcdonald, Thomasson, Biggers, Grimes, and related families. By Margaret McDonald Jeter. Tucson, Ariz. M. M. Jeter. 1989. (LC)

BIGGERS – Shannon, Betty Biggers, 1921-
The long Biggers line. By Betty Biggers Shannon. Lubbock, Tex. Shannon. c1976. (LC)

BIGGS – Campbell, Kathryn Hutcherson
John Biggs. Dallas, Tex. Campbell. 1979. (DAR)

BILL – Vicars, Valeska Buchholz
    Adams family: Lorenzo Dow Adams, Joshua Adams and their descendants: collateral lines of Lewellen, Bills, Mohundro, Hardin, Ballenger, and Gaither. By Valeska Buchholz Vicars. Seabrook, Tex. 1980? (LC)

BISHOP – Branen, Winnie
    Ancestors and descendants of Lewis Conley Bishop. Marshall, Okla. Bishop – Tolman – Branen Ancestors, Inc..., c1980. (DAR)

BIXBY – Wynne, Diana Jones, 1942-
    Ancestry and descendants of Jesse Bixby, 1815-1891. Researched and compiled by Diana Day Jones Wynne. Houston, Tex. D. D. J. Wynne. 1982. (LC)

BLACK – Black, William A.
    Black, seven generations from William Black of Lunenburg and Halifax Counties in Virginia, 1757, to William Stanley Black, 1974. Black, Tex.; Scottsdale, Ariz. Black: Black, 1974. (DAR)

BLACK – Eckhardt, Ura L.
    Black family assorted notes, no. 1-2, 4, 1960-1970. By Ura L. Eckhardt. Houston, Tex. 1970. (FW)

BLACKBURN – Bullard, Lucille Blackburn
    William Thomas Blackburn of Virginia and his Texas grandchildren. Lucille Blackburn Bullard. Jefferson, Tex. L. B. Bullard. C1985. (LC)

BLACKMORE – Holtzclaw, Clarice
    De(s)cendants of Newton Blackmore, Austin, Texas, June, 1968. By Clarice Holtzclaw. Austin, Tex. Printed by O. Jung, 1968. (LC)

BLACKSTOCK – Karl, Roy C. (Roy Calvin)
    The families and descendants of Thomas Newton Blackstock. By Roy C. Carl. Freeport, Tex. R. C. Carl. c1988. (LC)

BLACKWELL – Hawthorne, Frank Howard, 1923-
    Kissin' kin & lost cousins: a genealogy of the Blackwell, Capps, Dubose, Greene, Howard, Powell, Wille, Lynne, Yuratich, and related families. By Frank Howard Hawthorne. Montgomery, Ala. F. H. Hawthorne. 1989. (LC)

BLAIR – Blair, Lucy Echels, 1918-
    John Blair of Guilford County, North Carolina, and some of his descendants. Compiled by Lucy Echels Blair. Lamesa, Tex. B. Blair. 1979. (LC)

BLAKENEY – Blakeney, John Oscar
    The Blakeneys in America and some collaterals. Little Rock, Ark. Blakeney. 1928. (DAR)

BLALOCK – Blalock, Delton D. (Delton Dennis), 1940-
Blalock and related families: pioneers in Virginia, the Carolinas, Georgia, Alabama, and Texas, 1597-1988. By Delton D. Blalock. Montgomery, Ala. D. D. Blalock. 1988. (LC)

BLALOCK – Bowman, Myreline
The Blalocks and related families, Cass County, Texas. By Myreline Dailey Bowman. Atlanta, Tex. M. D. Bowman. 1977? (LC)

BLANDIN – Smith, Lois Eudora Bell
The descendants Joseph L. Blandin (1799-1854). Fort Worth, Tex. Smith. 1964. (DAR)

BLANKS – Wilson, John H.
The Blanks family. Compiled by John H. Wilson. With the collaboration of Lee Howell Blanks and his wife Elizabeth Hawkins Blanks of Amherst County, Virginia. 1st Ed. Fort Worth, Tex. 1971. (LC)

BLANKS – Wilson, John H.
Blanks family. Comp. By John H. Wilson. Fort Worth, Tex. 1971. (FW)

BLANTON – Mayfield, Jewel White, 1914-
Genealogical research of ancestors and descendants: Blanton weds Moore, 1885. By Jewel White Mayfield. Abilene, Tex. J. W. Mayfield. c1981. (LC)

BLASINGAME – Johnson, N. L.
Descendants of George Washington Blasingame and Harriet Melissa Rooks. By N. L. Johnson. Waco, Tex. (n.d.). (FW)

BLASSINGAME – Blassingame, W. Doak
The Blassingame families. By W. Doak Blassingame. Including various spellings of the name: Blasingame, Blassingham, Blassingim, etc. Wolfe City, Tex. University Press. c1973. (LC)

BLEDSOE – Eckhardt, Ura L.
Bledsoe family assorted notes. By Ura L. Eckhardt. Houston, Tex. 1970. (FW)

BLEWETT – Blewett, George Edgar
William Blewett who settled in North Carolina in 1746; a history and genealogy of him and his descendants. By George Edgar Blewett. Fort Worth, Tex. 1954. (LC)

BLUE – Kelly, Douglas F.
The Scottish Blue family from Carolina to Texas. By Douglas F. Kelly. Lumberton, N.C. D. F. Kelly. 1981, c1982. (LC)

BLUMBERG – Blumberg, Carl F.
The Carl F. and Catherine Ruff Blumberg klan book. By Carl F. Blumberg. Sequin, Tex. C. F. Blumberg, 1938. (MH)

BLUME – Blume, Irwin H.
  First hundred years of the "Blume" family of Fayette and McLennan County, Texas, 1853 to date. By Irwin H. Blume. Bellaire, Tex., 1975. (FW)

BLUNT – Overlander, Rufus M.
  Blount family of North Carolina and allied families Miller, Dyer, Gray. Seabrook, Tex. Rufus M. Overlander III, 1987. (LC)

BOAZ – Boaz, Hiram A.
  The Thomas Boaz family in America. Dallas, Tex. Boaz, 1949. (DAR)

BOBB – Ellis, Luella May Waggoner
  The Bobb family and associated families of Hoge, Armstrong, Naggle, Longsdorf and Waugh. Yuma, Ariz. Ellis, 1963. (DAR)

BOGGS –
  Report to the Boggs family Reunion, Lake Jackson, Texas. (n.p.) 1965. (SF)

BOGGS – Tally-Frost, Stephenie H.
  Genealogy of the Boggs family descendants, and related families. By Stephenie H. Tally-Frost. Corpus Christi, Tex., 1965. (FW)

BOHMFALK – Bohmfalk, John H.
  History of the Friede Bohmfalk family, Nov. 7, 1848 to Aug. 21, 1966. By John H. Bohmfalk. San Antonio, Tex. 1966. (FW)

BOHUN –McConnell, Richard Bland, 1902-
  Ancestral peregrinations: a series of genealogical charts dealing with some phases of de Bohun ancestry and with that of a few of the maternal lines involved. Assembled and presented by Richard B. McConnell. Houston, Tex. C. G. Fleetwood, 1979. (LC)

BOLEN – Bolling, Alexander R. (Alexander Russell), 1922-
  The Bolling family: eight centuries of growth. By Alexander R. Bolling, Jr. Baltimore: Gateway Press. Dallas, Tex. A. R. Roling, Jr. 1990. (LC)

BOLLING – Bolling, Ruth (J.)
  Tales of a Texas ranch. By Ruth (J.) Bolling. San Antonio, Tex. Naylor Co. 1959. (FW)

BOLTON – Abernethy, Arvord Milner, 1906-
  Into the setting sun went the Abernethys, the Boltons the Davises, the Talbots. Hamilton, Tex. A. M. Abernethy, 1986. (LC)

BOND – Prewitt, Lorene Bond
  Bond-Wheeler genealogy with related families. Dallas, Tex. Prewitt, 1972. (DAR)

BONNER – Thornton, Sue Bonner
  The Bonner family history. Waco, Tex. Texan Press, 1972. (DAR)

BONNER – Thornton, Sue Bonner
  The Bonner family history. By Sue Bonner Thornton. Waco, Tex. Texian Press, 1972.
  (LC)

BONNIFIELD – Hooper, Virginia S. (Virginia Sharp), 1927-
  Bon(n)ifield-Bonifant: descendants on male lines from James Bonevant in Prince Georges County, Maryland in 1713: an updating of descendants of Gregory Bonnifield (1726-1794) by Charles J. Maxwell, 1949, Dallas, Texas, with the addition of the Bonifant lines. By Virginia S. Hooper. Santa Clara, Calif. V. S. Hooper. 1984.
  (LC)

BONNIFIELD – Maxwell, Charles Joseph
  The Bonnifield family. Dallas, Tex. Maxwell, 1918. (DAR)

BONNIFIELD – Maxwell, C. J.
  Descendants of Gregory Bonnifield. (1726-1794). Dallas, Tex. Maxwell, 1949. (DAR)

BONNIFIELD – Maxwell, Charles Joseph
  The Bonnifield family. By Charles Joseph Maxwell. Dallas, Tex. Ginn & Co., 1918.
  (LC)

BOONE – Boone, Pecos Pate
  The Boone boys: frontiersmen and their great wild west show. By Pecos Pate Boone. Christoval, Tex. Boone. c1976. (LC)

BOONE – Campbell, Dorothy Spears, 1937-
  George Boone, son of Edward Boone, killed by the Indians in 1780, and nephew of Daniel Boone, the famed explorer: a history of the Boone family, including descendants of George and Patty Hazelrigg Boone and George and Hester Locke Boone. By Dorothy Spears Campbell, Shirley Spears Nowicki. Arlington, Tex. D. S. Campbell. c1982. (LC)

BOOTH – Boothe, Ross
  Boothe genealogy. By Ross Boothe. Gonzales, Tex. 1958. (LC)

BOOTHE – Boothe, Ross
  Boothe genealogy. Gonzales, Tex. Boothe. 1958. (DAR)

BOROWICZ -- Mueller, Valeria Vierus, 1936-
  The Borowicz family history. By Valeria Vierus Mueller. Houston, Tex. V. V. Mueller. c1985. (LC)

BORRER – Hallmark, William Otis, 1931-
  Borrer: descendants of Elijah Borrer and Celia Williams Borrer and their related families. Compiled by William Otis Hallmark, Sr. Burnet, Tex. Eakin Publications. 1979. (LC)

BOSWELL – Pippenger, Jean Boswell, 1927-
Descendants of Edward Boswell: Prince William County, Virginia and Orange County, North Carolina. Compiled by Jean Boswell Pippenger and Imogene May Boswell. Baltimore: Gateway Press. Richardson, Tex. J. B. Pippenger. 1986. (LC)

BOUNDS – Bounds, Charles L.
History of the Bounds family. By Charles L. Bounds. Decatur, Tex. 1926. (LI)

BOWDEN – Murphey, Joe Earl, 1929-
Profiles: a history of the Todd and Bowden families. By Joe Earl Murphey. Arlington, Tex? J. E. Murphy. c1985. (LC)

BOWDOIN – Eckhardt, Ura L.
Bowdoin family, no. 1-4, 1950-1969. By Ura L. Eckhardt. Houston, Tex. 1969. (FW)

BOWIE – Willingham, Willie Cleone White, 1915-
Family reference book of the lineage of Jim Williams – Barber, Buie, Crawford, White, Williams, Woodward, Hugh, Williams – Jones, Rogers, Williams; Enoch A. White – Brannans, Gartmans, Marshalls, McMillians, Pearsons, Whites, Youngs; Dallas P. Willingham – Baker – Brummett, Willingham; J. M. Livingston – Cornelius, Livingston, Mason, Moore, Myers, Willingham. By Willie Cleone White Willingham. Gustine, Tex. W. C. W. Willingham. c1986. (LC)

BOWLES – Shamlian, Barbara Sue, 1936-
The genealogical record of the Boal family. Compiled by Barbara Sue Shamlian. Tekarkana, Tex. B. S. Shamlian. 1982? (LC)

BOWMAN – Page, Leila Bowman A.
History of the George Washington Bowman and Fiser families of Mooreville, Falls County, Texas. By Leila Bowman A. Page. Galveston, Tex. Edited and published by P. C. Wilson, Jr. 1962. (LC)

BOWMAN – Page, Leila Bowman A.
History of the George Washington Bowman and Fiser Families of Mooreville, Falls County, Texas. Galveston, Tex. 1962. (NGS)

BOYCE – Boies, Robert B. (Robert Brice), 1920-
Genealogy of the Boies Family of Pennsylvania and adjoining counties in Eastern Ohio & James Boies of Milton, Mass. By Robert B. Boies, Sr. 1st Ed. McAllen, Tex. R. B. Boies, Sr. c1986. (LC)

BOYD – Perry, Max, 1919-
The descendants of the Robert Boyd and the Charles Boyd families of Chester County, South Carolina. By Max Perry. Midland, Tex. M. Perry. c1987. (LC)

BOYSON – Trumbull, Dorothy May Boyson
Continuing a special heritage: a family history, Sherman, Boyson, Trumbull. By Dorothy May Boyson Trumbull. 1st Ed. Austin, Tex. Nortex Press. c1990. (LC)

BRADBURY – Stedman, Ardath Tolson
The ancestry of Laura Delcena Bradbury. Denton, Tex. The Copy Factory, 1977.
(DAR)

BRADFIELD – Bradfield, Quida (Ragsdale)
The Bradfield family; history. By Quida (Ragsdale) Bradfield. Garland, Tex. Garland News Pub. Co. 1956. (LC)

BRADY – Brady, Ruth S.
Some descendants and related families of Robert Brady (1786-1853) and Catharine Scott Brady (1790-1861). By Ruth S. Brady. Marble Falls, Tex., 1975. (KH)

BRANDENBERGER –
Brandenberger: a family history. By Evelyn Duke Brandenberger and Frances Brandenberger Cole. Bellaire? Tex. Brandenberger. C1975. (LC)

BRANN – Brann, Mildred C. (W.)
Descendants of Nicholas Brann; a Revolutionary War soldier of Westmourland (!) Co., Va. By Mildred C. (W.) Brann. Dallas, Tex., 1942. (FW)

BRASHEAR – Brashear, Henry Sinclair
The Brashear-Brashears family, 1449-1929. Texarkana, Tex. Brashear. 1929. (DAR)

BRASHEARS – Brashear, Henry Sinclair
The Brashear-Brashears family, 1449-1929. By Henry Sinclair Brashear. 1st Ed. May, 1929. Texarkana, Tex. 1929. (LC)

BRASWELL – Braswell, Roy Bennett
Following the Braswells on the move westward in America, 1600-1973. By Roy Bennett Braswell. Pampa, Tex., 1974. (FW)

BRASWELLS – Braswell, Roy Bennett
Following the Braswells on the move westward in America, 1600-1974. Pampa, Tex. 1974. (NGS)

BRATT – Biasca, Cynthia Brott
Descendants of Albert and Arent Andriessen Bradt. By Cynthia Brott Biasca. Wolfe City, Tex. Henington Pub. Co. c1990. (LC)

BREAUX – Seymour, Geneva Bailey
Breaux. By Geneva Bailey Seymour. Lubbock, Tex. G. B. Seymour. c1981. (LC)

BREEDING – Breeding, Seth Darnaby
The first members of the Breeding family to come to Texas. By Seth Darnaby Breeding. Austin? 1955? (LC)

BREMER – Robinson, Robert R., 1940-
Die Bremerverwandtschaft in Deutschland und in Texas=The Bremers and their kin in Germany and in Texas. By Robert R. Robinson, Jr. (Robert R. Robinson-Zwahr). Wichita Falls, Tex. Nortex Press. c1977-1979.

BREVARD – Reese, Cynthia Jones, 1938-
The genealogical study of David Reese: with allied families: Polk, Brevard, Davidson, Caldwell, White, Alexander, McKnit, Bradley. By Cynthia Jones Reese. Wichita Falls, Tex. C. J. Reese. c1990. (LC)

BREWER – Brewer, H. Leon (Harold Leon), 1922-
The history of the Brewer and Pafford families. By H. Leon Brewer. Edited and published by Dixie Brewer O'Callaghan. Irving, Tex. O'Callaghan. 1979. (LC)

BRICE – Brice, Agnes
History of the Brice family. By Agnes Brice. Edited by Mitzi Musick Barnett. Fort Worth, Tex. American Reference Pub. Co.., 1972. (LC)

BRIGHAM – Salmon, David D., 1944-
The Tennessee origins of the Texas Brigham family: narrative, data and charts: includes charts of the Viertel and Salmon collateral lines. Written and collated by David D. Salmon. Oakland, Calif. Salmon. c1977. (LC)

BROOKS – Haack, Robert D. (Robert Davis), 1961-
A genealogy and kinology of the paternal history, Jerri Gayle Roden. By Robert D. Haack. Corpus Christi, Tex. R. D. Haack. c1983. (LC)

BROOME – Broome, George
Bibliography of items indexed by George Broome and preserved on microfilm in genealogy collection, Amarillo Public Library, Amarillo, Texas. By George Broome. (n.d.). (FW)

BROUGHTON – Broughton, M. Leon
Broughton memories. By M. Leon Broughton. 3d. Ed. Dallas, Tex., 1972. (LC)

BROUGHTON – Broughton, Milton Leon
Broughton memories. By Milton Leon Broughton. Tyler, Tex. 1961 (c1962). (LC)

BROUGHTON – Broughton, M. Leon
Broughton memories. Compiled and edited by M. Leon Broughton. 2d. Ed. Rev. Tyler, Tex. 1964. (LC)

BROUGHTON – Smith, Leni
My family, the Broughtons. By Leni Smith. Palestine, Tex., 1964. (LC)

BROUILLARD – Roderick, Jacqueline Brouillard, 1917-
My Brouillard ancestors, 1668-1983. By Jacqueline Brouillard Roderick. El Paso, Tex. J. B. Roderick. c1984. (LC)

BROWN – Ayres, Mildred Royal, 1920-
Royal-Brown heritage: with genealogical notes of related families. Mildred Royal Ayres and Frances Royal Foley. Austin, Tex. Nortex Press. c1984. (LC)

BROWN – Brown, Dorothy Louise Knox, 1920-
Lineages and genealogical notes: a compilation of some of the lineages and family lines in the genealogy of Dorothy Louise (Knox) Brown and Dorinda Alice Brown with genealogical notes. By Dorothy Louise (Knox) Brown. 3d. Ed. Dallas, Tex. D. L. K. Brown. 1981. (LC)

BROWN – Brown, Shepherd Spencer Neville, 1920-
Brown-Stanton-Evans-Sherman families and collateral lines, 1420-1987. By Shepherd Spencer Neville Brown. Waco, Tex. S. S. N. Brown. 1987. (LC)

BROWN – Hafertepe, Kenneth, 1955-
Ashton Villa: a family and its house in Victorian Galveston, Texas. Kenneth Hafertepe. Austin, Tex. Texas State Historical Society. c1991. (LC)

BROWN – Hughes, Dorothy Dillard
Our Hughes ancestors: a story of searches and discoveries, including maternal lines of Varvel, Ewing, Huntzinger, Sawyer, Brown, Hale/Haile, Craghead, and lists of descendants. By Dorothy Dillard Hughes. Lubbock, Tex. D. D. Hughes. c1989. (LC)

BROWN – McKnight, Grace, 1911-
Descendants of Thomas Brokenberry Brown. Compiled by Grace McKnight. Ferris, Tex. G. McKnight. c1983. (LC)

BROWN – Rugeley, Helen Hoskins, 1911-
Brown, William and Margaret (Peggy Fleming), descendants of (especially No. 50, Col. Joseph Brown, 1772-1868, the principle source of our early genealogy). Compiled by Helen (1507 Hoskins) Rugebey. Austin, Tex. H. H. Rugeley. c1983. (LC)

BROWNFIELD – Perry, Max, 1919-
The descendants of the Brownfield and Porter families. By Max Perry. Midland, Tex. M. Perry. c1987. (LC)

BROWNING – Mason, Cyrus, 1828 or 9-1915-
The poet Robert Browning and his kinfolk. By his cousin Cyrus Mason, edited and with an afterword by W. Craig Turner. Waco, Tex. Baylor University Press, Markham Press Fund. c1983. (LC)

BRUCKNER – Brucker, Wallace Hawn, 1908-
Johann Adam Brucker and his American descendants. By Wallace Hawn Brucker. El Paso, Tex. Guynes Print Co. 1978. (LC)

BRYAN -- Darling, Kenneth P.
Bryan-Bowmar. Houston, Tex. Darling, 1979. (DAR)

BRYANT – Pope, Jennings Bland, 1914-
The Bryants of Spartanbury, beginning with William Briant (c1741 Va.-c1834 SC.). By Jennings Bland Pope. Austin, Tex. Pope. 1980. (LC)

BUCHALEW – Green, Gerry
Mary's people, the Buckelews. By Gerry Green. Nursery, Tex. Words from Woods. c1985. (LC)

BUCKLES – Buckles, Ronald J., 1917-
The Buckles family: 250 years in America. By Ronald J. Buckles. Brackettville, Tex. Buckles. 1976? (LC)

BUFFINGTON – Buffington, Ralph M.
Buffington pedigree. By Ralph M. Buffington. Rev. Ed. Houston, Tex., 1967. (FW)

BUFFINGTON –
The Buffington family in America; a source book for further research; a joint venture for the Buffington family. By Clara Dunagan Rhome (and others), Ralph M. Buffington, editor. Houston, Tex., 1965. (LC)

BUFFINGTONS – Boveington, Vincent Joseph
English origins of the American Buffingtons. Houston, Tex. 1975. (NGS)

BULLLOCK – Ray, Worth Stickley
Colonial Granville County and its people. Loose leaves from "The lost tribes of North Carolina." By Worth Stickley Ray. Austin, Tex. 1945. (LC)

BUMPAS – Cherry, Mootie Clemmons
The story of the Bumpas family from Plymouth Massachusetts to the prairies of Texas. S.l.: Cherry? 1943? (DAR)

BUMPASS – Jones, William Moses
A genealogy of three branches of the Bumpass family. Houston, Tex. Monument Publishing Co., 1962. (DAR)

BURGER – De Vore, Shirley Ann Staley
Hodde genealogy search: some allied families: Buerger, Downey, Helm, Geisler, Lohmann, Mielenz, Mullendore, Pecore, Staley, and Wolf. By Shirley Ann Staley De Vore. 1st Ed. Norman, Okla. S. A. S. De Vore. c1988. (LC)

BURKETT – Fisher, Ruby Millicent Burkett
A concise genealogy of David Burkett and Horace Eggleston (an allied family). By Ruby Millicent Burkett Fisher. Dallas, Tex. Cundiff Print Co., 1972. (LC)

BURKETT – Schluter, Helen Gomer
The Thomas Jefferson Felts family of Mississippi and Sabine County, Texas including the Burkett and Polk Families. By Helen Gomer Schluter. Fort Worth, Tex. H. G. Schluter. 1988. (LC)

BURKETT – Seltzer, Maxine Burkett, 1928-
The history of the Burkett-Gilliam generations. Fort Worth, Tex. M. B. Seltzer. c1976. (LC)

BURLESON – Burleson, Richard E.
One southern branch of the Burleson family in America. Byran, Tex. Burleson, 1978. (DAR)

BURNETT – Blevins, Ray E. (Ray Ernest), 1920-
Burnetts from Virginia to Wayne County, Kentucky. By Ray E. Blevins. Round Rock, Tex. R. E. Blevins. c1986. (LC)

BURNS – Stewart, Estella M. Burns
The Burns family and allied lines of North Carolina, Alabama and Texas. Comp. By Estella M. Burns Stewart. Huntsville, Tex. 1969. (FW)

BURNS – Stewart, Estella Mae Burns
The Burns family and allied lines of North Carolina, Alabama, and Texas. Huntsville, Tex. 1969. (NGS)

BURT – Mathis, Robert B.
The Mathew Burt family of Virginia and Deep South. By Robert B. Mathis. Killeen, Tex. 1976. (FW)

BURT – Chancellor, J. C.
Ancestors of Annie Laurie Burt chancellor. By J. C. Chancellor. Odessa, Tex. West Tex. Off. Supply, 1964. (FW)

BURTON – Arthaud, John B.
Notes on the Richard and John Burton families, New York and Mass., 1850-1973; and allied Dapson (Dabson), Ellis and Haradon families... By John B. Arthaud. Houston, Tex., 1974. (FW)

BURTON – Arthaud, John Bradley
Notes on the Richard and John Burton families, New York and Massachusetts, 1850-1973, and allied Dapson (Dabson), Ellis, and Haradon families. Compiled and private (sic) printed by John Bradley Arthaud. Houston, Tex. Arthaud. 1974. (LC)

BURTON – Irwin, C. Thomas (Clyde Thomas), 1931-
Gorgon head and golden tongue. By C. Thomas Irwin. Houston, Tex. C. T. Irwin. 1989? (LC)

BURTON – Morris, Louise Elizabeth (Burton)
Lineages and genealogical notes. Dallas, Tex. Morris, 1967. (DAR)

BURTON – Morris, Louise Elizabeth (Burton)
Lineages and genealogical notes; a compilation of some of the lineages and family lines in the genealogy of Louise Elizabeth Burton (Mrs. Harry Joseph Morris). Dallas, Tex. 1967. (NGS)

BURWELL – Eckhardt, Ura L.
Burwell family notes, no. 1, 1965-70. By Ura L. Eckhardt. Houston, Tex. 1970. (FW)

BUSH – Foxworth, Sarah Payne, 1910-
Foxworth, Bush, Payne, Bledsoe & allied lineages: Lenoir, Pope, Regan, Elkin, Quisenberry, Morter, Foster, Mitchell, Johnston, Ogilvie, Birdsong, Higgins, etc. By Sarah Payne Foxworth and Michal Martin Farmer. Dallas, Tex. Farmer Genealogy Co. c1985. (LC)

BUSSEY – Guittard, Lynn Bussey, 1949-
The Bussey family genealogy. By Lynn Bussey Guittard. Fort Worth, Tex. Miran Publishers. c1979. (LC)

BUTLER –
Ancestors and descendants of Mrs. Lucia (Butler) Ford, decendant of the Duke of Ormond, and her husband Charles Ambrose Ford, of Fannin County, Texas. (n.p., 1969). (LC)

BUTLER –
Ancestors and descendants of Mrs. Lucia (Butler) Ford, descendant of the Duke of Ormond; pioneer settler of Ector, Fannin County, Texas, 1835. Bonham? Tex. 1971. (LC)

BUTLER – Allen, Catherine
Ancestors and descendants of Mrs. Lucia (Butler) Ford, descendant of the Duke of Ormond, and her husband Charles Ambrose Ford, of Fannin County, Texas. By Catherine Allen. (LC)

BUTLER. See also:

Atwater	Lewis
Bramshott	Long
Chance	Mackey
Farnham	Mills
Gentry	Ranney
Lawson	Roberts

BUTLER – Eckhardt, Ura L.
Butler family, no. 1-5, 1965-70. By Ura L. Eckhardt. Houston, Tex. 1970. (FW)

BUTTER – Dailey, Leonard Howard, Mrs., 1936-
The Butters, Giles, and allied families, 1816-1985. Compiled by Mrs. Leonard Howard Dailey, Jr. nee Rose Butter Dailey. Beaumont, Tex. R. B. Dailey. c1985. (LC)

BUTTERY – Buttery, Lester L.
Butterys of Texas. By Lester L. Buttery. Cuero, Tex., 1958. (FW)

BUTTON – Button, William Garland
A part of the Button family of Virginia and its westward migration to Kentucky, Texas, Oklahoma, and California from 1666 to 1959. By William Garland Button. Waco, Tex. Button, 1959. (LC)

BUTTRILL – Buttrill, Carrol Oliver, 1916-
The Buttrill family: a genealogy with touches of family history and recollections. By Carrol O. Buttrill and Louis E. Reid, Jr. 1st Ed. Beaumont, Tex. Buttrill and Reid. 1983. (LC)

BUTTRILL – Buttrill, Carrol Oliver
The Buttrill family: a genealogy with touches of family history and recollections. By Louis E. Reid, Jr. Beaumont, Tex. 1983. (NGS)

BUTTRILL – Wulfkuhle, Virginia A.
The Buttrill Ranch complex, Brewster County, Texas: evidence of early ranching in the Big Bend. By Virginia A. Wulfkuhle. Austin, Tex. Historical Commission. 1986. (LC)

BYARS – Thaten, Nell B.
Byars family history: with information or records on following allied lines; James H. Bounds, James C. Bounds, Jacob Hardin, Wright Gatlin, Joshua Richards, George Richard, Jonas Bedford, Peter Raymond. By Nell B. Thaten. Fort Worth, Tex. Miran Pub., 1976. (FW)

BYERS – Craig, Marion Stark
My Byers-Bonar-Shannon and allied families. Little Rock, Ark. Craig, 1976, c1977. (DAR)

BYERS – Garbert, Norma Y. Harris (Norma Yvonne Harris), 1934-
Descendants and forebears of James Kuykendall Byers and Ary Ann Burch: a southern family. By Norma Y. (Harris) Garbert; based on original research by Harold Carner, Jessica Christine (Byers) Carner. Baltimore: Gateway Press. Chatsworth, CA. N. H. Barbert. 1989. (LC)

BYERS – Thaten, Nell Byars
Byars family history: with information or records on following allied lines, James H. Bounds, James G. Bounds, Jacob Hardin, Wright Gatlin, Joshua Richards, George Richards, Jonas Bedford, Peter Raymond. By Nell Byars Thaten. Fort Worth, Tex. Miran Publishers. c1976. (LC)

BYLER – Byler, Roger Louis, 1912-
Jacob Byler of North Carolina who died in 1804 and his descendants. By Roger Louis Byler. Sweeny, Tex. R. L. Byler. c1985. (LC)

BYRD – Beard, Marjorie Pierce, 1924
Growing up on Preston Road: a family portrait, 1844-1964. By Marjorie Pierce Beard. 1st Ed. Austin, Tex. Nortex Press. c1989. (LC)

BYRD -- Martindale, Mary Jo, 1907-
Byrd—Stephenson and other lineages: a genealogy. By Mary Jo Martindale, compiler. Fort Worth, Tex. Miran Publishers. c1978. (LC)

BYRNE – Byrne, Jamie
 Short history of the Byrne family from County Wicklow, Ireland to the Byrne Colony at Lomar, Aransas Co., Texas. By Jamie Byrne. Austin, author, 1966. (FW)

BYRNE – Byrne, Jamie
 A short history of the Byrne Family from County Wicklow, Ireland to the Byrne Colony at Lamar (Arausas Co., Texas). Austin, Tex. 1966. (NGS)

BYRON – Byrom, Henry Harbin, 1919-
 Some descendants of Ezekial Byrom of Southfarnham Parish, Essex County, Virginia (1790). By Henry Harbin Byrom. 1st Ed. Fort Worth, Tex. H. H. Byrom. 1941. (LC)

BYRON – Roberts, Eunice Byram, 1884-
 Byram-Crawford and allied families genealogy. Compiled by Eunice Byram Roberts. Rev. Ed. Wichita Falls, Tex. Nortex Press. 1976. (LC)

C –

CABANISS – Green, John Plath
 Henry Cabaniss and his descendants. Dallas, Tex. Green. 1956. (DAR)

CAFFEY – Caffey, David L., 1947-
 The old home place: farming on the West Texas frontier. By David L. Caffey. Burnet, Tex. Eakin Press. c1981. (LC)

CALAME – Whatley, Pegge Yeldell, 1932
 Longbothan-Calame family. By Peggy Yeldell Whatley. Tarrant County, Tex. P. Y. Whatley. 1987. (LC)

CALDWELL – Anderson, Mrs. John Q.
 Caldwell. College Station, Tex. Anderson. 1959. (DAR)

CALDWELL – Anderson, Mrs. John Q.
 Caldwell workbook. Houston, Tex. Anderson. 1966. (DAR)

CALDWELL – Anderson, Marie Loraine (Epps)
 Caldwell, Epps, McEachin-MacQueen, McNutt-Gillespie. By Marie Loraine (Epps) Anderson. College Station, Tex., 1959. (LC)

CALDWELL – Caldwell, William W. (William Wallace), 1927-
 David Caldwell, 1705-1781, and his descendants in the United States of America. By William W. Caldwell. Parkdale, Ariz. J. Caldwell Files. 1987. (LC)

CALDWELL – Texas DAR, G. R. C.
 Caldwell, Grammer, Hitchcock and other Bible records. 1952. (DAR)

CALDWELL – Whelchel, Mary Lou Caldwell
 Caldwell-Cook-Morriss-Whelchel. Houston, Tex. Whelchel, 1968. (DAR)

CALHOUN – Calhoun, Edwin
Archibald Calhoun and descendants. By Edwin Calhoun. San Antonio, Tex. 1974. (FW)

CALLAHAN – Callahan, Michael A. (Michael Alan), 1942-
The Callahan's, Sligo to Dakota, 1863: the descendants of Peter Callahan and his wife Margaret Kevill and of Cornelius Callahan and his wife Catharine Finian, who came from County Sligo, Ireland, to Union County, South Dakota, including all descendants through the Baxters, Donnellys, McInerney, and O'Herons. By Michael A. Callahan. Dallas, Tex. M. A. Callahan, 1979. (LC)

CALLAHAN – Callahan, Michael A.
The Callahan's, Sligo to Dakota, 1863, descendents of Peter Callahan and Margaret Kevill; Cornelius Callahan and Catherine Finian. Dallas, Tex. 1979. (NGS)

CALLENDER – Robinson, Mrs. Alice (Vance)
Callender genealogy; ancestors and descendants of Nathaniel Callender and Olive Kellogg. By Mrs. Alice (Vance) Robinson. San Antonio, Tex. Vance Printery. 1911. (LC)

CAMAC – Cammack, Cecil C. (Cecil Cagle), 1908-
John and Margaret Purtle Cammack, their descendants and connecting lines. Compiled and written by Cecil C. Cammack. Tyler, Tex. C. C. Cammack, 1983. (LC)

CAMBERN – Marsh, Lois Cambern
Cambern family in Texas, 1831-1972. Washington, D.C. (s.n., 1972). (DAR)

CAMBERN – Marsh, Lois Cambern
They came to stay. Quanah, Tex. Marsh, 1974. (DAR)

CAMP – Carter, Nell Jones
Camp, Jones, and related families of Connecticut, Illinois, Missouri, Virginia, Carolina, Georgia, Alabama, Mississippi, Texas, and points west. Tallahasse, Fla. Carter, 1977. (DAR)

CAMP – Carter, Nell Jones, 1910-
Camp, Jones, and related families of Connecticut, Illinois, Missouri, Virginia, Carolina, Georgia, Alabama, Mississippi, Louisiana, Texas, and points west. By Nell Jones Carter. 1st Ed. Tallahassee: Carter. 1977. (LC)

CANTRELL – Benson, Mrs. W. E.
The Cantrell-Newman genealogy. Bowie, Tex. Benson, 196? (DAR)

CANTRELL – Benson, Mrs. W. E.
The Cantrell-Newman genealogy. Compiled by Mrs. W. E. Benson, Mrs. Jack Slayden. Bowie, Tex. W. E. Benson. 198-. (LC)

With: The Cantrill-Cantrell genealogy. Susan Cantrill Christie. Brooklyn, N.Y. S. C.

CANTRELL – Wright, Mildred S.
George Washington Cantrell and his wife, Martha Elizabeth Lea Carver of Tennessee: their ancestry and descendants. Compiled by Mildred Sulser Wright. Beaumont, Tex. M. S. Wright. c1983. (LC)

CARAWAY – Elliott, Zola F. (Zola Florence), 1912-
Kinship, our mother's line: Caraway, Williams, and Dowdle. By Zola F. Elliott. Austin, Tex. Z. F. Elliott. 1989. (LC)

CARDWELL – Cardwell, Robert J.
Robert Cardwell of Campbell County, Virginia. El Paso, Tex. Cardwell, c1980. (DAR)

CARDWELL – Cardwell, Robert
Robert Cardwell of Campbell County, Virginia. Compiled by Robert Cardwell. El Paso, Tex. R. J. Cardwell, c1980. (LC)

CAREY – Rigsby, Michael H. (Michael Hall), 1935-
The ancestry of Laura Elaine Rigsby. By Michael H. Rigsby, Carolyn E. Rigsby. Houston, Tex. M. H. Rigsby. c1987. (LC)

CARLEY – Carley, Wm. H.
Information on the Kerley, Cearley and Carley families of the South. By Wm. H. Carley. San Angelo, Tex. 1945. (FW)

CARRICO – Carrico, Horner E.
Descendants of Peter Carrico of Charles County, Maryland. By Horner E. Carrico. Dallas, Tex., 1950. (FW)

CARROLL – Carroll, R. Francis (Rupert Francis), 1910-
The heritage of our children: family history of Carroll, Robinson, Strain, Stephens, Mitchell, Eiland, Daniel, Whatley, Bird, Trawick, Bryant, Ping, Bradley, Bush, Chambers, McMullen, Fulgham, McWhorter, Stewart, Woodward, Dobritz, Zahn, Albrecht, Harsdorff. By R. Francis Carroll. Corpus Christi, Tex. R. F. Carroll, 1981. (LC)

CARROLL – Strickland, David N. (David Neil), 19947-
Carroll, Echols, Clement, Driver & related families. Carrollton, Tex. David N. Strickland. 1988. (LC)

CARRUTH – Carruth, Lela Grant, 1918-
From whence ye came: Carruth, Craighead, Davis, Grant, Hawkins, Miller, Mills, Noblitt, Packwood, Tyler, Wood and related famililes. By Lela Grant Carruth. Burnet, Tex. Nortex Press. c1982. (LC)

CARSON – Carson, Frederick Thomas
A history of the Carson family, and the allied families: Cooke, Kimbrough, and Henderson; being an account of the forebears and the descendants of Doctor William Cooke Carson and Dorcas Elizabeth Kimbrough of Tennessee and Texas. By Frederick Thomas Carson. (n.p.). 1956. (LC)

CARTER – Carter, Glenmore R. (Glenmore Rust), 1907-
   The Carters of Virginia: Bernard Carter branch. Glenmore R. Carter? Keene, Tex. G. R. Carter. 1986. (LC)

CARTER – Cartier, Mistrot
   The Carter-Davidson history. By Mistrot Cartier. Houston? Tex. 1965. (LC)

CARTER – Eckhardt, Ura L.
   Carter family assorted notes, no. 1-10. By Ura L. Eckhardt. Houston, Tex. 1969. (FW)

CARTER – Gray, Faye J.
   My grandmother's Smiths and Carters. By Faye J. Gray. Commanche? Tex. 1967. (LA)

CARTER – Griffin, Phyllis Ansley, 1936-
   A history of descendants, Thomas Ansley, Warren County, Georgia. By Phyllis Ansley Griffin. Denton? Tex. Griffin. c1979. (LC)

CARTER – Taff, Edward Hill Carter
   The Carter family tree (1662-1962): John Carter and Elizabeth (Hill) Carter branch. By Edward Hill Carter Taff. Houston, Tex. 1961. (LC)

CARTHEW – Carthew-Yorstown, C. M.
   (Abstracts of the) Carthew Yorstown family (genealogy). By C. M. Carthew-Yorstown. Dallas, Tex. (n.d.). (FW)

CASEY – Casey, Clifford B.
   Bakers' dozen; we were thirteen, the Caseys of Tuscola, Taylor Co., Texas. By Clifford B. Casey. Seagraves, Tex. Pioneer Bk. Pub. 1974. (FW)

CATCHINGS -- Catchings, T. C.
   The Catchings and Holiday families and various related families in Virginia, Georgia, Mississippi and other southern states. Atlanta, Ga. A. B. Caldwell Pub. co. 1919. (DAR)

CATES – Leard, Greta Cates, 1938
   The Cates chain: the Hiram Cates family from Tennessee to Texas & around the world, 1814-1988. Research by Sitaska Riley Merritt & Greta Cates Leard; written by Greta Cates Leard. Wolfe City, Tex. Published for the author by Henington Pub. Co. c1988. (LC)

CATTERTON – Catterton, Conn D., 1908-
   American Cattertons. By Conn D. Catterton. Arlington, Tex. Woodland West Office Supply. c1982. (LC)

CHADWICK – Taylor, Bill N.
   A concise history of the Chadwick family with especial reference to Stokley Rowan Chadwick and some notations on the Jacob Fisher family, (an allied family). Longview, Tex. Taylor. 1966? (DAR)

CHALK -- Hyman, Minna Chalk
The Chalk family of England and America, 1066-1942. Hyman, Tex. Hyman. 1942? (DAR)

CHALK – Hyman, Mrs. Minna Chalk (Scott)
The Chalk family of England and America, 1066-1942. By Mrs. Minna Chalk (Scott) Hyman. Hyman, Tex. Press of the Naylor Company, 1942. (LC)

CHALK – Williams-Walker, Naylan Gaile Linton
Allied families of Chalk, Massie, Oates, Linton, 1066-1987. Compiled and edited by Naylan Gaile Linton Williams-Walker. Victoria, Tex. G. Walker. 1988? (LC)

CHAMBERLAIN – Eckhardt, Ura L.
Chamberlain family assorted notes. By Ura L. Eckhardt. Houston, Tex. 1970. (FW)

CHAMBERS – Chambers, Mildred Aldrich
Charles Chambers genealogy. Compiled by Mildred Aldrich Chambers. Midland, Tex. M. A. Chambers. 1985? (LC)

CHANCE – Chance, Hilda
Chance of Ohio, Virginia, North Carolina, Georgia, Texas, Tennessee, Kentucky, Delaware, Maryland, Pennsylvania, Michigan, California, Indiana, New Jersey. By Hilda Chance. Liberty, Pa. 1970. (LC)

CHANCELLOR – Chancellor, Johnson Camden
The Chancellors, Odessa, Tex. Chancellor, 1963. (DAR)

CHANCELLOR –CHANDLER Chancellor, Johnson C.
The Chancellors. By Johnson C. Chancellor. Odessa, Tex. The West Texas Office Supply Co. 1963. (FW)

CHANCELLOR – Chancellor, Johnson C.
The ancestors of Annie Laurie Burt Chancellor... By Johnson C. Chancellor. Odessa, Tex., 1964. (SL)

CHANDLER – Foster, Gladys Edith Richards
Chandler and Richards families. Fort Worth, Tex. Foster & Foster, 1961. (DAR)

CHANDLER – Spray, Barbara C.
Chandler and Peacock cousins with Petty and Hayhurst families. By Barbara Chandler Spray. Amarillo, Tex. B. C. Spray. 1985. (LC)

CHASE – Chase, Mary Henrietta
Descendants of Aquila Chase and Robert Seeley. Dallas, Tex. Chase, 1963. (DAR)

CHASTAIN – Chastain, James Garvin
A brief history of the Huguenots and three family trees: Chastain-Lochridge-Stockton. By James Garvin Chastain. El Paso, Tex. Print. by Baptist Publishing House. 1933. (LC)

CHENAULT – Chenault, Wm. O.
Rambling Chenaults. By Wm. O. Chenault. Dallas, Tex., 1955? (FW)

CHILDERS – Jenkins, Frank Duane
The family of Thomas & Lottie (Brewer) Childers, Sr. Ballinger, Tex. Jenkins, 1974. (DAR)

CHISHOLM – Chisholm, Fannie G.
The four state Chisholm trail. By Fannie G. Chisholm. San Antonio, Tex., 1966? (NY)

CHISHOLM – Taylor, T. U.
Jesse Chisholm. By T. U. Taylor. Bandern, Tex. Frontier Times. c.1939. (LC)

CHRISTIAN – Doshier, Inez Christian
Christian-Terrill genealogy. Amarillo, Tex? Doshier, Nelson, McFarlan? 1955? (DAR)

CHRISTIAN – Doshier, Inez C.
James Terrill Christian family. Copied from records by Inez C. Doshier. Amarillo, Tex. (n.d.) (FW)

CHRISTIAN – Hicks, William, Mrs.
The yesterdays behind the door. By Mrs. Hicks Beach. Dallas, Tex. Christinne Carthew-Yorstoun, 1973. (LC)

CHRISTOPHER – Eckhardt, Ura L.
Assorted notes on the Christopher family, no. 1-2, 1964-1970. By Ura L. Eckhardt. Houston, Tex., 1970. (FW)

CHRYSLER – Crisler, William Neville, 1924-
A genealogy, history, and chronology of the Kreisler-Crisler family of the United States of America, or, more particularly, the descendants of Matthais Kreisler and Barbara Von Schellenberg Kreisler... Commenced in 1938 by the author, William Neville Crisler, Jr. Dallas? W.N. Crisler, Jr. c1981. (LC)

CHURCH – Koutnik, Dorothy King
Church, Lake, Lee, Love. Dallas, Tex. ?1968. (NGS)

CLABAUGH – Harrell, Elizabeth J.
The Clabaughs: an account of the life and times of Frederick Clabaugh of Maryland in 1742 and his descendnats who migrated to East Tennessee, then on to Alabama and Texas: with a special chapter on Henry Haggard, 1746-1842, a frontier Baptist preacher of Virginia, East Tennessee and Alabama, and his family. By Betty Harrell. Los Altos, Calif. B. Harrell. c1982. (LC)

CLAIBORNE – Eckhardt, Ura L.
   Claiborne family, no. 1-2, 1966-70. By Ura L. Eckhardt. Houston, Tex. 1970. (FW)

CLAIBORNE – Threlkeld, Harriette Pinnell
   Supplement to The Claybourn family, written and compiled by Verner Marvin Claybourn, Harriette Pinnell Threlkeld, Rose Marie Brown Williams. By Threlkeld and Williams; assisted by Josephine Scarborough Claybourn. McKinney, Tex. H. P. Threlkeld. 1979. (LC)

CLARK – Clark, A. G.
   Reminiscences of a centenarian; as told by Amasa Gleason Clark, veteran of the Mexican War. By A. G. Clark. San Antonio, Tex. Naylor. 1972. (FW)

CLARK – Clark, Eunice Newbold
   Clarks from Pennsylvania and allied families: from early 1700s to 1984. By Eunice Newbold Clark. Dallas, Tex. E. N. Clark. c1984. (LC)

CLARK – Clark, James W.
   Richard Clark of Virginia, 1732-1811, with a brief history of his descendants, and their westward migration through Montgomery County, Kentucky; Putnam and Montgomery Counties, Indiana; Dallas County, Iowa; and Jewell County, Kansas. Abilene, Tex. Clark, 1971. (DAR)

CLARK – Clark, James Warren
   Richard Clark of Virginia, 1732-1811. Abilene, Tex. 1971. (NGS)

CLARK – Clark, John W.
   Some descendants of William Clark of Sabine County, Texas. Fort Worth, Tex. American Reference Pub. Co., c1971. (DAR)

CLARK – Clark, John W.
   Some descendants of Wm. Clark of Sabine County, Texas. By John W. Clark. Fort Worth, Tex. Amer. Ref.. Pub. Co., c1971. (LC)

CLARK – Clark, Joseph L.
   Thank God, we made it! A family affair with education. By Joseph L. Clark. Austin, Tex. Univ. of Texas. 1969. (FW)

CLARK – Clark, Pat
   Ancestors of my children – Clark/James/Myers. By Pat Clark. Fort Worth, Tex. P. and R. Clark. 1981. (LC)

CLARK – Clark, Ruby L.
   History and lineage of a Clark family, 17th century-20th century. By Ruby L. Clark. Gainesville, Tex., 1966. (NY)

CLARK – Clark, Victor E. (Victor Earl), 1919-
   The Highland Scot Clarks from the Isle of Jura, Scotland: letter #1, December 10, 1980. From Victor E. Clark, Jr. Dallas, Tex. V. W. Clark. 1984. (LC)

CLARK – Crawford, William Lusk, 1907-
Ancestors & friends: a history & genealogy. By William Lusk Crawford, Sr. Dallas, Tex. Farmer Genealogy Co. c1978. (LC)

CLARK – Eckhardt, Ura L.
Clark family, no. 1-11, 1952-1970. By Ura L. Eckhardt. Houston, Tex. 1970. (FW)

CLARK – Shannon, Betty Biggers, 1921-
Our Clark legacy. By Betty Biggers Shannon. Austin, Tex. B. B. Shannon. c1990. (LC)

CLARK(E) –
Richard Clark of Virginia, 1732-1811; with a brief history of some 750 of his descendants and their westward migration through Montgomery Co., Ky., Putnam and Montgomery Co., Ind.; Dallas Co., Iowa; and Jewell Co., Kans. Abilene, Tex. 1971. (FW)

CLAY –
The Clay family. Houston, Tex. Clay Family Assoc. 1966. (LA)

CLAYTON – Clayton, Belva
Thomas Nelson Clayton: his descendants-his ancestors; a family history and genealogical research. By Belva Clayton. Fort Worth, Tex. Mason Print. Co. 1973. (LC)

CLELAND – Oliver, Glenn William
Cleland Cousins; and allied families of Baker, Blair, Collins, Fisher, Gowdey, Haylett, Hume, Moody, Oliver, Richards, Ross, Wells, etc. Also by Rebekah D. Oliver. Dallas, Tex. 1962. (NGS)

CLEM – Clem, Inus B.
Clem family: 1765-1976. By Inus B. Clem. Dallas, Tex. Falcon. 1976. (FW)

CLEMENTS – Strickland, David N. (David Neil), 1947-
Carroll, Echols, Clement, Driver & related families. Carrollton, Tex. David N. Strickland. 1988. (LC)

CLOUD – Rugeley, Helen Hoskins, 1911-
Cloud, Woolsey, and allied families. Data compiled by Rosa (Woolsey) Howze; produced by Amanda (Howze) Amsler; edited by Margaret (Howze) Purcell; supplemental researched and written by Helen (Hoskins) Rugeley. Austin, Tex. M. H. Purcell. c1987. (LC)

COATES – Tucker, D. A. (Duard Arnold), 1919-
Coats kin: from North Carolina to Tennessee to Arkansas. By D. A. tucker. Houston, Tex. D. A. Tucker. 1987. (LC)

COBB – Bivins, Viola Cobb
Memoirs. Mrs. J. B. Bivins. Longview, Tex. Bivins. 194? (DAR)

COBB – Cobb, Lester Ray
William H. Cobb tree and related families. By Lester Ray Cobb, compiler and auth. Fort Worth, Tex. Arrow, Curtis Print Co., Pub. Division, 1974. (LC)

COBB – Cobb, Lester R.
William H. Cobb tree and related families. By Lester R. Cobb. Fort Worth, Tex. Arrow Curtis Print Co. 1971. (FW)

COBB – Cobb, Rodney Dale
Our Cobb family: a history of our origins in the royal colony of North Carolina, Robertson County of Tennessee, and Cass County of Texas. Written by Rodney Dale Cobb; genea. research by Herschel Neill Cobb. Sacramento, Calif. Cobb. c1975. (LC)

COBB – Turner, Virgin? (McKinney) Turner
The Cobb family of "Rocky Mount," Piney Flats, Tennessee, 1613-1972. By Virgin? (McKinney) Turner. Published under the supervision of Pauline Massengill DeFriece. Dallas, Tex., 1973. (LC)

COCKE – Eckhardt, Ura L.
Cocke family, 1-9, 1960-1970. By Ura L. Eckhardt. Houston, Tex. 1970. (FW)

COCKRELL – Cockrell, Monroe F.
Francis Marion Cockrell of Warrensburg, Mo. and Alexander Cockrell 1 of Dallas, Texas. By Monroe F. Cockrell. (Chicago) 1947. (LC)

COCKRELL – Cockrell, Monroe Fulkerson
Sarah Horton Cockrell in early Dallas. By Monroe Fulkerson Cockrell. Evanston? Ill. 1961. (LC)

COKER – Hill, Euel Ray, 1934-
The Hills of Tennessee and Texas. By Euel Ray Hill; edited by Theron Lavon Smith. El Paso, Tex. E. R. Hill. 1982. (LC)

COLBERT – Taliaferro, Velma
Memoirs of a Chickasaw squaw. By Velma Taliaferro; edited with introductory note by Molly Levite Griffis. Norman, Okla. Levie of Apache. c1987. (LC)

COLE – Cole, Gary C.
Across the frontier; a history of the Cole family from the 13th century. By Gary C. Cole. Garland? Tex. 1973. (LC)

COLE – Eckhardt, Ura L.
Cole family, no. 1-8, 1960-1970. By Ura L. Eckhardt. Houston, Tex. 1969. (FW)

COLE – Hightower, Jack English, 1926-
The family of William Clayton Hightower and Mai Cole: their ancestors and descendants, a genealogy/family history. By Jack English Hightower. Austin, Tex. J. E. Hightower. 1988. (LC)

COLE – Killgore, D. E.
The ancestors and descendants of William Rappleye Cole. Clarkwood, Tex. M. T. Cole, 1956. (DAR)

COLEMAN – Coleman, James P.
The Robert Coleman family, from Virginia to Texas, 1652-1965. Ackerman, Miss. Coleman, 1965. (DAR)

COLEMAN – Coleman, James P.
The Robert Coleman family, from Virginia to Texas, 1652-1965. By James P. Coleman, with the assistance of many others. Ackerman, Miss. Coleman. 1965. (LC)\

COLEMAN – Croom, Emily Anne
Coleman kin. Houston, Tex. Croom, 1973. (DAR)

COLEMAN – Dickson, Roy S. (Roy Shelton), 1933-
The descendants of James A. Dickson, ca. 1820-1864, of Tennessee and Texas: allied families, Coleman, Fulbright, Harkey, Nall, Tippen. By Roy S. Dickson, Jr. Bartllesville, Okla. R. S. Dickson. c1987. (LC)

COLEMAN – Eckhardt, Ura L.
Coleman family, no. 1-8, 1960-1970. By Ura L. Eckhardt. Houston, Tex. 1970. (FW)

COLEMAN – Winston, Mary Frances Coleman, 1927-
A collection of Coleman family mementoes. Updated ed. By Mary Frances Coleman Winston. Austin, Tex. Historical Publications. 1988. (LC)

COLEMAN – Winston, Mary Frances Coleman, 1927-
A collection of Coleman family mementoes. By Mary Frances Coleman Winston. Austin, Tex. M. F. C. Winston. 1983. (LC)

COLLADAY – Jones, Wayne V., 1902-
Jacob Woodward Colladay and his descendants. Compiled by Wayne V. Jones. Houston, Tex. Jones. 1976. (LC)

COLLADAY – Jones, Wayne Van L.
Jacob Woodward Colladay and his descendants. By Wayne Van L. Jones. Houston, Tex. D. Armstrong Co. 1976. (FW)

COLLADAY – Jones, Wayne Van Leer
Jacob Woodward Colladay and his descendants. Houston, Tex. 1976. (NGS)

COLLINS – Collins, Archibald O.
Ole Man Mose and his chillun; the story of Moses Collins of South Carolina, Georgia, Alabama, and Mississippi, and his descendants. By Archibald O. Collins. Aransas Pass, Tex. Biog. Press, 1974. (FW)

COLLINS – Collins, Vinson A.
A story of my parents Warren Jacob Collins and Tolitha Eboline Valentine Collins, including their 65 years of married life together... and many of their descendants... By Vinson A. Collins. Dallas, Tex. C. P. Collins, Jr. 1962. (DP)

COLLINS – Darling, Kenneth P.
Collins-Bryan. Houston, Tex. Darling. 1980. (DAR)

COLLINS – Splawn, Jennie L. (Jennie Lillian), 1885-1960-
Genealogy of the Splawn and Collins family. By Jennie L. Splawn. Lubbock, Tex. Texas Tech Press. 1986. (LC)

COLVIN – Hayes, Florence, 1932-
My family remembered. By Florence Hayes. Houston, Tex. F. M. S. Hayes. 1987. (LC)

COMBEST – Covington, Mildred Lerlene Rowell, 1916-
John Combest and his descendants. By Lerlene Rowell Covington. Burleson, Tex. L. R. Covington. c1987. (LC)

COMPTON – Blalock, Delton D. (Delton Dennis), 1940-
British and American Comptons from the colonial era to the modern day in New York, New Jersey, Virginia, Tennessee, Alabama, and Texas, 1634-1984. Compiled by Delton D. Blalock. 1st Ed. Hanceville, Ala. D. Blalock. 1984. (LC)

COMSTOCK – Comstock, Ernest B.
Family history and allied families: Baker, Titus, Vrooman, West, Bingham, etc. By Ernest B. Comstock. Dallas, Tex., 1930. (FW)

COMSTOCK –
The ancestry of Ernest Bernard Comstock, Dallas, Texas. Including family connections with Comstock, West, Vroom, Baker... et al. Dallas, Tex. 1936. (FW)

CONARD – Bowen, Amy M.
Descendants of John Conard of Loudoun County, Virginia. By Amy M. Bowen. San Antonio, Tex. Darley. 1939. (FW)

CONNOR – Baer, Mabel Van Dyke
Connor families of North Carolina and Texas and collateral families of Murr and Reed Reid. 1974? (DAR)

CONVERSE – Wynne, Robert L.
Ancestry of Deacon Edward Converse, 1590-1663. Dr. & Mrs. Robert L. Wynne. Houston, Tex. R. L. Wynne. 198-. (LC)

COOK – Cell, Robert F.
Tax records, selected family names, Franklin County, Pennsylvania, 1796-1847: for selected names of the Cell family. By Robert F. Cell. Edinburg, Tex. R. F. Cell. c1990. (LC)

COOK – Cook, Tressie
Cook-Heard & allied families, Barton, Bullock, Fitzpatrick & Smith. Dallas, Tex. Farmer Genealogy Co., c1978. (DAR)

COOK – Cook, Tressie, 1903-
Cook-Heard & allied lines: Barton, Bullock, Fitzpatrick & Smith. By Tressie Cook. Dallas, Tex. Farmer Genealogy Co. c1978. (LC)

COOK – Eckhardt, Ura L.
Cook family, no. 1-10, 1959-1970. By Ura L. Eckhardt. Houston, Tex. 1970. (FW)

COOK – Edwards, Lula Cook, 1938-
Friends and families: a genealogy of the family of Columbis Marion Cook and Mary Robertson Cook. By Lula Cook Edwards. Waxahachie, Tex. L. C. Edwards. c1989. (LC)

COOK – Kelsey, Mary Wilson
Robert Wilson, 1750-1826 of Blount County, Tennessee; some of his descendants and related families including Gould, Cook, Brooks, Huson, Shearer, Stribling. By Mary Wilson Kelsey. Houston, Tex. M. W. Kelsey. c1987. (LC)

COOKE – Cooke, Velma M.
Things that count; the story of the Cooke family. By Velma M. Cooke. Baytown, Tex? 1974. (FW)

COOLEY – Miller, Kathryn Mercedes Cooley
My Cooley-Walters ancestry from Fairchance, Penn. and surrounding areas. By Kathryn Mercedes Cooley Miller. Houston, Tex. K.M.C. Miller. c1987. (LC)

COOPER – Cooper, Clarence Lavaugn
Cooper family index: Southern United States federal population censuses, 1790-1850. Houston, Tex. C. L. Cooper. c1978. (LC)

COOPER –
Cooper from then… 'till now. By Peggy Cooper Garrett and Joe Garrett. Abilene, Tex. Quality Print Co., 1973. (LC)

COOPER – Morrow, Betty Moss
McGee-Cooper-Synnott. By Betty Moss Chaney-Morrow. Teague, Tex. B. M. Chaney-Morrow. c1990. (LC)

COOPER – Roberts, Lesbia W.
Hugh Cooper (1720-1793) of Fishing Creek, S.C. and his descendants. By Lesbia W. Roberts. Fort Worth, Tex. McElhaney Print., 1975. (FW)

COOPER – Roberts, Lillian
Hugh Cooper, 1720-1793, of Fishing Creek South Carolina and his descendants. Fort Worth, Tex. Roberts, 1975. (DAR)

COOPER – Scott, Evalyn Parrott
Links that bind, vol. I, Cooper family notes. Sundan, Tex. Sundan Bacon-News, c1967. (DAR)

COPELAND – Jantz, Virginia Copeland, 1923-
Copeland, Bostick, Patton, and allied families: including Martin, Clement, Thompson, and Cobb. By Virginia Copeland Jantz. Waco, Tex. V. C. Jantz. c1981. (LC)

COPELAND – Jantz, Virginia Copeland
Copeland, Bostick, Patton, and allied famililes, Martin, Clement, Thompson, Cobb families. Waco, Tex. c1981. (NGS)

CORBIN – Eckhardt, Ura L.
Corbin, Bertrand and Eltonhead families assorted notes. By Ura L. Eckhardt. Houston, Tex. 1970. (FW)

CORETH – Gayne, Minetta Altgelt, 1924-
Lone star and double eagle: Civil War letters of a German-Texas family. By Minetta Altgelt Gayne. Fort Worth, Tex. Texas Christian University Press. c1982. (LC)

CORLEY –Corley, Bill J.
Two hundred years of Corley generations (and related family names). Edited by Bill J. Corley. Duncanville, Tex. Printing Express, 1984. (LC)

CORN – Wilbert, Hulda, 1903-
Kernels of Korn: the historical events of a pioneer family. By Hulda Wilbert. Burnet, Tex. Nortex Press. c1982. (LC)

CORSE – Craig, Betty Lee Berry
The Corse family. Austin, Tex. Craig, 1978. (DAR)

CORSE – Craig, Betty Lee Berry, 1928-
The Corse family. By Betty Lee Berry Craig. Austin, Tex. B.L.B. Craig. 1978. (LC)

COSBY – Ball, Greg, 1962-
Family charts of the Cozby, Skeen, Walker, Rawson, Brumbelow, and Smith families. By Greg Ball. 2nd Ed. San Antonio, Tex. G. Ball. 1989. (LC)

COTHAM – Balinas, Verby Lee Cotham
A Cotham book. Compiled by Verby Lee Cotham Balinas. Houston, Tex. V. L. C. Balinas. c1981. (LC)

COTHAM – Balinas, Verby Lee Cotham, 1919-
More named Cotham. Supplement to A Cotham book. By Verby Lee Cotham Balinas. Houston, Tex. V. L. C. Balinas. c1984. (LC)

COTTON – Gregory, Peggy H.
Cotton picking volume one. Houston, Tex. Gregory, c1976. (DAR)

COUNTRYMAN – Countryman, Ardell
Countryman family history: including a reproduction of Contryman genealogy, 1925.
By Ardell and Grace Countryman. Dallas, Tex. Curtis Media Corp. 1986, [1987]. (LC)

COVINGTON – White, Eurie (Covington)
Covington cousins; a genealogy of the Covingtons and some of the related families.
By Eurie (Covington) White. Dallas, Tex. Nolden Print. Co. c1956. (LC)

COVINGTON – White, Eurie (Covington)
Covington cousins. Dallas, Tex. c1956. (NGS)

COWLISHAW – Evans, Alfred W.
George Cowlishaw of Pilsley, England and Trinidad, Colorado. San Antonio, Tex. Evans, c1977. (DAR)

COWLISHAW – Evans, Alfred W., 1941-
George Cawlishaw of Pilsley, England and Trinidad, Colorado. Compiled by Alfred W. Evans. San Antonio, Tex. Evans. c1977. (LC)

COX – Jaeckel, Karl T., 1955-
The family of Granville H. Cox, 1822-1888, of early Ashe County, North Carolina, and Atchison County, Missouri. By Karl T. Jaeckel. El Paso, Tex. 1980. (LC)

COX – Manz, Mabel Ann Anderson, 1914-
Ancestors and descendants of Wesley and Huldah Wilson Cox of Madison County, Iowa. Compiled by Mabel Anderson Manz; primary research by Elinor Anderson Gaines, also, information gathered by Hazel Bardmess Cox; edited, typed, and published by Mabel Anderson Manz. Austin, Tex. M. A. Manz. 1983. (LC)

COX – Wallace, B. C.
Cornelius Jackson Cox and Huldah Ann Kemp Cox; their families, their descendants.
By B. C. Wallace. Happy, Tex., 1973. (FW)

CRABTREE –
The Crabtrees of southwest Virginia; abstracts of historical information, census and service records, genealogies (and) legends. Compiled by Arah Miller Fritz and Margaret Milam McProud. Pecos, Tex. Hawks Print. Co. 1965. (LC)

CRAIN – Crain, John M.
John Malone Crain family tree. By John M. Crain. Amarillo, Tex., 1962. (FW)

CRAIN – Crain, Solon P.
Ten sons of Oliver. San Angelo, Tex. Newsfoto Yearbooks, 1972. (DAR)

CRAIN – Crain, Solon P.
Ten sons of Oliver. By Solon P. Crain. San Angelo, Tex. Newsfoto Yearbooks. 1972. (NY)

CRAMER – Woff, Dolores Cramer
  The descendants of Nathan Cramer – Alazana Fish, including allied families and genealogical notes: Applegate, Ball, Bean, Cheney, Cox, Cranmer, Fessenden, Hennsley, Lyon, Mourning, Stookey, Wright. By Delores Cramer Woff. Odessa, Tex., 1972. (LC)

CRANE –
  Ten sons of Oliver. By Solon P. Crain (and) Marguerite Starr Crain. San Angelo, Tex. Newsfoto Yearbooks. 1972. (LC)

CRANSHAW – Wilkins, Hazel Crenshaw, 1919-
  Crenshaws and connections [i.e. connecting] families: Davis, Burgess, Lavenders, Hargis, Hoppers, Dials, Fanchers. Compiled by Hazel Crenshaw Wilkins. Gilmer, Tex. H. C. Wilkins. c1981. (LC)

CRAWFORD – Crawford, William Lusk
  Ancestors & Friends: A history & genealogy. Clark, Crawford, Lusk, Blount families. Dallas, Tex. c1978. (NGS)

CRAWFORD – Edward Crawford Family
  Edward Crawford's family: with special emphasis on those descendants who lived in or passed through Macoupin County, Illinois with eventual concentration in Illinois, Missouri, Oregon, Texas, Tennessee. By Crawford Family members. 1st Ed. [Illinois]. Crawford Family Book Committee. 1988. (LC)

CRAWFORD – Nitske, Betty Fugatt, 1916-
  We were a Texas people: Crawford, Fugatt, Fugitt, Hurley, Parsons. By Betty Fugatt Nitske. Ltd. Ed. (LC)

CRAWFORD – Smith, Lee R.
  Van Elizabeth Miller Smith and her known forebears; a documented genealogy. By Lee R. Smith. Miami, Tex. 1965. (NY)

CRENSHAW – Eckhardt, Ura L.
  Assorted notes on the Crenshaw family, no. 1-3, 5, 1964-1970. By Ura L. Eckhardt. Houston, Tex. 1970. (FW)

CRESWELL – Eckhardt, Ura L.
  Creswell family, no. 1-2, 4, 1965-1968. By Ura L. Eckhardt. Houston, Tex. 1968. (FW)

CRETIEN – Cretien, C. F.
  Early days in Dallas and Oak Cliff, Texas. By C. F. Cretien. Dallas, Tex. 1963. (FW)

CROCKETT – Crockett, Beatrice M.
  James Robert Crockett family history. By Beatrice M. Crockett. Waco, Tex. 1958. (FW)

CROCKETT – Duhe, Janis Vessels
  The Crocket bridge builders. By Janis Vessels Duhe. Cypress, Tex. J. V. Duhe. 1987. (LC)

CROCKETT – Eckhardt Ura L.
Crockett family assorted records. By Ura L. Eckhardt. Houston, Tex. 1970. (FW)

CROCKETT – Jones, Kathryn E.
Crockett cousins. By Kathryn E. Jones. Graham, Tex. K. E. Jones. c1984. (LC)

CROFT – Cell, Robert F.
Tax records, selected family names, Franklin County, Pennsylvania, 1796-1846: for selected names of the Cell family... By Robert F. Cell. Edinburg, Tex. R. F. Cell. c1990. (LC)

CROOK – Allen, Virginia Crook King
Some descendants of James Crook and Mary Williams Crook and several related families: [1746-1978]. Virginia (Crook) King Allen, Martha (King) Neubauer. Austin, Tex? M. K. Neubauer. 1978. (LC)

CROOK – Roberts, Leonard
Sang Branch settlers; folksongs and tales of a Kentucky mountain family. By Leonard Roberts. Music transcribed by C. Buell Agey. Austin. Published for the American Folklore Society by the University of Texas Press. 1974. (LC)

CROWE – Crow, Jewell (Lofland)
History of William Crow of Virginia and his descendants in America, and related families: their settlements, migrations, marriages, military achievements. By Jewell (Lofland) Crow. Dallas? C1961. (LC)

CROWELL – Hervey, Joyce Parker, 1943-
Just folk: the Crowell family. By Joyce Parker Hervey. Houston? Tex. J. P. Hervey. c1984. (LC)

CULBERTSON – Culbertson, Ambrose B.
John Culbertson, Ransom Thacker, John Cummings and related families. By Ambrose B. Culbertson. Fort Worth, Tex. (n.d.). 1961? (FW)

CULLUM –
Cullums synonymous. (Descendants of Rev. Marcus H. Cullum and Elizabeth Jane Davis). Dallas, Tex? 1970. (FW)

CULLUM – Cullum, Earl Owen
The Cullum colonels of Dallas, Texas. Prepared by Earl Owen Cullum. [S.1.] Cullum. 1977. (LC)

CULLUM – Cullums Synonymous
The Marcus Hiram Cullum Family. Dallas, Tex. ?1968. (NGS)

CUMMINGS – Cummings, Nettie Jo
Our heritage: Barnett, Blair, Cunningham, Endsley, Holmes, Hughings, Hunter, Lovett, Lowery, McNeely, Sanders, Simpson, Smiley, Wilson, McAfee. By Nettie Jo Cummings. Fort Worth, Tex. Miran Publishers. 1974. (LC)

CURBELO – Seymour, Geneva Bailey
Corbello. By Geneva Bailey Seymour. Lubbock, Tex. G. B. Seymour. c1984. (LC)

CURRY – Ericson, Carolyn Reeves
Curry cousins, 1785 to 1974. Nacogdoches, Tex. Ericson, c1975. (DAR)

CURRY – Ericson, Carolyn (R.)
Curry cousins, 1785 to 1974. By Carolyn (R,) Ericson. Nacogdoches, Tex. C. R. Ericson. 1975. (FW)

CUSTARD – Castor, Gaylord Bernard
Castor/Custard: the progenitors and other kinsfolk of Henry and Nancy Castor: a condensed family history. By Gaylord Bernard Castor. El Paso, Tex. G. B. Castor. 1984. (LC)

D –

DABBS – Dabbs, Jack Autrey
Dabbs family genealogy, U.S. By Jack Autrey Dabbs. Austin, Tex. J. A. Dabbs. 1986. (LC)

DALBY – Dalby, Norman Leonard
The Dalbys of Northeast Texas. S.l.: Dalby, 1970. (DAR)

DALE – Neal, Clarice G.
The Dales of eastern shore, Maryland, and Tennessee. By Clarence Neal. Austin, Tex. C. Neal. c1986. (LC)

DALE – Neal, Clarice
The Dales of Eastern Shore Maryland and Tennessee. Austin, Tex. c1986. (NGS)

DAMRON – Allen, Catherine
George Damron and wife Delilah Catherine (Fisher) Damron who settled in Fannin County, Texas, 1829. S.l.: Allen, 1968. (DAR)

DAMRON – Allen, Catherine
The Damron family; pioneer settlers of Fannin County, Texas, 1829. By Catherine Allen. (n.p., 1968). (LC)

DAMERON – Allen, Juanita Catherine, 1908-
Dr. George Damron, born 1796, Tennessee, and his descendants: pioneer settler Bonham and Ector, Fannin County, Texas, 1829. Houston, Tex. J. Allen. c1982. (LC)

DAMRON –
The Damron family; pioneer settlers of Fannin County, Texas, 1829. (n.p., 1968). (LC)

DAMRON – Herriage, Vivian L. N.
Pioneer settlers and their descendants of Ector, Fannin County, Texas: Damron and Nelms families. By Vivian L. N. Herriage. Bonham, Tex., 1967. (FW)

DAMRON –
First settlers; our great, great, great grandparents George and Delilah Fisher Damron and their descendants, of Bonham and Ector, Fannin County, Texas, in the Red River Valley. By Vivian and Brenda Newingham. Bonham, Tex. 1968. (LC)

DANDRIDGE – Barton, Thomas E.
From Virginia with love. By Thomas E. Barton. Sherman, Tex. TEBSCO. c1985. (LC)

DANIEL – Devine, Zanetta A. D.
The George Mayfield Daniel family in Texas. By Zonetta A. D. Devine, 1961. (FW)

DARBY – Cawthon, John Ardis
The inevitable quest. San Antonio, Tex. Naylor Co. c1965. (DAR)

DARDEN – Darden, Newton Jasper
Darden family history, with notes on ancestry of allied families: Washington, Lanier, Burch, Strozier, Dodson, Pyles, McNair, Barnett; a memorial of Dearden-Durden-Dardens of the United States of America, particularly in Virginia, Georgia, Tennessee, Alabama, Mississippi, and Texas. By Newton Jasper Darden. Edited, rev., and enl. By Leroy W. Tilton. (Washington?). 1957. (LC)

DARLING – Darling, Kenneth P.
Family histories. Houston, Tex. Darling, 1979. (DAR)

DARTER – Darter, Bertha Van M.
The Darter-Tarter-Daughters family. By Bertha Van M. Darter. Austin, Tex. The Darter Assoc. International, 1976. (GF)

DAVENPORT – Eckhardt, Ura L.
Davenport family, no. 1-2, 1965-1970. By Ura L. Eckhardt. Houston, Tex. 1970. (FW)

DAVIDSON – Davidson, J. M.
Emigration of William Mitchell Davidson and family from Buncombe County, North Carolina, to Texas in 1844; sketch of family history. By J. M. Davidson. (n.p., 1927?). (LC)

DAVIDSON – Reese, Cynthia Jones, 1938
The genealogical study of David Reese: with allied families: Polk, Brevard, Davidson, Caldwell, White, Alexander, McKnitt, Bradley. By Cynthia Jones Reese. Wichita Falls, Tex. C. J. Reese. c1990. (LC)

DAVIS – Abernethy, Arvord Milner, 1906-
Into the setting sun went the Abernethys, the Boltons, the Davises, the Talbots. Hamilton, Tex. A. M. Abernethy. 1986. (LC)

DAVIS – Davis, Thomas Jefferson, 1863-1953-
Our Davis family history. By Thomas Jefferson Davis. Cone, Tex. R.D. Travis. [197?]. (LC)

DAVIS – DeVerter, Ruth Hendricks
The genealogy of the Davis family. Baytown, Tex. DeVerter, c1957. (DAR)

DAVIS – DeVerter, Ruth (Hendricks)
The genealogy of the Davis family, Middlesex County, Virginia, and Montgomery County, Kentucky. By Ruth (Hendricks) DeVerter. Baytown, Tex., 1957. (LC)

DAVIS – Eckhardt, Ura L.
Assorted notes on the Davis family, no. 1-5, 1965-1970. By Ura L. Eckhardt. Houston, Tex. 1970. (FW)

DAVIS – Eckhardt, Ura L.
Davis: assorted records on the Davis family. By Ura L. Eckhardt. Houston, Tex. 1972. (FW)

DAVIS – Scarborough, Jewel Davis
The Davis family and their connections. Abilene, Tex. Scarborough, c1952. (DAR)

DAVIS – Sheriff, Pauline Callaway, 1918-
Davis data: John and Mary (Mooney) Davis: their ancestors and descendants as we know them, from North Carolina, South Carolina, Georgia, Alabama, Arkansas, Texas, Oklahoma and elsewhere. By Pauline Callaway Sheriff. Hollis, Okla. P. C. Sheriff. 1988. (LC)

DEVOUS – Hansborough, John W.
Genealogy of the Devous family. By John W. Hansborough. Austin, Tex. 1976. (FW)

DEWEES – McCarley, Marenne D.
Journey into yesterday, a family history, 1696 to 1969; Seay and DeWeese lines. By Marenne D. McCarley. Dallas, Tex., 1969. (FW)

DAWSON –
The genealogical history of the Thomas Dawson family and its descendants in America. By Everett T. Dawson and Buna Robertson Dawson. Austin, Tex. Aus-Tex. Printers. 1974. (LC)

DAWSON – Ebrom, Janet Dawson, 1949-
Dawson-Deaton pioneers to Texas. By Janet Dawson Ebrom & Gregory Alan Dawson. San Antonio, Tex. Dawson Books. c1989. (LC)

DAY – DeVerter, Ruth (Hendricks)
The Day and Hendrix(cks) families, including Poe and allied lines. By Ruth (Hendricks) DeVerter. Baytown, Tex. c1963. (LC)

DEAN – Wood, Margarette Hall, 1926-
The history of John Huson: from North Carolina to Alabama, his Huson, Huston, Houston descendants, and the allied pioneer families of Clepper, Robinson, Denn, and Gilmore. By Margaret Hall Wood. Baltimore, Gateway Press. (n.d.). (LC)

DEATON – Ebrom, Janet Dawson, 1949-
Dawson-Deaton pioneers of Texas. By Janet Dawson Ebrom. San Antonio, Tex. Dawson Books. c1989. (LC)

DECKER – Martin, Erna (Leinweber)
The Decker family history; genealogy gathered from the 18th century through the 20th century (1981). Hondo, Tex. 1982. (NGS)

DELANEY – Scott, Mary Rebecca Dulany
Gone to Texas: a compendium of the Dulany, Haddox, Heaton, Holland and Martin families. By Mary Rebecca Dulany Scott. Tomball, Tex. M. R. D Scott. c1989. (LC)

DELOZIER – Edwards, Richard Laurence, 1911-
Ancestors and descendants of the Edwards-Mathis, Delozier, and related families that pioneered through Virginia, Carolinas, Tennessee, Kentucky, Illinois, Missouri, Kansas, and spread to descendants in thirty-seven states and two provinces in Canada. By Richard Laurence Edwards. 1st Ed. Coffeyville, Kan. R. L. Edwards. c1985. (LC)

DELZELL – Delzell, Hugh Wayland, 1919-
Delzell ties: a history of the family of John Dalzell of Blount County, Tennessee. Compiled and published by Hugh Wayland Delzell. Wichita Falls, Tex. Delzell. c1977. (LC)

DENHAM – Denman, Rita B.
The Denman family from North Carolina to Texas. By Rita B. Denman. Richardson, Tex. R. B. Denman. 1990. (LC)

DENNARD – Dennard, Norris, 1919-
Dennard heritage. By Norris Dennard. Houston, Tex. Dennard Heritage Foundation. 1985. (LC)

DENNIS – Blazer, Margaret Coleman, 1924-
The Dennis and Coleman family tree. Rio Ranch, N. Mex. M. C. Blazer. 1985? (LC)

DENNY – Denny, Arthur, 1944-
William M. Denny of Titus County, Texas: born Apr. 1832 in Tennessee, died 5 Apr. 1917 in Titus County, Texas. Garland, Tex. A. Denny. c1987. (LC)

DESHAY – Nogues, DeWitt C. (DeWitt Collier), 1910-
Desha genealogy: a survey. DeWitt C. Nogues. Austin, Tex. ATEX Austin Inc. c1983. (LC)

DESHONG –
Louise DeShong, Revolutionary soldier; his ancestors and descendants. Ennis, Tex. Morton's, 1964. (LC)

DESHONG – Autry, Mahan Blair
Louis DeShong, Revolutionary soldier, his ancestors and descendants. Corsicana, Tex. Autry? (Ennis, Texas; Morton's). 1964. (DAR)

DEVEREUX – Winfrey, Dorman H.
Julien Sydney Devereux and his Monte Verdi Plantation. Waco, Tex. Texian Press, 1964, c1962. (DAR)

DEVERTER – DeVerter, Paul L.
The DeVerter family. Baytown, Tex. DeVerter, 1958. (DAR)

DEVERTER – DeVerter, Paul Logan
The DeVerter family. By Paul Logan DeVerter. Baytown, Tex., 1958. (LC)

DEW – Dew, Sarah Mae
The Dew line from England to Virginia and the Carolinas to Alabama, Mississippi, Arkansas, Texas, and Louisiana, with some records of other states. By Sarah Mae Dew. Magnolia, Ark. S. M. Dew. 1988. (LC)

DEW – Dews, Eli Madison, 1914-
The restless branch of the Dews family tree. By Eli Madison Dews. Rev. Ed. Orlando, Fla. E. M. Dews. 198-. (LC)

DICKSON – Reynolds, Harriet Dickson
Michael Dickson, 1788-1856 and some of his descendants. Houston, Tex. Reynolds. (DAR)

DIKEMAN – Dikeman, M. M.
The Dikeman family in Texas. Houston, Tex. Dikeman, 1959. (DAR)

DIKEMAN – Dikeman, Matthew M.
Dikeman family in Texas. By Matthew M. Dikeman. Dallas, Tex? 1959. (FW)

DINWIDDIE – DeVerter, Ruth (Hendricks)
The Duncan and Dinwiddie families, with allied lines; Scotalnd; Virginia; Shelby, Scott, Boone, and Bourbon Counties, Kentucky; Rush and Hendricks Counties, Indiana, and westward migrations as far as California. By Ruth (Hendricks) DeVerter. Baytown, Tex. 1969. (LC)

DIXON – Dickson, Roy S. (Roy Shelton), 1933-
The descendants of James A. Dickson, ca. 1820-1864, of Tennessee and Texas: allied families, Coleman, Fulbright, Harkey, Nall, Tippen. By Roy S., Dickson, Jr. Bartlesville, Okla. R. S. Dickson. c1987. (LC)

DIXON – Sample, Trixie Dixon, 1908-
Dixons, from Virginia to Texas. By Trixie Sample. Owensboro, Ky. Cook-McDowell Publications. 1981. (LC)

DOBBS – Ladd, Edward J.
Gone to Alabama; a history of the Dobbs and Gilbreath families. Compiled by Edward J. Ladd. Fort Worth, Tex. Miran Publishers. c1972. (LC)

DOBBS – Ladd, Edward Johnson
Gone to Alabama; a history of the Dobbs and Gilbreath families. Fort Worth, Tex. c1972. (NGS)

DODDRIDGE – Tucker, Faye Christman, 1907-
Doddridge and Teter: some ancestors and descendants. By Faye Christmas Tucker. Dallas, Tex. F. C. Tucker. 1986. (LC)

DODGE – Birt, Gladys Dodge
Dodge family. Dallas, Tex. Birt, 1975. (DAR)

DODSON – Dodson, Mrs. C. T.
Ancestors of Robert Dodson and his descendants. S.l.: Dodson? Austin, Tex. Dailey Diversified Services. 1965. (DAR)

DODSON – Dodson, Mrs. C. T.
Ancestors of Robert Dodson and his descendants. Written by Mrs. C. T. Dodson. Illustrated by Miss Oneida Uzzell. Austin, Tex., 1965. (LC)

DONNELL – Donnell, Charles E.
Genealogy of Donnell, Langford and other families. By Charles E. Donnell. Plainview, Tex. Author. 1949. (DP)

DOOM –
Doom families of America. Edited by Merle Ganier. Fort Worth, Tex.: M. Ganier. c1988. (LC)

DOUBRAVA – Miller, Dorothy S.
Czech pioneers in Texas: Vincenc Doubrava and Frantisha Novak Doubrava and their descendants. By Dorothy S. Miller. Bryan, Tex. Wallace. 1979. (LC)

DOUGLAS – Douglass, Malcolm Curtiis
History, memoirs, and genealogy of the Douglass family. By Malcolm Curtis Douglass. Houston, Tex. Biggers Print. Co., 1957. (LC)

DOUGLASS – Douglass, Malcolm Curtis
History, memoirs and genealogy of the Douglass family. Houston, Tex. Biggers Printing Co. 1957. (DAR)

DOUTHAT – Douthitt, Billie
Genealogy of the Ward, Douthitt, Murphy, Heard & Cox families of Leon County, Texas. By Billie Douthitt. Edited by Stephenie H. Tally-Frost. Corpus Christi, Tex. Professional Printing & Lithographing. 1968. (LC)

DOWDLE – Elliott, Zola F. (Zola Florence), 1912-
Kinship, our mother's line: Caraway, Williams and Dowdle families. By Zola F. Elliott. Austin, Tex. Z. F. Elliott. 1989. (LC)

DOWDLE – Elliott, Zola F. (Zola Florence), 1912-
Our family: the Elliott-Dowdle lines, 1827-1989. By Zola F. Elliott. Austin, Tex. Z. F. Elliott. 1989. (LC)

DOWNEY – De Vore, Shirley Ann Staley
Hodde genealogy search: some allied families: Buerger, Downey, Helm, Geisler, Lohmann, Mielenz, Mullendore, Pecore, Staley, and Wolf. By Shirley Ann Staley De Vore. 1st Ed. Norman, Okla. S. A. S. De Vore. c1988. (LC)

DOWNS – Barclay, Margaret
The Downs of Orange and Wilkes. By Margaret Barclay. Waco, Tex., c1959. (LC)

DRAPER – Draper, John B.
Draper-Loveless-Ayres (families). By John B. Draper. Austin, Tex., 1976. (FW)

DRESSER – Boyd, Frederick T.
Dresser family. S.1.: Boyd? Austin, Tex. Ginny's Copying Service. 1977. (DAR)

DRESSER – Boyd, Frederick T. (Frederick Tilgham), 1913-
Dresser family: twelve generations in America, (1638-1976). Compiled by Frederick T. Boyd. [S.1.: s.n.], 1977. Austin, Tex. Ginny's Copying Service. (LC)

DREYER – Boehl, Beverly
Koehler, Dreier, Rath, Thieme, and Boehl families: a genealogical delineation of German immigrants in De Witt County, Texas. By Beverly Boehl. Garland, Tex. B. Boehl. c1986. (LC)

DRIVER – Strickland, David N. (David Neil), 1947-
Carroll, Echols, Clemen, Driver & related families. Carrollton, Tex. David N. Strickland. 1988. (LC)

DUCKETT – King, Margaret Johnson, 1929-
The Ducketts, from Maryland to Texas. By Margaret Johnson King, with Henry L. King. Cary, N.C. M. J. King. C 1989. (LC)

DUCKWORTH – Jackson, Gene Lawrence, 1923-
Zachary Taylor French and Rachel Evelyn Duckworth: their ancestors and descendants. By Gene Lawrence Jackson. Baltimore, Md. Gateway Press. Fort Worth, Tex. 1991. (LC)

DUDERSTADT – Franklin, Frances S.
Family of John Duderstadt and Jane Davis Duderstadt. By Frances S. Franklin. Commerce, Tex., 1960. (FW)

DUGAN – Gracy, Alice Duggan
Thomas Hinds Duggan, descendant and ancestor. By Alice Duggan Gracy; maps and illustrations by Watt Harris, Jr. Austin, Tex. Gracy. c1976. (LC)

DUGGAN – Gracy, Alice Duggan
Thomas Hinds Duggan, descendants and ancestors. Austin, Tex. c1976. (NGS)

DUKE – Duke, Columbus W.
Sentimental journeys to Duke, Shackelford, Crockett, and more than four hundred allied families. By Columbus W. Duke. Lubbock, Tex. Keels. 1974. (FW)

DUNBAR – Schilling, Ethel D.
A short sketch of William Dunbar and his son John Samuel Dunbar... and reminiscences of the life of Z. P. Cottle, pioneer of Texas, by his son, W. Z. Cottle. By Ethel D. Schilling. n.p., 1952. (SP)

DUNBAR – Dunbar, Lorene B. B.
From across the sea and over the hills they came: the forebears of 4 Dunbars. By Lorene B. B. Dunbar. El Paso, Tex. Dunbar. 1976? (SL)

DUNCAN – Barrett, Linnie Wright
...Duncan families of Virginia... their descendants and some allied families... By Linnie Wright Barrett. Dallas, Tex. McCraw Publishing Co., 1940. (LC)

DUNCAN – DeVerter, Ruth Hendricks
The Duncan and Dinwiddie familes with allied lines. Baytown, Tex. DeVerter. c1969. (DAR)

DUNCAN – DeVerter, Ruth (Hendricks)
The Duncan and Dinwiddie famillies, with allied lines; Scotland; Virginia; Shelby, Scott, Boone, and Bourbon Counties, Kentucky; Rush and Hendricks Counties, Indiana; and westward migrations as far as California. By Ruth (Hendricks) DeVerter. Baytown, Tex. 1969. (LC)

DUNLAP – Caraway, William Oates
Genealogy, descendants of Alexander Dunlap including Hodge – Atchison – Crockett – Rice – Bailey – Hazelrigg – Richard – Wyatt and allied families – early Virginia and Kentucky pioneers. Sugar Land, Tex. Caraway. 1956? (DAR)

DUNLAP – Dunlap, Jay Feel
A genealogical record of the Lewis Alexander and Nancy Melanda Dunlap branch of the John and Mariah Dunlap family tree. Fort Worth, Tex. Dunlap. 1975. (DAR)

DUNLAP –Dunlap, Jay Teel
A genealogical record of the Lewis Alexander and Nancy Melanda Dunlap branch of the John and Mariah Dunlap family tree. Compiled by Jay Teel Dunlap. Fort Worth, Tex. Dunlap. 1974. (LC)

DUNN – Dunn, William Edward
The James McMurry Dunn family of Texas and Kentucky; the migration of their ancestors from County Derry, Northern Ireland, to Pennsylvania, thence to the Province of Maryland, and their further migration to Kentucky and Texas. Preliminary Ed. By William Edward Dunn. Washington, 1960. (LC)

DUNN –
Family genealogy of Mr. J. B. (Jewell Beatrice) Dunn... Houston, Tex. 1967. (LC)

DUNN – Dunn, J. B. (Jewell Beatrice)
Genealogy of Dunn and Reagan families of South Carolina, Georgia, and Wisconsin. By J. B. (Jewell Beatrice) Dunn. Houston, Tex. 1968. (LC)

DUTTON – Dutton, W. F.
Duttons of Dutton, England, and the Duttons of America, Philadelphia branch. By W. F. Dutton. Houston, Tex? Author. 1956. (FW)

DUTY – McKinney, Thelma D.
Converging paths. By Thelma D. McKinney. Fort Worth, Tex. Manney Co., 1972. (LC)

DYER – Overlander, Rufus M.
Blount family of North Carolina and allied families Miller, Dyer, Gray. Seabrook, Tex. Rufus M. Overlander III. 1987. (LC)

DYER – Wright, Elizabeth Ann
James Dyer, descendants and allied families. Dallas, Tex. Wright. c1954. (DAR)

E –

EARLY – Early, Cleland Edward, 1919-
The Early families of Knox and Whitley counties, Kentucky, with allied families. By Cleland Edward Early. Houston, Tex. D. Armstrong Co. 1988, c1989. (LC)

EARLY – Hampton, Margaret Woods
Descendants of John Early of Virginia (1729-1744). By Margaret Woods Hampton. Fort Worth, Tex. Miran Publishers. 1973. (LC)

EARLY – Hampton, Margaret Woods, 1900-1987-
Descendants of John Early of Virginia (1729-1774). Fort Worth, Tex. Miran Publishers. 1973. (LC)

EARLY – Hampton, Margaret Woods
Descendants of John Early of Virginia (1729-1774). Fort Worth, Tex. Miran Publishers. 1973. (DAR)

EARLY – Hampton, Margaret Woods
Descendants of John Early of Virginia (1729-1774). Fort Worth, Tex. 1973. (NGS)

EASLEY – Eckhardt, Ura L.
Easley family, no. 1, 3-5, 1960-1970. By Ura L. Eckhardt. Houston, Tex. 1970. (FW)

EASTMAN – McCulley, William Straight, 1909-
Roger Eastman, some descendants and ascendants: undiscovered by Guy Scobie Rix, 1901. Pieced together by William Straight McCulley. Bryan, Tex. W. S. McCulley. 1979. (LC)

EASTWOOD – Hammond, Murieldean Easterwood, 1927-
Our family, the Easterwoods. Compiled by Murieldean Easterwood Hammond, Erith Easterwood Wallis. Sweeny, Tex. M. E. Hammond. Corsicana, Tex.: E. E. Wallis. c1980. (LC)

EAVES – Wood, Jimy Brady, 1929-
What God hath blessed. By Jimy Brady Wood; compiled and edited by Dot Adkins. 1st Ed. Richardson, Tex. Rockwell International Print. Services Dept. c1976. (LC)

EBY – Eby, James B.
My two roads. By James B. Eby. Ed. 2. Houston, Tex. Pacesetter Pr. 1976. (FW)

ECHOLS – Strickland, David N. (David Neil), 1947-
Carroll, Echols, Clement, Driver & related families. Carrollton, Tex. David N. Strickland. 1988. (LC)

ECKERT – Orrison, Estella Hartmann
Eckert record: story of George Bernhardt Eckert and his descendants, 1793-1957. By Estella Hartmann Orrison. San Angelo, Tex., 1957. (LC)

ECKHARD –
History of an Eckhar(d)t family whose three sons (John, Henry, George) came to America before 1850. Including records of a Pullman family. A genealogy compiled and arr. by charles M. Reinoehl and George B. Eckhhart. Bryan, Tex. Mimeographed by the Scribe Shop, 1952. (LC)

ECKHART – Reinoehl, Charles M.
History of an Eckhar(d)t family. Bryan, Tex. Eckhart. 1952. (DAR)

ECKLUND – Reibold, Dorothy Marty, 1922-
The Ecklin family story: the descendants of John R. and Jane Ecklin. By Dorothy Mary Reibold. Wolfe City, Tex. Henington Pub. Co. c1988. (LC)

ECKMAN – Barr, Ruth Eckman (Mrs. James L.)
Descendants of Hans Jacob Eckman of Pennsylvania and Maryland, and miscellaneous Eckmans. By Ruth Eckman Barr (Mrs. James L.). Austin, Tex. 1969. (LC)

EDMISTON – Edmiston, Prentess P.
A branch of the Edmiston family tree from Ireland to North Carolina to Pennsylvania to Virginia to Tennessee to Arkansas and to Texas, A.D. 1700 to 1964. By Prentess P. Edmiston. Harlingen, Tex. 1964. (LC)

EDWARDS – Eckhardt, Ura L.
Edwards family, no. 1-9, 1959-1970. By Ura L. Eckhardt. Houston, Tex. 1970. (FW)

EDWARDS – Edwards, Richard Laurence, 1911-
Ancestors and descendants of the Edwards-Mathis, Delozier, and related families that pioneered through Virginia, Carolinas, Tennessee, Kentucky, Illinois, Missouri,

Kansas, and spread to descendants in thirty-seven states and two provinces in Canada. By Richard Laurence Edwards. 1st Ed. Coffeyville, Kan. R.L. Edwards. c1985. (LC)

EGAN – Peterson, Louise Egan, 1896-
Descendants of Valentine Egan and related families. By Louise Egan Peterson. Richardson, Tex. Peterson. 1979. (LC)

EIDT – Moser, August C.
Family tree: William Eidt (1838-1905) native of... Germany and Catherine Deniger... native of New Orleans, La. By August C. Moser. Dallas, Tex., 1969. (FW)

ELCHERT – Koop, Myra C. Studer
Ancestors and descendants of Johannes Kolbe: a history of the Elchert's, Kelbe's and Kelbley's. By Myra C. Studer Koop. Plano, Tex. M.C.S. Koop. 1988? (LC)

ELFERT -- Thompson, Lois M. Elfert (Lois Marie Elfert), 1923-
One foot in Louisiana: T. C. and Grand Elfert Mother. By Lois M. Elfert Thompson. Dallas, Tex. Taylor Pub. Co., c1983. (LC)

ELLIOTT – Cain, Janet Elliott
Descendants of George Elliott, pioneer settler of Atlanta: including historical background & related Terry family. By Janet Elliott Cain. Houston, Tex. J. E. Cain. c1980. (LC)

ELLIOTT – Elliott, Zola F. (Zola Florence), 1912-
Consanquinity: my father's line: McCuistons, Nelsons, Hollans & Elliotts. By Zola F. Elliott. Austin, Tex. Z. F. Elliott. 1989. (LC)

ELLIOTT – Elliott, Zola F. (Zola Florence), 1912-
Our family: the Elliott-Dowdle lines, 1827-1989. By Zola F. Elliott. Austin, Tex. Z. F. Elliott. 1989. (LC)

ELLIOTT – Reynolds, Troy Harper
Family history for descendants of John Elliott. Houston, Tex. Reynolds. 1975. (DAR)

ELLIS – Ellis, Harry H. (Harry Howard), 1914-
The family of Lt. John and Elizabeth (Freeman) Ellis of Sandwick, Massachusetts. Compiled by Harry H. Ellis. Dallas, Tex. H. H. Ellis. c1983. (LC)

ELLIS – Ellis, Ollie, 1915-
Tales & trails of four families: Coleman, Ellis, Estes, Henderson. Compiled by Ollie & Nina Ellis. Kerrville, Tex. O. & N. Ellis. c1979. (LC)

ELLISON – Erath, Clara Ellison
Descendants of John and Robert Ellison, Fairfield County, South Carolina. By Clara Ellison Erath. Allied families: Adger, Patterson, Capers. Houston, Tex., 1972. (LC)

ELLISON – Pitts, Alice E.
Strong-Ellison-Henderson family history. By Alice E. Pitts. McKinney, Tex., 1976. (FW)

EMBREY – Weaver, Oliver C. (Oliver Cornelius), 1914-
John and Prudence (Emrey) Lloyd, their descendants, and some allied families: Allen, Cowling, Embree, Gilbert, Kelly, McCracken, McGee, Northern, O'Rear, Slaughter, Stewart, Tarrant, Tankersley. By Oliver C. Reed, Jr. Birmingham, Ala. c1990. (LC)

EMERY –
James Wallace Emery (1829-1902) and his descendants; with a summary on his 7 forefathers. Anthony, James, etc. who lived in New Eng. Between 1635 and 1864. Fort Worth, Tex., 1974. (FW)

ENDSLEY – Griffin, Phyllis Ansley, 1936-
A history of descendants, Thomas Ansley, Warren County, Georgia. By Phyllis Ansley Griffin. Denton? Tex. Griffin. c1979. (LC)

ENGLISH – Watson, Nadine English, 1905-
English family history. By Nadine English Watson. Baltimore: Gateway Press. Wichita Falls, Tex. 1985. (LC)

EPPES – Allison, Edna Finney
Eppes, Epps, Epes genealogy & history & related families. By Edna Finney Allison. San Angelo, Tex? 1974. (LC)

ERNST – York, Miriam Korff
Friedrich Ernst of industry: research on life, family, acquaintences, and conditions of the times. By Miriam Korff York. [Texas]. M. K. York. 1989. [Giddings, Tex.: Nixon Printing Co.]. (LC)

ERWIN – Detty, Marie S.
Our courageous ancestors: facts and fables, 1600-1974. By Marie S. Detty. Austin, Tex. San Felipe Pr., 1975. (FW)

ETTER – Etter, Richard L.
We people called Etter. A Texan branch with related families. By Richard L. Etter. Houston, Tex., 1962. (PH)

EVANS – Brown, Shepherd Spencer Neville, 1920-
Brown-Stanton-Evans-Sherman families and collateral lines, 1420-1987. By Shepherd Spencer Neville Brown. Waco, Tex. S. S. N. Brown. 1987. (LC)

EVANS – Davis, Marie Evans, 1930-
There's no wonder we act the way we do: allied families, Adkinson, Atkins, Booker... [et al]. By Marie Evans Davis. Cullman, Ala. Gregath Co. 1985. (LC)

EVANS – Evans, Grace Moran
The Evans, Poole, and Gathright families. Compiled and published and documentary records by Grace Moran Evans. Nevada, Tex., c1956. (LC)

EVANS – Eckhardt, Ura L.
Evans family, no. 1-2, 1964-1970. By Ura L. Eckhardt. Houston, Tex. 1970. (FW)

EVANS – Evans, Marvin D.
Evans. Fort Worth, Tex. Evans. 1953. (DAR)

EVANS – Reddell, Thelma E.
Evans, Americans of royal descent. By Thelma E. Reddell. Fort Worth, Tex. Miran Pub., 1974. (FW)

EVETTS – Haley, J. Evetts (James Evetts), 1901-
Rough times, tough fiber: a fragmentary family chronicle. By J. Evetts Haley. Canyon, Tex. Palo Duro Press. 1976. (LC)

EWING – Brown, Marguerite
Ewing – McCulloch – Buchanan genealogy. Dallas, Tex. Royal Publishing Co. 1957. (DAR)

EWING – Ewing, Milam Myrl, 1900-
Edley Ewing, the Texas pioneer and his descendants. By Milam Myrl Ewing. Tulsa, Okla. Ewing. 1976. (LC)

EWING – Ewing, Milam Myrl
Edley Ewing, the Texas pioneer and his descendants. Tulsa, Okla. 1976. (NGS)

EWING – Ewing, Milam Myrl
Edley Ewing, the Texas pioneer and his descendants. Tulsa, Okla. Ewing. 1979. (DAR).

EWING – Ewing, Presley Kittredge
The Ewing genealogy with Cognate branches. Houston, (Tex?). Hercules Ptg. & Book Co. 1919. (DAR)

EWING – Hughes, Dorothy Dillard
Our Hughes ancestors: a story of searches and discoveries, including maternal lines of Varvel, Ewing, Huntzinger, Sawyer, Brown, Hale/Haile, Craghead, and lists of descendants. By Dorothy Dillard Hughes. Lubbock, Tex. D. D. Hughes. c1989. (LC)

EXLINE –
Genealogy of the Exline and Axline family. By Edythe Wilson Thoesen, Emma Miller Exline and Leo L. Holz. Dallas? Tex., 1952. (LC)

F –

FAITH – Robbins, Loyce Margaret Smith, 1901-
Faith, a genealogy. By Loyce Margaret Smith Robbins. El Paso, Tex. R. E. Faith. 1979? (LC)

FALES – Fail, Welton Ruel, 1912-
The Fail – Fales and related families: a tribute to our patriot ancestor, Dixon Fail. By Welton Ruel Fail. Wolfe City, Tex. Henington Pub. Co. Lancaster, Tex. 1987. (LC)

FANT – Fant, Alfred E.
Fant genealogy. Austin, Tex. Fant. 1975. (DAR)

FANT – Fant, Alfred E.
Fant genelaogy: comprising 2,809 individual entries noting available biographical facts. Compiled by Alfred E. Fant. Austin, Tex. Fant. 1975. (LC)

FARRIS – Davis, Sherry Ann Schauer, 1939-
The Farris family: rootin, shootin, and tootin. By Sherry Ann Schauer Davis. Houston, Tex. Davis, c1978. (LC)

FARWELL –
The Farwell family... a history of Henry Farwell and his wife Olive (Welby) Farwell of Boston, England, and Concord and Chelmsford, Mass., 1605-1927, with twelve generations of their descendants; also lineages of many allied families, with a hundred and fifty ullustrations from original photographs, daguerreotypes, oil portraits, etc.; records of John Dennis Farwell, completed and compiled by Jane Harter Abbott and Lillian M. Wilson. Orange, Tex. F. H. Farwell and Fanny B. Farwell, 1929. (LC)

FASH – Hall, Theta McCrory
Fash-Faesch-Boniface. By Theta McCrory Hall. Fort Worth, Tex. Miran Publishers, 1973. (LC)

FAUBION – Faubion, Bernard H.
Addendum number one to Faubion and allied families. Bernard H. Faubion, Marybeth Faubion Rule; Mary Laverne Faubion, editing. Georgetown, Tex. M. L. Faubion. c1983. (LC)

FAUBION –
Faubion and allied families. Collectors-coordinators, Ann Faubion Armstrong... [et al.]; Mary Laverne Faubion, editing. Georgetown, Tex. M. L. Faubion. c1982. (LC)

FAULKENBERRY – Tumlinson, Rebecca L.
Tennessee to Texas: It happened like this: stories of research and remember. By Rebecca L. Tumlinson, Limited 1st Ed. Channelview, Tex. Tumlinson, 1979. (LC)

FAULKNER – Falconer, George Alexander, 1914 –
The descendants of George and Martha Falconer: a genealogy of a Canadian and American family, 1814-1980, with a historical perspective. By George Alexander Falconer. Houston, Tex. G. A. Falconer. 1980. (LC)

FAULKNER – Tucker, D. A. (Duard Arnold), 1919-
John Faulkner: North Carolina to Georgia to Arkansas. By D. A. Tucker. Houston, Tex. D. A. Tucker. 1987. (LC)

FEAZLE – McCarley, LaJoy DeShane, 1928-
George L. Feazle of Spring Valley, his ancestors and de[s]cendants: a biographical & historical genealogy. Compiled by LaJoy Deshane McCarley. Fort Worth, Tex. L. D. McCarley. 1980. (LC)

FEE – Pearson, Ralph E.
A history of the Fee family. Austin, Tex. 1969-(71?). (FW)

FELTS – Schluter, Helen Gomer
The Thomas Jefferson Felts family of Mississippi and Sabine County, Texas including the Burkett and Polk families. Conpiled by Helen Gomer Schluter. 1988. (LC)

FENN – Fenn, Doyle
Fenn family, descendants of Andrew Jackson Fenn. By Doyle Fenn. Deer Park, Tex. 1968. (LC)

FENNER – Barrett, Ruth Leslie
The Fenner forebears of Samuel Fenner Leslie, 1877-1969: their lives, their descendants, their kin in North Carolina, Virginia, Tennessee, Alabama, Mississippi, Arkansas, and Texas. By Ruth Leslie Barrett. Windom, Tex. R. L. Barrett. 1987. (LC)

FERGUSON – Ferguson, Charles W.
Ferguson family tree. By Charles W. Ferguson. Dallas, Tex. Ferguson, 1972. (FW)

FERGUSON – Ferguson, Charles W.
Ferguson family genealogical chart. By Charles W. Ferguson. Dallas, Tex. Ferguson, 1974. (FW)

FERGUSON – Ferguson, Leota
This Ferguson clan. By Leota Ferguson. Coleman, Tex. J. & L. Ferguson, 1967? (DP)

FERGUSON – Ferguson, William Otto, 1908-
We Fergusons and related families. By William Otto Ferguson. Monroe, La. W. O. Ferguson. 1985? (LC)

FESMIRE – Khalid, Alice Ann Fesmire, 1949-
Fesmire, a family history and genealogy: Martin Fesmire and his descendants in North Carolina and Tennessee, with branches in Indiana, Ohio, Mississippi, Texas and Oklahoma. By Alice Ann Fesmire Khalid. Baton Rouge, La. Land and Land Printers. 1982. (LC)

FEUEBACHER –
Family of Alvin Frederick Feuerbacher and wife Emma Theresa Feuerbacker (nee Hernsdorf). Austin, Tex. 1976. (FW)

FIELD – Eckhardt, Ura L.
Field family assorted notes, no. 1. By Ura L. Eckhardt. Houston, Tex. 1970. (FW)

FIELD – Field, Charles Kellogg, 1927-
A genealogical and biographical history of the Field family of Massachuetts and Vermont and the French-Henry families of Virginia and Texas: a union of North and South. By Charles Kellogg Field, III. 1st Ed. Baltimore, Md.: Gateway Press. c1985. (LC)

FIKE – McLendon, Connie Fyke, 1922-
   The story of Fyke Road. By Connie Fyke McLendon and Dorotha Good Russell; narrative by Connie Fyke McLendon. Carrollton, Tex. C. F. McLendon. 1978 [i .e.1980]. (LC)

FILLMORE – Fillmore, Thelma L. (Thelma Louise)
   Fillmore: eleven generations, John "The Mariner (1)", John "The Captain (2)". Researched and compiled by Thelma L. Fillmore (TLF). Wichita Falls, Tex. T. L. Fillmore. 1983. (LC)

FINCH – Finch, Orville Henry
   The lives and times of a family named Finch, from 1806-1954. By Orville Henry Finch. Amarillo? Tex., 1954. (LC)

FINNEY – Hatch, Jo Ann Finney
   Ten southern families: Finney, Jones, Morgan, Scott, Williamson & Posey, also Hennessey, Adams, Beddoe & Stark. Compiled by Jo Ann Finney Hatch. Pinedale, Ariz. J. F. Hatch. 1986. (LC)

FISH – Eckhardt, Ura L.
   Fish family, no. 1-2, 1964-70. By Ura L. Eckhardt. Houston, Tex. 1970. (FW)

FISHER – Eckhardt, Ura L.
   Fisher family, no. 1-2, 1966-1970. By Ura L. Eckhardt. Houston, Tex. 1970. (FW)

FISHER – Fischer, Ernest G. (Ernest Gus), 1902-
   The Texas families of Spiegelhauer and Fischer: as viewed and reviewed by descendants. Baltimore: Gateway Press. 1986. (LC)

FISHER – Fisher, Ovie Clark
   The Texas heritage of the Fishers and the Clarks. By Ovie Clark Fisher. Salado, Tex. Anson Jones Press. 1963. (LC)

FITZHUGH – Fitzhugh, Marie
   Three centuries passed (the Fitzhugh family). By Marie Fitzhugh. San Antonio, Tex. Naylor Co. 1975. (LC)

FLACK – Overstreet, Carolyn Lindemann, 1933-
   On the Flach family trail = Auf den Spuren der Famillie Flach. By Carolun Lindemann Overstreet. 1st Ed. Austin, Tex. Eakin Press. c1984. (LC)

FLANDERS – Hardison, Lewis M. (Lewis Merrill), 1913-
   A branch of the Flanders family, where there is a problem in the 6th generation. Prepared by Lewis M. Hardison. Kerrville, Tex. L. M. Hardison. 1982. (LC)

FLEETWOOD – Shirren, Adam John
   The chronicles of Fleetwood House. By A. J. Shirren. Houston, Tex. Pacesetter Press. 1977? (LC)

FLEURY – Newton, Leroy L., 1927-

Genealogical report, Newton and Flury and allied families: from Maryland, Virginia, Alabama, South Carolina, Georgia, southern Arkansas, Red Lands in Indian Territory, Oklahoma, and other places. By Leroy L. Newton; edited by Claireeta D. Newton, Latricia L. Newton. Altus, Okla? L. L. Newton. c1987. (LC)

FLINT – Flint, Edwin W. (Edwin Waldo), 1921-
The Flint heritage: Wales to Iowa. By Edwin W. Flint. Austin, Tex. E. W. Flint. 1984. (LC)

FLORENCE – Florence, Charles Wesley, 1912-
We, the Florances/Florences. By Charles Wesley Florence, Jr. San Antonio, Tex. C. W. Florence, 1981. (LC)

FLORES – Padgett, James Foyil
A documented history of the Flores family. Ennis, Tex. Padgett. 1963. (DAR)

FLORES – Padgett, James F.
Documented history of the Flores family, 1725-1963, and related families. By James F. Padgett. Ennis, Tex., 1963. (FW)

FLOURNOY – Rathbone, Bettye S.
Some of the ancestors of Francis Flournoy, Sr. of Chesterfield County, Virginia. Compiled by Bettye S. Rathbone. Austin, Tex. Nortex Press. c1985. (LC)

FLOURNOY – Spiller, Wayne
Branches from the Flournoy family tree. Waco, Tex. Spiller. c1976. (DAR)

FLOURNOY – Spiller, Wayne
Branches of the Flournoy family. By Wayne Spiller. Seagraves, Tex. Pioneer Bk. Pub., 1976. (FW)

FLOURNOY – Spiller, Wayne, 1911-
Branches from the Flournoy family tree. Compiled by Wayne Spiller. Voca, Tex. W. Spiller. c1976. (LC)

FLOYD – Floyd, Mildred, 1911-
The Floyd family: Wales to Va.., N.C., (S.C.?), Ga., Ala., Miss., & Texas: evidences of all families involved, threads of ancestors, allied famillies. By Mildred Floyd. Dallas, Tex. Floyd. c1978. (LC)

FOHN – Fohn, Nicholas H., 1941-
Fohn memories: heritage of a Castro colony immigrant family in Texas. By Nicholas H. Fohn. Uvalde, Tex. N. H. Fohn. 1981. (LC)

FOLLMER – Folmar, L. W., 1919-
Colonial ancestors of the Fulmers of South Carolina and the Folmars of Alabama. Compiled and published by L. W. Folmar. 2nd Ed. Austin, Tex. L. W. Folmar. 1981. (LC)

FOOTE – Fouts, Luther S. (Luther Samuel)
Luther Samuel Fouts and forebears. By Luther S. Fouts, Jr. 1st Ed. Roswell, Ga. WH Wolfe Associates. C1989. (LC)

FORD –
Ancestors and descendants of Mrs. Lucia (Butler) Ford, descendant of the Duke of Ormond; pioneer settler of Ector, Fannin County, Texas, 1835. Bonham? Tex. 1971. (LC)

FORD – Allen, Juanita Catherine, 1908-
Mrs. Lucia Butler Ford, descendant of a duke of England, pioneer settler of Extor, Texas, Fannin County, 1828. By Juanita Allen. Houston, Tex. Allen. c1960. (LC)

FORDNEY – Hersman, Theodota Guerin
Descendants of Joseph Warren Fordney. By Theodota Guerin Hersman. Dallas, Tex., 1972. (LC)

FORE – Covington, Mildred Lerlene Rowell, 1916-
The Fore family. By Mildred Lerlene Rowell Covington. Burleson, Tex. L. R. Covington. 1979. (LC)

FORMAN – Ghormley, Pearl
Yesterday, today and tomorrow; a genealogy of the Foreman, Hays, Ghormley, Williams and Brockett families. By Pearl Ghormley. San Antonio, Tex. Naylor Co. 1966. (LC)

FORSTON – Johnson, M. G.
Forston and Driskill family letters. By M. G. Johnson. Dallas, Tex., 1971. (FW)

FORT –
A family called Fort, the descendants of Elias Fort of Virginia. By Homer T. Fort, Jr. and Drucilla Stovall Jones. Midland, Tex. West Texas Print Co. 1970. (LC)

FORTIER – Cochran, Estelle Mina (Fortier)
The Fortier family, and allied families. By Estelle Mina (Fortier) Cochran. San Antonio? Tex. c1963. (LC)

FOSTER – Boyd, Margie Milner, 1925-
Rigsby relatives and related families, Shephard, Foster, Lawson, Virginia, North Carolina, Georgia, Texas, 1693-1900s: also Barclay, Bean, Burke... Margie Milner Boyd. Port Arthur, Tex. M. M. Boyd. 1986. (LC)

FOSTER – Dennis, Gerneva Foster, 1923-
Forster, Foster, and their royal descendants of England – 823 AD, Virginia – 1635 AD, U.S.A. – 1900 AD. Compiled by Gerneva Foster Dennis. Abilene, Tex. Published for the author by A.A.A. Printing Co. c1990. (LC)

FOSTER –Firebaugh, V. P.
Descendants of George Foster of Carlisle, Massachusetts (with his forefathers back to John, who came to Salem, Mass., early in the seventeenth century). By V. P. Firebaugh. Odessa? Tex. Author, 1964? (FW)

FOSTER – Foster, Thomas Boyd
Family sketches. Houston, Tex. Alexander Love Chapter. 1978, 1979. (DAR)

FOUST – Jernigan, LaDora Foust, 1932-
The Foust family of Alabama. LaDora Foust Jernigan. Houston, Tex. L. F. Jernigan. 1981. (LC)

FOWLER – Arthur, Glenn Dora Fowler
Annals of the Fowler family with branches in Virginia, North Carolina, South Carolina, Tennessee, Kentucky, Alabama, Mississippi, California and Texas. Austin, Tex. Ben C. Jones & Co. 1901. (DAR)

FOWLER – Arthur, Mrs. James Joyce (Glenn Dora Fowler Arthur)
Annals of the Fowler family, with branches in Virginia, North Carolina, South Carolina, Tennessee, Kentucky, Alabama, Mississippi, California and Texas. Comp. and ed. By Mrs. James Joyce Arthur (Glenn Dora Fowler Arthur). Austin, Tex. The Author. 1901. (LC)

FOWLER – Fowler, Grover Parsons
The house of Fowler; a history of the Fowler families of the South, embracing descendants of John Fowler of Virginia and branches in North Carolina, South Carolina, Georgia, Tennessee, Kentucky, Alabama, Texas, also records of allied families... Compiled and published by the author, Grover Parsons Fowler. Hickory, N. C., 1940. (LC)

FOX – Smith, Craig W. (Craig Woods), 1913-
Be they remembered: the ancestry of Craig Woods Smith. By Craig W. Smith. [Texas?] C. W. Smith. 1990. (LC)

FOXWORTH -- Foxworth, Sarah Payne, 1910-
Foxworth, Bush, Payne, Bledsoe & allied lineages: Lenoir, Pope, Regan, Elkin, Quisenberry, Morter, Foster, Mitchell, Johnston, Ogilvie, Birdsong, Higgins, etc. Sarah Payne Foxworth and Michal Martin Farmer. Dallas, Tex. Farmer Genealogy Co. c1985. (LC)

FRANCIS – Coalston, Eula DeRee Francis, 1918-
Our Francis family and relatives. Compiled by Eula DeRee Francis Coalston. Humboldt, Tenn? E.D.F. Coalston. 1989. (LC)

FRASER – Owens, Erma Lee, 19926-
The Fraziers and the Younses: their ancestors, their descendants and their in-laws. By Erma Lee Owens, Letha McGrew. 3rd Ed. [Texas?]. E. L. Owens. 1986. (LC)

FREAD – Dodson, Mrs. C. T.
The Fread and Rockfeller families in 'the good old days' and 'the present days', 1590-1969. Austin, Tex. Dodson. 1969. (DAR)

FREAD – Dodson, Mrs. C. T.
The Fread and Rockefeller families in the good old days and the present days, 1590-1969. Written by Mrs. C. T. Dodson. Illustrated by Oneida Uzzell. Auustin, Tex. Aus-Tex Duplicators, Inc., 1969. (LC)

FREE – Free, Margaret Bernice (Madara)
Some of the descendants of John Free (ca. 1804-ca. 1809). Alvin, Tex. 1976. (NGS)

FRENCH –Braswell, Irene (F.)
Families of Frenches, Williamsons, Shafers, Braswells in America, 1710-1975. Irene (F.) Braswell. Pampa, Tex., 1975. (FW)

FRENCH – Collier, Myra Butler, 1924-
French. [compiled [sic] by Myra Butler Collier]. San Antonio, Tex. M. B. Collier. [1979]. (LC)

FRENCH – Jackson, Gene Lawrence, 1923-
Zachary Taylor French and Rachel Evelyn Duckworth: their ancestors and descendants. By Gene Lawrence Jackson. Baltimore, Md.: Gateway Press. Fort Worth, Tex. 1991. (LC)

FRICK – Katsenis, Ardath Edwards, 1934-
The Frick, Fricks, Frix Family of the South, or, the three brothers. Compiled and edited by Ardath Edwards Katsenis. Tujunga, Calif. A. E. Katsenis. 1984. (LC)

FRIERSON – Evans, Blanche Frierson, 1904-
The Haskell County, Texas, Friersons, 1906-1981. By Blanche Frierson Evans. Pecos, Tex. B. F. Evans. c1982. (LC)

FROMHERTZ – Wilson, John H. (John Human), 1900-
Fromhart family history; descendants of John Fromhart (or Fromhertz) of Bergalingen, Tex., pref. 1968. (LC)

FRONABARGER – Blair, Eric L.
Miss Lallie's kinfolks. By Eric L. Blair. Lake Jackson, Tex. 1968. (LC)

FROSH – Frosch, Daniel, 1912-
Unto the seventh generation: a narrative about the lives of David and Sarah Frosch, their forebears, relatives, and descendants. By Daniel Frosch. Houston? Tex. D. Frosch. c1987. (LC)

FROST –Rickaway, Ruth Hollar
Benjamin Frost, a Texan from Tennessee. By Ruth Hollar Rickaway. Houston, Tex. R. H. Rickaway. c1981. (LC)

FRYER – Price, Barbara Fryer, 1946-
   Fryer's delight. By Barbara Fryer Price. Fairfield, Tex. B. F. Price. c1989. (LC)

FUCHS – Schiller, Nelson Lorenz
   Genealogy of Lorenz and Friedericke Fuchs of Carmine, Fayette County, Texas, 1847-1949. By Nelson Lorenz Schiller. Austin? Tex., 1949. (LC)

FULBRIGHT – Dickson, Roy S. (Roy Shelton), 1933-
   The descendants of James A. Dickson, ca. 1820-1864, of Tennessee and Texas: allied families, Coleman, Fulbright, Harkey, Nall, Tippen. By Roy S. Dickson, Jr. Bartlesville,, Okla. R. S. Dickson. c1987. (LC)

FULLER – Lane, Hassie Olivia Fuller, 1909-
   Descendants of Oliver T. Fuller of Greene Co., NY: with some of their ancestors and other allied families. By Hassie Olivia Fuller Lane; edited [by] Nina M. Fuller. Belton, Tex. H. O. F. Lane. c1991. (LC)

FUNDERBURK – Funderburg, Alvin K., 1916-
   Descendants of Jacob & Eve (Boone) Funderburg. By Alvin K. Funderburg. Dallas, Tex. Taylor Pub. Co. c1978. (LC)

FUNK – Strock, Richard M., 1915-
   Some Strock, Harbaugh, Funk, and Reynolds families of Washington and Frederick Counties, Maryland, and of Franklin County, Pennsylvania: including some descendants in Colorado, Illinois, Kansas, Michigan, Missouri, Ohio, Texas, etc.: organized around the direct and collateral lineage of the authors (brothers), with direct lineage extending back to the immigrants. Richard M. Strock and Robert F. Strock. Cincinnati, Ohio. R. M. Strock. 1988. (LC)

FUQUA – Irwin, Alya Dean Smith
   Fuqua—a fight for freedom. Houston, Tex. Irwin. 1974. (DAR)

FUQUA – Irwin, Alya Dean (Smith)
   Fuqua – a fight for freedom: allied families, Alexander... By Alya Dean (Smith) Irwin. Houston, Tex. Irwin. 1974. (LC)

FUQUA – Iirwin, Alya Dean Smith
   Fuqua – A fight for freedom. Also Alexander, Word, Fouquet families. Houston, Tex. 1974. (NGS)

FURY – Klingman, Helen Linz
   Grandma's legacy. Dallas, Tex. Klingman. 1970. (DAR)

G –

GAINES – Clark, Robert M. (Robert Murel), 1948-
   Hardie, Vincent, Gaines, and related families: from Virginia to Texas. By Robert M. Clark, Jr. [United States?: R. M. Clark, c1989]. (LC)

GALEENER –
Book of remembrance. Houston, 1965? (LC)

GALVEZ –
Spain furnishes authentic coat of arms of Galvez; wealth of history disclosed in quest of official shield. (Galveston, Tex., 1926). (PH)

GAMBILL – Johnson, William Perry
Gambill of Texas and Virginia. 1972. (DAR)

GAMBRELL – Deviney, Esther Gambrell
Gambrell album. Austin, Tex. Aus-Tex Duplicators. 1974. (DAR)

GAMBRELL – Deviney, Esther Gambrell
A Gambrell album. By Esther Gambrell Deviney. Austin, Tex. Aus-Tex Duplicators. 1974. (LC)

GANIER – Ganier, Merle, 1914-
Ancestors and descendants of Francois Ganier of France and Louisiana. By Merle Ganier. Fort Worth, Tex. M. Ganier, c1980. (LC)

GANTT – Terry, Jessie B. Gantt
Bud and Sis at the turn of the Century. By Jessie B. Gantt Terry. San Antonio, Tex. Naylor Co. 1976. (NY)

GAR – Prewitt, Lorene Bond
Dear Granddaughter. Dallas, Tex. Prewitt. 1968. (DAR)

GARDNER –
The Gardner, Wheeler, Moran, and Herndon families: documented records. Nevada, Tex. c1959. (LC)

GARRETT –
The genealogy in part of Stephen and William Garrett of Buckingham, Virginia, with some historical data of the families. By Rev. Clyde B. Garrett and Miss Mary E. Gaither. Marshall, Tex. Printed by the Marshall News Messenger Pub. Co., 1926. (LC)

GARRETT – Garrett, Edward R. (Edward Ray), 1924-
Garrett: 100 years from Normandy. By Edward R. Garrett. Houston, Tex. E. R. Garrett. c1989. (LC)

GARRETT – Wolfram, Joydelle Garrett
Our heritage: the roots and twigs of one Garrett family tree. Researched and compiled by Joydelle Garrett Wolfram, assisted by Marian Garrett Gibbs. [S.1.:s.n.]. c1980. ([San Angelo, Tex.]: Taylor Pub. Co.). (LC)

GARRISON – Garrett, Martha H.
Descendants of Caleb Garrison, Sr. and his wife, Sarah Fleming, 1797-1966. John R. Ross. Angleton, Tex. Printed by Times Printers, n..d. (LA)

GARRISON – Garrison, Lloyd Russell
The descendants of John Garrison of Sumner County, Tennessee. Denton, Tex. Terrill Wheeler Printing Co. 1961. (DAR)

GARRISON – Garrison, Lloyd Russell
The descendants of John Garrison of Sumner County, Tennessee. By Lloyd Russell Garrison. Denton, Tex. Terrill Wheeler Print. Co. 1961. (LC)

GARTMAN – Watts, Frederick L.
The Gartman papers. By Frederick L. Watts. 1st Ed. Plano, Tex. Littlebooks. 1990. (LC)

GARZA – Rubio, Abel G., 1929-
Stolen heritage: a Mexican-American's rediscovery of his family's lost land grant. Abel G. Rubio; edited and with foreword by Thomas H. Kreneck. 1st Ed. Austin, Tex. Eakin Press. c1986. (LC)

GARZA – Garza, Lionel, 1921-
Brief history of both banks of the Rio Grande and the San Antonio rivers: 450 years of history and genealogy of the ascendants and descendants of Mucio Garza and Romana Barrera. Researched and compiled by Lionel Garza. Kingsville, Tex, B. Torres Print Co. 1986. (LC)

GARZA–SADA -- Saragoza, Alex
The Monterrey elite and the Mexican State, 1880-1940. By Alex M. Saragoza. 1st Ed. Austin: University of Texas Press. 1988. (LC)

GASSAWAY – Gazaway, Kathryn DeWitt, 1932-
Genealogical history of the Jesse Gazaway family. Compiled by Kathryn (DeWitt) Gazaway. Utopia, Tex. K. D. Gazaway. 1989. (LC)

GASTON – Perry, Max, 1919-
American descendants of William Gaston and Mary Olivet Lemon. Compiled by Max Perry. Midland, Tex. M. Perry. c1989. (LC)

GEBHARDT – Gully, Sharon Shaw, 1952-
Our Copehart family. By Sharon Shaw Gully. Richardson, Tex. S. S. Gully. c1983. (LC)

GEDDIE – Geddie, Jack
The families Geddie & McPhail. Fort Worth, Tex. Henry L. Geddie. 1959. (DAR)

GEORGE – George, Thomas R.
George family record: descendants of Col. John George of Virginia. [Thomas R. George]. Houston, Tex. H. George Graphic Design. 1978. (LC)

GEORGE – George, Thomas R.
George family record; descendants of Col. John George of Virginia. Houston, Tex. 1978. (NGS)

GERON – Woodward, Jewell Daphne Gerron
Solomon Geron and his descendants. Fort Worth, Tex. Woodward. 1968. (DAR)

GERON – Woodward, Jewell Daphne Gerron
Solomon Geron and his descendants, 1761-1968. By Jewell Daphne Gerron Woodward. Illustrated by Oneida Uzzell. Fort Worth, Tex. Printed by the Manney Co., 1968. (LC)

GERON – Woodward, Jewell Daphne Gerron
Solomon Geron and his descendants, 1761-1968. Fort Worth, Tex. 1968. (NGS)

GERMAN-TEXAS – Goyne, Minetta Altgelt
German-Texas family. By Minetta Altgelt Goyne. Fort Worth, Tex. Texas Christian University Press, c1982. (LC)

GIBSON – Hill, Euel Ray, 1934-
The Hills of Tennessee and Texas. By Euel Ray Hill, edited by Theron Lavon Smith. El Paso, Tex. E. R. Hill. 1982. (LC)

GIBSON – Roach, Arminta Roach
The Gibson family. Compiled by Arminta Roach Roach. Apple Springs, Tex. A. R. Roach. 1987. (LC)

GIDDENS – Ivey, Emily Woodall, 1936-
Genesis four, "We begat!": Giddens family history. By Emily Woodall Ivey. Hummble, Tex. JaBar Pub. c1985. (LC)

GILBERT – Schwartze, Annie James (Andrews)
Gilbert genealogy, starting with Abram Gilbert and Elizabeth West Gilbert in Newberry, South Carolina, and following their descendants through Georgia, Alabama, and Texas. By Annie James (Andrews) Schwartze. (n.p., 194-). (LC)

GILES – Bullard, Lucille Blackburn
Genealogical sketches of Elijah Giles – James Smith families. Jefferson, Tex. Bullard. 1965. (DAR)

GILES – Bullard, Lucille (Blackburn)
Genealogical sketches of Elijah Giles – James Smith families. By Lucille (Blackburn) Bullard. Jefferson, Tex., 1965. (LC)

GILL –
Acres of love: the life and times of Levi Thomas Gill and Ethel Lee (Wilkerson) Gill. Written by their children and grandchildren; edited by Wayne S. Gill. San Antonio, Tex. W. S. Gill, 1983? (LC)

GILL – Eckhardt, Ura L.
Gill family assorted records, no. 2. By Ura L. Eckhardt. Houston, Tex. 1970. (FW)

GILLILAND – Greenwood, Martrue Hutcheson
The loving Irish – the Gilllilands. Compiled by Martrue Hutcheson Greenwood. Bluff Dale, Tex. (Gilliland Family of Texas Association). 1970. (LC)

GILMORE – Boyd, Margie Milner, 1925-
The Robert Harllee McNeill and Lela Harper Gilmore family: their ancestors and descendants. Compiled by Margie Milner Boyd. Beaumont, Tex. M. M. Boyd. 1990. (LC)

GISH – Huffaker, Josephine Costello, 1918-
Christian Gish of Virginia. Compiled by Josephine Costello Huffaker. Baltimore: Gateway Press; Dallas, Tex. 1989. (LC)

GIST – Addison, Eddie Gist Williams
Pine cones and cactus. By Eddie Gist Williams Addison (as told to Thelma Lacy). San Angelo, Tex. Anchor Pub. Co. c1980. (LC)

GIVENS – Givens, Dorothy Hall, 1909-
The Texas-Oklahoma clan of Daniel Givens descendants: supplenent II to A Givens-Hall family history from pre-Revolutionary times to 1970. Compiled by Dorothy Hall Givens. Radford, Va. Commonwealth Press. 1976, c1977. (LC)

GIVENS – Givens, Dorothy H.
More Daniel Givens descendants: Supplement to I to A Givens-Hall family history from pre-revolutionary times to 1970. By Dorothy H. Givens. Radford, Va. Commonwealth Print. 1977. (FW)

GIVENS –
Texas-Oklahoma clan of Daniel Givens descendants, supplement II to A Givens-Hall family history from pre-Revolutionary times to 1970. Radford, Va. Commonwealth Print. 1977. (FW)

GIVENS – Jones, Chester L.
Short history of Givens family from 1719; Doelle family from 1837; Jones family from 1849; Gray family from 1818. By Chester L. Jones. Dallas, Tex. 1971. (FW)

GLEN – Landy,, Louise Glenn
The genealogies of two John Glenns. By Louise Glenn Landy. San Angelo? Tex. Landy. c1977. (LC)

GODBEY – Pitts, Alice
The Godby-Godbey book. By Alice Ellison Pitts. Rev. McKinney, Tex. A. E. Pitts. 1981. (LC)

GOLDEN – Cherry, Martha Grant, 1942-
Golden chains of love. By Martha Grant Cherry. San Antonio, Tex. M. G. Cherry. c1981. (LC)

GOOCH – Hume, Gladys Gooch
Gooch family history. Compiled by Gladys Gooch Hume; research by Clayton Reed, Susan Swaney, Virginia Gooch Watson. Eastland County, Tex. G. G. Hume, 1989? (LC)

GOOD – Britt, Cloma, 1917-
William Mason Goode, Mary Catherine Fry: Dublin, Ireland-Virginia-Missouri, Young County, Texas: from there to here, 1829-1983. By Cloma McDuff Britt. Azle, Tex. C. M. Britt. c1983. (LC)

GOODWIN – Eckhardt, Ura L.
Goodwin family, no. 1-2, 1961-1970. By Ura L. Eckhardt. Houston, Tex. 1970. (FW)

GOODWIN – Gadbury, Ruth, 1916-
Goodwin-Hill and related families. By Ruth Godwin Gadbury; sketches, Mary Word Hood. Lometa, Tex. R. G. Gadbury. c1980. (LC)

GORDON – Flack, Jessie Gordon
Genealogy of the Gordon – Macy, Hiddleson – Curtis, and allied families. Tulsa, Okla. Flack. 1967. (DAR)

GORDON – Gordon, Frank Newton
Descendants of Reverend Edward Clifford Gordon. By Frank Newton Gordon. Kingsville, Tex. Printed by Tex-Mex. Printery. 1952. (LC)

GORDON – Hodges, Frances Beal Smith
Gordons of Spotsylvania County, Virginia, with notes on Gordons of Scotland. By Frances Beal Smith Hodges. Wichita Falls, Tex. Wichita Multigraphing Company. c1934. (LC)

GORDON – Marshall, Ermine Northcutt
Gordons of the deep South. Austin, Tex. Marshall. 1961. (DAR)

GORDON – Marshall, Ermine N.
Gordons of the deep South. By Ermine N. Marshall. Austin, Tex. Printed by the Steck Co. 1961. (FW)

GORDON – McCurdy, John C.
A letter to Clyde from John C. McCurdy. Slaton, Tex? J. C. McCurdy. 1987? (LC)

GOSE – Yost, Thelma Pearl Chitwood
The Gose book. Fort Worth, Tex. Don Cowan Co. 1970. (DAR)

GOSE – Yost, Thelma Pearl Chitwood
The Gose book: the descendants of Stephen Mathus and Mary Frances Gerking Gose, Decatur, Wise County, Texas. By Thelma Pearl Chitwood Yost. Fort Worth, Tex. D. Cowan Co. Printers. 1970. (LC)

GOSE – Yost, Thelma Pearl Chitwood
The Gose Book; the descendants of Stephen Mathus and Mary Frances Gerking Gose, Decatur, Wise County, Texas. Fort Worth, Tex. 1970. (NGS)

GOSSELIN – Harrison, Lorraine Gosselin
Gabriel's grandchildren. Odessa, Tex. L. G. Harrison. 1985. (LC)

GOULD – Kelsey, Mary Wilson
Robert Wilson, 1750-1826 of Blount County, Tennessee: some of his descendants and related families including Gould, Cook, Brooks, Huson, Shearer, Stribling. Compiled from the papers of Mary Wilson Kelsey, James Cook Wilson, and Louise Kirk; illustrations from the Mavis and Mary Kelsey Collection of Art and Americana at the Sterling Evans Library, Texas A&M University. 1st Ed. Houston, Tex. M. W. Kelsey. c1987. (LC)

GRACEY – Gracy, Alice Duggan
The Gracy family of New York and Texas. By Alice Duggan Gracy; maps by Watt Harris, Jr. Austin, Tex. A. D. Gracy. c1986. (LC)

GRAHAM – Millis, Mary Ruth, 1929-
A Graham chronicle: records of the Craig and Graham families of Graham, and including Kintners of Indiana, Hunts of Kentucky. Compiled and annotated by Mary Ruth Millis. Dallas, Tex. Millis. 1977. (LC)

GRAHAM – Rhoades, Clara L. S.
Ancestors and heirs of the Paralee Graham and Daniel Sanders family of Mercer County. By Clara L. S. Rhoades. Pampa, Tex., 1971. (DP)

GRANGER – Seymouor, Geneva Bailey
Granger. By Geneva Bailey Seymour. Lubbock, Tex. G. B. Seymour. c1981. (LC)

GRANT – Smith, Flora Grant
Descendants of Marshall (Mike) Grant and Melissa Jane Cassiday. San Antonio [sic], Tex. Grant. 1978. (DAR)

GRAVES – Graves, Louise
Graves, twelve generations, some descendants and kin of Captain Thomas Graves, progenitor, ancient planter in colony of Virginia 1608, to and including Henry Lee Graves, Dallas, Texas, 1977. Dallas, Tex. Graves. 1977? (DAR)

GRAVES – Graves, Louise, 1905-
Graves: twelve generations, some descendants and kin: Captain Thomas Graves, progenitor, ancient planter in colony of Virginia, 1608 to and including Henry Lee Graves, Dallas, Texas, 1977. Louise Graves, compiler. Dallas, Tex. 1977. (LC)

GRAVES – MacDonald, Stewart Lincoln
The story of Wesley Graves: 1802-1890, and his descendants. Springdale, Ark. MacDonald. 1966. (DAR)

GRAY – Eckhardt, Ura L.
Gray family, no. 1-2, 4, 1965-1970. By Ura L. Eckhardt. Houston, Tex. 1970. (FW)

GRAY – Gray, Lewis, 1916-
A family history, Gray – Avery and related families. By Lewis Gray and Ruby Gray. Burkburnett, Tex. Maple-Gray Press. c1980. (LC)

GRAY – Gray, Millie, 1800-1851-
The diary of Millie Gray, 1832-1840 (nee Mildred Richards Stone, wife of Col. Wm. Fairfax Gray) recording her family life before, during and after Col. Wm. F. Gray's

journey to Texas in 1935; and the Small journal, giving particulars of all that occurred during the family's voyage to Texas in 1838. Houston, [Tex.]. Printed in the name of Rosenberg Library Press. Galveston, Tex., by the F. Young Pub. Co. 1967. (LC)

GRAY – Overlander, Rufus M.
Blount family of North Carolina and allied families Miller, Dyer, Gray. Seabrook, Tex. Rufus M. Overland III, 1987. (LC)

GREELEY – Barton, Thomas E.
From Virginia with love. By Thomas E. Barton, Sherman, Tex. TEBSCO. c1985. (LC)

GREEN – Russell, Lauretta
John Green, pioneer Alabama legislator, and his descendants. San Antonio, Tex. Russell. 1967. (DAR)

GREENE – Welsh, Dorothy Green
The Greene Family. Dallas, Tex. 1965. (NGS)

GREENFIELD – Vick, James Andrew, 1929-
Greenfield, Colonel Thomas, immigrant to Maryland: some of his ancestors and descendants. By James Andrew Vick. Waco, Tex. J. A. Vick. 1989. (LC)

GREER – Greer, Jack T.
Leaves from a family album (Holcombe and Greer). By Jack T. Greer. Waco, Tex. Texian Pr. 1975. (FW)

GREER – Wakefield, Eliza (McCleve)
Texas and the Greers. By Eliza (McCleve) Wakefield. Carlsbad? N. M., 1953. (LC)

GREGORY – Gregory, Marolf Preston, 1902-
The Daniel Gregory family and allied families. Marolf Preston Gregory. Houston, Tex. M. P. Gregory. c1980. (LC)

GREINER – Becker, Dorothy Robertson
Some early related families of Lancaster County, Pennsylvania. Fort Worth, Tex. Miram Publishing. c1979. (DAR)

GRIFFIN – Eckhardt, Ura L.
Griffin family, no. 1-14, 1959-1969. By Ura L. Eckhardt. Houston, Tex. 1969. (FW)

GRIGSBY – Lacy, Lawson Keener
The descendants of John and Sarah (Rosser or Prosser) Grigsby. Longview, Tex. Lacy. 1961, c1963. (DAR)

GRIGSBY – Lacy, Lawson Keener (Mrs. Rogers Lacy)
The descendants of John and Sarah (Rosser or Prosser) Grigsby. Compiled by Lawson Keener Lacy (Mrs. Rogers Lacy). Longview, Tex. Dec. 30, 1961. (LC)

GRIMWOOD – Grimwood, James M.
Grimwood sketches, 1562-1982: the lineage of William H., Isaac O., and Joseph C. Grimwood. By James Maurice Grimwood. Houston, Tex. J. M. Grimwood. 1982. (LC)

GROSS – Hall, William C., 1939-
The Andrew Jackson Gross genealogy: being a history of Andrew Jackson Gross, born in Pa. and all his descendants from Hardin Co., Ohio to Iowa and thence to all parts of the United States. Compiled by William C. Hall. Nevada? Iowa. Hall. c1978. (LC)

GROSS – Underwood, Mary Pauline Walker, 1918-
Look backward my child; history and roster of two families whose paths merged in 1870, exactly one hundred years ago: William Dunbar Gross and Isham Shearer. Centennial Ed. Lubbock, Tex. Midwest Reproductions. 1970. (LC)

GUENTHER – Guenther, Imogen Ireson
The Guenther family genealogy. Sugar Land, Tex. Guenther. 1946. (DAR)

GUESS – Guess, Mary Lupton
Something of the Guess-Guest family. Austin, Tex. Guess? 1961. (DAR)

GUEST – Martin, Alta Louise Biggs, 1915-
Guest-Guess, history and lineage in America. Compiled by Alta Louise Biggs Martin from Guest-Guess and related families and other records. Atlanta, Tex. Mrs. C. A. Martin. 1981. (LC)

GULLETT – Cullar, W. Clytes Anderson (Willie Clytes Anderson), 1920-
French carriages on the Trinity: the Guillot family of Dallas. By W. Clytes Anderson Cullar and Lawrence Elie Guillot. Dallas, Tex. L. E. Guillot. c1986. (LC)

GUNDERMAN – Spray, Barbara C.
Gunderman and Wullenjohn cousins with Hampel and Noll families. By Barbara Chandler Spray. Amarillo, Tex. B. C. Spray. 1978? (LC)

GUNN – Gunn, Beth, 1913-
[Gunn family genealogy]. [Arlington, Tex.: B. Gunn, 1984?]. (LC)

GUNN – Gunn, Drewey Wayne
Gunn: a genealogy, including information about related lines: Dowell, Moore, Ratliff, Anderson, Walker, Miles, Roark, Smith, Kallam, Hill, and other families. By Drewey Wayne Gunn. Corpus Christi, Tex., 1972. (LC)

GUNN – Plant, Louise Gunn, 1926-
Rev. Samuel and Catherine Sherrill Gunn and their descendants. Paducah, Tex. L. G. Plant, 1983. (LC)

GUNTHER –
Gunter. Compiled, written, edited by Edwin D. Gunter... [et al.]. [Jacksonville, Tex.]. E. D. Gunter. [c1983]. (LC)

GURLEY – Simmons, Julia Clare Gurley
The Gurley-Simmons families as related to the Spotswood-Moore-West-Dandridge families of Virginia. Houston, Tex. Simmons? 1968. (DAR)

GURLEY – Simmons, Julia Clare Gurley
The Gurley-Simmons families as related to the Spotwood-Moore-West-Dandridge families of Virginia. By Julila Clare Gurley Simmons. Houston? Tex. 1968. (LC)

H –

HAACK – Haack, Robert D. (Robert David), 1961-
The Haack family: our family heritage. By Robert D. Haack. Grand Prairie, Tex. R. D. Haack. c1989. (LC)

HADDOCK – Koontz, Dewie Lucas, 1917-
The Haddock family of Cypress Inn, Wayne Co., TN., and descendants. Compiled by Dewie Lucas Koontz. Arlington, Tex. D.L. Koontz. c1989. (LC)

HADDOCK – Scott, Mary Rebecca Dulany
Gone to Texas: a compendium of the Dulaney, Haddox, Heaton, Holland and Martin families. By Mary Rebecca Dulany Scott. Tomball, Tex. M. R.D. Scott. c1989. (LC)

HAGGARD – Ray, Jennie Haggard
History of the Haggard family in England and America, 1433, to 1899, to 1938. Dallas, Tex. Regional Press. 1938. (DAR)

HAGGARD – Ray, Jennie Haggard
History of the Haggard family in England and America 1433 to 1899 to 1938. By Jennie Haggard Ray. Dallas, Tex., 1938. (LC)

HAGGERTY – Eckhardt, Ura L.
Haggerty family, no. 1-4, 1963-1970. By Ura L. Eckhardt. Houston, Tex. 1970. (FW)

HAGLER -- Haegelin, Hilmer Bernard, 1907-
The Haegelin family: six generations with allied lines of Zinsmeyer, Biry, Simon, Riff, Lebold, Schuchart and others. Researched by Hilmer Bernard Haegelin, Margaret Hoffman Haegelin. Hondo, Tex. H. B. Haegelin, c1984. (LC)

HALEY – Dougherty, Miriam Hayley, 1917-
The Hayley family. By Miriam (Hayley) Dougherty. Quitmon, Tex. M. H. Dougherty. 1984. (LC)

HALEY – Haley, J. Evetts (James Evetts), 1901-
Rough times, tough fiber: a fragmentary family chronicle. By J. Evetts Haley. Canyon, Tex. Palo Duro Press. 1976. (LC)

HALL – Eckhardt, Ura L.
Hall family, no. 1-14, 1959-1970. By Ura L. Eckhardt. Houston, Tex. 1970. (FW)

HALL – Hall, Marvin F.
History of the Hall – Ayers – Holland family: Virginia, North Carolina, Georgia, Tennessee, Texas. Scarsdale, N. Y. Hall. 1976. (DAR)

HALL – Jantz, Virginia Copeland, 1923-
Pierce, Pace, Hall, Minton, and Huie families. By Virginia Copeland Jantz. Waco, Tex. V. C. Jantz. c1986. (LC)

HALL – Johnstone, Hazel Hall, 1917-
Feet of clay: history of the L. L. Hall family. By Hazel Hall Johnstone. [Tex.]. H. H. Johnstone. c1984. (LC)

HALL – Meier, Gladys Hall
History of the Hall family and allied lines. Brownsville, Tex. Meier: Martindale. 1959. (DAR)

HALL –
History of the Hall family and allied lines. By Gladys Hall Meier and Robert Rene Martindale. Brownsville, Tex., 1959. (LC)

HALLER – Schmidt, Ernestine Peters, 1909-
The Haller Haus. Researched and compiled by Ernestine Peters Schmidt & Otto Carl Schmidt, Jr. 2nd Ed. San Antonio, Tex. E. P. Schmidt: O.C. Schmidt. [c1983]. (LC)

HALLETT – Finkelstein, Mrs. Dave
John and Margaret Hallett; American pioneers, founders of Hallettsville, Texas, 1852. By Mrs. Dave Finkelstein. Hollettsville? Tex., 1961. (LC)

HALLMAN – Hallman, E. S.
Hallman-Clemens genealogy with a family's reminiscence. By E. S. Hallman. Pub. by the E. S. Hallman family, Tuleta, Tex. Hesston, Kans., Record Print. 1949. (FW)

HALVERSON – Albertson, Dorothy Earle
Mid-night sun (Norway) to Texas. Compiled by Dorothy Earle Albertson. Tyler, Tex., 1942 (i.e.1944). (LC)

HAMILTON –
Hamilton family of Charles County, Maryland. (Houston, Tex., Standard Printing Co., 1930). (LC)

HAMILTON – Kelley, Maria Louisa Hamilton
Hamilton family of Charles County, Maryland. Houston, Tex. Kelley:Cherault. 1930. (DAR)

HAMILTON – Kelley, Maria L. H.
Hamilton family of Charles County, Md. By Maria L. H. Kelly. Houston, Tex., Standard Print., 1930. (FW)

HAMILTON – Tucker, D. A. (Duard Arnold), 1919-
Hamilton kin of Martha "Mat"Tucker. Compiled by D. A. Tucker. Houston, Tex. D. A. Tucker. 1987. (LC)

HAMMOND – Eckhardt, Ura L.
Hammond family, no. 1-9, 11, 1959-70. By Ura L. Eckhardt. Houston, Tex. 1970. (FW)

HAMMOND – Ingle, John, 1960-
The Hammond's family tree of life. [Fort Worth, Tex.]. J. Ingle. [1982]. (LC)

HAMPTON –Meynard, Virginia G. (Virginia Gurley), 1919-
The venturers: the Hampton, Harrison, and Earle families of Virginia, South Carolina, and Texas. By Virginiia G. Meynard. Easley, S. C. Southern Historical Press, c1981. (LC)

HAMPTON – Meynard, Virginia Gurley
The venturers; the Hampton, Harrison, and Earle Families of Virginia, South Carolina and Texas. Easley, SC. c1981. (NGS)

HAND – Bourgeois, May Hander, 1906-
They chose Texas: the Hander family from Denmark. By May Hander Bourgeois and Frances Brandenberger Cole. [S.l.]. Bourgeois. c1979. (LC)

HANITCH – Dempsey, Helen H.
The Hanitch family of Alsfeld, Germany and Dayton, Ohio, with related families. By Helen H. Dempsey. San Antonio, Tex., 1950. (LA)

HANKS – Baber, Adkin
The Hanks family of Virginia and westward; a genealogical record from the early 1600s, including charts of families in Arkansas, the Carolinas, Georgia, Illinois, Indiana, Iowa, Kentucky, Missouri, Oklahoma, Ohio, Pennsylvania and Texas. Compiled and edited, in collaboration with a number of Hanks descendants by Adin Baber. Kansas, Ill., privately printed by the author. 1965. (LC)

HANKS – Johnson, Gladys Hanks
Genealogy of the Hanks and allied families. By Gladys Hanks Johnson. Lano? Tex. 1965. (LC)

HANSBOROUGH – Hansborough, John W., 1908-
History and genealogy of the Hansborough-Hansbrough family with data on the Hanbury, Garrard, Lash, Devous, Davis, Wathen, and Bell families. [J. W. Hansborough]. Austin, Tex. J. W. Hansborough. c1981. (LC)

HAPGOOD – Huffmaster, James T.
Ancestors of James Hapgood and Mary C. Estabrook of Acton, Mass., comprizing [sic] the names of about fifty of the early settlers and the line of decent from each ancestor. Galveston, Tex. Huffmaster. 1925. (DAR)

HARBAUGH – Strock, Richard M., 1915-
Some Strock, Harbaugh, Funk, and Reynolds families of Washington and Frederick Counties, Maryland, and of Franklin County, Pennsylvania: including some descendants in Colorado, Illinois, Kansas, Michigan, Missouri, Ohio, Texas, etc: organized around the direct and collateral lineage of the authors (brothers), with

direct lineage extending back to the immigrants. Richard M. Strock and Robert F. Strock. [Cincinnati, Ohio]. R. M. Strock. [1988]. (LC)

HARBOR – Williams, Louis J., 1892-
The Harbours in America (Harber, Harbor, Harbur, Harbour, Arbour): with brief sketches of some early Virginia related famililes—Arrowsmith, Dalton, Fuson, Hall, Houchins, Pedigo, Pillson, Reynolds, Ross, Spurlock, Truman, Witt. By Louis J. Williams in collaboration with William Tyler Ross. 1st Ed. Lubbock, Tex. Harbour-Harbor-Harber Family Association. c1982. (LC)

HARDEMAN – Wilson, Francis W.
The Hardeman impact on early Texas history. By Francis W. Wilson. Luling, Tex. F. W. Wilson, c1986. (LC)

HARDING – Trammell, Camilla Davis
Seven Pines: its occupants and their letters, 1825-1872. By Camilla Davis Trammell. Houston: C. D. Trammell; Dallas, Tex. Distributed by Southern Methodist University Press. 1986. (LC)

HARDISON –Hardison, Lewis M. (Lewis Merrill), 1913-
One branch of the Hardison family. By Lewis M? [sic] Hardison. Kerrville, Tex. L. M. Hardison. [198?]. (LC)

HARDWICKE – Hardwicke, Robert E.
Notes on the Hardwicke family; together with two charts attached as supplement. Fort Worth, Tex. Hardwicke. 1940. (DAR)

HARDY – Arpee, Marion B. (Marion Bernice), 1915-
The Hardey family of Charles County and Piscataway, Maryland, and their Missouri descendants. Compiled by Marion B. Arpee, nee Hardey. Rev. Ed. Harlingen, Tex. M. B. Arpee. 1980. (LC)

HARDY – Clark, Robert M. (Robert Murel), 1948-
Hardie, Vincent, Gaines, and related families: from Virginia to Texas. By Robert M. Clark, Jr. United States? R. M. Clark, c1989. (LC)

HARDY – Hardee, David L.
The Eastern North Carolina Hardy-Hardee family in the South and Southwest. Raleigh, N. C. Hardee. 1964? (DAR)

HARGIS – Hamner, Laura Vernon
Somebody might come; a story of modern southern hospitality in the hills of Alabama. With illus. by Marietta Byrnes (and others). By Laura Vernon Hamner. Dallas. American Guild Press. c1958. (LC)

HARGRAVE – Vowell, Emily M. H.
Hargrave family lineage, descendants of John W. Hargrave and Willie E. Farmer. By Emily M. H. Vowell. El Paso, Tex., 1970. (FW)

HARLLEE –
(Stuart) Harlee, Andrew and Agnes (Cade) Fulmore, Benjamin and Mary Curry, Samuel and Amelia (Russell) Kemps, John and Hannah (Walker) Bethea, Sterling Clack and Frances (King) Robertson, Samuel and Sophia Ann (Parker) Dickey, their antecedants, and collateral relatives, with chapter concerning state and county records and the derivation of counties of Alabama, Florida, Georgia, Mississippi, North Carolina, Pennsylvania, South Carolina, Tennessee, Texas Kinfolks, a genealogical and biographical record of Thomas and Elizabeth and Virginia. Prepared and published by William Curry Harlee, assisted by numerous collaborators. New Orleans, La. Printed by Searcy & Pfoff, Ltd. 1934-37. (LC)

HARMAN – Harman, L. L.
Historical life of Lewis Givens Harman, 1826, Tenn., 1902, Texas. By L. L. Harman. (FW)

HARPER – Peacock, Ruby Leona Henderson, 1925-
Twigs and branches from the Archer-Harper-Henderson-Reeves family tree. By Ruby Leona Henderson Peacock. Roaring Springs, Tex. R.L.H. Peacock. 1984? (LC)

HARRELL – Harrell, Wanda Frazier, 1942-
Under the rainbow: the Harrells. By Wanda Frazier Harrell. Anton, Tex. W. F. Harrell. c1986. (LC)

HARRINGTON – Harrington, George H.
Manuscript of Harrington family genealogy gazetter. By George H. Harrington. Austin, Tex. 1941. (LC)

HARRIS – Byler, Roger Louis, 1912-
Rev. Robert Harris Harris: ancestry, ministry, descendants, 1818-1909. By Roger Louis Byler. Sweeney, Tex. R. L. Byler. c1983. (LC)

HARRISON –
Descendants of Michael Moulton Harrison and related pioneer families of the Republic of Texas, including Reams, Hutson, Jackson, Heffington. Compiled by Sallie Stewart Harrison and Ethel Stewart Cole. Houston? 1972. (LC)

HARRISON – Harrison, Thomas P., Jr.
The Harrisons of Andersonville, South Carolina. By Thomas P. Harrison, Jr. Austin, Tex., 1973. (LC)

HARRISON. See also:
                    Armistead
                    Irwin
                    Lewis
                    MacDonell

HARRISON – Sarrafian, Katherine Harrison
The Harrison family in Texas, 1830-1966. Compiled by Katherine Harrison Sarrafian. Waco? Tex. 1966. (LC)

HARRISON. See also:

Berry	Hood	Peden
Beville	Johnson	Pocahontas
Brown	Lewis	Smith
Byrd	Ligon	Torrence
Echols	O'Connor	Wilson
Funsten	Page	

HARROUN – Comstock, E. B.
Harroun family in America, descendants of Alexander Harroun of Colerain, Mass. By E. B. Comstock. Dallas, Tex.. (n.d.). (FW)

HARROUN – Comstock, Ernest B.
The history of the Harroun family in America, seven generations; descendants of Alexander Harroun of Colrain, Mass., 1691-1784. Compiled and published by Ernest B. Comstock. Dallas, Tex. 1940. (LC)

HART – Carley, William H.
Information on the Hart, Teague, Onley, Waldron, and Jeter families of The South. San Angelo, Tex. Carley. 1945. (DAR)

HART – Greenwood, Kathy L., 1949-
Heart-Diamond. Kathy L. Greenwood; introduction by Elmer Kelton; illustrations by Charles Shaw. 1st Ed. Denton, Tex. University of North Texas Press. c1990. (LC)

HART – Tarrance, Mary Gilmore (Rea)
Hart, Rea, Turner, Tarrance and allied families. Dallas, Tex. Tarrance. 1963. (DAR)

HARTMAN – Orrison, Estella Hartmann, 1914-
The Philip Hartmann heritage, 1830-1979. Written and compiled by Estella Hartmann Orrison. Waco, Tex. Orrison. c1980. (LC)

HARTSFIELD – Hartsfield, Samuel Jackson
Hartsfield of America. By Samuel Jackson Hartsfield. (S.1.: s.n., 1972?). Tyler, Tex. Chief Printing Co. (LC)

HARVEY – Hervey, Donald G. (Donald Gable), 1941-
Mayflower to the moon, Herveys & Gables. By Donald G. Hervey. Houston, Tex. Passim Press. c1980. (LC)

HARVEY – Krueger, Jessie Harvey
The Harvey's from back thar in Kentucky (an anthology of the Harvey Clan) 1799 to 1963. By Jessie Harvey Krueger. Fort Worth, Tex. Printed by Manney Co., 1964. (LC)

HASHIM – Garcia, Joan Ellis, 1936-
Our family tree grew from a very strange bush: an Arabic-Anglo-Hispanic family history. By Joan Ellis Garcia. 1st American Ed. Quanah, Tex. Nortex Press. c1978. (LC)

HATZENBUEHLER –
Texas cousins: Hatzenbuehler, Hawpre, Sypert, Thompson (family newsletter). (FW)

HAVINS –
The history of the descendants of John and Mary Havins. By Havins-Havens Assoc. Abilene? Tex., 1962. (NY)

HAWKINS – Gage, Duane
John Henry Hawkins and his kin. Tarrant Co., Tex. Gage. 1978. (DAR)

HAWKINS – Hawkins, John Wesley
A brief history of the William Alden and Anna Eddy Hawkins family; who came from Indiana to Texas in 1848. Westbrook, Tex. Jack R. Hawkins. 1961? (DAR)

HAWKINS – Hawkins, John W.
Brief history of the William Alden and Anna Eddy Hawkins family, who came from Indiana to Texas in 1848. By John W. Hawkins. Groesbeck, Tex. J. W. Hawkins, 1962. (FW)

HAWKINS – SoRelle, Laura (C.)
Hawkins-Harold family history. By Laura (C.) SoRelle, Amarillo, Tex. 1962. (FW)

HAXTON – Mayes, C. Vale
Haxton genealogy and allied lines. Fort Worth, Tex. Miran Pub. c1979. (DAR)

HAXTON – Mayes, C. Vale (Charles Vale), 1906-
Haxton genealogy and allied lines. By C. Vale Mayes and Bertha Clark. Fort Worth, Tex. Miran Publishers. c1979. (LC)

HAYNES – Simmons, Julia Clare Gurley
Some descendants of Henry Haynes (b. 1701). Compiled by Julia Clare Gurley Simmons. Houston, Tex. Simmons. 1965. (LC)

HAYNES – Eckhardt, Ura L.
Haynes family, no. 1-5, 7-11. 13. 1960-1970. By Ura L. Eckhardt. Houston, Tex. 1970. (FW)

HAYNIE – Rossman, Loyce (Haynie)
A Haynie genealogy: their 1650 Virginia roots, 1839 Texas trunk, nine limbs, many branches, twigs and some leaves. By Loyce (Haynie) Rossman. Fredericksburg? Tex. 1963. (LC)

HAYNIE – Rossman, Loyce (Haynie)
A Haynie genealogy: their 1650 Virginia Roots, 1839 Texas Trunk,, Nine Limbs, many branches, twigs and some leaves. ?Fredericksburg, Tex. 1963. (NGS)

HEABERLIN – Heaberlin, Sam J. (Sam Joe), 1913-
The Heaberlins in East Texas: including the related family of Joe Elton Stribling. By Sam J. Heaberlin, compiler and narrator. Lufkin, Tex. Pineywoods Print. 1988. (LC)

HEAD – Eckhardt, Ura L.
Head family, assorted record, no. 1-13, 15-19, 1955-70. By Ura L. Eckhardt. Houston, Tex. 1970. (FW)

HEAD – Smith, Rachel S.
Album of the Head, Rodman, Selby, Stovall, Smith, Tate line, 1749-1966. By Rachel S. Smith. Albany, Tex., 1963. (FW)

HEADLEE – Headlee, Miss Rollie
The Headlee family in America. By Miss Rollie Headlee, edited and revised by Emmet Jerome Headlee. Denton, Tex. 1936. (LC)

HEARD – Heard, Harold
Descendants of John Heard, Sr., Wilkes County, Ga. By Harold Heard. Amarillo, Tex. (n.d.). (FW)

HEARD – Heard, Harold
Early records of Heards. By Harold Heard. Amarillo, Tex. (n.d.). (FW)

HEARD – Heard, Harold, 1903-
Early records of Heards. Amarillo, Tex. [1971?]. (LC)

HEARD – Heard, Harold
Heard families in Arkansas, 1830, 1840, 1850, 1860, 1870 and 1880, U. S. Census records of Arkansas. By Harold Heard. Amarillo, Tex. (196-). (DP)

HEARD – Heard, Harold
The Heard family; articles and extracts about the family. By Harold Heard. (Amarillo, Tex., 196-). (DP)

HEARD –
Heard-Hurd families. (n.p.) 1962? (FW)

HEARD –
Descendants of Charles Heard. Amarillo, Tex. (1967?) (LC)

HEARD – Heard, Harold
Miscellaneous collections of the Heard family. By Harold Heard. Amarillo, Tex. 1967. (DP)

HEARD – Heard, Harold
Miscellaneous collections of the Heard family. By Harold Heard. 2d Series. Amarillo, Tex. (1967?). (DP)

HEARD – Heard, Harold
Southern Heard families. By Harold Heard. (Amarillo? Tex., 1968?). (LC)

HEARD – Heard, Harold
Descendants of John Heard, Sr. of Wilkes Co., Ga. By Harold Heard. Amarillo, Tex. (197-?). (LC)

HEARD – Heard, Harold
Miscellaneous collections of Heards. By Harold Heard. (Amarillo? Tex., 1970?). (LC)

HEARD – Heard, Harold
Early records of Heards. By Harold Heard. Amarillo, Tex. (1971?). (LC)

HEARD – Heard, Harold
Heard families in Arkansas: 1830, 1840, 1850, 1860, 1870, and 1880 U. S. Census records of Arkansas. By Harold Heard. (Amarillo? Tex., 1970?). (LC)

HEARST – Hurst, John Simeon, 1909-1981-
Hurst and allied families. By John Simeon Hurst, Jr. Lancaster, Tex. H. R. Hurst, c.1984. (LC)

HEATON – Scott, Mary Rebecca Dulany
Gone to Texas: a compendium of the Dulany, Haddox, Heaton, Holland and Martin families. By Mary Rebecca Dulany Scott. Tomball, Tex. M.R.D. Scott. c1989. (LC)

HEINER – Hensell, John
Chronicles of a German family; or, Heiners of Germany, Pennsylvania, Kentucky and Texas. By John Hensell. Houston, Tex. (J.Hensell, 1958). (NY)

HELMS – Hellums, Earle C.
The Hellums family, 1765 to 1984: beginning with John Hellums Sr. in Laurens County, South Carolina. By Earle C. Hellums. [Texas?]. E. C. Hellums. c1984. (LC)

HENDERSON – Bish, LaVerne (Hutchens)
The Olden Days. Henderson, King, Montgomery, Shields families. Austin, Tex. 1973. (NGS)

HENDERSON – McWhorter, Lotie, 1913-
Mary (Barry) (1795-1888) & William Barry Henderson (1787-1863): their forebears & descendants. Compiled & edited by Lottie McWhorter and Lou Ann Mackey Melton; major contributors, Blanche Abney... [et al.]. Baltimore; Gateway Press. Longview, Tex. 1987. (LC)

HENDERSON – Peacock, Ruby Leona Henderson, 1925-
Twigs and branches from the Archer-Harper-Henderson-Reeves family tree. By Ruby Leona Henderson Peacock. Roaring Springs, Tex. R.L.H. Peacock. 1984? (LC)

HENKEL –Hoskinson, Josie V. (H.)
A history of the family of George August Edward Henkel who emigrated to Texas from Germany in 1846 and generations of the Henkel-Schoenwerk families in Germany. By Josie V. (H.) Hoskinson. Norman, Okla., 1956. (NY)

HENNECKE – Treybig, Arliss, 1934-
Descendants of Jacob Hennecke and Mary Braden: a statistical history: including references to Braden, Burtschell, Glueck, and Hennecke families in Texas. By Arliss Treybig. Rev. El Campo, Tex. A. Treybig. 1981. (LC)

HENNIGER -- Henniger, Monroe R.
Nicholaus Henniger and his descendants, 1794-1964. By Monroe R. Henniger. Austin, Tex., 1964. (FW)

HENNING – Haning, James Leslie, 1923-
Matthew Haning (c. 1730-1807) and descendants. By James Leslie Haning. Baltimore: Gateway Press. San Antonio, Tex. 1987. (LC)

HENRY – Eckhardt, Ura L.
Henry family, no. 1-13, 1959-1970. By Ura L. Eckhardt. Houston, Tex. 1970. (FW)

HERBERT – Richardson, C. Kathryn
Our Herbert heritage. Azle, Tex. Richardson. c1969. (DAR)

HERRING – Grimwood, James M.
Herring highlights, 1642-1984: the lineage of Baaylis E., Hines H., and Daniel M. Herring. By James Maurice Grimwood, Lola Herring Kennedy. Houston, Tex. J. M. Grimwood. 1984. (LC)

HERRING – Grimwood, James M.
Herring Highlights, 1642-1984: the lineage of Baaylis E., Hines H., and Daniel M. Herring. Houston, Tex. 1984. (NGS)

HEUSINGER – Heusinger, Edward W.
The Heusinger family in Texas. San Antonio, Tex. Heusinger. 1945. (DAR)

HEUSINGER – Heusinger, Edward W., F.R.G.S.
The Heusinger family in Texas. By Edward W. Heusinger, F.R.G.S. San Antonio, Tex. Standard Printing Company. 1945. (LC)

HICKCOX – Zeitler, Vernon Arthur, 1917-
Upon the shoulders of giants: Zeitler, McFeaters, Hickox, Moorhead, Leckendorn... Vernon Arthur Zeitler, Thelma Poorbaugh Zeitler. Lake Jackson, Tex. V. A. Zeitler. 1986. (LC)

HICKMMAN – Cell, Robert F.
Tax records, selected family names, Franklin County, Pennsylvania, 1796-1847: for selected names of the Cell family... Transcribed by Robert F. Cell. Edinburg, Tex. R. F. Cell. c1990. (LC)

HICKMAN – Wolf, Leonora Stoll, 1928-
Christian Heckmann and Louisa Raabe and their descendants: Germany to America, 1833-1987. Compiled by Leonora Stoll Wolf. Texas: L. S. Wolf. c1988. (LC)

HICKS – Hicks, Burnis Gertrude, 1912-
Lineage of Captain Fabius Haywood Hicks, 1835-1987. By Burnis Gertrude Hicks. Amarillo, Tex. B. G. Hicks. c1987. (LC)

HICKS – Hix, Gayle D.
Hix (Hicks) heads of families, 1790-1850: New York. Houston, Tex. G. D. Hix, 1980? (LC)

HICKS – Hix, Gayle D.
Hix (Hicks) heads of families, 1790-1850, Vermont, New Hampshire, Massachusetts. Houston, Tex. G. D. Hix, 1981? (LC)

HICKS – Mayfield, Fay Hicks, 1897-
Hicks history, 1773-1976: story of Isaiah Luther and Melissa Ida Hicks and their descendants. By Fay Hicks Mayfield. Abilene, Tex. Mayfield. c1976. (LC)

HICKS – Woods, Gary D.
The Hicks, Adams, Bass, Floyd, Pattillo and collateral lines, letters, 1840-1868. By Gary D. Woods. Salado, Tex. A. Jones. 1963. (NY)

HIESTAND – Trimble, David B.
Hiestand family of Page County, Virginia. By David B. Trimble. San Antonio, Tex. 1974. (FW)

HIGHTOWER – Baker, Mondeleen M.
Lloyd and related families. Childress, Tex.? M. M. Baker. 1987. (LC)

HIGHTOWER – Barton, Thomas E.
From Virginia with love. By Thomas E. Barton. Sherman, Tex. TEBSCO. c1985. (LC)

HIGHTOWER – Hightower, Jack English, 1926-
The family of William Clayton Hightower and Mai Cole: their ancestors and descendants, a genealogy/family history. Compiled by Jack J. E. Hightower. 1988. (LC)

HILDEBRAND – Harrell, Helen Odum, 1924-
The Heldebrand heritage. Helen Odum Harrell. New Braufels, Tex. Harrell. c1980. (LC)

HILL – Bartlett, Robert Merrill, 1898-
Those valiant Texans: a breed apart. By Robert M. Bartlett. Portsmouth, NH. P. E. Randall. c1989. (LC)

HILL – Hill, Euel Ray, 1945-
The Hills of Tennessee and Texas. By Euel Ray Hill; edited by Theron Lavon Smith. El Paso, Tex. E. R. Hill. 1982. (LC)

HILL – Hill, Geo. A., Jr.
The Hill family of Fayetteville, typical Texians; an address by Geo. A. Hill, Jr. Houston, Tex. 1936. (LC)

HILL – Hill, Joe Meredith
Family history: Hill, Meredith, Lowery. By Joe Meredith Hill. Dallas, Tex., 1966. (FW)

HILL --
Huntington-Hills-Roddis-Kreger-Culhane-Inskeep and allied families: ancestors of our grandchildren. Compiled by Jedediah Huntington Hills and Vera Mae Kreger Hills. Privately printed. San Antonio, Tex. Schneider Print. Co. 1969. (LC)

HILLMAN – Wynne, Diana Jones, 1942-
Ancestry and descendants of John M. Hillman and Harriet E. Louthan: with allied families of Lackey, Henderson, Bowles, and Mickesell. Compiled by Diana Jones Wynne. Houston, Tex. D. J. Wynne. 1982. (LC)

HILLSBERRY – Lemons, Nova A.
Through the orchard. Supplement: Arterberry, Hillsberry, Lemons, Ragsdale. By Nova A. Lemons. Dallas, Tex. N. A. Lemons. c1990. (LC)

HILLYER – Heck, Lorena Hilyer
Hillyer family, first years in Texas. 1961? (DAR)

HINDMAN – Hindman, Juanita Lewis
Postpioneers. Fort Worth, Tex. Branch-Smith. 1973. (LC)

HINER – Hensell, John
Chronicles of a German family. Houston, Tex. Hensell. 1958? (DAR)

HINER – Hensell, John
Through 900 years, Hiner and related famillies (Hiner, Heiner, Hainer, Hyner, etc.). By John Hensell. Houston, Tex. Hiner Reunion Assoc. of Texas. (196?). (FW)

HINKLEY – Hinckley, E. Charles
Hinckley: heritage & history. By E. Charles Hinckley. 2nd Ed. Fort Worth, Tex. Hinckley. 1976. (LC)

HINKLEY – Hinckley, E. Charles
Hinckley: heritage & history. By E. Charles Hinckley. 3rd Ed. Fort Worth, Tex. E. C. Hinckley. 1982. (LC)

HINOJOSA – Arpee, Marion B. (Marion Bernice), 1915-
The Hinojosa family of northeastern Mexico and the lower Rio Grande Valley: its background and history. By Marian B. Arpee. Harlingen, Tex. M. B. Arpee. 1985. (LC)

HINOJOSA – Arpee, Marion B. (Marion Bernice), 1915-
Lieutenant Diego Hinojosa of El Neuvo Reyno de Leon, Mexico. By Marion B. Arpee. Harlingen, Tex. M. B. Arpee. 1988. (LC)

HIXSON – Free, Margaret Madara
Hixson Trails, from New Jersey to Canada and back; descendants of Timothy and Naomi (Corwin) Hixson of New Jersey and Ontario, with Corwin, Winthrop and Gedney ancestral lines of Salem, Massachusetts. Alvin, Tex. 1982. (NGS)

HOCK – Steger, Mel
A Schrapfer-Hoch history. Houston, Tex. M. Steger, 1985. (LC)

HOCKADAY – Hockaday, Olin S.
History of the family of Thomas Hart Benton Hockaday, 1835-1956. By Olin S. Hockaday. Fort Worth, Tex., 1956. (FW)

HOCKADAY – Hockaday, Olin S(cott)
Descendants of Thomas Hart Benton Hockaday (1835-1918) and Maria Elizabeth Kerr (d. 1881). By O(lin) S(cott) Hockaday. Fort Worth, Tex? March 9, 1959. (LC)

HODDE – De Vore, Shirley Ann Staley
Hodde genealogy search: some allied families: Buerger, Downey, Helm, Geisler, Lohmann, Mielenz, Mullendore, Pecore, Staley, and Wolf. By Shirley Ann Staley De Vore. 1st Ed. Norman, Okla. S.A.S. De Vore. c1988. (LC)

HODGES – Dameron, Kyle, 1941-
The descendants of William Fields Hodge & Sophia Brownlow McClellan of Fayette County, Texas. Compiled by Kyle Dameron. Tulsa, Okla. K. Dameron. 1986. (LC)

HODGES – Knox, Barbara Roach, 1923-
Robert Hodge et al. of Livingston County, Kentucky. Compiled by Barbara Roach Knox. Fort Worth, Tex. B. R. Knox. c1983. (LC)

HOELSCHER – Gold, Theresa Gros, 1941-
The Hoelscher family of Texas: history and genealogy of Anton and Mary Katherine Hoelscher (eight generations), 1846-1978. Compiled by Theresa Gros Gold and Donald T. Hoelscher; family histories by Jackie Wooley Lipski. San Antonio, Tex. Gold. 1979? (LC)

HOELSCHER – Gold, Theresa Gros
The Hoelscher Family of Texas, 1846-1978. San Antonio, Tex. ?1979. (NGS)

HOFFMAN – Lehmann, Elizabeth A. J., 1907-
From Hesse, Germany, to Texas—1846: the Valentin Hoffman family, early German pioneers in Washington County, Texas. [Texas]. Elizabeth A. J. Lehmann. c1981. (LC)

HOFFMAN – Turnbo, Charles Alton, 1942-
Huffman heritage, 1770-1985. By Charles Turnbo & Sue Shields. Fort Worth, Tex. C. Turnbo; Burleson, Tex.: S. Shields. 1985. (LC)

HOGSETT –
Genealogy of the James Wesley Jacobs family, 1826 to 1967: Adam Lang family, 1826 to 1967: John Hogshead-Hogsett family, 1710 to 1967. Pampa, Tex., 1967. (FW)

HOLLAND – Eckhardt, Ura L.
Holland family notes, no. 1-21. By Ura L. Eckhardt. Houston, Tex., 1969. (FW)

HOLLAND – Elliott, Zola F. (Zola Florene), 1912-
Consanquinity: my father's line: McCuistons, Nelsons, Hollands & Elliotts. By Zola F. Elliott, author, editor, compiler, and publisher. Austin, Tex. Z. F. Elliott. 1989. (LC)

HOLLAND – Holland, Kirk Davis
Holland: a history of the Virginia Holland families from 1620 to 1963. By Kirk Davis Holland. Salado, Tex. Reproduced by the Anson Jones Press. 1963. (LC)

HOLLAND – McCall, Pearl Davis
The Holland-Jackson record. Salado, Tex. Anson Jones Press. 1959. (DAR)

HOLLAND – McCall, Pearl (Davis)
The Holland-Jackson record with related Hoyle-Swofford history. By Pearl (Davis) McCall. Salado, Tex. Anson Jones Press. 1959. (LC)

HOLLAND – McCall, Pearl (Davis)
The Holland-Jackson record with related Hoyle-Swofford history. Salado, Tex. 1959. (NGS)

HOLLAND –
Valley Forge forward: Thomas Holland, R.S. – [S.l.: s.n.], c1985. Austin, Tex. Nortex Press. (LC)

HOLMES – Shook, Tonya Holmes, 1935-
Displaced Cherokee: come home, come home. By Tonya Holmes Shook. Wichita Falls, Tex. Published for the author by Humphrey Printing Co.; Hastings, Colo. c1986. (LC)

HOLMSLEY – Cunningham, Carrie Holmsley
Historical record of the Holmsley family. By Carrie Holmsley Cunningham. Amarillo, Tex., 1958. (LC)

HOLMSLEY – Cunningham, C. H.
Historical record of the Holmsley family. By C. H. Cunningham. Amarillo, Tex., 1958. (FW)

HOLT – Marshall, Mrs. Arch Bruce (Maudie Marie Holt)
The descendants of Michael Holt. Compiled by Mrs. Arch Bruce Marhsall (Maudie Marie Holt). Houston? Tex., 1967. (LC)

HON – Wynne, Diana Jones, 1942-
Descendants of Jonas Hon, 1740-1838 and Joseph Hon, 1742-1825/35. Compiled by Daphne Hon Ramsay; copied by Mrs. Robert L. Wynne. Houston, Tex. Mrs. R. L. Wynne, 1981. (LC)

HOOK – Wilson, Callie Coe, 1917-
A pride of kin. By Callie Coe Wilson and Ellen Walker Rienstra. College Station: Texas A&M University Press. c1985. (LC)

HOOPER – Hooper, William E. (William Edward), 1924-
Seven trails into the past: a compilation of some of the lineages and family lines of Hooper, Poarch, Wilbanks, Spence, Clardy, LaFoy, Watkins, and Lumpkin, with genealogical notes. By William E. Hooper. Mesquite, Tex. W. E. Hooper. 1980. (LC)

HOOPES – Fuller, Gerald Ralph, 1919-
The Hoopes family record: a genealogical record of the Hoopes family, descendants of Daniel Hoopes of Westtown, Chester County, Pennsylvania. Compiled and edited by Gerald R. Fuller, June Markus Hoopes, Lillian Fredsall Webster. Houston, Tex. Hoopes Family Organization. 1979[1983]. (LC)

HOOPES – Fuller, Gerald Ralph
The Hoopes family record; a genealogical record of the Hoopes family, descendants of Daniel Hoopes of Westtown, Chester County, Pennsylvania. Also June M. Hoopes and Lillian F. Webster, cp. Houston, Tex. 1979-83. (NGS)

HOPKINS – Eckhardt. Ura L.
Hopkins family, no. 1-4, 1960. By Ura L. Eckhardt. Houston, Tex. 1967. (FW)

HOPSON – Hopson, George R.
Some very fine folks; Hopson. By George R. Hopson. San Angelo, Tex. San Angelo Genealogical and Historical Soc., 197-. (FW)

HORNBURG –
The Hornburg story. By Edna H. Elkins, et al. Austin, Tex. J. G. Garcia. 1974. (FW)

HORTON – Horton, Guy L.
Memoirs of S. H. Horton. Dallas, Tex. G. L. Horton. 1975. (DAR)

HOSTETTER – Campbell, Kathryn Hutcherson
Francis Hostetter, St. Charles, Missouri – 1806. Dallas, Tex. Campbell. 1972. (DAR)

HOUSE – Boles, Audrey I. H.
House that George built: a genealogy of George Washington House and his descendants. By Audrey I. H. Boles. Plainview, Tex. Wayland Baptist College, 1972. (FW)

HOUSE – Estes, Carolyn Hull, 1933-
Hull's heritage: a genealogical history. By Carolyn Hull Estes. Fort Worth, Tex. C. H. Estes. 1986. (LC)

HOUSE – Sutton, Mack C.
Descendants of Labon House. Compilers & researchers, Helen Varnell... [et al.]: contributors, Frances Irene House Schaefer... [et al.]; typed & compiled by Mack S. Sutton. Austin, Tex. M. C. Sutton. 1983. (LC)

HOUSTON – Huston, Cleburne
Bold legacy. Waco, Tex. Texian Press. 1968. (DAR)

HOUSTON – Huston, Cleburne
Bold legacy; the story of the Houston-Huston ancestors, 1150 to 1800. By Cleburne Huston. Waco, Tex. Printed by Texian Press, 1968. (LC)

HOUSTON – Morrow, Temple Houston
Houston genealogy, complete as to descendants of General Sam Houston. Compiled by Temple Houston Morrow. Drafted by Otho C. Morrow. Fort Worth, Tex., 1932. (LC)

HOUSTON –
Following General Sam Houston from 1793 to 1863. Etchings by Bernhardt Wall... historical sketches by Amelia Williams. Austin, Tex. The Steck Company. c1935. (LC)

HOUSTON – Shuffler, Ralph Henderson
The Houstons at Independence. By Ralph Henderson Shuffler. Waco, Tex. Texian Press. 1966. (LC)

HOWE – Whitley, Olga Rolater
The Howe line. Commerce, Tex. Whitley. 1967. (DAR)

HOWELL –
Ancestors and descendants of Samuel Howell, member of the Committee of Correspondence, etc. ... Rewritten. San Antonio, 1953. (NY)

HOWELL – Eckhardt, Ura L.
Howell family, no. 1-5, 1964-1970. By Ura L. Eckhardt. Houston, Tex. 1970. (FW)

HOWZE – Amsler, Amanda (H.)
History of our branch of the Howze family. By Amanda (H.) Amsler. El Paso, Tex., 1967. (NY)

HUDSON -- Hart, Donald Claire
Hudson records of North Carolina. Donald Claire Hart. Longview, Tex. Hudson Fmily Association (South). 1982. (LC)

HUDSON – Hart, Donald Claire
Hudson records of Virginia. Donald Claire Hart. Longview, Tex. Hudson Family Association (South). 1984. (LC)

HUDSON – Hudson, Betty Jo
Hudson immigrants and the geography of early settlement. Betty Jo Hudson and Phillip Wayne Rhodes. Longview, Tex. Hudson Family Association (South). 1981. (LC)

HUDSON – Hudson, Malcolm H.
Hudsons of the South in the 1790 census. Longview, Tex. Hudson Family Association. c1976. (DAR)

HUDSON – Hudson, Malcolm H.
Hudsons of the South in the 1790 census: a research aid for genealogists. By Malcolm H. Hudson; edited by Tom Hudson for Hudson Family Association (South). Longview, Tex. The Association. c1976. (LC)

HUDSON – Hudson, Malcolm H.
Hudsons of the South in the 1790 Census. Longview, Tex. 1976. (NGS)

HUDSON – Hudson, Malcolm H.
Hudson marriages in Virginia: a research for genealogists. Compiled by Malco[l]m H. Hudson; indexed by David Hudson; edited by Bettye Atkins Cartwright for Hudson Family Association (South). Longview, Tex. The Association. c1980. (LC)

HUDSON – Shull, William A.
Hudson marriages in North Carolina. Compiled by William A Shull, Jr., edited by Cleve Hudson for Hudson Family Association (South). Longview, Tex. the Association. c1984. (LC)

HUDSON – Stamps, Lonita Ayers
Our Hudson Heritage. Lubbock, Tex. Stamps. c1980.. (DAR)

HUDSON – Stamps, Lonita Ayers, 1921-
Our Hudson heritage. Compiled by Lonita Ayers Stamps, Weldon Isaac Hudson. Lubbock, Tex. L. Stamps. c1980. (LC)

HUESKE – Wolf, Leonora Stoll, 1928-
History of August Hueske (Huske) and Emilie Grauwunder and their descendants, 1834-1987. Compiled by Leonora Stoll Wolf. New Braunfels, Tex? L. S. Wolf. c1988. (LC)

HUFFAKER – Nolan, Ione Adamson
The Huffaker family. Fort Worth, Tex. Branch-Smith, Inc. 1966. (DAR)

HUFFAKER – Nolan, Ione A.
Huffaker family; a collection of genealogical records on descendants of Michael and Catherine Huffaker. By Ione A. Nolan. Fort Worth, Tex. Branch-Smith, 1966. (FW)

HUFFINGTON – Huffington, J. M.
Huffington family history. Sugar Land, Tex. Huffington. 1968. (DAR)

HUFFMASTER – Huffmaster, James T.
Huffmaster-Hoffmeister family record. Galveston, Tex. Huffmaster. 1922. (DAR)

HUFFMASTER – Huffmaster, James T.
Poetic productions of my old age. By James T. Huffmaster. Galveston, Tex. O. Springer, Print. 1920. (LC)

HUFFMASTER – Huffmaster, James T.
Huffmaster-Hoffmeister family records. Comp. by James T. Huffmaster. Galveston, Tex. Oscar Springer Print. 1922. (LC)

HUFFMASTER – Huffmaster, James T.
  Ancestors of James Hapgood and Mary C. Estabrook of Acton, Mass. ... By James T. Huffmaster. Galveston, Tex., 1925. (NY)

HUGHES – Finstad, Suzanne, 1955-
  Heir not apparent. Suzanne Finstad. Austin, Tex. Texas Monthly Press. c1984. (LC)

HUGHES – Hughes, Dorothy Dillard
  Our Hughes ancestors: a story of searches and discoveries, including maternal lines of Varvel, Ewing, Huntzinger, Sawyer, Brown, Hale/Haile, Craghead, and lists of descendants. By Dorothy Dillard Hughes. Lubbock, Tex. D. D. Hughes. c1989. (LC)

HUGULEY – Huguley, Harold C. (Harold Clyde), 1924-
  The Huguleys-who are we?: a study of our beginnings in America, where our immigrant ancestors settled, where they died and what happened to some of their descendants, particularly our own line of decent from one Charles Huguelet who arrived at the Philadelphia, Pennsylvania Port 14 September, 1754. Compiled and written by Harold C. Huguley. Amarillo, Tex. H. C. Huguley. c1980. (LC)

HULL – Estes, Carolyn Hull, 1933-
  Hull's heritage: a genealogical history. By Carolyn Hull Estes. Fort Worth, Tex. C. H. Estes. 1986. (LC)

HUMPHREYS – Humphreys, Allan S.
  Humphreys genealogy. Some descendants of John Humphreys, of Chester County, Pa., ten generations of whom have made their home in the southern states. By Allan S. Humphreys. Fayetteville, Ark. 1954. (FW)

HUNNICUTT – Hunnicutt, Lahoma
  Hunnicutt and allied families. By Lahoma Hunnicutt. Amarillo, Tex., 1967. (FW)

HUNT – Tuccille, Jerome
  Kingdom: the story of the Hunt family of Texas. Jerome Tuccille. Otttawa, Ill. Jameson Books. c1984. (LC)

HUNTER – Barkley, Laura G. H.
  Hunter-Sneed and allied families. By Laura G. H. Barkley. Austin, Tex., 1963. (FW)

HUNTER – McLean, W. H.
  Adam Hunter, Ayrshire Scot emigrant to Macoupin County, Ill. By W. H. McLean. Fort Worth, Tex., 1975. (FW)

HUNTER – McLean, William Hunter
  From Ayr to Thurber: three Hunter brothers and the winning of the West. Compiled by William Hunter McLean. 1st Ed. Fort Worth, Tex. Fort Worth Genealogical Society. c1978. (LC)

HUNTER – Hunter, Victor E.
  Hunter family history, 1810-1965. By Victor E. Hunter. Dallas, Tex., 1965. (FW)

HUNTER – Hunter, Walter M.
The Hunters of Medford County, Virginia; notes and documents on the family of James Hunter, regulator leader of N. C. including forebears in Pennsylvania, Virginia, North Carolina, Louisiana and Texas. By Walter M. Hunter. Cottonport, La. Polyanthos. 1973. (FW)

HUNTINGTON – Hills, Jedeiah Huntington
Huntington-Hills-Roddis-Kreger-Culhane-Inskeep and allied families. San Antonio, Tex. Hills: Hills. 1969. (DAR)

HURD – Heard, Harold, 1903-
Heard families in Mississippi, 1820, 1830, 1840, 1850, 1860, 1870: U. S. Census records of Mississippi. Compiled by Harold Heard. Amarillo, Tex. H. Heard. [19--]. (LC)

HURDLE – Zollar, Hattie P. Hurdle
The A. J. Hurdle family heritage. Compiled by Hattie P. Hurdle Zollar. Austin, Tex. Zollar. 1975. (LC)

HURT – Hurt, Ronald Wayne, 1944-
Tidewater to Texas: the Hurt family, a history. By Ronald Wayne Hurt. Dallas. Minuteman. 1990. (LC)

HUTCHESON – Greenwood, Martrue Hutcheson
Here it is-Hutcheson genealogy. Fort Worth, Tex. Hutcheson Reunion Association. 1966. (DAR)

HUTCHINS – Bish, LaVerne (H.)
"Olden days." By LaVerne (H.) Bish. Austin, Tex. Aus-Tex Dup., 1973. (FW)

HUTCHINS – Hudgins, Edgar H., 1911-
Hudgins, Virginia to Texas. Edgar H. Hudgins. Houston, Tex. Larksdale. c1983. (LC)

HUTCHINSON – Hutcheson, Edward C.
The freedom tree; a chapter from the saga of Texas. By Edward C. Hutcheson. Waco, Tex. Printed by Texian Press, c1970. (LC)

HUTCHINSON – Hutchinson, Frederick McAlpine
The Hutchinson family of Laurens County, South Carolina, and descendants. By Frederick McAlpine Hutchinson. Houston, Tex. A. Jones Press. 1947. (LC)

I –

INSALL – Pieratt, Shirley Insall
Cade Insall, Texas ranger--and his people. By Shirley Insall Pieratt. San Antonio, Tex. S. I. Pieratt. c1984. (LC)

IRWIN – Dettty (i.e.. Detty), Marie Erwin
Our courageous ancestors: facts and fables, 1600-1974. By Marie Erwin Dettty (i.e. Detty). Austin, Tex. San Felipe Press. 1975.

IRWIN – Irwin, C. Thomas (Clyde Thomas), 1931-
Gorgon head and golden tongue. By C. Thomas Irwin. Houston, Tex. C. T. Irwin. 1989? (LC)

IRWIN – McBlair, Robert
The Irwin family. Dallas, Tex. McBlair:McBlair. 1977? (DAR)

ISAACKS – Isaacks, S. J.
The Isaacks clan in America and Texas. El Paso, Tex. Isaacks. 1935. (DAR)

J –

JACKSON –Poole, Mamie Jackson, 1909-
Change of address. By Mamie Jackson Poole. Groom, Tex. M. J. Poole. c1983. (LC)

JACKSON – Short, Aimee Jackson
Jackson – Taylor and related families. Dallas, Tex. Royal Pub. Co. 1960. (DAR)

JACKSON – Short, Aimee (Jackson)
Jackson-Taylor and related families. By Aimee (Jackson) Short. Dallas. Royal Pub. Co. c1960. (LC)

JACKSON – Smith, Renee Jackson, 1925-
William Jackson (-1710), Surry County, Virginia: a twelve generation line of descent. By Renee Jackson Smith. Dallas, Tex? R. J. Smith. 1983? (LC)

JAMES – Eckhardt, Ura L.
James family, no. 1-13, 1965-1970. By Ura L. Eckhardt. Houston, Tex. 1970. (FW)

JAMESON – Jameson, Robert O.
Some descendants of David and Mary (Gates) Jameson of central Georgia. By Robert O. Jameson. Dallas, Tex. 1961. (FW)

JARBOE – Jarboe, Bob, 1923-
A history of a Jarboe family: related lines, Tattershall, Greenwell, Thomas, Coale, Beall, Smith, Edmonston, Cleland, Collins, Davis, McClue, Kenton. By Bob and Mary Jarboe. Richardson, Tex. Jarboe. 1974. (LC)

JARRY -- Jarry, Paul R. S.
W. A. F. Jarry and his descendants of Shelby County, Texas. By Paul R. S. Jarry. Dallas. Jarry. 1974. (FW)

JEFFRIES –
  Joseph Arthur Jeffries Fauquier County, Virginia, 1840-1919. Compiled and edited by Helen Jeffries Klitch. San Antonio, Tex. P. Bate Associates. c1989. (LC)

JENKINS – Carruth, Margaret Ann Scruggs, 1892-
  Jenkins and Speight. By Margaret Ann Scruggs (Mrs. Carruth). Dallas, Tex. 1969. (LC)

JENKINS – Jenkins, Jack S.
  Greenberry Jenkins of Cherokee County, Texas. San Antonio, Tex. Jenkins. 1968. (DAR)

JENKINS – Jenkins, Jack S.
  Greenberry Jenkins of Cherokee County, Texas; his ancestors and descendants. With biographical sketches of families: Bailey, Evans, Harris, Hornbuckle, and Medford. Compiled by Jack S. Jenkins. Assisted by A. C. Jenkins (and others). San Atonio, Tex., 1968. (LC)

JENKINS – Jenkins, Jacks S., 1914-
  Greenberry Jenkins of Cherokee County, Texas: his ancestors and descendants: with biographical sketches of families, Bailey, Evans, Harris, Hornbuckle, and Medford. Compiled by Jack S. Jenkins; assisted by A. C. Jenkins… [et al.]. Rev. Ed. San Antonio, Tex. J. S. Jenkins. 1983. (LC)

JENNINGS – Jennings, H. M. (H. Marvin)
  Jennings in Texas: census index, 1850 & Soundex 1880-1900. Data compiled by H. M. Jennings. Waco, Tex. Jennings. 1982. (LC)

JENNINGS – Pope, Jennings Bland, 1914-
  Some Jennings ancestors, their descendants, and allied families. By Jennings Bland Pope. Austin, Tex. Pope, c1977. (LC)

JENNINGS –
  Jennings, the descendants and ancestors of Robert B. Jennings, Senior and his wife, Tabitha (Lockhart) Jennings. Compiled by Sarah Hattie Hazel Delgado… [et al.]. 1st Ed. Wolfe City, Tex. Henington Pub. Co., Arlington, Tex. T. E. Jennings. 1988. (LC)

JETER – Debenport, Jane Clancy, 1935-
  The descendants of Joseph Ratcliff of Bienville Parish, Louisiana: including the families of Jeter, Wimberly, Davis, Dubberly, Wood, Hardy, Carmichael, Mathews, Norris, McKinney. Compiled by Jane Clancy Debenport. Midland, Tex. J. C. Debenport. c1988. (LC)

JETER – Estes, Carolyn Hunt, 1933-
  Hull's heritage: a genealogical history. By Carolyn Hunt Estes. Fort Worth, Tex. C. H. Estes. 1986. (LC)

JOHNS – Irwin, C. Thomas (Clyde Thomas), 1931-
  Gorgon head and golden tongue. By C. Thomas Irwin. Houston, Tex. C. T. Irwin. 1989? (LC)

JOHNSON – Bearss, Edwin C.
Lyndon B. Johnson National Historic Site, Blanco & Gillespie Counties, Texas; historical data. By Edwin C. Bearss. [Denver] Denver Service Center, U. S. National Park Service. 1971. (LC)

JOHNSON – Baker, Koma Jo Johnson
Footprints to Wildcat Ferry (and beyond). Amarillo, Tex. (s.n.). 1981. (DAR)

JOHNSON – Clarkson, A. E.
Family record of Elisha Johnson (also spelled Johnston) who married Lydia Griffin about 1803 or 1804; they lived in East Haddon, Conn. By A. E. Clarkson. Houston, Tex. 1938. (FW)

JOHNSON – Harrison, Sallie Stewart
The Jared Johnson family. By Sallie Harrison and Ethel Cole. Houston, Tex. S. Harrison. Brady, Tex. E. Cole. 1986? (LC)

JOHNSON – McCurdy, John C.
A letter to Clyde from John C. McCurdy. Slaton, Tex? J. C. McCurdy. 1987? (LC)

JOHNSON – Whitley, Edythe Rucker
Kith and kin of our President: Lyndon Baines Johnson. By Edythe Rucker Whitley. (Nashville). 1967. (LC)

JOHNSON – Willis, Adelaide Rutherford
Johnson – Seawright – Miller and allied lines. Abilene, Tex. Jones. 1980. (DAR)

JOHNSTON – Johnston, Elbert Felton
Johnston of Caroline County, Virginia. Wolfe City, Tex. Henington Pub. Co. 1964. (DAR)

JOHNSTON – Johnston, Floyd Allen
Lt. Benjamin Johnston. Dime Box, Tex. Johnston. 1969. (DAR)

JOLLY – Baker, Nellie Fern, 1933-
Nelson Jolly, Sr., and his family of Breckinridge County, Kentucky. By Nellie Fern Baker. Baltimore: Gateway Press. Brandon, Tex. 1983. (LC)

JONES – Doshier, I. C.
Jones and allied families. By I. C. Doshier. Amarillo, Tex., 1961? (FW)

JONES – Reeder, Hazel Jones, 1917-
The family: Jones, Mason, and Maltby. By Hazel Jones Reeder. Amarillo, Tex. H. Reeder. c1983. (LC)

JONES – Smith, Cecil B.
Portions of Jones-Smith family genealogy. By Cecil B. Smith. Austin, Tex. 1970. (FW)

JOPLIN – Eason, Dorothy Jopling
The Jopling-Joplin family with some of their connections in England and America. Compiled by Dorothy (Jopling) Eason, Sarah (Moseley) Fricks, Lucille (Jopling) Adams. Texarkana, Tex., 1979? (LC)

JORDAN – Eckhardt, Ura L.
Jordan family assorted notes, no. 1-6, 1960-1969. By Ura L. Eckhardt. Houston, Tex. 1969. (FW)

JORDAN – Jordan, Gilbert John, 1902-
Yesterday in the Texas hill country. By Gilbert J. Jordan; foreword by Terry G. Jordan. 1st Ed. College Station: Texas A&M University Press. c1979. (LC)

JORDAN –
Ernst and Lisette Jordan: German pioneers in Texas. By Gilbert J. Jordan and Terry G. Jordan. Austin, Tex. Printed by Von Boeckmann-Jones Co., 1971. (LC)

JORDAN – Russey, John Wesley
The family history of Charles Wesley Jordan of Georgia. San Antonio, Tex. Russey. 1971. (DAR)

JORDAN – Russey, John W., Jr.
The family history of Charles Wesley Jordan of Georgia. Compiled by John W. Russey, Jr. San Antonio, Tex. 1971. (LC)

JURRY –
W. A. F. Jarry and his descendants of Shelby County, Texas. By Paul R. S. Jarry, Juanita Jarry Bowlin, and Ernest C. Hatton. Dallas, Tex. Jarry. 1974. (LC)

K -

KAISER – Keyser, Willet, 1906-
The Keyser family: Henry's children. Keyser, Willet. 2nd Ed. Houston, Tex. Keyser. 1988. (LC)

KAMPMANN – Johnson, Francis W.
History of Texas and Texans… By Francis W. Johnson. Chicago & New York. The American Historical Society. 1914. (LC)

KAPINOS – Guthrie, Martha Dee Schwartz, 1913-
Our kin – past and present: the Kapinos family. Research, compiled, and published by Martha Dee Schwartz Guthrie. Limited Ed. Dallas, Tex. M.D.S. Guthrie. 1983. (LC)

KAY –Shook, Marion Horton
Carolina round up. Dallas, Tex. Shook. 1965. (DAR)

KEAHEY – Reeves, Emma Barrett
Keahey clansmen and their kin, Slay, Summerall, Smith. By Emma Barrett Reeves. Waco, Tex. Texian Press. 1969. (LC)

KEAHEY – Reeves, Emma Barrett
Keagey Clansmen and their kin, Slay, Summerall, Smith. Waco, Tex. 1969. (NGS)

KEATING – Keating, Cecil A.
Keating and Forbes families and reminiscences of C. A. Keating, A.D. 1758-1920. Dallas, Tex. Keating. 1920. (DAR)

KEATING --
Keating and Forbes families and reminiscences of C. A. Keating, A.D. 1758-1920. Dallas, Tex. Wilkinson Print. Co. 1920. (LC)

KEENER – Lacy, Lawson Keener (Mrs. Rogers Lacy)
The descendants of William and Rachel Keener. Compiled by Lawson Keener Lacy (Mrs. Rogers Lacy). Longview, Tex. 1964. (LC)

KEESEE – Eckhardt, Ura L.
Keesee family, no. 1-4, 1965-1970. By Ura L. Eckhardt. Houston, Tex. 1970. (FW)

KELBLEY – Koop, Myra C. Studer
Ancestors and descendants of Johannes Kolble: a history of the Elchert's, Kelble's, and Kelbley's. Compiled by Myra C. Studer Koop. Plano, Tex. M.C.S. Koop. 1988? (LC)

KELLER –Kellough, Gene Ross
The ancestry of John Stevens Kellough: with associated lines of Stevens, Conant, Dodge, Carroll, and others... including numerous "old letters" loaned by Wilma Emery Putnam of Hartland, Vermont. By Gene Ross Kellough. Trinidad, Tex. G. R. Kellough, 1981. (LC)

KELLEY –
The family history of Virginia L. Kelly. Longview? Tex. 19--. (LC)

KELLEY – Kelly, Lloyd E.
The Charles Kelly family (1769-1963). By Lloyd E. Kelly. (n.p., 1963). (LC)

KELLEY – McCullough, William Wallace
Doctor William Dennis Kelley (1825-1888), Texas physician and surgeon. Galveston, Tex. McCullough. 1961. (DAR)

KELLEY – Smithers, Debra Winfield, 1952-
Tanglewood chronicles: a pedigree of branches of the Smithers, Kelley, Winfield, Johnson, and allied families. Compiled by Debra Winfield Smithers. Baltimore: Gateway Press. Corpus Christi, Tex. 1983. (LC)

KELLEY – Stearns, Monyene
The Kelley clan: descendants of John Kelley. By Monyene Stearns. Waco, Tex. Print Mart. c1983. (LC)

KELSEY – Kelsey, Mavis Parrott
Samuel Kelso/Kelsey, 1720-1796: Scotch-Irish immigrant and Revolutionary patriot of Chester County, S.C. Also Mills, Gill, Pagan, Wylie, Morrow, Jones, Sealy, Jaggers, Reeves, Mauldin, Moore, Stevenson, McAlexander fam. Houston, Tex. c1984. (NGS)

KELSO – Andrews, Karolyn Kelso
Kelso and Harding. Houston, Tex. Andrews. 1974. (DAR)

KELSO – Kelsey, Mavis Parrott
Samuel Kelso/Kelsey, 1720-1796: Scotch-Irish immigrant and revolutionary patriot of Chester County, South Carolina: his origin, descendants, and related families including newly published information on the Mills, Gill, Pagan, Wylie, Morrow, Jones, Sealy, Jaggers, Reeves, Moor, Stevenson, McAlexander and other families... Compiled and published by Dr. and Mrs. Mavis Parrott Kelsey, Sr. 1st Ed. Houston, Tex. M. P. Kelsey. c1984. (LC)

KEMPNER – Hyman, Harold Melvin, 1924-
Oleander odyssey: the Kempners of Galveston, Texas, 1854-1980s. By Harold M. Hyman. 1st Ed. College Station: Texas A&M University Press. c1990. (LC)

KENDALL – Kendall, John S.
Notes on the Kendall family of Virginia, West Virginia, Kentucky, and Texas. With references to allied families. By John S. Kendall. New York, 1939. (NY)

KENISELL – Waller, Beulah Kenisell
Genealogical notes and lineages: a compilation of some of the lineages and family lines in the genealogy of George W. Kenisell, with genealogical notes. Researched, compiled, edited, published by Beulah Kenisell Waller. Dallas, Tex. B. K. Waller. 1974. (LC)

KENT – Eckhardt, Ura L.
Kent family, no. 1-5, 1959-1968. By Ura L. Eckhardt. Houston, Tex. 1968. (FW)

KERLEY – Carley, William H.
Information on the Kerley, Cearley, and Carley families of the South. San Angelo, Tex. Carley. 1945. (DAR)

KERN – Kern, P. E.
The Kern genealogy. By P. E. Kern. El Paso? Tex., 1917. (LC)

KERSHNER – Maxwell, Mary Kershner
The Kershner families of Maryland, 1731-1977. By Mary Kershner Maxwell. Houston, Tex. Kershner Family Association. 1978-1981. (LC)

KESSINGER – Ratjen, Phyllis, 1939-
Solomon and Elizabeth Kessinger and their descendants. Compiled by Phyllis Ratjen and Mary Jo Smith. Happy, Tex. P. Ratjen. c1988. (LC)

KEY – Key, Della Tyler
The Keys in Texas and related families. Amarillo, Tex. Lawrence Macager Key: Della Tyler Key. 1965. (DAR)

KEY – Key, Della (Tyler)
The Keys in Texas, and related families; the genealogy and history of the Key family, Groves family, Burrows family, McGehee, Potts, and others. By Della (Tyler) Key. Amarillo, Tex. L. M. Key. 1965. (LC)

KEY – Key, Edward S.
Key, 1776-1972. By Edward S. Key. Houston, Tex. 1972. (FW)

KEY – Key, Edward Seth
Key, 1776-1972. Also by Irene T. Sevier. Houston, Tex. 1972. (NGS)

KEY – Key, Edward Seth
Key, 1776-1972, 2nd Ed. Bedias, Tex. 1908. (NGS)

KEY – Key, Hobart, Jr.
By my strong hand; the motto of Clan MacKay of Southerland, Scotland; an account of some of the lives and adventures of the Key family of Prince George County, Maryland, and Marshall, Texas from the earliest times to the present. Compiled and illustrated from material in the family records. By Hobart Key, Jr. Marshall, Tex. Port Caddo Press. 1965. (LC)

KEY – Key, Marcus M.
The family of John Key, Sr., of Virginia and allied families of Virginia and Georgia. 1950. (DAR)

KIDWELL – Kidwell, Priscilla
Some of the descendants of John Kidwell, 1730-1973. Bedford, Tex. 1973. (NGS)

KILLEN – Taylor, Juanita, L. K.
Killen kith and kin: a genealogical record of Daniel and Saluda Killen who came to Texas in the early 1850s. By Juanita L. K. Taylor. Port Neches, Tex., 1972. (FW)

KINCAID – Kincaid, Eugene Davis, 1941-
A genealogical history of the name of Kincaid with certain descents. By Eugene Davis Kincaid III. Uvalde, Tex. E. D. Kincaid III. c1987. (LC)

KING –
Papers of William King, 1849-1866, Barry County, Missouri to Johnson County, Texas. Compiled by Merry Herdman Allen. Bedford, Tex. Allen. c1979. (LC)

KING – King, Oscar Benjamin
Our King family. Fort Worth, Tex. King. c1970. (DAR)

KING – King, Oscar Benjamin
Our King family; their ancestors, in-laws, and descendants. By Oscar Benjamin King. Fort Worth, Tex. Manney Co. 1970. (LC)

KING – King, Russell B.
Pioneer, Thomas King, Springville, Alabama, 1813-1956. By Russell B. King. Houston, Tex. Premier Print., 1957. (FW)

KINGSLEY – Indexes
A Description of the Hazel Evalyn Kingsley Rucidlo papers now on microfilm. Fort Worth, Tex. Fort Worth Genealogical Society. 1981. (LC)

KINSEY – Kinsey, Margaret Riser
The U.S. according to us. By Margaret Riser Kinsey. Lamesa, Tex. 1970. (LC)

KIRK – Marshall, Maudie Marie Holt
Southern Kirk and Carrell families. Houston, Tex. Marshall. c1971. (DAR)

KIRK – Marshall, Mrs. Arch Bruce
Southern Kirk and Carrell families. Compiled by Mrs. Arch Bruce Marshall (Mat- - Marie Holt). Houston, Tex., 1971. (LC)

KIRKPATRICK – Kirkpatrick, D. M.
American Kirkpatrick family. Houston, Tex. Kirkpatrick. 1972. (DAR)

KIRKPATRICK – Kirkpatrick, Jane, 1946-
Homestead. By Jane Kirkpatrick. Dallas. Word Pub. c1991. (LC)

KITTRELL – Kittrell, Pleasant Williams, 1805-1867-
The Kittrell journal, 1853-1867. By Pleasant Williams Kittrell; introduction by John Payne. Bryan, Tex. Family History Foundation. 1980. (LC)

KITTRELL – Kittrell, Pleasant Williams
The Kittrell Journal, 1853-1867. Bryan, Tex. 1980. (NGS)

KLEBERG – Eckhardt, Ura L.
Kleberg and Von Roeder families, no. 1-2, 1965-1969. By Ura L. Eckhardt. Houston, Tex. 1969. (FW)

KLEPPER –Mehrkam, Lucille Clepper, 1923-
History and genealogy of the family of Jacob Klepper/Clepper family and Malcolm McAlpine family: including allied branches of the Gilliam, Birdwell, Duncan, Woods, Estill, Forehand, Stifflemire, Cloyd, and Doddridge families. By Lucille (Clepper) Mehrkam; edited by Ernestine (Lloyd) Jackson, Jacqueline Jackson and Alixe (McAlpine) Taylor. Houston, Tex. L. C. Mehrkam. 1986. (LC)

KLINGMAN – Klingman, H. M. L.
Grandma's legacy: the family history of Christine Helen Klingman... By H. M. L. Klingman. Dallas, Tex. 1970. (FW)

KNIGHT –
Knight letter. Fort Worth, Tex. 1968. (FW)

KNIGHT – Ganier, Merle, 1914-
Some descendants of Jacob Knight of Pennsylvania and Louisiana. By Merle Ganier; cover by Delores Hurd. Fort Worth, Tex. Ganier. c1979. (LC)

KNIGHT – Knight, Mary Zelmere, 1886-1970-
Henry Knight and his descendants. By Mary Zelmere Knight and Elizabeth Daniel Law; edited by Merle Ganier. Fort Worth, Tex. M. Ganier. c1987. (LC)

KNOX – Brown, Dorothy Louise Knox
Lineages and genealogical notes. Dallas, Tex. Brown. 1981. (DAR)

KNOX –
Lineages and genealogical notes; a compilation of some of the lineages and family lines in the genealogy of Dorothy Louise Knox (Mrs. Fred Ross Brown), with genealogical notes. (1st Ed. Dallas? 1972). (LC)

KNOX – Knox, William P. (William Paul), 1938-
Knox tracks: following the trail of a Knox family from North Carolina to Texas: including the descendants of William Shields Knox. By William P. Knox. Amarillo, Tex. Knox Books. 1987. (LC)

KNOX – Wood, Christine
Knox memorial. Descendants of William Knox, who died 1778 Berkeley County, Va. ... By Christine Wood. Lubbock, Tex., 1971 or 1972. (FW)

KNOX – Wood, Christine Knox
Knox memorial. Lubbock, Tex. 1972. (NGS)

KOEHLER – Boehl, Beverly
Koehler, Dreier, Sager, Rath, Thieme, and Boehl families: a genealogical delineation of German immigrants in DeWitt County, Texas. By Beverly Boehl; edited by Judith Koehler Ludvigsen. Garland, Tex. B. Boehl. c1986. (LC)

KOEN – Koen, Ottis Vaughn
The glory trail: Keon and kin, coast to coast, including references to hundreds of allied families. By Ottis Vaughn Koen. 1st Ed. Austin, Tex. Koen. 1974. (LC)

KOTHMANN –
The Kothmanns of Texas, 1845-1931. By Selma Metzenthin Raunick and Margaret Schade; original compiler Mrs. E. Marschall. Austin, Tex. Press of Von Boeckmann-Jones Company. 1931. (LC)

KRUEGER – Krueger, Ben J.
Andrew and Auguste. By Ben J. Krueger. Austin, Tex. Press of Von Boeckmann-Jones Co., 1970. (LC)

KUCKER – Darden, Nora K.
Kickers of Washington County, Texas. By Nora K. Darden. (n.p., 1973). (FW)

KUYKENDALL – Delaney, Anne Kuykendall
A history of the Kuykendall family in Texas. 1942. (DAR)

KUYKENDALL – Delaney, Anne K.
History of the Kuykendall family in Texas. By Anne K. Delaney. Commerce, Tex. 1942. (FW)

KYKENDALL – Brannen, J. L. W.
Family record on Kuykendall, Osborne, Richmond, Collier, Warren, Brannen and allied families. By J. L. W. Brannen. Amarillo, Tex. 1950. (FW)

KYLE – Kellough, Gene Ross
The ancestry of Gene Ross: including the Ross line and associated lines of Bennett, Grimes, Llewellyn, Knighton, Turnbull and Kyle. By Gene Ross Kellough; including wills, letters, and contents of Kyle estate sale, plus "Samplings" the account of growing up in Texas 1909 through 1937. Seneca, S.C. By G. R. Kellough. 1986. (LC)

L –

LACY – Chace, Harriet E. N.
The Walter Garner Lacy Branch of the Lacy family of Colonial Virginia. Waco, Tex. Walter Garner Lacy. 1925. (DAR)

LAIL – Lale, Max Sims
From whence we came: the Sims and Lale families in Oklahoma. By Max Sims Lale. 1st Ed. Marshall, Tex. Port Caddo Press. c1984. (LC)

LAIN – Lain, Nadine
Lain, Lourance, Lorance and related families. By Nadine Lain. Dallas, Tex. 1961? (FW)

LAKE – Koutnik, D. K.
Church, Lake, Lee, Love. By D. K. Koutnik. Dallas, 1968? (DP)

LAMMERT –
F. W. Lammert family: a family history, 1884-1984. Katy, Tex. T&E Publishers. c1985. (LC)

LANCASTER – Rogers, Mary Nixon
Lancaster. Rosenberg, Tex. Rogers. 1975. (DAR)

LANCASTER – Rogers, Mary N.
Lancaster, from Virginia to Texas. By Mary N. Rogers. Rosenberg. Tex., 1975. (FW)

LANDERS – Davis, Sherry Ann Schauer, 1939-
My Landers family from ship to shore. By Sherry Schauer Davis. Houston, Tex. Davis. 1978. (LC)

LANDRETH – Miller, Naomi Drake
Zachariah and Nellie Fender Landreth and their descendants. Corpus Christi, Tex. Miller. 1966. (DAR)

LANDRETH – Miller, Naomi D.
Zachariah and Nellie Fender Landreth and their descendants. By Naomi D. Miller. Corpus Christi, Tex. 1955. (FW)

LANDRUM – Price, Etna Reed, 1887-1960-
In search of tomorrow. By Etna Reed Price; compiled and arranged by Novalyne Price Ellis. Brownwood? Tex. N. P. Ellis. c1983. (LC)

LANDRY – Evans, Norma Pontiff, 1937-
Grandpa with a stick, Joseph Theolin Landry: his ancestors and descendants. By Norma Pontiff Evans. Special Ed. First family reunion. Beaumont, Tex. Evans. 1980. (LC)

LANE – Hall, Frank Nelson
A Lane genealogy. Compiled by Frank Nelson Hall. Denton, Tex. 1965. (LC)

LANE – Heiskell, Roy H. (Roy Heildreath), 1915-
Lane, early family history and genealogy. By Roy H. Heiskell. Weslaco, Tex. R. H. Heiskell. 1980. (LC)

LANE – Lain, Nadine, 1903-
Lain, Lowrance, Lorance, and related families. Compiled and edited by Nadine Lain. Dallas, Tex. Lain. 1978? (LC)

LANE – Sisk, Luther L. (Luther Lafayette), 1902-
The Texas Laynes. Luther L. Sisk. Escondido, Calif. L. L. Sisk. 1982. (LC)

LANGFORD – Wade, Ronald E.
The Langford legacy: the generation of James and Martha Langford, 1653-1986. By Ronald E. Wade. 1st Ed. Longview, Tex. R. E. Wade. c1986. (LC)

LANHAM –
Genealogical records and manuscripts of the Lanham family. Dallas, Tex. D.A.R., 1963. (FW)

LANTZER – Bailey, Janet Moore, 1940-
Ancestors and descendants of Samuel Lantzer. By Janet Moore Bailey. Irving, Tex. J. M. Bailey. c1986. (LC)

LARNER – Larner, Ray A., 1895-1978-
The Larner book: Wm. Larner, 1812-1850 & his descendants. By Ray A. Larner, Sr. & Marilyn Larner Hicks. Dallas, Tex. M. L. Hicks. c1987. (LC)

LARSEN – Larson, Jerry Laverne, 1931-
The sons of Lars: a genealogy of the Larson and Smith families of southwest Missouri. By Jerry Laverne Larson. Universal City, Tex. J. L. Larson. c1987. (LC)

LARUE – Mather, Otis M.
Six generations of Larues and allied families. Dallas, Tex. 1921. (NGS)

LATHAM – Bailey, W. H.
Genealogy of the Latham, Hill,, Montfort, Littlejohn, McCulloch, Campbell and Brownrigg families. By W. H. Bailey. Houston, Tex., 1899. (FW)

LATHAM – Cropsey, Harold U.
Genealogical history of the William Harris Latham family of Thetford, Vermont... 1620-1976. By Harold U. Cropsey. San Antonio, Tex., 1976. (MH)

LATTING – Latting, Richard Baggett, 1901-
The Richard Gano Latting, Sr., family. By Richard Baggett Latting, Jr.; including "The Latting Family" by John Jordan Latting. Austin, Tex. R. B. Latting. 1980. (LC)

LAWHON – Harrison, Sallie Stewart
David E. Lawhon and his descendants, 1811-1971. By Sallie Stewart Harrison. Houston, 1972. (LC)

LAWSON – Eckhardt, Urah L.
Lawson family, no. 1-4, 1963-69. By Urah L. Eckhardt. Houston, Tex. 1969. (FW)

LAWSON – Runyon, Robert
Genealogy of the descendants of Anthony Lawson of Northumberland, England. By Robert Runyon. Brownsville, Tex., 1952. (LC)

LAYTON – Murrie, P. S.
Layton-Harris descendants. By P. S. Murrie. Houston, Tex., 1975. (FW)

LEAGUE – Willie, Betty
The League family of Virginia and South Carolina. Amarillo, Tex. Willie. 1976. (DAR)

LEBARON – LeBaron, Verian M.
The LeBaron story. By Verian M. LeBaron. Lubbock, Tex. Keels & Co. c1981. (LC)

LEDBETTER – Ledbetter, Roy C.
Ledbeters from Virginia. Dallas, Tex. Wilkinson Printing Co. 1964. (DAR)

LEDBETTER – Ledbetter, Roy Clifford
Ledbetters from Virginia. ?Dallas, Tex. 1964. (NGS)

LEDFORD – Ledford, Mary Ellen
The Ledford-Basham-Bryant book. By Mary Ellen Ledford. Irving, Tex. M. E. Ledford, 1989. (LC)

LEE – Eckhardt, Ura L.
Lee family, no. 1-2, 1967-1970. By Ura L. Eckhardt. Houston, Tex. 1970. (FW)

LEE – Flowers, Develand
Descendants of Isaac and Elizabeth Preutt Lee. By Develand Flowers. Fort Worth, Tex. A.B.C. Print. Co. 1967. (LC)

LEE – Ragan, C. K.
Moses Lee (1817-71) and his family. By C. K. Ragan. Houston, Tex., 1964. (FW)

LEE – Rose, Ben Lacy, 1914-
The Lea ancestry of Margaret Lea, wife of Gen. Sam Houston. By Ben L. Rose & Margaret M. Marty. Richmond, Va. B. L. Rose. 1987. (LC)

LEHMAN – Lehmann, Elizabeth A. J., 1907-
Roots and branches of Ludwig Lehmann, 1700s-1983: the times in which they lived. [Texas]. Elizabeth A. J. Lehmann. c1983. (LC)

LEHMKUHL – Manz, Mabel Ann Anderson, 1914-
The Lehmkuhls of Uetersen. Compiled by Mabel Ann (Anderson) Manz. Austin, Tex. M. A. A. Manz. 1981. (LC)

LEIFESTE – DeVos, Ruby E. (Ruby Eckert), 1920-
Look unto the hills: the Leifeste family in the United States. Compiled and edited by Ruby E. and Julius E. DeVos. [Texas?]. R. E. DeVos. 1985. (LC)

LEIPER – Shumaker, Esther Agnes Leiper
Genealogical lineage of Priscilla Jones Macon Leiper; Macon, Fitzhugh, Ashton, Washington families. By Esther Agnes Leiper Shumaker. Houston, Tex. Harper Leiper Studios. 1969. (LC)

LEMMEN – Lemons, Nova A.
Through the orchard. Supplement: Arterberry, Hillsberry, Lemons, Ragsdale. By Nova A. Lemons. Dallas, Tex. N. A. Lemons. c1990. (LC)

LEONARD – McKinney, Leonard Laurence, 1908-
The Leonard family of Davidson County, North Carolina and Benton County, Arkansas. Authors, Leonard Laurence McKinney and Lawrence Carl McKinney. 1st Ed. Wichita Falls, Tex. Texoma Instant Print. c1979. (LC)

LESLIE – Barrett, Ruth Leslie
The Leslie line: ancestors of five Leslie brothers. By Ruth Leslie Barrett. Windom, Tex. R. L. Barrett. 1990. (LC)

LESSENGER – Lessenger, James E. (James Ernest), 1948-
The Lessenger family history. By James E. Lessenger and Waunita Gibbons. Porterville, Tex. W. Gibbons. 1988. (LC)

LEWIS –
The Lewis family of Mt. Holly and the Ark-La-Tex. John Aylmer Lewis... [et al.]. Ruston, La. C. N. Cargill. 1978. (LC)

LEWIS – Frazier, Irvin, 1898-
The family of John Lewis, pioneer. Compiled by Irvin Frazier; text by Mark W. Cowell, Jr.; edited by Lewis F. Fisher. Rev. Ed. San Antonio, Tex. Fisher Publications. c1985. (LC)

LEWIS – Hardison, Lewis M. (Lewis Merrill), 1913-
One branch of the Lewis family, whose line can not be proved before 1755: search for ancestors of Abijah Lewis. Prepared by Lewis M. Hardison. Kerrville, Tex. L. M. Hardison. 1982. (LC)

LEWIS – Hindman, Juanita Lewis
Postpioneers. Fort Worth, Tex. Branch-Smith. 1973. (LC)

LEWIS – Williams, Barbara Lewis, 1941.
400 years with a New England Lewes-Lewis family. Baltimore: Gateway Press. Beaumont, Tex. 1990. (LC)

LEWIS – Wilson, R. B. (Rena Beth), 1940-
My family, Shields, Price, McKenzie, Lewis... By R. B. Wilson. Rockport, Tex. R. B. Wilson. c1990. (LC)

LIDE – McCurdy, Anne Ayers Lide, 1911-
Pleasant places: a goodly heritage. By Anne Ayers Lide McCurdy. Austin, Tex. Eakin Publications. c1982. (LC)

LIGHTFOOT – Lightfoot, Sallie L.
Lightfoot family. By Sallie L. Lightfoot. Paris, Tex. S. L. Lightfoot. 1952? (NY)

LIGHTFOOT – Eckhardt, Urah L.
Lightfoot family, no. 1. 1961-1970. By Urah L. Eckhardt. Houston, Tex. 1970. (FW)

LIGON – Miller, Margaret Hardwick
Ligons and their kin of Graves County, Ky. Corsicana, Tex. Miller. 197-? (DAR)

LINDEMAN – Boswell, Imogene May, 1927-
The ancestors and descendants of Henry D. Lendermon: Randolph County, North Carolina, Greenville County, South Carolina, Maury County, Tennessee, Carroll County, Tennessee, Marshall County, Mississippi. Compiled by Imogene May Boswell and Jean Boswell Pippenger. Wolfe City, Tex. Henington Pub. Co.; Carrollton, Tex. 1988. (LC)

LINDSEY – Dutton, Anecia Floradell
Lindseys and descendants. Odessa, Tex. Dutton; Marshall, Texas: McMillan. 1972. (DAR)

LINDSEY – Ritchey, Jenevieve Lindsey
Lindsey family. Bonham, Tex. Ritchey. 1978. (DAR)

LINDSEY – Rowley, Retha Vaughn (Hamberlin)
Lindsey; book of rememberance; golden memoirs. By Retha Vaughn (Hamberlin) Rowley. Winona? Tex., 1963. (LC)

LINK – Eckhardt, Ura L.
Link family, no. 1-8, 1954-1970. By Ura L. Eckhardt. Houston, Tex. 1970. (FW)

LINTON – Williams-Walker, Naylan Gaile Linton
Allied families of Chalk, Massie, Oates, Linton, 1066-1987. Compiled and edited by Naylan Gaile Linton Williams-Walker. Victoria, Tex. G. Walker, 1988? (LC)

LIPPERT – Lippard, Delmas V. (Delmas Valgene), 1928-
The Lippard family in North America. By Delmas V. Lippard. Austin, Tex. Morgan Print and Pub. 1989. (LC)

LIPTRAP – Liptrap, James M., 1951-
The Liptrap family in America, 1785-1985: the descendants of Isaac Liptrap, 1752-1819. Compiled by James M. Liptrap. Houston, Tex. J. M. Liptrap. 1985. (LC)

LITTLE – Shumaker, M. M. B.
Little genealogy. By M. M. B. Shumaker. Dallas, Tex. (n.d.). (FW)

LITTON – Hayes, Florence, 1932-
My family remembered. By Florence Hayes. 1st Ed. Houston, Tex. F. M. S. Hayes. 1987. (LC)

LLEWELLYN – Vicars, Vallleska Buchholz
Adams family: Lorenzo Dow Adams, Joshua Adams and their descendants: collateral lines of Llewellen, Bills, Mohundro, Hardin, Ballenger, and Gaither. By Valeska Buchholz Vicars. Seabrook, Tex. V. B. Vicars. 1980? (LC)

LLOYD – Baker, Mondeleen M.
Lloyd and related families. Childress, Tex? M. M. Baker. 1987. (LC)

LLOYD – Eckhardt, Ura L.
Lloyd family, nos. 1-4, 1961-70. By Ura L. Eckhardt. Houston, Tex. 1970. (FW)

LOCKE – Tiller, Linda Locke
Our Locke family: descendants of Wm. C. Locke and his wife, Jane Wilson Elliott. By Linda Locke Tiller. Garland, Tex. Tiller, 1975. (LC)

LOCKETT – Scarborough, Jewel Davis
The Locketts. Abilene, Tex. Scarborough. c1951. (DAR)

LOCKETT – Scarborough, Jewel (D.)
Southern kith and kin; a record of my children's ancestors. By Jewel (D.) Scarborough. Abilene, Tex. Printed by Abilene Print Co. 1951-58. (NY)

LOCKHART –
Jennings, the descendants and ancestors of Robert B. Jennings, Senior and his wife, Tabitha (Lockhart) Jennings. Compiled by Sarah Hattie Hazel Delgado... [et al.]..
1st Ed. Wolfe City, Tex. Henington Pub. Co. Arlington, Tex. 1988. (LC)

LOELOFF – Brandenberger,, E. D.
Loloff, Loloff, Loeloff family. By E. D. Brandenberger. Houston, Tex. 1976. (FW)

LOFLAND – Crow, Jewell Lofland
History of the family of Lofland in America and related families. Dallas, Tex. Crow. 1956. (DAR)

LONDON – Cox, Opal London
200 years of London family in America. Enid, Okla. Cox. 1976. (DAR)

LONG –
Our Long line. Llano, Tex. 1971. (FW)

LONG – Horn, Mrs. Maud
Family history: Atchley, Griffith, Long, Maples, Scoggin, etc. ... Compiled, printed, published by Mrs. Maud Horn. Houston, Tex. 1937. (LC)

LOOMIS – Loomis, Louise, 1912-
Judge Loomis of Marion County, Texas: the family history of Richard Asbury Loomis beginning in 1789. Compiled by Louise Loomis. Beaumont, Tex. L. Loomis. 1983. (LC)

LOPEMAN – DuBois, Delanne Lopeman, 1931-
The Lopeman family: in search of a legend. By Delanne Lopeman DeBois. Houston, Tex. D. L. DuBois, c1983. (LC)

LOVE – Murchison, Beatrice, 1895-
Trees of lineage. By Beatrice Murchison. Waco, Tex. B. Murchison, 1998-? (LC)

LOVING – Cullar, Willie Clytes Anderson
The Loving family in Texas. Dallas, Tex. Cullar. 1953. (DAR)

LOVING – Cullar, Willie C. A.
Loving family in Texas, 1843-1953. By Willie C. A. Cullar. Dallas, Tex., 1953. (FW)

LOWDERMILK – Ball, Evelyn Vancil Lowdermilk
A new colonial family history; lines of Lowdermilk, Brown, Hudson and Moore, Vancil, Donner, together with some relatives. Okmulgee, Okla. 1977. (NGS)

LOWDERMILK – Quenon, Raymond H.
The descendants of George Washington Loudermilk. By Raymond H. and Aline "Loudermilk" Quenon. Fort Worth, Tex. R. H. and A. L. Quenon, c1981. (LC)

LOWRY – Hurst, John Simeon, 1909-1981-
"**A family history.**" Researched & compiled by John Simeon Hurst, Jr. Lancaster, Tex. M. Hurst. 1985. (LC)

LUCKETT – Luckett, Helen Hart
The Lucketts of Georgia. Fort Worth, Tex. Luckett. c1976. (DAR)

LUCKETT – Luckett, Helen H.
The Lucketts of Georgia: a genealogical history of Thomas Hussey Luckett and William Rhody Luckett of Wilkes, Warren, Tatiaferro County, Georgia ... By Helen H. Luckett. Fort Worth, Tex. 1976. (NY)

LUCKETT – Luckett, Helen Hart
The Lucketts of Georgia: a genealogical history of Thomas Hussey Luckett and William Rhody Luckett of Wilkes, Warren, Taliaferro Counties, Georgia. Fort Worth, Tex. c1976. (NGS)

LUKER – Luker, Vera Goodman
The Luker families: a history & genealogy. By Vera Goodman Luker. Dallas, Tex. V. G. Luker. c1983. (LC)

LUNGER – Lunger, Harold L.
Descendants of Jacob Lunger of Derrs (1811-1896) with a discussion of his ancestry: a preliminary report. Authored and compiled by Harold Lehman Lunger. Granbury, Tex. H. L. Lunger. 1981. (LC)

LUTER – West, Belle Lewter
Luter-Lewter family of England, Virginia, North Carolina, and states south and west. Durham, N.C. West. 1974. (DAR)

LYLE –
Life of Judge M. Llyle, an autobiography. Fort Worth, Tex. H. L. Geddie Co. 1964. (FW)

LYON – Mitchell, M. E. B.
One branch of the Lyon family. By M. E. B. Mitchell. Waco, Tex., 1955. (FW)

M –

MABERRY – Willingham, Lois Glenn Maberry
The Maberry Clan. By Lois Glenn Maberry Willingham. Dallas, Tex. 1969? (LC)

MACBEAN – Bean, Bernie
The Clan MacBean in North America. By Bernie Bean. Cut and Shoot, Tex. Clan MacBean. 1976. (FW)

MACDONALD – McDonald, Clarinda Pauline
Our pioneer heritage. By Clarinda Pauline McDonald. Dallas? Tex. c1961. (LC)

MACKENZIE – Wilson, R. B. (Rena Beth), 1940-
My family, Shields, Price, McKenzie, Lewis... By R. B. Wilson. Rockport, Tex? R. B. Wilson. c1990. (LC)

MACKEY – Hoskinson, Josie V.
Mackeys and Eberlys of Texas. Norman, Okla. Bishop. 1965. (DAR)

MACKEY – Hoskinson, Josie V. H.
Mackeys and Eberlys of Texas, and allied families of McIlwaine, Elgin, Harrison, Adams, Smallwood, Stone, Troope and Perry of Ky., Tenn., Md., and Va. Also by Julia R. Bishop. Norman, Okla. 1965. (NGS)

MACON – Shumaker, Esther Agnes Leiper
Genealogical lineage of Priscilla Jones Macon Leiper. Houston, Tex. William Harper Leiper. 1969. (DAR)

MACON – Shumaker, Esther A. L.
Genealogical lineage of Priscilla Jones Macon Leiper: Macon, Fitzhugh, Ashton, Washington families. By Esther A. L. Shumaker. Houston, Tex., 1969. (FW)

MACQUEEN – MacQueen, Ena
MacQueen, McDonald, Jones, Swift, and other families. Sweetwater, Tex. MacQueen. 1964. (DAR)

MACY –Pearson, Ralph E.
Macy family history. Austin, Tex. R. E. Pearson, 1982? (LC)

MADARA –Free, Margaret Bernice (Madara)
Some of the descendants of William Madara (1787-1868). Alvin, Tex. 1976. (NGS)

MADISON – Gadbury, Ruth
A branch of the Madison tree, with supplements: Ware, Sample, Barley (and) Rusler. By Ruth Gadbury. Sketches by Mary Hood. Austin, Tex. Printed by Shelby Print., 1974. (LC)

MAGEE – Moore, Clarence Elbert
Genealogy of Patrick Magee and his wife Rosanna (McCullar) Magee. By Clarence Elbert Moore. Fort Worth, Tex. 1967. (LC)

MAGEE – Morrow, Betty Moss
McGee-Cooper-Synnott. Prepared by Betty Moss Chaney-Morrow. Teague, Tex. B. M. Chaney-Morrow. c1990. (LC)

MAHLANDT – Steger, Mel
A Steger-Schlittler-Mahlandt history. Book prepared by Mel Steger. Houston, Tex. 1986. (LC)

MAI – Ford, Ethel T.
The Mai-Maze dictionary (includes families from Adams to Young). By Ethel T. Ford. Amarillo, Tex. (IG)

MALLORY – Griffith, Madge Mallory
Some Mallorys and Bells and related families. Dallas, Tex. Mallory. 1968? (DAR)

MALLORY – Griffith, M. M.
Some Mallorys and Bells and related families. By M. M. Griffith. Dallas, Tex., 1968. (FW)

MALLORY – Mallory, J. R.
Some Mallorys and Bells. Greenville, Tex. Greenville Printing Co. c1950. (DAR)

MALLORY – Mallory, James R.
Some Mallorys and Bells. By James R. Mallory. Greenville, Tex. Greenville Pr., 1950. (FW)

MALLORY – Moyer, Julia M.
John Mallory, Virginia soldier, 1777-1782. Paris, Tex. Will H. Lightfoot. 1939. (DAR)

MALLORY – Vandiver, Eva Mallory, 1919-
Southern genealogies of the Mallory, Vandiver, and related families. Compiled by Eva Mallory Vandiver. Mineola, Tex. E. M. Vandiver. 1987. (LC)

MALONEY – Fowler, Charles A.
Maloney family biographical record; as portrayed through the life of Samuel N. (and) Nancy E. (Cupp) Maloney, 1806-1974. Ed. 3. By Charles A. Fowler. Lubbock, Tex. 1974. (FW)

MANDOLA –
The Mandola family history. Houston, Tex.: J. Coles, A. Tilotta, T. Richie, c1987. (LC)

MANN – Mann, James C.
Mann family. Arlington, Tex. Mann. 1971. (DAR)

MANZ – Montz, M. M.
The Montz family of Louisiana; 1721-present. By M. M. Montz; (with illus. by Buddy Halyard). Houston, Tex. Montz. c1975. (LC)

MARKS – Rhine, Nanneitta Raines, 1894-1979-
The saga of the little red chair. As told by Nanneitta Raines Rhine; co-author, Mary Sue R. Moseley; illustrations, Carolyn Munoz Harney and Nita Moseley Munoz. 2nd Ed. El Paso, Tex? M.S.R. Moseley. 1982. (LC)

MARKS – Sizemore, Deborah Lightfoot
The LH7 Ranch in the city's shadow: from longhorns to the Salt Grass Trail. By Deborah Lightfoot Sizemore. Denton, Tex. University of North Texas Press. 1991. (LC)

MARR –
The Marrs family. By John P. Marrs and others. Amarillo? Tex., 1930? (LC)

MARRIOTT – Eckhardt, Ura L.
Marriott-Farrow-Farrar & Eppes families assorted notes. By Ura L. Eckhardt. Houston, Tex., 1970. (FW)

MARRS – Rogers, Bea
Marrs and allied families. Stephenville, Tex. Rogers. 1966. (DAR)

MARSHALL – Eckhardt, Ura L.
Marshall family. By Ura L. Eckhardt. Houston, Tex. 1969. (FW)

MARSHALL – Eckhardt, Ura L.
Marshall, Horn(e) and Isham families assorted notes. By Ura L. Eckhardt. Houston, Tex. 1970. (FW)

MARTIN –
Martin family quarterly. Vol. 1. – 1975. Dallas, Tex. Farmer Genealogy Co. (FW)

MARTIN – Brinkley, Beatrice Martin
Records of Martin-Crawford-Rodes-Dishman families in Virginia, Kentucky, and Texas. 1972? (DAR)

MARTIN – Fagg, Jenny M.
A family history of Thomas Martin, Sr., a North Carolinian American Revolutionary soldier. By Jenny M. Fagg. Fort Worth, Tex. Arrow Curtis Print. Co., 1976. (FW)

MARTIN – Fagg, Jenny Martin, 1930-
A family history of Thomas Martin, Sr., a North Carolinian American Revolutionary soldier. By Jenny Martin Fagg. 1st Ed. Fort Worth, Tex. Arrow/Curtis Print Co. 1976. (LC)

MARTIN – Farmer, Michal Martin, 1946-
Adam Martin (1755-1835) and Thomas Roy Musick (1757-1842), St Louis County, Missouri, pioneers: their ancestors, descendants, and related families, Hildebrand, Peira, Roy, and Neville. By Michal Martin Farmer. 1st Ed. Wolfe City, Tex. Henington Pub. Co. c1989. (LC)

MARTIN – Gallaway, Irene Dabney
The Martin family. Fayetteville, Ark. Sentinel Print. 1906. (DAR)

MARTINEZ DEL RIO – Walker, David W. (David Wayne), 1948-
Kinship, business, and politics: the Martinez del Rio family in Mexico, 1824-1867. By David W. Walker. 1st Ed. Austin: University of Texas Press. 1986. (LC)

MASEAR – Anderson, Sue Masear, 1946-
The Masear mystery, including Condill, Corey, Legner, Libby. By Sue Masear Anderson. Midland, Tex. S. M. Anderson. c1983. (LC)

MASON – Gable, Bertha L.
Tenn.-Ark.-Mo.: Windsor Mason trail, 1787-1987. Clarksville, Tex. B. L. Gable. c1987. (LC)

MASSENGILL – Cravens, Margaret
Massengales and the Pattersons. By Margaret Cravens. Waco, Tex. Humphrey Print., 1975. (FW)

MASSEY – Blue, William H.
Index of names in Massey family in America (book 2 of Massey genealogy, by Frank A. Massey, 1974). By William H. Blue. Fort Worth, Tex., 1974. (SP)

MASSEY – Kelsey, Mavis Parrott, 1912-
The family of John Massie, 1743-c.1830, Revolutionary patriot of Louisa County, Virginia: including early emigrants to Kentucky and Texas and related families, Bachman, Baker, Ballinger, Burrus, Clopton, Duke, Harris, Jackson, Keener, Mills, Overton, Parrott, Poer, Riddell, and Walton. Compiled by Mavis Parrott Kelsey and Mary Wilson Kelsey. Houston, Tex. Kelsey. c1979. (LC)

MASSEY – Massey, Frank A.
Massey genealogy. Fort Worth, Tex. King and Massey. 1947-1980. (DAR)

MASSEY – Massey, Frank A.
Massey genealogy. Fort Worth, Tex. King and Massey. 1974. (LC)

MASSEY – Massey, Frank A.
Massey genealogy – addendum. By Frank A. Massey. Fort Worth, Tex. King and Massey. 1979. (LC)

MASSEY – Massey, Frank A.
Massey on censuses. By Frank A. Massey. Fort Worth, Tex. King and Massey. 1980. (LC)

MASSEY – Massey, Frank A.
Massey Genealogy. Fort Worth, Tex. 1974. (NGS)

MASSEY – Massey, Frank A.
Massey Genealogy. Addendum, with index for Book II. Fort Worth, Tex. 1979. (NGS)

MASSEY – Massey, Frank A.
Massey on Censuses. Fort Worth, Tex. 1980. (NGS)

MASSIE – Kellsey, Mavis Parrot
The family of John Massie, 1743-c.1830, Revolutionary patriot of Louisa County, Virginia. Houston, Tex. Kelsey. c1979. (DAR)

MASSIE – Kelsey, Mavis Parrot
The family of John Massie, 1743-c-1830, Revolutionary patriot of Louisa County, Virginia. Early emigrants to Ky. and Tx. Backman, Baker, Bollinger, Walton families. Houston, Tex. 1979. (NGS)

MASTERS – Masters, Wesley W.
Masters family, descendants of Samuel Masters. By Wesley W. Masters. Deer Park, Tex. 1967. (FW)

MATHIS – Edwards, Richard Laurence, 1911-
Ancestors and descendants of the Edwards-Mathis, Delozier, and related families that pioneered through Virginia, Carolinas, Tennessee, Kentucky, Illinois, Missouri, Kansas, and spread to descendants in thirty-seven states and two provinces in Canada. Authored, compiled, edited, and published by Richard Laurence Edwards. 1st Ed. Coffeyville, Kans. R. L. Edwards. c1985. (LC)

MATTHEWS – Holden, Frances Mayhugh, 1913-
Lambshead before Interwoven: a Texas range chronicle, 1848-1878. By Frances Mayhugh Holden; drawings by John Guerin. 1st Ed. College Station: Texas A&M University Press, c1982. (LC)

MATTHEWS – Mathews, G. C.
Biography of Burrell Matthews. By G. C. Matthews. Amarillo, Tex., 1966. (FW)

MATTHEWS – Matthews, Sallie Reynolds, 1861-
Interwoven: a pioneer chronicle. By Sallie Reynolds Matthews; drawings by E. M. Schiwetz. 4th Ed. College Station: Texas A&M University Press, c1982. (LC)

MATTHEWS – Wilson, Laura, 1939-
Watt Matthews of Lambshead. Photographs and text by Laura Wilson; introduction by David McCullough. Austin, Tex. Texas State Historical Society. c1989. (LC)

MAUDIE – Marshall, Maudie M. (H.)
Forebears and descendants of an early Houston family. By Maudie M. (H.) Marshall. Houston, Tex. A. B. Marshall, 1975. (FW)

MAULE – Nicholson, Richard L.
Genealogy of the Maule family, with a brief account of Thomas Maule, of Salem, Massachusetts, the ancestor of the family in the United States. By Richard L. Nicholson. San Antonio? Tex. 1925? (LC)

MAVERICK – Green, Rena Maverick
Memoirs of Mary A. Maverick arranged by Mary A. Maverick and her son Geo. Madison Maverick. San Antonio, Tex. Alamo Printing Co. 1921. (DAR)

MAXEY –
Maxey records found in Lamar County, Texas. Paris, Tex., 1956. (FW)

MAY – Boswell, Imogene May, 1927-
The descendants of Claiborne B. May: South Carolina, St. Clair County, Alabama, Talledega County, Alabama, Green County, Alabama: including a compendium of other May families. Compiled by Imogene May Boswell, Reba Kirksey Cooper, Donna May Lonon. Carrollton, Tex. Pippenger and Boswell Researchers. 1990. (LC)

MAY – May, B. David
  The descendants of Caleb and Margaretta (Patrick) May, 1781 to 1985. By Bruce David May and Nadine Carol (Preece) May. Baltimore: Gateway Press. Houston, Tex. 1985. (LC)

MAY –May, B. David
  Our family heritage: some east Kentucky roots. By Bruce David May, and Nadine Carol (Preece) May. Baltimore: Gateway Press. Houston, Tex. 1985. (LC)

MAY – Mays, Ivan K.
  The Mays family; a sequel to "The Mays Family" by Samuel Edward Mays. By Ivan K. Mays. Austin, Tex. 1970. (LC)

MAYFIELD – Mayfield, Fay Hicks
  Memorabilia of Albert and Ann Mayfield and their descendants, 1850-1969. By Fay Hicks Mayfield. Abilene? Tex. 1969. (LC)

MAYS – Mays, Ivan
  The Mays family. Austin, Tex. Mays. 1970. (DAR)

MAYS – Mays, Samuel Edward
  Genealogy of the Mays family and related families to 1929 inclusive. Plant City, Fla. Mays. 1929. (D AR)

MEADOWS – Farmer, Michal M.
  Daniel Meadows and his descendants, 1779-1976. By Michal M. Farmer. Dallas, Tex. Farmer Genealogy Co. 1976. (FW)

MEADOWS – Farmer, Michal Martin, 1946-
  Daniel Meadows and his descendants, 1779-1976. By Michal Martin Farmer. Dallas, Tex. Farmer Genealogy Co. 1976. (LC)

MEDLAN – Samuels, Nancy Timmons
  Medlan Medley. Fort Worth, Tex. [s.n., 1965]. (DAR)

MEEKS – Harrison, Sallie C. S.
  Descendants of Nathan Meeks and wife, Sarah C. Jones. By Sallie C. S. Harrison. Fort Worth, Tex. B. Hanson. (1976?). (FW)

MEEKS – Harrison, Sallie Stewart
  Descendants of Nathan Meeks and wife, Sarah C. Jones. Compiled by Sallie Stewart Harrison and Ethel Stewart Cole. Fort Worth, Tex. B. Hanson Print. [1980?]. (LC)

MEELER – Meeler, John W.
  Meeler and related patronymics. Researched, transcribed, edited, annotated, indexed by John W. Meeler. [United States]. J. W. Meeler. c1985. (LC)

MEGEE – Megee, Vernon Edgar
Ancestral trails; with genealogical notes on the following families: Megee, Ford, Futrell, Dunbar (and) Stover. By Vernon Edgar Megee. Austin? Tex. 1969. (LC)

MELUGIN – McKay, Douthitt Melugin, 1904-
A memorial to the Melugin family of America. By Douthitt Melugin McKay. Austin, Tex. Eakin Press [i.e. publications]. San Antonio, Tex. 1981. (LC)

MENDENHALL – Beeson, Henry Hart
The Mendenhalls. Houston, Tex. Beeson. 1969. (DAR)

MENEFEE – Powell, Doris D.
The genealogy of Laban Menefee. Cleburre, Tex. Powell. 1972. (DAR)

MENEFEE – Powell, Doris D.
Genealogy of Laban Menefee. By Doris D. Powell. Cleburne, Tex. 1972. (DP)

MENIL (Art Collections) – Ernst, Max, 1891-1976-
[Innere Gesicht. English]. Inside the sight. Houston, Tex. Institute of the Arts, Rice University. c1973. (LC)

MERCER – Mercer, Don W. (Don Wayland), 1926-
Mercer family research: including other related families. Alawine, Batchelor, Biggs, Green, Hopper, Ives, Jones, King, Melton, Patterson, Rice, Richards, Robinson, Sawyer, Sillivan, Simmons, Simson, Smith, Swanson, Swinfard, Thompson, Webb, White, Whittington, and many others. By Don W. Mercer. Houston, Tex. Mercer. 1985. (LC)

MERCER – Mercer, Don W.
Mercer family research. Houston, Tex. 1985. (NGS)

MEREDITH – Trube, Mattie Ellen Brown
Your family and mine. Houston, Tex. Trube. 1973. (DAR)

MEREDITH – Trube, Mattie E. B.
Your family and mine. By Mattie E. B. Trube. Houston, Tex., 1973. (FW)

MERRILL – Hardison, Lewis M. (Lewis Merrill), 1913-
One branch of the Merrill family. By Lewis Merrill Hardison. Kerrville, Tex. L. M. Hardison. [198-?]. (LC)

MERRILL – Merrill, David L.
Journey to the Southland: a history of one line of the Merrill family in America from its arrival in 1670 to the present. By David L. Merrill. Fort Worth, Tex. Author, 1965. (FW)

MERRITT – Merritt, King, 1933-
Historical perspectives of Charles Merritt, ca. 1652-1718: including his family and some descendants. By King Merritt, Jr. Baltimore: Gateway Press. El Paso, Tex. 1987. (LC)

METCALF – Metcalf, Lois Nicholson
  Metcalfs and Metcalfes. Temple, Tex. Ford Office Machines Co. 1973. (DAR)

METCALF – Metcalf, Lois N.
  Metcalf and Metcalfes. By Lois N. Metcalf. Temple, Tex., 1973. (FW)

METTS – Metts, Albert Caswell, Jr.
  Metts Ancestors in America: The Direct Line. San Antonio, Tex.. 1984. (NGS)

METZ – Metts, Albert Caswell, 1921-
  Metts ancestors in America: the direct line. By Albert Caswell Metts, Jr. San Antonio, Tex. A. C. Metts, Jr. 1984. (LC)

MEW – Whipple, Judith
  History and Journal of Letters of George William Knight Mew. Portland, Tex. 1975. (NGS)

MEYER – Greer, Georgeanna H.
  The Meyer family: master potters of Texas. By Georgeanna H. Greer. San Antonio, Tex. Pub. for the San Antonio Museum Assoc. by Trinity University Press. 1971. (NY)

MILES – Eckhardt, Ura L.
  Miles family, no. 1-3, 1964-1970. By Ura L. Eckhardt. Houston, Tex. 1970. (FW)

MILLER – Baird, Josie
  A Miller family tree grows into a forest. Rotan, Tex. Baird. c1965. (DAR)

MILLER – Baird, Josie
  A Miller family tree grows into a forest. By Josie Baird. Rotan, Tex. 1965. (LC)

MILLER – Gavlak, Nancy Miller Thompson Smith, 1929-
  The Norwegian and American ancestry of Mamie Clarice Miller Thompson, 1545-1982. Compiled by Nancy Miller Thompson Smith Gavlak. Bedford, Tex. N. T. Gavlak, c1983. (LC)

MILLER – Miller, W. M.
  Descendants of John G. Miller and wife Elizabeth Goodell. Dallas, Tex. Miller. 1951? (DAR)

MILLER – Overlander, Rufus M.
  Blount family of North Carolina and allied families Miller, Dyer, Gray. Seabrook, Tex. Rufus M. Overland III, 1987. (LC)

MILLER – Sanderfer, Sylvia Jean Miller, 1941-
  Jonathan Miller family tree. Researched and compiled by Sylvia Jean Miller Sanderfer. Creedmoor, Austin, Tex. S.J.M. Sanderfer. 1978. (LC)

MILNER – Hershey, Virginia Sharpe
  Those southern Milners: a collection of record abstracts for the Southern States between 1606 and 1850, with biographical and historical sketches, family records, and

genealogies up to 1900. Researched and compiled by Virginia Sharpe Hershey. [S.1.]. Hershey, c1980. (LC)

MILSAPS – Gormanous, Netie Milsaps, 1936-
The Milsaps family: patriotic, God loving, hard working Americans. By Nettie Milsaps Gormanous. Spring, Tex. N. M. Gormanous. c1990. (LC)

MILWARD – Macdonald, Margaret Taylor
The Milward family of Lexington, Kentucky, 1803-1969. By Margaret Taylor Macdonald. 1st Ed. Dallas? 1970. (LC)

MILWARD – MacDonald, Margaret Taylor
The Milward family of Lexington, Kentucky, 1803-1969. ?Dallas, Tex. 1970. (NGS)

MIMS – Eckhardt, Ura L.
Assorted notes on the Mimms (Mims) family, no. 1-2, 4-5, 1965-1968. By Ura L. Eckhardt. Houston, Tex. 1968. (FW)

MINEAR – Maxwell, Charles Joseph
Descendants of John Minear. Dallas, Tex., [s.n., 1948]. (DAR

MINEAR – Maxwell, Charles Joseph
The Minear family. Dallas, Tex. Maxwell. 1926. (DAR)

MINEAR – Maxwell, Charles Joseph
The Minear family (Minear, Menear, Myneer, Manear, Mineer). By Charles Joseph Maxwell. Dallas? Tex. Ginn & Co. 1926. (LC)

MINEAR – Maxwell, Charles Joseph
Descendants of John Minear, 1732-1781. By Charles Joseph Maxwell. Dallas, Tex. 1948. (LC)

MINIER – Weaver, Sarah Minier (Sanborne)
The Minier family, especially descendants of George W. Minier, of Minier, Illinois. By Sarah Minier (Sanborne) Weaver. Donna, Tex. 1926. (LC)

MISTROT – Cartier, Mistrot
The Mistrot-Segura story in Louisiana and Texas. By Mistrot Cartier. Houston, Tex. 1965. (LC)

MITCHELL – Allen, Estill Franklin
Cousins: handbook and family history of Mitchell, Allen, Gilleland, and related families from Virginia into Georgia, North Carolina, Kentucky, Tennessee, Missouri, Mississippi, Illinois, Iowa, Arkansas, Louisiana, Oklahoma, New Jersey, Texas, California, Florida, and Idaho, mid 1700s to 1980. By Estill Franklin Allen and cousins. Bornwood, Tex. Howard Payne University. c1981. (LC)

MITCHELL – Eckhardt, Ura L.
Mitchell family, no. 1-11, 1959-1969. By Ura L. Eckhardt. Houston, Tex. 1969. (FW)

MITCHELL –
Homer R. Mitchell, 1871-1956. Dallas, Tex., 1956. (FW)

MITCHELL – Irwin, C. Thomas (Clyde Thomas), 1931-
Gorgon head and golden tongue. By C. Thomas Irwin. Houston, Tex. C. T. Irwin. 1989? (LC)

MITCHELL – Mitchell, Homer R.
Mitchell family, descendants of James and Nancy Campbell Mitchell. By Homer R. Mitchell. Dallas, Tex., 1952. (FW)

MIXON – Mixson, John Leslie
The Mixon-Mixson family. By John Leslie Mixson. Fort Worth, Tex. American Reference Publishers. c1969-72. (LC)

MIXSON – Mixson, John Leslie
The Mixon-Mixson Family. Fort Worth, Tex. 1969. (NGS)

MONSON –
Ten million acres; the life of William Benjamin Munson. By Donald Joseph in collaboration with Mary Tonkin Smith. Denison, Tex. Priv. Print. (New York, William E. Rudge's Sons) 1946. (LC)

MONTAGUE – Montague, John V.
Genealogy of John V. Montague, Middlebury, Connecticut; born April 5, 1878, Bandera, Texas; died Aug. 15, 1960, Middlebury, Conn. This history and genealogy was compiled, designed and drafted by John V. Montague. Middlebury, Conn. c1961. (LC)

MONTGOMERY – Montgomery, Floyd Monroe
Montgomery's of America: 1850 census extracts. By Floyd Monroe Montgomery. San Antonio, Tex. F. M. Montgomery. c1987. (LC)

MONTGOMERY – Sanders, Alma F.
Montgomery, Williams and Menefee families. By Alma F. Sanders. Sweetwater, Tex. Sanders. 1976. (FW)

MONTGOMERY – Sanders, Alma Fay, 1907-
The Montgomery, Williams and Menefee families. By Alma Fay Sanders. Sweetwater, Tex. Sanders. 1976. (LC)

MOODY – Moody, Mary C.
The Moodys and related families. Arlington, Tex. M. C. Moody: V. B. Moody. c1979. (DAR)

MOODY – Moody, Mary C.
The Moodys and related families. Compiled and edited by Mary C. Moody, Virgil B. Moody. Collectors Ed. Arlington, Tex. M. C. Moody. c1979. (LC)

MOODY – Park, Clara Lorene Cammack, 1911-
Francis Moody (1769-1821): his ancestors, descendants, and related families, and all Moodys in the early records of Chesterfield County, Virginia. Compiled by Clara Lorene (Cammack) Park; research assistant, Wilbur Goolsby Park, Sr. Baltimore: Gateway Press. El Paso, Tex. c1984. (LC)

MOONEY – Sheriff, Pauline Callaway, 1918-
Davis data: John and Mary (Mooney) Davis: their ancestors and descendants as we know them, from North Carolina, South Carolina, Georgia, Alabama, Arkansas, Texas, Oklahoma, and elsewhere. By Pauline Callaway Sheriff, Mary Beth Davis Lightfoot, Alma Davis Bomer. Hollis, Okla. P. S. Sheriff. 1988. (LC)

MOORE – Coleman, M. J. (Maraan Jerrel), 1941-
Now comes [sic] the descendants of John A. & Mary Moore. By M. J. Coleman. Houston, Tex. M. J. Coleman, c1988. (LC)

MOORE – Eckhardt, Ura L.
Moore family, no. 1-10, 1966-1970. By Ura L. Eckhardt. Houston, Tex. 1970. (FW)

MOORMAN – Eckhardt, Ura L.
Moorman family, no. 1-2, 1963-1970. By Ura L. Eckhardt. Houston, Tex. 1970. (FW)

MOOSBERG – Sherman, June Moosberg, 1948-
The Trofast-Moosberg family: a genealogy. Compiled by June Moosberg Sherman. Lockney, Tex. J. M. Sherman. 1986. (LC)

MOREHOUSE – Higginbotham, George S.
Genealogy of Morehouse, Ashley, Woodhead and many others. By George S. Higginbotham. Fort Sam Houston, Tex., 1936. (FW)

MORGAN – Burton, Angela (M.)
Nellie B., tales of a Texan. By Angela (M.) Burton. Prairie Village, Kan. Squire Publishers, 1970. (KH)

MORONEY – Gilman, V. B.
Certain descendants of Joacobus and Ann McCarthy Moroney. By V. B. Gilman. Dallas, Tex., 1963. (FW)

MORRIS – Morris, Franklin
The Isaac Morris family, with the connecting families. By Franklin Morris. Editor, Maudie Ladell Fletcher. Amarillo, Tex. 1941. (LC)

MORRIS – Morris, Franklin
The Isaac Morris family. Amarillo, Tex. Fletcher. 1941. (DAR)

MORRIS – Morris, Whit
A Morris family of Mecklenburg County, North Carolina. San Antonio, Tex. Morris. c1956. (DAR)

MORRIS – Tate, Mary M., 1944-
The descendants of Amos Morris and Sarah Mitchell. Compiled by Mary M. Tate. Rev. Denton, Tex. M. M. Tate, 1987. (LC)

MORSE – Marshall, Mrs. Arch Bruce
Forebears and descendants of an early Houston family. Houston, Tex. Mrs. James Peyton Stanifer Griffith and Arch Bruce Marshall. c1975. (DAR)

MORSE – Marshall, Mrs. Arch Bruce (Maudie Marie Holt Marshall)
Forebears and descendants of an early Houston family. Research and compiled by Mrs. Arch Bruce Marshall (Maudie Marie Holt Marshall). Houston? Tex. Mrs. J.P.S. Griffith. c1975. (LC)

MORSE – Marshall, Maudie Marie Holt
Forebears and descendants of an early Houston Family. Morse, Marshall, Stilliman, Frisbie, Thornton families. ?Houston, Tex. 1975. (NGS)

MORSE – Morse, Edward C.
Blood of an Englishman... By Edward C. Morse. Abilene, Tex. Jones of Texas. 1943. (LC)

MORSE – Morse, Edward Clarke
Blood of an Englishman. Morse family. Abilene, Tex. 1943. (NGS)

MOSLEY – Moseley, Thomas Byrd, 1915-
A Moseley genealogy: England, Holland, Virginia, the Carolinas, Georgia, Alabama, Mississippi, Louisiana, Texas, to the West Coast. Researched, compiled and written by Thomas Byrd Moseley, Jr. Baltimore: Gateway Press. Clifton, Tex. 1985. (LC)

MOSS – Moss, Paul
The Moss family. Odessa, Tex. Moss. c1964. (DAR)

MOSS – Moss, William Paul
Biographical sketches of the Mosses: Paul Moss, Thaddeus A. Moss, Howell Moss, Howell C. Moss, Henry Moss, Amanda Holden Moss. By William Paul Moss. Odessa? Tex. c1960. (LC)

MOSS – Moss, Paul
The Moss family: William Paul Moss, Thaddeus Augustus Moss, Amanda Holden Moss, Howell Moss, Crestus Howell Moss, Henry Moss, their families and progenitors. Compiled and written by Paul Moss. Odessa? Tex. 1964. (LC)

MOUNT – Mount, Brent
Mount. Gatland, Tex. Mount; Okmulgee, Okla. 1974. (DAR)

MOUNT – Mount, Julius Allen
History and genealogical record of the Mount and Flippin families. Corpus Christi, Tex. Mount. 1954. (DAR)

MOUSER – Mouser, Lafrona Foshee
A genealogy of the Mouser ancestry including the Best and other families. Oklahoma City? Mouser. c1978. (DAR)

MOWREY – Eckhardt, Ura L.
Mowrey family, no. 1-3, 1960-1968. By Ura L. Eckhardt. Houston, Tex. 1968. (FW)

MOYER – Jung, Paula Moyer
The Moyer family. Dallas, Tex. Jung. 1974. (DAR)

MULLEN – Mullins, Alice Doraee Tankersley, 1932-
Branches of a tree: the Mullins legacy. Written and compiled by Alice Doraee Tankersley Mullins. Lubbock, Tex? A. D. T. Mullins. 1989. (LC)

MULLINEAUX – Mullinax, Otto B, 1912-
Some Mullinax roots, South Carolina to Texas. By Otto B. Mullinax. Austin, Tex. L. Shock. c1982. (LC)

MULVANEY –
Mulvany migration in N. America from the land of the shamrock. Phyllis Kilmer, editor; H. A. Kilmer, co-editor and consultant. Lubbock, Tex. Craftsman Printers, c1983. (LC)

MURCHISON – Murchison, Beatrice, 1895-
Trees of lineage. By Beatrice Murchison. Waco, Tex. B. Murchison. [198?]. 1960. (LC)

MURFF – Murff, Paul B.
The genealogy of Randolph S. Murff. Floydada, Tex. Murff and Murff. c1955. (DAR)

MURFF – Murff, Paul B.
Genealogy of Randolph S. Murff, 1784-1955. By Paul B. Murff. Floydada, Tex. 1955. (FW)

MURFF – Murff, Paul B. (Paul Bernard), 1897-1978-
The genealogy of Randolph S. Murff, 1784-1955. By a great, great grandson, Paul B. Murff, assisted by wife Vaughan Evelyn Murff. Floydada, Tex. Rev. Ed. Greenville, S.C.: M. B. Ashmore. c1982. (LC)

MURPHREE – Bates. O. D.
The descendants of Daniel (1) Murphree and Benjamin and Nancvy Murphree Ellis. Irving, Tex. Bates. 1974. (DAR)

MURPHY – McDaniel, Isabel Murphy
Murphy family of Houston, Texas. [S.l.:s.n. 1963-1972]. (DAR)

MURRAY – Cudd, Lois Murray, 1919-
And that's the way it was. By Lois Murray Cudd. [S.l.: s.n.]. c1980. Wichita Falls, Tex.: Quick Print. (LC)

MUSICK – Farmer, Michal Martin, 1946-
Adam Martin (1755-1835) and Thomas Roy Musick (1757-1842), St. Louis County, Missouri, pioneers: their ancestors, descendants, and related families, Hildebrand, Peira, Roy, and Neville. By Michal Martin Farmer. 1st Ed. Wolfe City, Tex. Henington Pub. Co. c1989. (LC)

MYERS – Adams, Dorothy M. K. (Dorothy Myers Knowlton), 1918-
Myers history: some descendants of Hans Meier of Pequea, Lancaster County, Pennsylvania. By Dorothy M. K. Adams. Houston, Tex. D. M. K. Adams. 1987. (LC)

MYERS – Myers, William
Myers history. By William Myers. Dallas, Tex., 1909. (FW)

MC –

MCADAM – McAdams, Kelly Edgar, 1903-
The McAdams family of Walker County, Texas. By Kelly Edgar and Ina May Ogletree McAdams. Austin, Tex. K. E. McAdams, c1985. (LC)

MCADAM – Towell, Roy H. (Roy Harrison), 1915-
Isaac Towell & his family: including Towell, McAdams, Whitworth, Shaw, Fitzgerald & others, 1764-1990. By Roy H. Towell, Jr. Beaumont, Tex. R. H. Towell. c1990. (LC)

MCALLEY – Fowler, Louise Bishop, 1927-
David and Mary (McElyea) Spence: their ancestors and descendants. By Louise Bishop Fowler. Baltimore: Gateway Press. Ore City, Tex. 1986. (LC)

MCALLISTER – Eckhardt, Ura L.
MacCallister family, no. 1-2, 1965-1968. By Ura L. Eckhardt. Houston, Tex. 1968. (FW)

MCALPINE – Mehrkam, Lucille Clepper, 1923-
History and genealogy of the family of Jacob Klepper/Clepper family and Malcolm McAlpine family: including branches of the Gilliam, Birdwell, Duncan, Woods, Estill, Forehand, Stifflemire, Cloyd, and Doddridge families. Edited by Ernestine (Lloyd) Jackson, Jacqueline Jackson, and Alixe (McAlpine) Taylor. Houston, Tex. L. C. Mehrkam. 1986. (LC)

MCBLAIR – McBlair, George
McBlair family genealogical record. By George McBlair. Dallas, Tex. 1973. (FW)

MCCABE – Hall, Martin Grant, 1938-
Pearson – McCabe: a genealogy and collection of family stories. Martin Grant Hall. Dallas, Tex. M. G. Hall. 1990. (LC)

MCCALL – McCall, Kenneth Scott
A study of one McCall family in the nineteenth century: Georgia, Mississippi, Louisiana, Texas. Compiled by Kenneth Scott McCall. Ardmore, Okla. K. S. McCall. 1979. (LC)

MCCANN – Hett, Karen McCann, 1939-
James McCan and Sarah S. Viser: history and genealogy of their descendants, 1828-1983. Compiled by Karen McCann Hett. Edna, Tex. K. M. Hett. c1983. (LC)

MCCANTS – Jones, Robbie McCants, 1923-
McCants, Wall, and related families. By Robbie McCants Jones. Houston, Tex. D. Armstrong. c1982. (LC)

MCCARLEY – McAfee, Jane Berry
The McCarley memories. Farmersville, Tex. Search-N-Print. c1980. (DAR)

MCCARLEY – McAfee, Jane Berry, 1945-
The McCarley memories. By Jane Berry McAfee. Farmersville, Tex. Search-N-Print. c1980. (LC)

MCCARTER – McCarter, Herbert H.
Robert A. B. Carter in Navarro County, Texas. Houston, Tex. D. Armstrong Co. c1979. (DAR)

MCCLANAHAN – Baker, Sibyl McClanahan, 1922-
McClanahan families from Tennessee to Missouri. By Sibyl McClanahan Baker. Bedford? Tex. Baker. 1979. (LC)

MCCLELLAN – McClellan, Aubrey Lester
Descendants of William Brownlow McClellan. Wolfe City, Tex. Henington Pub. Co. c1966. (DAR)

MCCLELLAN – McClellan, Aubrey Lester
Descendants of William Brownlow McClellan. By Aubrey Lester McClellan. 2nd Ed. Wolfe City, Tex. Printed by Henington Pub. Co. 1966. (LC)

MCCLELLAN – Woodward, Jewell Daphne Gerron, 1902-
Ancestors of Rufus McLelland and his descendants, 1783-1975. By Jewell Daphne Gerron Woodward; edited by George C. Woodward, Jr. Fort Worth, Tex. J.D.G. Woodward. [c.1982]. (LC)

MCCLUNEY – McCluney, Olivia L.
The name is McCluney. By Olivia L. McCluney. Houston (Texas). Press of Premier, 1974. (FW)

MCCLURE – Baxter, Nancy Niblack
The movers: a saga of the Scotch-Irish. By Nancy N. Baxter. Austin, Tex. Guild Press. c1987. (LC)

MCCORMICK – McCormick, Andrew Phelps
Scotch-Irish in Ireland and in America, as shown in sketches of the pioneer Scotch-Irish families McCormick, Stevenson, McKenzie, and Bell, in North Carolina, Kentucky, Missouri and Texas. By Andrew Phelps McCormick. (New Orleans), 1897. (LC)

MCCORMICK – McCormick, Edna H.
William Lee McCormick, a study in tolerancce; with genealogy. By Edna H. McCormick. Dallas, Book Craft. 1952. (FW)

MCCORMICK – Tyler, John S.
McCormicks of Kintyre. By John S. Tyler. Dallas, Tex? 1955. (FW)

MCCOWN – McCown, Leonard Joe
Simeon McCown, 1863-1925. By Leonard Joe McCown. Irving, Tex. L. J. McCown. 1986. (LC)

MCCRACKEN –Berry, Josephine
They went west: historical western genealogy. By Josephine Berry & Veda Magee, collaborator, Gay Blair; illustrators, note pages by Doris Flegal, dedication page by Karen Maddox. Rosston, Tex. Berry, c1978. (LC)

MCCRARY – Reynolds, Harriet Dickson
Colonel Robert McCrary (1732-1804) of North Carolina. Houston, Tex. Reynolds. 1966. (DAR)

MCCUISTON – Daggett, Carleen M.
Noah McCuiston, pioneer Texas cattleman. By Carleen M. Daggett. Waco, Tex. Texan Pr., 1975. (FW)

MCCULKLEY – McCulley, William Straight
The McCulley family tree. Bryan, Tex. McCulley. 1968. (DAR)

MCCULLEY –
The McCulley family tree; a history of Solomon and Sarah McCulley and some of their descendants to the eigth generation. Compiled by William Straight McCulley with the assistance of Frances J. Baldwin (and others). Bryan? Tex. 1968. (LC)

MCCUMBER – Macomber, Edward Milton, 1930-
Connections: a pedigree record of the direct ancestors of Edward Milton Macomber, with partial lineage of 112 related surnames... [By Edward Milton Macomber]. Rev. Austin, Tex. E. M. Macomber. 1987, c1985. (LC)

MCCUNE – Campbell, Kathryn Hutcherson
William McCune, the Pennsylvanian. Dallas, Tex. Campbell. 1974. (DAR)

MCDERMOTT – McDermott, Ella M.
Irish heritage of allied members of McGivern's, McDermott's, Gallagher's, Gillespie's. By Ella M. McDermott. San Antonio, Tex. Clegg Co. 1976. (FW)

MCDERMOTT – McDermott, Ella May, 1892-
Irish heritage of allied members of McGivern's, McDermott's, Gallagher's, Gillespie's. By Ella May McDermott. San Antonio, Tex. Clegg Co. c1976. (LC)

MCDONALD – McDonald, Pauline
Our pioneer heritage. Dallas, Tex? McDonald. c1961. (DAR)

MCDONALD – McDonald, Robert E.
Clan McDonald. By Robert E. McDonald. San Antonio, Tex? Printed by A. D. Orme. 1968. (FW)

MCDONALD – McDonald, W. T.
The McDonald family. By W. T. McDonald, Sr. Bryan, Tex. W. T. McDonald. 1984. (LC)

MCDUFF – Britt, Cloma, 1917-
Trails of the McDuffs, Ginns. By Cloma Britt. Azle, Tex. C. Britt. c1981. (LC)

MCELROY – McLeroy, Tom
History of John Mackelroy family of Baltimore County, Maryland and allied families. By Tom McLeroy. Center, Tex. T. McLeroy. [198?]. (LC)

MCEWAN – McCuan, Noble McKeel, 1920-
The Family McCuan. By Noble McKeel McCuan, Jr. Grapevine, Tex. N. M. McCuan. 1980 printing. (LC)

MCFEATTERS – Zeitler, Vernon Arthur, 1917-
Upon the shoulders of giants: Zeitler, McFeaters, Hickox, Moorhead, Hechendorn... Vernon Arthur Zeitler, Thelma Poorbaugh Zeitler. Lake Jackson, Tex. V. A. Zeitler. 1986. (LC)

MCGAFFEY – McGaffey, George Washington
The genealogical history of the McGaffey family. Waxahachie, Tex. Ola McGaffey Upshaw. 1966. (DAR)

MCGAVIN – Robbins, Eugene W. (Eugene Weldon), 1925-
Robbins/McGuffey family history. By Eugene W. Robbins. Spicewood, Tex. E. W. Robbins. [1990]. (LC)

MCGEE – Bennett, Inez R. M.
Genealogical record of the MacGhie family in America. By Inez R. M. Bennett. Dallas, Tex. 1960. (FW)

MCGIFFIN – McGiffin, James Quail
The McGiffin story. By James Quail McGiffin. Baytown, Tex. 1952. (LC)

MCGREGOR – Price, Caroline Beall
Ancestral beginnings in America of the McGregor, Magruder, Beall, Price, Phillips, Bland, McKisick, Miller, Dickson, Lawson, Henderson, Young and related families. Austin, Tex. Price. 1928. (DAR)

MCGREGOR –Price, Caroline Beall
Ancestral beginnings in America of the McGregor, Magruder, Beall, Price, Phillips, Bland, McKisick, Miller, Dickson, Lawson, Henderson, Young and related families. Austin, Tex. Price. 1928. (DAR)

MCKINLEY – Honea, Patricia McKinley Murphree
The Stephen McKinley family of Hamilton County, Texas: a history. By Patricia McKinley Murphree Honea. Fort Worth, Tex. P. M. M. Honea. [1986]. (LC)

MCKINNEY – Garver, Lois
The descendants of Collin and Daniel McKinney. Austin, Tex. 1984. (NGS)

MCKNIGHT – Peak, Texarado McKnight
The McKnight families and their descendants. Austin, Tex. Peak. 1965. (DAR)

MCKNIGHT – Peak, Texarado McKnight
The McKnight family and their descendants. Austin, Tex. Peak. 1969. (DAR)

MCKNIGHT – Peak, Texarado M.
The McKnight families and their descendants, also, the Wallace and Alexander families. By Texarado M. Peak. Austin, Tex., 1965. (FW)

MCKNIGHT – Matthews, G. C.
Biography of McKnight, Newsom, Matthews. By G. C. Matthews. Amarillo, Tex. (n.d.). (FW)

MCLAUGHLIN – McLaughlin, Steven K. (Steven Kent), 1952-
The McLaughlin genealogy: descendants of James and Mary McLaughlin of Muff (now Eglinton), County Londonderry, Ireland: related families, Brown, Johnston, Lossee, Morford, Parker, Speir, Woods. Compiled by Steven K. McLaughlin. Dallas, Tex. S. K. McLaughlin. 1990. (LC)

MCLAUGHLIN – McLaughlin, Steven K. (Steven Kent), 1952-
The McLaughlins. By Steven K. McLaughlin & Evelyn Z. McCann. 3rd Ed. [Dallas, Tex.]. S. K. McLaughlin. [1988]. (LC)

MCLEAN – McLean, Wm. H.
Descendants of John McLean, school master from Isle of Jura, Scot., emigrant to the U. S. ... By Wm. H. McLean. Fort Worth, Tex., 1971. (FW)

MCLEAN – McLean, William Hunter
Descendants of John McLean, 1797 to 1971. Fort Worth, Tex. 1971. (NGS)

MCLELLAND – Woodward, Jewell Dauphne Gerron
Ancestors of Rufus McLelland and his descendants, 1783-1975. Fort Worth, Tex. c1982. (NGS)

MCMINN – Brittain, Virginia (T.)
The McMinn family in America. 1st Ed. By Virginia (T.) Brittain. Passadena, Tex. V. T. Brittain, 1967. (FW)

MCNALL – MacNaul, Albert G. (Albert George), 1910-
The MacNaul/McNaul family and related families. Researched and written by Albert G. & Mary Alice MacNaul. New Braunfels, Tex. A. G. and M. A. MacNaul. c1990. (LC)

MCNEIL – Boyd, Margie Milner, 1925-
The Robert Harllee McNeill and Lela Harper Gilmore family: their ancestors and descendants. Compiled by Margie Milner Boyd. Beaumont, Tex. M. M. Boyd. 1990. (LC)

MCPHERSON – McPherson, Samuel A.
History of the McPherson family. By Samuel A. McPherson. Waxahachie, Tex. Pub. by the author, 1927. (DP)

MCQUISTON – Elliott, Zola F. (Zola Florence), 1912-
Consanquinity: my father's line: McCuistons, Nelsons, Hollands & Elliotts. By Zola F. Elliott, author, editor, compiler and publisher. Austin, Tex. Z. F. Elliott. [1989]. (LC)

MCWHORTER – Tenney, Mary McWhorter
McWhorter, Barry, and allied families. Sugarland, Tex. Joe M. Huffington. 1967. (DAR)

MCWHORTER – Wright, Shelley McWhorter
Some descendants of David McWhorter (McWhirter) (ca. 1741-1789) and his wife Mary Poston (Posten) McWhorter, (1750-1846). Longview, Tex. Mr. & Mrs. E. R. McWhorter. 1978. (DAR)

N –

NAVARRO – Navarro, Susan Daugherty
From legend to reality: the DeBerry-Navarro story. By Susan Daugherty Navarro. Pecos, Tex. 1964. (LC)

NEAL – Neal, Betty Christene, 1942-
Journey into yesteryear: the Neal family and related families. Author, Betty Christene Neal. Whitewright, Tex. B. C. Neal. c1988. (LC)

NEAL – Neal, Hazel Frances Copeland, 1905-
Descendants of Alfred Neal family, Alfred Neal and Elizabeth Polk Neal. Compiled, edited & published by Hazel Frances Copeland Neal, co-publisher Dollie Ruth Neal Ballenger. San Angelo, Tex. Neal. 1979. (LC)

NEALE – Eckhardt, Ura L.
Neale-O'Neale family, no. 1-4, 1965-1970. By Ura L. Eckhardt. Houston, Tex. 1970. (FW)

NEELEY – Neeley, Bonnie J. (B.)
John Neeley 1770?-1804 of Warren County, Ohio and some of his descendants who lived in Jay County, Ind. By Bonnie J. (B.) Neeley. Fort Worth, Tex. Miran Pub. 1975. (FW)

NEIGHBORS – Neal, John Whitman Monroe, 1904-1973-
Neighbors. By John Whitman Monroe Neal; Annette Roy Hunt, compiler' Luther Cleveland Nabors, Grover Cooley Nabors, editors. [S.1.:s.n.]. c1976. (LC)

NELMS – Allen, Juanita Catherine, 1908-
Mrs. Mary Belle Crain Nelms, born 1792, Tennessee: pioneer settler, Bonham and Ector, Fannin County, Texas, 1842. Ector, Tex? Juanita Allen. c1982. (LC)

NELMS – Allen, Juanita Catherine, 1908-
Reverend John A. Nelms, Methodist Minister: pioneer settler, Bonham and Ector, Fannin County, Texas, 1842. By Juanita Allen. Houston, Tex. J. Allen. c1980. (LC)

NELMS – Dodd, Ella Frances Mainer, 1905-
This family called Nelms. Compiled by Ella Frances Mainer Dodd. Crockett, Tex. Crockett Commercial Printers. 1987. (LC)

NELMS –
Families of Reverend John A. Nelms, Methodist Minister, and wife, Mary Bell Crain Nelms; C. C. Nelms and wife, Delilah Damron Nelms; George Damron and wife, Delilah Fisher Damron; Moses Allen and wife, Malvina Owens Allen; A. Ford and wife, Lucy Ford; Dr. Wm. Hunter and wife, Minerva Hunter; all of whom were among the first settlers at Ector, Fannin County, Texas, in the days of the Republic of Texas. By Vivian and Brenda Newingham. (Herriage) Bonham, Tex. 1966. (LC)

NELMS – Newingham, Vivian
Ancestors and their descendants of our great, great, great grandparents: Reverend John A. Nelms, Methodist Minister, and his wife, Mary Belle Crain Nelms, who settled in Fannin County, Texas, in the days of the Republic of Texas. Compiled and edited by Vivian Newingham Herriage and Brenda Newingham. Bonham, Tex. 1968. (LC)

NELSON – Elliott, Zola F. (Zola Florence), 1912-
Consanquinity: my father's line: McCuistons, Nelsons, Hollands & Elliotts. By Zola F. Elliott, author, editor, compiler, and publisher. Austin, Tex. Z. F. Elliott. 1989. (LC)

NEMKEY – Willis, Meta Memkey, 1899-
My ancestors. By Meta Nemkey Willis. San Antonio, Tex. Willis. c1977. (LC)

NEVILL – Nevill, Ivan B.
Genealogy of the Nevill family. Houston, Tex. Nevill. 1964. (DAR)

NEVILL – Nevill, Ivan B.
Genealogy of the Nevill family. By Ivan B. Nevill. Houston, Tex., 1964. (NY)

NEVILLE – Hodges, Frances Beal Smith
The Neville family of England and the United States. Wichita Falls, Tex. Watt Ella Nevils Watson. 1964. (DAR)

NEVILLE – Hodges, Frances B. (S.)
The Neville family of England and the United States. By Frances B. (S) Hodges. Wichita Falls, Tex. Priv. Pub. by W. E. Nevils Wilson, 1964. (FW)

NEVILLE – Neville, Joseph B.
A 360 year history of one Neville family, 1612-1972. Tucson, Ariz. Neville. 1974. (DAR)

NEWMAN – Benson, W. E., Mrs.
The Cantrell-Newman genealogy. Compiled by Mrs. W. E. Benson, Mrs. Jack Slayden. Bowie, Tex. W. E. Benson. [198-]. (LC)

NEWTON – Clark, Jemmie (Newton)
Pioneer Newtons of southwest Texas, and genealogies. By Jemmie (Newton) Clark. Redlands, Calif. c1959. (LC)

NEWTON – Newton, Leroy L., 1927-
Genealogical report, Newton and Flury and allied families: from Maryland, Virginia, Alabama, South Carolina, Georgia, southern Arkansas, Red Lands in Indian Territory, Oklahoma, and other places. By Leroy L. Newton; edited by Claireeta D. Newton, Latricia L. Newton. Altus, Okla? L. L.Newton. c1987. (LC)

NICHOLLS – Nicholls, Guy
The Nicholls family. [S.1.: Rio Grande Printing and Pub. Co. 1976]. (DAR)

NICHOLS – Nichols, George Louis, 1917-
A Nichols genealogy: a branch of the family descended from Thomas and Hannah Griffin Nichols of Newport, Rhode Island, and Sarah Alexander Nichols of East Greenwich, Rhode Island. Compiled by George Louis Nichols. Houston, Tex. G. L. Nichols. 1987. (LC)

NICHOLS – Nichols, M. Q. (Milford Quinton), 1920-
White roots: a Nichols genealogy. By M. Q. Nichols. Bridge City, Tex. M. Q. Nichols. 1983. (LC)

NICHOLSON – Holmes, Janice Nicolson, 1919-
Nicolson history, 1655-1985: nine generations of direct descendants of the Robert Nicolson who patented 500 acres in Charles City County in the Virginia Colony on January 3, 1655/56. Rev. Fort Worth, Tex. [J. N. Holmes]. 1985. (LC)

NIMITZ – Sister Joan of Arc
My name is Nimitz. By Sister Joan of Arc. San Antonio, Tex. Standard Print. Co. 1948. (LC)

NIXON –
The early Nixons of Texas; with genealogies. By Dr. and Mrs. Pat Ireland Nixon, Jr. El Paso, Tex. C. Hertzog. 1956. (LC)

NIXON – Owen, Ruby Fay Stringer
History of the family of Dr. Eldred Scott Simpkins Nixon. Athen, Tex. Owen. 1977. (DAR)

NOACK – Kasper, Evelyn (N.)
Family history of Johann and Maria Noack. By Evelyn (N.) Kasper. La Grange, Tex? 1968? (FW)

NOFZIGER – Hofziger, Harley
Genealogy: Christ R. Nofziger, 1827-1968. By Harley Hofziger. [n.p., 1968?]. (FW)

NOLD – Watson, May (M.)
Nold family history and genealogical background. By May (M.) Watson. Corpus Christi, Tex., 1941. (FW)

NORMAN – Norman, Lois L.
Normans of Normandy Hall. Wolfe City, Tex. University of Texas. 1976. (DAR)

NORRID – Norrid, Henry H.
History of the Norrid family and related families. By Henry H. Norrid. Amarillo, Tex., 1973. (FW)

NORTHCUTT – Northcutt, Dolly
Northcutt. Longview, Tex. Morris Pub. Co. 1938. (DAR)

NORTHCUTT – Northcutt, Dolly
The Northcutt families of Kentucky. Longview, Tex. Northcutt. c1960. (DAR)

NORTHCUTT –
Northcutt and allied families. By Dolly Northcutt and Amelia Sparkman Castleberry. Longview, Tex. Morris Pub. Co. 1938. (LC)

NORTON – Smith, Erma Dell Melton, 1913-1976-
The descendants of Mercer (Messer) Norton. 1750?-1800? and his wife Martha. Compiled by Erma Dell Melton Smith and Mildred Dulaney. Mart, Tex. M. Dulaney. 1983, c1984. (LC)

NORWOOD –
"General" John Norwood and related lines. Compiled by William Howard Norwood in cooperation with James Harvey Norwood, Sr., and Henry Offie Norwood. Dallas, Tex. Trumpet Press. 1964. (LC)

NORWOOD – Jones, E. N.
Norwood-Ott and allied lines: Powell, Brown, Higgins, Massey. By E. N. Jones. Dallas, Tex. 1954. (FW)

NOVAK – Novak, Rynell Stiff, 1929-
The Novak "connections": family history of Joseph Robert Novak and Rynell Stiff Novak. Compiled by Rynell Stiff Novak. Denton, Tex. R. S. Novak. c1983. (LC)

NULISCH – Nulisch, Nany Rohde, 19936-
Named Nulisch: the history of the Nulisch family in Texas. By Nancy Rohde Nulisch. Dallas, Tex. N. R. Nulisch. c1988. (LC)

O –

OATES –
Genealogy: Oates-Case-Porter. From the research of Cora Case Porter. Edited by Renfro and Likie Herndon. Fort Worth? Tex., 1973. (LC)

OATES – Williams-Walker, Naylan Gaile Linton
Allied families of Chalk, Massie, Oates, Linton, 1066-1987. Compiled and edited by Naylan Gaile Linton Williams-Walker. Victoria, Tex. G. Walker, 1988? (LC)

OBERHOLTZER – Turn, Helen Overholser, 1923-
Samuel Overholtzer of Virginia and some of his descendants. By Helen Overholser Turn. Belton, Tex. Center Press. 1981. (LC)

O'BRIEN – Merk, George L.
Some descendants of Philip and Dolly O'Bryan: parents of John, Henry, Joseph and Benedict O'Bryan. Compiled by George L. Merk. Rev. Ed. Prepared by Joseph E. O'Bryan. Abilene, Tex. J. E. O'Bryan. 1988. (LC)

O'BYRNE – O'Byrne, Ceclia Christina
The O'Byrne Mill; digging for facts and fantasies. By Cecilia Christina O'Byrne. Gladewater, Tex. Acme Duplicating Services. c1970. (LC)

ODOM – Eckhardt, Ura L.
Odom family, no. 1-5, 1959-1970. By Ura L. Eckhardt. Houston, Tex. 1970. (FW)

OERTLI – Steger, Mel
An Oertli history. Prepared by Mel Steger. Houston, Tex. M. Steger. 1984. (LC)

OFFER – Girard, Mary Offer, 1937-
The history of the Offer family: a record of two brothers, Adam Hermann Joseph and Johann Julius August Offer, who imigrated to Texas and were the proginators of the Offer family in Texas. Compiled by Mary Offer Girard. Cullman, Ala. Gregath Co. c1987. (LC)

OGDEN –Fenn, Alice McGee, 1905-
Descendants of Francis Purdy (ca. 1610-1658) and ancestors of related families of Brundage, Brown, Ogden, Strang, Smith, Carman, Loveland who married into Purdy families and descendants of John Eliot (1604-1690) and St. Arnulf (580-640) who married into Purdy families. Compiled by Alice M. Fenn. Tulsa, Okla. A. M. Fenn. 1990. (LC)

OGELTREE – Ptomey, Kyser Cowart, 1915-
John Ogeltree, Sr., 1740-1822: two hundred twenty five years of descendants: and the allied lines of Phillips, Turner, Sanders, French, Riggins, Martin, and McBrayer. By Kyser Cowart Ptomey. Houston. K. C. Ptomey. c1986. (LC)

O'HARA – Hall, Susan V. Harrah, 1921-
People and places of days gone by. Researched and written by Susan V. Harrah Hall. Allen, Tex. M. L. H. Caquelin. 1984? (LC)

OHRNDORFF – Drake, Julia A.
The Christian Ohrndorff family in Germany. By Julila A. Drake. 1st Ed. San Angelo, Tex. Anchor Pub. Co. 1968. (NY)

OLDHAM – Bliss, Nancy Hamilton
Of eagles and old islands: the Arnolds and the Oldhams and their descendants. By Nancy Hamilton Bliss, Ann Hamilton Pippin. Kirkwood, Mo. N. H. Bliss; Greenville, Tex. A. H. Pippin. c1988. (LC)

OLIVE –
James Olive family, Wake County, N. C. Fort Worth, Tex. Olive Family Association. c1965. (DAR)

ONDERDONK – Steinfeldt, Cecilia
The Onderdonks: a family of Texas painters. By Cecilia Seinfeldt. San Antonio. Published for the San Antonio Museum Association by Trinity University Press. 1975, c1976. (LC)

ORANGE-NASSAU, HOUSE OF – Duyverman, J. P.
Uit de geheime dagboeken van Aeneas Mackay dienaar des konings 1806-1876. J. P. Duyverman. Houten: De Haan. c1987. (LC)

O'ROARK – Roark, Morris L.
Roarks (O'Rourke) of Ireland… and… the Nathan Roark family in America. By Morris L. Roark. San Antonio, Tex., 1959. (FW)

ORR – Evans, Marvin D.
The Orrs of Miller County, Arkansas. Fort Worth, Tex. Evans. 1951. (DAR)

OSMOND – Osmond, Charles H.
The Osmond family: the story of Jonathan Osmond, born 1771, Bucks Co., Pa., his ancestors and descendants, tog. with related families: Buckman, Conrad, Jones, Strickland, Stinson, and Thomas. By Charles H. Osmond. Fort Worth, Tex. C. H. Osmond. 1964. (SP)

OUSLEY – Anderson, Ollie Mae Ousley, 1921-
From Tennessee to Texas. By Ollie Mae Ousley Anderson. [S.1.]. O. M. O. Anderson. 1980. (LC)

OUSLEY – Weddell, Monty Thomas Ousley, 1943-
Our English heritage and Ousley genealogical history. By Monty Thomas Ousley Weddell. Dallas, Tex. Consumer Management Service, 1981. (LC)

OWEN – Cunningham, T. M.
Owen family history. Denton, Tex. Cunningham. c1940. (DAR)

OWEN – Cunningham, T. M.
Owen family history, with an incomplete genealogy of the Daniel family. By T. M. Cunningham. Denton, Tex. 1940. (LC)

OWEN – Frizzell, Bonner
History of the family of Judge David Allen Owen. Palestine, Tex. Frizzell. 1962. (DAR)

OWEN – Frizzell, Bonner
History of the family of Judge David Allen Owen, son of Samuel Tine and Sarah Ward (Knight) Owen. By Bonner Frizzell. Palestine, Tex. 1962. (LC)

OWEN – Texas DAR
Genealogical record of the Owen DeJuzan, Garrett and allied families. 1944. (DAR)

OWEN – Wynne, Birdie Farrar
All roads led to Texas. Dallas, Tex. Wynne. c1969. (DAR)

OWEN – Wynne, Birdie F.
All roads lead to Texas… Owen-Humphrey, Farrar, Abernathy, Bowdon, Bradford, Ashley-Lasater, Wynne. By Birdie F. Wynne. (1968). (SL)

P –

PABST – Pope, Jennings Bland
Pabst-Bobst-Pobst-Pope family in the South. Austin, Tex. Pope. c1978. (DAR)

PABST – Pope, Jennings Bland
Pabst/Bobst/Pobst/Pope family in the South. Austin, Tex. 1978. (NGS)

PACE – Casey, Alvin Harold, 1915-
Shelton, Wininger, and Pace families. By Harold Casey and Robert Casey. 1st Ed. Dallas, Tex. Brooks Pub. Co. Stillwater, Okla. c1988. (LC)

PACE – Jantz, Virginia Copeland, 1923-
Pierce, Pace, Hall, Minton, and Huie families. By Virginia Copeland Jantz. Waco, Tex. V. C. Jantz. c1986. (LC)

PAGE – Baskin, Jane Page Osborn, 1924-
McKineth A. Page family data sheets. Compiled by Jane Page Osborn Baskin and Carol Jane Baskin Tatum. McKinney, Tex. J. P. O. Baskin. 1990. (LC)

PARK – Becker, Doorothy Robertson, 1905-
The Parke family: earliest pioneers of New Jersey with later generations who pioneered in Old Frederick Co.., Va. & on into Ohio and Indiana. Compiled by Dorothy Robertson Becker (nee Fritzinger). Fort Worth, Tex. Miran. c1979. (LC)

PARK – Hazelwood, Jean (P.)
History of the family of Pearson Money Park and Mary Elizabeth Teater Park. By Jean (P.) Hazelwood. Fort Worth, Texas, author. 1969. Revised – Fort Worth, Tex. 1970. (FW)

PARK – Piper, Blanche Park, 1895-
I remember – because I was there. By Blanche P. Piper. Waco? Piper. c1975. (LC)

PARKE – Becker, Dorothy Robertson
The Parke family. Fort Worth, Tex. Miran. c1979. (DAR)

PARKER – Campbell, Kathryn Hutcherson
John Parker. Dallas, Tex. Campbell. 1980. (DAR)

PARKER – Parker, Gladys Harris
Robert Arthur Parker: a Texas pioneer, ancestors, descendants, related families. Researched and compiled by Gladys Harris Parker (Mrs. William Harold Parker), Anna Beth Heffernan (Mrs. William H. Heffernan), Pearl Scott Rattan (Mrs. Ward Rattan). Irving, Tex. A. B. Heffernan. 1985. (LC)

PARNELL – Dowdy, Henry G.
Parnell-Camp genealogy and records. By Henry G. Dowdy. Fort Worth, Tex. Miran Pub. 1976? (FW)

PARROTT – Kelsey, Mavis Parrott
Benjamin Parrott, c.1795-1839, and Lewis Stover, 1781-1850/60, of Overton County, Tennessee, and their descendants. Houston, Tex. Dr. & Mrs. Mavis Parrott Kelsey. c1979. (DAR)

PARROTT – Kelsey, Mavis Parrott
Benjamin Parrott, c1795-1839 and Lewis Stover, 1781-1850/60 of Overton County, Tennessee and their descendants. Houston, Tex. 1979. (NGS)

PARROTT – Scott, Evalyn Parrott
The Parrott family history. Sudan, Tex. c1967. (NGS)

PARTRIDGE – Finch, Thomas A.
Partridge-Finch genealogy. By Thomas A. Finch. San Antonio, Tex., 1916. (FW)

PARTRIDGE – Finch, Thomas Alber
The Partridge-Finch genealogy. San Antonio, Tex. 1916. (NGS)

PASCHAL – Paschal, Rosa Price (Mrs. John Jones Paschal)
Some Paschal ancestors, descendants, and allied families. Compiled by Rosa Price Paschall (Mrs. John Jones Paschal). Wolfe City, Tex. Southern Baptist Press. 1969. (LC)

PASCHALL – Johnston, Mary E.
Elisha Paschall family genealogy, born 1735, Revolutionary War patrioit. Katy, Tex. Johnston. 1973. (DAR)

PASCHALL – Johnston, Mary E. S.
Elisha Paschall family genealogy: born 1735, Revolutionary War patriot. By Mary E. S. Johnston. Katy, Tex., 1973. (FW)

PATILLO – Crosse, Melba C.
Patillo, Pattilo, Pattulo and Pittillo families. Compiled by Melba C. Crosse. Fort Worth, Tex. American Reference Pub. Co., 1972. (LC)

PATTERSON – Dodson, Lois
Ancestors of John Burkett, Albert, Spencer, Patterson, and John Johnson and their descendants in Alabama, Texas, Oklahoma. By Lois Gerron Dodson and Larry Jay Gage. Austin?Tex. Dodson. c1980. (LC)

PATTERSON – Patterson, Marjorie S. (Marjorie Sherrill), 1906-
Patterson, here and there. Compiled by Marjorie S. Patterson, Yvonne Gertrude Parson, Arthur F. Parson. [Fort Worth? Tex.: s.n.]. 1979. (LC)

PATTERSON – Paris, George
The Paterson letters: ties of a scattered family, 1811-1890. Compiled and edited by George Paris. [United States?]. G. Paris. c1989. (LC)

PATTERSON – Patterson, Edna Earle Fleming
Patterson-Harrison, Fleming-Burgess, Bierbower-Fox and allied families. Houston, Tex. Lady Washington Chapter (Texas) DAR. 1972. (DAR)

PATTON –Swanson, Ernest C. (Ernest Carl), 1930-
Descendants of Isaac Patten, Sr., and his wife, Jane Norris: an early pioneer family in Sullivan County, Indiana. Compiled by Ernest C. Swanson. Baltimore: Gateway Press; El Paso, Tex. E. C. Swanson [distributor]. 1985. (LC)

PAXTON – Paxton, W. M.
The Paxtons: their origin in Scotland, and their migration through England and Ireland, to the colony of Pennsylvania, whence they moved South and West, and found homes in many states and territories... By W. M. Paxton. Platte City, Mo. Landmark Print. 1903. (LC)

PAYNE – Foxworth, Sarah Payne, 1910-
Foxworth, Bush, Payne, Bledsoe & allied lineages: Lenoir, Pope, Regan, Elkin, Quisenberry, Morter, Foster, Mitchell, Johnston, Ogilvie, Birdsong, Higgins, etc. By Sarah Payne Foxworth and Michal Martin Farmer. Dallas, Tex. Farmer Genealogy Co. c1985. (LC)

PEACOCK – Spray, Barbara C.
Chandler and Peacock cousins with Petty and Hayhurst families. By Barbara Chandler Spray. Amarillo, Tex. B. C. Spray. 1985. (LC)

PEARCE – Matthews, James Alonzo
Pearce, Bartlett, Matthews, Smart, and allied families. Compiled by James Alonzo Matthews, Jr. Midland, Tex. Lucille Pearce. c1983. (LC)

PEARCE – Srom, Zelma Hayley
The Pearces' pioneering days in Texas. 1976. (NGS)

PEARSON – Diller, Corinne Hanna, 1954-
Quaker Pearsons: being descendants of Lawrence Peirson, 1607-1673 of Cheshire, England. Collected by Corinne Hanna Diller. Houston, Tex. C. H. Diller. 1985. (LC)

PEARSON – Hall, Martin Grant, 1938-
Pearson – McCabe: a genealogy and collection of family stories. Martin Grant Hall. Dallas, Tex. M. G. Hall. 1990. (LC)

PEAVY – Morrow, Betty Moss
Peevy/Peavy/Pevey/Puvey. Compiled by Betty Moss Morrow. Teague, Tex. B. M. C. Morrow. c1990. (LC)

PECKENPAUGH – Brace, Edwin T., 1903-
Peckinpaughs, Pickenpaughs, Beckenbaughs, Peckinpahs, and Peckenpaughs: descendants of Johann Adam & Anna Maria Beckenbach. Compiled by Edwin T. & Atha Peckenbaugh Brace. Rev. Ed. Baltimore: Gateway Press. El Camp. Tex. 1984 (LC)

PECKHAM –
Genealogy of one branch of the Peckham family of Newport and Westerly, R.I. and its allied family. Compiled by William Perry and John Earle Bentley. Documentary evidence by Emilie Sarter. Dallas? Tex. 1957? (LC)

PECKHAM – Peckham, Charles W.
The Charles Peckham branch: Peckham genealogy, from England, Rhode Island, Pennsylvania, Ohio, Indiana, Wisconsin, Illinois, Texas, and elsewhere. By Charles Wesley Peckham. Lebanon, Ohio. C. W. Peckham. 1978. (LC)

PEGUES – Chambers, Mildred Aldrich
The Claudius Pegues family. Compiled by Mildred Aldrich Chambers. Midland, Tex. M. A. Chambers. 1986. (LC)

PEGUES – Pegues, Aston D.
Line of descent of Samuel Butler Pegues and Juliet King. Houston, Tex. Pegues; Crystal City, Tex. Lidwin. 1956. (DAR)

PEGUES – Pegues, Aston D.
Families descended from Samuel Butler Pegues (1778-1835) and his wife, Juliet (King) Pegues. By Aston D. Pegues. Houston, Tex. (n.d.). (FW)

PENCE – Eckhardt, Ura L.
Pence and Perkey families, no. 1-4, 1960-1967. By Ura L. Eckhardt. Houston, Tex. 1967. (FW)

PENDLETON – Ekhardt, Ura L.
Pendleton family assorted notes. By Ura L. Eckhardt. Houston, Tex. 1970. (FW)

PENNINGTON – Roberts, Virginia Culin
With their own blood: a saga of southwestern pioneers. By Virginia Culin Roberts. Fort Worth, Tex. Texas Christian University Press. c1991. (LC)

PERES – Shankman, Sam
The Peres family. Kingsport, Tenn. Southern Publishers. 1938? (DAR)

PEREZ – McAlear, Robert
Children of the Hummingbird: Perez and Najera of Mexico and Texas. Compiled by Robert McAlear. Nice, Calif. R. McAlear. c1984. (LC)

PERKINS – Letts, Hubert W. (Hubert Winfred), 1913-
Yankee land to Dixie land: a family genealogy. By Hubert W. Letts. Corpus Christi, Tex. Home Publishers. c1986. (LC)

PERRY – Perry, Hubert L.
The family tree of Daniel Perry, 1704-1970. By Hubert L. Perry. Caldwell, Tex., 1970? (FW)

PERRY – Perry, Max
The descendants of Perry – Peterson families. Midland, Tex. c1977. (DAR)

PERRY –Perry, Max, 1919-
The descendants of Perry-Peterson families: including allied families and genealogical briefs of Abercrombie, Bagwell, Brown, Hallmark, Kelly, Queen, Roach, Tuggle, Williams, and Williamson. Compiled by Max Perry. Midland, Tex. Perry. c1977. (LC)

PERRY – Phillips, A. I. P.
Perry and allied families from Colonial days to the present time. By A. I. P. Phillips. Bryan? Tex., 1933. (FW)

PERSON – Knox, Barbara Roach
Amos Person(s): his forebears and descendants. With supplemental Hodge genealogy. By Barbara Roach Knox. Fort Worth, Tex. Higgins Print Co. 1967. (LC)

PERSON – Pearson, Frederick John, 1919-
100 years of Pearsons: the descendants of John and Johanna Pearson who emigrated from Sweden to America in April, 1889. Compiled by Fred J. Pearson. Houston, Tex. 1976. (LC)

PESSEMIER – Siegert, Joan Emert, 1931-
The Pressemier portfolio: ancestors and descendants of Charles Louis Pessemier and his wife, Marie Justine Valley. Compiled by Joan Emert Siegert. 1st Ed. Garland, Tex. J. E. Siegert. 1982. (LC)

PETTY – Billingsley, Zora Petty
The Petty and Francis families. Amarillo, Tex. Billingsley. 1967. (DAR)

PETTY – Billingsley, Zora Petty
The Petty and Francis families and allied lines. By Zora Petty Billingsley. Amarillo, Tx. 1967. (LC)

PETTY – Billingsley, Zora P.
The Petty and Francis families and allied lines... By Zora P. Billingsley. Amarillo, Tex., 1967. Supplement No. 1-2 (cor., add. and index). Amarillo, Tex., 1969-71 (FW)

PETTY – Billingsley, Zora Petty
The Petty and Francis Families, with 1969 suppl. Amarillo, Tex. 1967. (NGS)

PETTY – Petty, Alfred M., Mrs.
1881-1981, Petty trees: a memorial. Marquex, Tex. A. M. Petty. [1981]. (LC)

PEYTON – Peyton, M. T.
Peyton-Quirk families. By M. T. Peyton. Midland, Tex. 1968. (LC)

PEYTON. See also: Barksdale   Palmer
                       Beal   Rogers
                       Crossley   Strong
                       Glasswell   Woolsey

PFEIFFER – Pfeiffer, Rudy, 1916-
Memorabilia: our families, mostly Texans. By Rudy & Jane Tarver Pfeiffer. San Antonio, Tex. R. Pfeiffer. 1981, c1982. (LC)

PHELPS – Ellis, Harry H. (Harry Howard), 1914-
The Phelps of Lawson's Bottom and most of their relatives. Compiled by Harry H. Ellis. Dallas, Tex. H. H. Ellis. [c1987]. (LC)

PHELPS – Twidwell, Minnie Beauchamp, 1908-
Historical genealogy of the Phelps fam[i]ly. By Minnie Beauchamp Twidwell. Burnet, Tex. Nortex Press, c1980. (LC)

PHILIPS – Philips, Jere C.
Short history of the Philips-Yarbrough families. Pauls Valley, Okla. R. L. Philips: M. S. Philips. 1928. (DAR)

PHILLIPS – Blalock, Delton D. (Delton Dennis), 1940-
Phillips, Fine, Sandlin, Self families in North Alabama, Texas, Oklahoma, and Arkansas. Compiled by Delton Blalock. 1st Ed. Hanceville, Ala. D. D. Blalock, 1984. (LC)

PHILLIPS – Phillips, John Wesley
Phillips family papers. Fritch, Tex. Phillips. 1978. (DAR)

PHILLIPS – Phillips, John Wesley
A short history of the Phillips family, descendants of Adam Phillips. Fritch, Tex. Phillips. 1976. (DAR)

PHILLIPS – Phillips, Myrtle Hannah
Wesley Ruel Phillips' diary. [S.l.: s.n.]. 1946? (DAR)

PICKENS – Sharp, Eron M.
Pickens families of the South. By Eron M. Sharp. Memphis, 1963. (DP)

PIERCE – Beard, Marjorie Pierce, 1924-
Growing up on Preston Road: a family portrait, 1844-1964. By Marjorie Pierce Beard. 1st Ed. Austin, Tex. Nortex Press. c1989. (LC)

PIERCE – Jantz, Virginia Copeland, 1923-
Pierce, Pace, Hall, Minton, and Huie families. By Virginia Copeland Jantz. Waco, Tex. V. C. Jantz. c1986. (LC)

PIERCE – Jantz, Virginia Copeland
Pierce, Pace, Hall, Minton, and Huie families. Waco, Tex. c1986. (NGS)

PIERCE – Strom, Zelma Hayley, 1903-
The Pearces' pioneering days in Texas. By Zelma (Hayley) Strom. [Menard? Tex.]. Strom. 1976. (LC)

PIERSON – Firebaugh, Vera Pierson
Charlie Pierson and 'Belle Cole'. Odessa, Tex. Forebaugh. 1960? (DAR)

PIERSON – Firebaugh, Vera Pierson
The Pierson and others related by blood or marriage, 1630-1975. Odessa, Tex. Firebaugh. 1975? (DAR)

PIERSON – Firebaugh, Vera J. I. (P.)
Charlie Pierson and Belle Cole; some of their descendants – more of their descendants. By Vera J. I. (P.) Firebaugh. Odessa, Tex? Author, 1962. (FW)

PIERSON – Firebaugh, Verna (P.)
Family Pierson and others related by blood or marriage, 1630-1975. By Verna (P.) Firebaugh. Odessa, Tex., 1975. (FW)

PINKERTON – Chandler, Raymond D. (Raymond Dee), 1926-
Pinkerton's, my journey from yesterday. Compiled by Raymond D. Chandler. Carswell A. F. B., Tex. R. D. Chandler. [1984]. (LC)

PINNELL –
The Pinnell-Royall Family Circle. Mesquite, Tex. (SP)

PIRKLE – Cagle, John A.
The Pirkles and their descendants in the U.S.A. Greenville, Tex. Cagle. c1933. (DAR)

PIRTLE – Pirtle, George W., 1902-
   From whence we came: a personal family biography. By George W. Pirtle, Sr. 1st Ed. Tyler, Tex. Story-Wright. 1976. (LC)

PIRTLE – Pirtle, George W.
   From whence we came: a personal family biography. By George W. Pirtle. 1st Ed. Tyler, Tex. Story-Wright. 1976. (NY)

PITTS – Anderson, Hazel Pitts
   Pitts family in America. San Antonio, Tex. Martin & Allardyce. 1978. (DAR)

PITTS – Anderson, Hazel Pitts, 1900-
   Pitts family in America: addenda. Compiled by Hazel Pitts Anderson. San Antonio, Tex. Martin & Allardyce. 1978, c1979. (LC)

PITTS – Eckhardt, Ura L.
   Pitts family, no. 1-12, 1968-1970. By Ura L. Eckhardt. Houston, Tex. 1970. (FW)

PLANK –
   Life and progress of the Plank pioneers; read at the reunion at Ike Schrocks in Aug. 1900. (LaFeris, Tex., 1926). (FW)

PLANK – Plank, Ezra E.
   Descendants of David H. Plank. By Ezra E. Plank. Canyon, Tex., 1964. (FW)

POINDEXTER – Brown, Dorothy Louise Knox, 1920-
   Lineages and genealogical notes: a compilation of some of the lineages and family lines in the genealogy of Dorothy Louise (Knox) Brown and Dorinda Alice Brown with genealogical notes. By Dorothy Louise (Knox) Brown. 3rd Ed. Dallas, Tex. D. L. K. Brown. 1981. (LC)

POINDEXTER – Landers, John Poindexter
   Poingdestre-Poindexter. Austin, Tex. R. D. Poindexter. 1977. (DAR)

POINDEXTER – Pondexter, R. W.
   Some account of the Poindexter family. 1918. (DAR)

POLK – Polk, Mary (R.)
   I remember... By Mary (R.) Polk. Bluff City, Tex., 1961? (FW)

POLK – Reese, Cynthia Jones, 1938-
   The genealogical study of David Reese: with allied families: Polk, Brevard, Davidson, Caldwell, White, Alexander, McKnitt. Compiled by Cynthia Jones Reese. Wichita Falls, Tex. C. J. Reese. c1990. (LC)

POLK – Schluter, Helen Gomer
   The Thomas Jefferson Felts family of Mississippi and Sabine County, Texas including the Burkett and Polk families. Compiled by Helen Gomer Schluter. Fort Worth, Tex. H. G. Schluter. 1988. (LC)

POLLARD – Geddie, Jack, 1920-
Southern Pollards. By Jack Geddie. Fort Worth, Tex. H. L. Geddie Co. 1971. (LC)

PONDER – Ewald, Annie Laurie
Family of Hezekiah Ponder of Buncombe County, N.C., S.C., Georgia and Texas. (NGS)

PONTIFF – Evans, Norma Pontiff, 1937-
Pontiff paths: 200 years in Louisiana. Compiled and edited by Norma Pontiff Evans; illustrated by Allen J. Pontiff, Jr., Nancy Jo Evans, Norma Pontiff Evans. Beaumont, Tex. N. P. Evans. c1982. (LC)

POPE – Pope, Jennings Bland, 1914-
Pabst, Bobst, Pobst, Pope family in the South. By Jennings Bland Pope. Austin, Tex. Pope. c1978. (LC)

PORTER – Garner, Billie Porter
The Porter cousins and their ancestors. San Antonio, Tex. Garner. c1967. (DAR)

PORTER – Gardner, Billie P.
Porter cousins and their ancestors, Wm. Porter, Isaac Sheldon (and) Amos Richardson. By Billie P. Gardner. San Antonio, Tex. 1967. (SW)

PORTER – Perry, Max, 1919-
The descendants of the Brownfield and Porter families. Compiled and published by Max Perry. Midland, Tex. M. Perry. c1987. (LC)

PORTER – Porter, Homer W., 1900-
A Porter family in America. By Homer W. Porter. Dallas, Tex. H. W. Porter. 1980. (LC)

PORTER – Porter, Homer W.
A Porter family in America. Dallas, Tex. 1980. (NGS)

PORTER – Porter, Mary E.
A family history: William Porter, Jr. of Rockbridge County, Virginia (1740-1804) and five generations of his descendants. Edmond, Okla. 1984. (NGS)

POTTER – Alleman, Helen Potter
Lineages of the children of David Magie Potter, 1851-1933 and Rowen Johnson Teas, 1867-1930. 1941. (DAR)

POWELL – Eckhardt, Ura L.
Powell family, No. 1-6, 1959-1969. By Ura L. Eckhardt. Houston, Tex. 1969. (FW)

PRATT – Shook, Marion, A. H.
Carolina roundup, Kay – Clink – Scales – Pratt and related families. By Marion A. H. Shook. Dallas, Tex. 1965. (FW)

PRESTON – Foster, Gladys E. R.
A record of some of the ancestors of Betty Louise Foster Preston and of the descendants of her great grandparents. By Gladys E. R. Foster. Fort Worth, Tex., 1964. (NY)

PRICE – Price, Carter O.
Genealogy record of the Dazwell Carter Price and Martha Ann (Oliver) Price families from 1825 to 1975. By Carter O. Price. (Rev. to Jan. 31, 1975). Austin, Tex. Price, 1975. (FW)

PRICE – Price, Carter O., 1903-
Supplement to Genealogy record of the Dazwell Carter Price and Martha Ann (Oliver) Price families from 1825 to 1975. Carter O.Price. Austin, Tex. C. O.Price. 1980. (LC)

PRICE – Mitchell, Jewell T.
Price marriages in Collin County, Texas, 1846-1960. By Jewell T. Mitchell. McKinney, Tex., 1961. (FW)

PRICE – Roach, Henry A., 1906-
Levi Lloyd Price, 1842-1920, and descendants. By Henry A. Roach. Glen Rose, Tex. Roach. 1978. (LC)

PRICE – Wilson, R. B. (Rena Beth), 1940-
My family, Shields, Price, McKenzie, Lewis... By R. B. Wilson. Rockport, Tex. R. B. Wilson. c1990. (LC)

PRIMROSE – Bryant, Bertie Primrose, 1927-
Primrose: forks of the rivers folks. By Bertie Primrose Bryant. Burnet, Tex. Nortex Press. c1981. (LC)

PRINCE – Prince, Fay H.
Prince is the name; the genealogy of 2 brothers (Jesse & Zachariah) and their descendants. By Fay H. Prince. Irving, Tex. J. H. Prince. 1968. (FW)

PRITCHARD – Symmonds, Dorothy
A history and genealogy of the Pritchett, Rimmer, Jacobs, Hamilton, Eldridge, Etheridge, Smith, Brown, and Davidson families from North Carolina, Tennessee, Illinois, Missouri, and Kansas in the early 1800s to 1900s. By Dorothy Symmonds. Bellaire, Tex. D. Symmonds. c1985—c1989. (LC)

PUCKETT – Peyton, Sue E. (P.)
Thomas Puckett (1792-1868) of Travis County, Republic of Texas (his ancestors and descendants). By Sue E. (P.) Peyton. Houston, Tex., 1955. (FW)

PUGH – Heard, Ida Mae Pou, 1910-
John Pou III and his descendants, 1788-1988. By Ida Mae Pou Heard; illustrated by the pen art of Jesse Grace Pou. Tenaha, Tex. Ida Mae Pou Heard. c1988. (LC)

PUMMILL – Lang, Dorothy Elizabeth, 1912-
My genealogical story: Lang-Rowe-Pummill-Loomis and related families. By Dorothy Elizabeth Lang. [United States: s.n., 1987]. (LC)

PURIFOY – Rose, Floretta Purifoy, 1918-
Henry Marshall Purifoy genealogy: ancestry and descendants of Henry Marshall Purifoy of Quachita County, Arkansas. Compiled and edited by Floretta Purifoy Rose. Texarkana, Tex. F. P. Rose, 1981. (LC)

PYBURN – Morrow, Betty Moss
Piborn/Pyborn/Pyburn family. Compiled by Betty Moss Chaney Morrow. Teague, Tex. B.M.C. Morrow. c1990. (LC)

Q –

QUACKENBUSH – Quackenbush, Gail Richard, 1950-
The Quackenbush family in America. By Gail Richard Quackenbush. Wolfe City, Tex. Henington Pub. Co. Dallas, Tex. G. R. Quackenbush. c1987. (LC)

QUINN – O'Quinn, D. P. (Dallas Patrick), 1921-
The O'Quinns, Ireland to Texas. By D. P. O'Quinn. Austin, Tex. D. P. O'Quinn. c1981. (LC)

QUINN – Quinn, Peter Wiley, 1889-1971-
Family history of Patrick (Peter) Quinn (1760-1800) and Esther (Martin) Quinn (1765-1810), Cork, County Cork, Ireland, married about 1782. Original records compiled by Peter Wiley Quinn (1889-1971); edited and rev., Mary Eleanor Williams, 1972-1973. [S.l.: s.n.]. c1973. (LC)

QUINN – Quinn, Vera Jones
Shamrocks to bluebonnets: the William Quinn Family. Compiled by Vera Jones Quinn. Burnet, Tex. Nortex Press. c1981. (LC)

R –

RADCLIFFE – Debenport, Jane Clancy, 1935-
The descendants of Joseph Ratcliff of Bienville Parish, Louisiana: including the families of Jeter, Wimberly, Davis, Dubberly, Wood, Hardy, Carmichael, Mathews, Norris, McKinney. Compiled by Jane Clancy Debenport. Midland, Tex. J. C. Debenport. c1988. (LC)

RAGSDALE – Lemons, Nova A.
Through the orchard. Supplement: Arterberry, Hillsberry, Lemons, Ragsdale. By Nova A. Lemons. Dallas, Tex. N. A., Lemons. c1990. (LC)

RAINES – Rhine, Nanneitta Raines, 1894-1979-
The saga of the little red chair. As told by Nanneitta Raines Rhine; co-author, Mary Sue R. Moseley; illustrations, Carolyn Munoz Harney and Nita Moseley Munoz. 2nd Ed. El Paso, Tex? M. S. R. Moseley. 1982. (LC)

RAINES – Threatt, Fredna R.
...and the Rains fame. By Fredna R. Threatt. Dallas, 1967. (NY)

RALEIGH – Marsh, Carl James, 1927-
Raleigh and related families. By Carl James Marsh. Tyler, Tex. C & L Publications. c1988. (LC)

RAMSEY – Ramsey, James Thomas
Genealogy of the Ramsey family in the Southern United States, 1740-1962. By James Thomas Ramsey. Houston, Tex. 1962. (LC)

RAMSEY. See also: Douglas
                      Fulton
                      Harrison
                      Phipps

RAMSEY – Ramsey, James Thomas, Jr.
The Ramseys of Edgefield; Samuel and Ealanor Ramsey of Edgefield County, South Carolina, and their descendants. Compiled and edited by James T. Thomas Ramsey, Jr. Houston? Tex., c1971. (LC)

RANDOLPH – Eckhardt, Ura L.
Randolph family notes, no. 1-2, 1965-1970. By Ura L. Eckhardt. Houston, Tex. 1970. (FW)

RANUZZI – Wells, Maria Xenia Zevelechi
The Ranuzzi manuscripts. Selected and described by Maria Xenia Zevellechi Wells. Austin. Humanities Research Center, University of Texas. c1980. (LC)

RANZAU – Wisseman, Charles L.
Ludwig Ranzau family. By Charles L. Wisseman. Kerrville? Tex. 1972. (FW)

RAWSON – Ball, Greg, 1962-
Family charts of the Cozby, Skeen, Walker, Rawson, Brumbelow, and Smith families. Compiled and indexed by Greg Ball. 2nd Ed. San Antonio, Tex. G. Ball. 1989. (LC)

RAY –
Newsletter. V. 1-2; Sept. 1973 – June, 1976. Joseph and Mary Ray Runions. Dallas, Tex. (NY)

RAY – Raguzin, Sue Nite, 1918-
The Ray/Robbins families: Texas pioneers. By Sue Nite Raguzin. Dickinson, Tex. S. N. Raguzin. 1986. (LC)

RAY – Tallant, Louise
    Rays then and now, 1635-1986. Editor and publisher, Louise Tallant. Purdon, Tex. L. Tallant. 1986. (LC)

RAYBURN – Eckhardt, Ura L.
    Rayburn family, no. 1-7, 1961-1970. By Ura L. Eckhardt. Houston, Tex. 1970. (FW)

READ – Key, Della Tyler
    Two Baptist pioneer preachers of Texas and their genealogy. By Della Tyler Key. (n.p., 1939?). (LC)

REDFERN – Pells, Louise Redfern, 1908-
    The Francis Redfearn family: a story of the family of Francis Redfearn (1777-1858), his wife, Ruth Milner (1779-1857), and their three sons and their daughters. By Louise Redfern Pells. Baltimore: Gateway Press. Corpus Christi, Tex. Mrs. H. W. Pells [distributor]. 1982. (LC)

REED –
    The Reed family in central Texas. [S.1.: s.n.] 1947? (DAR)

REED –
    The Reed family in central Texas. ?Austin, Tex. 1947. (NGS)

REED –
    The Reed family in Central Texas; a memorial on the marking of the graves of Michael and Martha Burnett Reed, July 13, 1947. Austin? 1947. (LC)

REED – Wynne, Robert L.
    Ancestry and descendants of Peter Hon Reed and Sarah E. Hon. Dr. & Mrs. Robert L. Wynne. Houston, Tex. R. L. Wynne. 1982? (LC)

REES – Eckhardt, Ura L.
    Our ancestor, Rev. Isham Reese of Dinwiddie Co., Va. and Jones Co., Ga. No. 1-7, 1960-1969. By Ura L. Eckhardt. Houston, Tex. 1969. (FW)

REESE – Reese, Cynthia Jones, 1938-
    The genealogical study of David Reese: with allied families: Polk, Brevard, Davidson, Caldwell, White, Alexander, McKnitt, Bradley. Compiled by Cynthia Jones Reese. Wichita Falls, Tex. C. J. Reese. c1990. (LC)

REESE – Reese, Jon O. (Jon Otie), 1940-
    Hope for a better age: from Wales to America with descendants of David Reese. By John O. Reese & Cynthia Jones Reese. Wichita Falls, Tex. J. O. Reese & C. J. Reese. c1987. (LC)

REESE – Reese, Rebecca Jean Ashley
    The lineage of Rebecca Jean Ashley Reese. Houston, Tex. Reese. 1975? (DAR)

REEVE – Peacock, Ruby Leona Henderson, 1925-
Twigs and branches from the Archer-Harper-Henderson-Reeves family tree. By Ruby Leona Henderson Peacock. Roaring Springs, Tex. R.L.H. Peacock. 1984? (LC)

REEVE – Reeves, Jonathan F.
The Reeves review. Comp. by a few descendants of William Reeves of Granville County, N.C., 1690-1751. Ed. By Jonathan F. Reeves. Lufkin, Tex. Pineywood Prt. 1976. (FW)

REEVES – Wood, Christine (K.)
Those Reeves girls; a study of the descendants of five sisters, with some descendants of each sister to present time, as many as nine generations. By Christine (K.) Wood. Lubbock, Tex. 1973. (FW)

REEVES – Wood, Christine Knox
Those Reeves Girls. Lubbock, Tex. 1973. (NGS)

RENCHER –
Rencher genealogy. Compiled by John Preston Rencher. By Evelyn McAbee Rencher. San Antonio, Tex. 1971. (LC)

RENEAU – Eckhardt, Ura L.
Reneau-Reno family, no. 1-2, 1961-1970. By Ura L. Eckhardt. Houston, Tex. 1970. (FW)

RENFREW –
William Renfro, 1734-1830; some descendants, relatives, and allied families. Collected and compiled by Josie Baird and Delila Baird. Rotan, Trex., 1973. (LC)

RENFREW – Renfro, Roy E. (Roy Edward), 1945-
Renfro revelations & relations. By Dr. & Mrs. Roy E. Renfro, Jr. Sherman, Tex. R. E. Renfro. 1980. (LC)

RENFRO – Baird, Josie
William Renfro, 1734-1830. Rotan, Tex. Baird: Baird. 1973. (DAR)

RENWICK –Renick, Dorothy Waties
Leaves, an ancestral chart. By Dorothy Waties Renick (Luttrell). Waco, Tex. Renick, c1980. (LC)

REUTHER – Toney, Virginia Lee Sims, 1927-
The Reuter/Riter family of Germany and Wetzel County, Virginia/West Virginia. By Virginia Lee Sims Toney. Houston, Tex. V.L.S. Toney. c1988. (LC)

REYNOLDS – Reynolds, Everette
Family records for Reynolds, Chatfield, Vines, Sapp. Houston, Tex. Reynolds:Reynolds. 1971. (DAR)

REYNOLDS –
The Reynolds Family Association, 1892-1976-1982: historical and genealogical collection. Compiled and edited by Linwood A. and Marcia Hurst Smith in conjunction

with and assisted by Dorothy Jellinghaus and Albert Rebholz. El Paso, Tex. M.H.S. Micro Data. c1983. (LC)

REYNOLDS – Strock, Richard M., 1915-
Some Strock, Harbaugh,, Funk, and Reynolds families of Washington and Frederick Counties, Maryland, and of Franklin County, Pennsylvania: including some descendants in Colorado, Illinois, Kansas, Michigan, Missouri, Ohio, Texas, etc.: organized around the direct and collateral lineage of the authors (brothers), with direct lineage extending back to the immigrants. Richard M. Strock and Robert F. Strock. Cincinnati, Ohio. R. B. Strock. 1988. (LC)

REYNOLDS – Wilson, Laura, 1939-
Watt Matthews of Lambshead. Photographs and text by Laura Wilson; introduction by David McCullough. Austin, Tex. Texas State Historical Association. c1989. (LC)

RHEIN – Rhine, Nannneitta Raines, 1894-1979-
The saga of the little red chair. As told by Nanneitta Raines Rhine; co-author, Mary Sue R. Moseley; illustrations, Carolyn Munoz Harney and Nita Moseley Munoz. 2nd Ed. El Paso, Tex.? M.S.R. Moseley. 1982. (LC)

RHODES – Haack, Robert D. (Robert David), 1961-
A genealogy and kinology of the paternal history, Jerri Gayle Rodin. Written and edited by Robert D. Haack. Corpus Christi, Tex. R. D. Haack. c1983. (LC)

RHODES – Trant, Velma Toades
Memoirs of my ancestry; genealogy of Valentine Roads and related families: Davis Miller, Keplinger, Neyswanger. By Velma Toades Trant. Kendleton, Tex. Bay Ridge Press. c1972. (LC)

RHODES – Williams, Elizabeth Lewis Mitchell, 1903-
The family of Myra Rhodes. By Elizabeth Lewis Mitchell Williams. Dallas, Tex. E.L.M. Williams. c1986. (LC)

RICE – Rice, Clyde, 1903
Nordi's gift. Clyde Rice. Portland, Ore. Breitenbush Books; Dallas, Tex. Distributed by Taylor Pub. Co., 1990. (LC)

RICE – Turner, Dean W.
From Normandy to Texas, 1066 to 1876 A.D. [S.1.] Turner, 1972? (DAR)

RICH – Hogan, Julia Rich
William Rich (Richee) Sr. Houston, Tex. Rich Family Association. 1968. (DAR)

RICHARDSON – Huey, N. L. R.
Richardson family. By N. L. R. Huey. Lufkin, Tex., 1965. (FW)

RICHESON – Ingram, Mary Richeson
Listen to the Bell. Bay City, Tex. Brock Printing. 1979. (DAR)

RIDDLE – Riddle, William M.
The first William Riddle: our ancestors in perspective with the history surrounding each generation. Tulsa, Okla. c1982. (NGS)

RIEKE –Jones, Wayne V., 1902-
The Rieke family of Bavenhausen and America: including chapters on the German families of Stapperfenne, Heger, Linneweber, Wehrman, Lehmeyer, Sandmeyer, Meyer, Bunte, Brockhausen, Ludeke-Saak, Freytag, Prussner, and Kluckhohn, with extensive accounts of their descendants in America named Rieke Kluckhohn, Hauswirth, Prussner, and Kappes and lesser accounts of many other families. Compiled by Wayne V. Jones. Houston, Tex. D. Armstrong Co., 1979. (LC)

RIGBY – Boyd, Margie Milner
Rigsby relatives and related families, Shephard, Foster, Lawson: Virginia, North Carolina, Georgia, Texas, 1693-1900s: also Barclay, Bean, Burke... By Margie Milner Boyd. Port Arthur, Tex. M. M. Boyd. 1986. (LC)

RIGBY – Rigsby, Michael H. (Michael Hall), 1935-
The ancestry of Laura Elaine Rigsby. Michael H. Rigsby, Carolyn E. Rigsby. Houston, Tex. M. H. Rigsby: C. E. Rigsby. c1987. (LC)

RIMMER – Perry, Max, 1919-
Descendants of Mary Remer and Rev. John Simpson and the Remer and Strait families. Compiled by Max Perry. Midland, Tex. M. Perry. c1989. (LC)

RIMMER – Symmonds, Dorothy
A history and genealogy of the Pritchett, Rimmer, Jacobs, Hamilton, Eldridge, Etheridge, Smith, Brown, and Davidson families from North Carolina, Tennessee, Illinois, Missouri, and Kansas in the early 1800s to 1900s. By Dorothy Symmonds. Bellaire, Tex. S. Symmonds. c1985-c1989. (LC)

RINEHART –Willingham, Lois Glenn Maberry, 1920-
Reinhardt-Shuford, Warlick-Hoyle lineage (1700-1979). By Lois Glenn Maberry Willingham. Dallas, Tex. Suburban Tribune, 1979. (LC)

RITCHIE – Jarboe, Mary Ritchie, 1923-
Ritchie/Shelledy family history: our people who came to Kansas Territory in 1855, John Ritchie and Mary Jane Shelledy, his wife. Richardson, Tex. M. R. Jarboe. 1984. (LC)

ROACH –
A Roach family history: James and Malinda McConnell Roach and their descendants. Compiled by Frank W. and Ruth D. Roach Medley. Lubbock, Tex. Kells. 1974. (LC)

ROACH – Medley, Frank W.
A Roach family history: James and Melinda McConnell Roach and their descendants. Also by Ruth R. Medley. Lubbock, Tex. 1974. (NGS)

ROACH – Perry, Max, 1919-
The descendants of the Roach family of York County, South Carolina: including allied families and genealogical briefs of Drennan, Springs, Workman, Hanna, Harris, Thomasson, McConnell, Sturgis, Reid, Edwards, Dodds, Polk, Latham. Compiled and published by Max Perry. Midland, Tex. M. Perry. c1983. (LC)

ROACH –
Luke Roach and his descendants, Va., N.C., Tenn., Miss., and Tex., 1787-197? Compilers, Virginia Roach Brooks, Elizabeth Roach Kotte, Rachel Tate Smith; edited by Rachel Tate Smith. Albany, Tex. Smith. c1975. (LC)

ROACH – Roach, Arminta Roach
Roach family history. Compiled by Arminta Roach Roach. Apple Springs, Tex. A. R. Roach. 1988. (LC)

ROADES – Trant, Velma Roades
Memoirs of my ancestry. Kendleton, Tex. Bay Ridge Press. 1972. (DAR)

ROARK – Roark, Morris L.
The Roarks (O'Rourke) of Ireland; a short history of the Roarks in Ireland and pedigree of the Nathan Roark family in America. By Morris L. Roark. San Antonio, Tex., 1950. (NY)

ROBINETT – Robinett, James M.
Allen Robinett and his descendants in America. By James M. Robinett. Beaumont, Tex. J. M. Robinett, 1967-70. (FW)

ROBBINS – Eckhardt, Ura L.
Robbins family, no. 1-3, 1957-1967. By Ura L. Eckhardt. Houston, Tex. 1970. (FW)

ROBBINS – Pearson, Ralph E.
Robbins family history. By Ralph E. Pearson. Austin, Tex. (n.d.). (FW)

ROBBINS – Raguzin, Sue Nite, 1918-
The Ray/Robbins family: Texas pioneers. By Sue Nite Raguzin. Dickinson, Tex. S. N. Raguzin. 1986. (LC)

ROBBINS – Robbins, Eugene W. (Eugene Weldon), 1925-
Robbins/McGuffey family history. By Eugene W. Robbins. Spicewood, Tex. E. W. Robbins. 1990. (LC)

ROBERTS – Roberts, Emily Griffith
Ancestral study of four families. Terrell, Tex. Roberts. 1939. (DAR)

ROBERTSON –
William Crockett Robertson: ancestors-descendants & related families. Frank Allen Robertson... [et al.]; compiler, Frank Allen Robertson. Houston, Tex. F. and K. Robertson. c1984. (LC)

ROBINETT – Robinet, James M.
Allen Robinett and his descendants in America. Beaumont, Tex. Robinett. 1967-1968. (DAR)

ROBINSON – Edwards, William Hopple
Ancestors of John Edwin Robinson and his sister Stella Adolphus Robinson of Alabama, Louisiana and Texas. Meriden, Conn. Edwards. 1957. (DAR)

ROBINSON – Edwards, William H.
Ancestors of John Robinson... of Ala., La., and Texas. By William H. Edwards. Meriden? Conn., 1956-7. (SL)

ROBINSON – Keith, Alice E. (R.)
Hugh Robinson of Scotland and his descendants in America and allied families. By Alice E. (R.) Keith. Fort Worth, Tex., 1936. (FW)

ROBINSON – Long, Elsie Viola Robinson
This Robinson line. Austin, Tex. Austin Printing Co. 1971. (DAR)

ROBINSON – Long, E. Viola Robinson
This Robinson line, 1468-1938. By E. Viola Robinson Long. 1st Ed. Austin, Tex. Printed by Austin Print. Co. 1971. (LC)

ROBINSON – Long, Elsie Viola Robinson
This Robinson line, 1468-1938. Austin, Tex. 1971. (NGS)

ROEBUCK – Crain, Betty Fay Griffin, 1933-
The Roebuck and Spring clans. Researched and compiled by Betty Fay Griffin Crain. Limited Ed. [Texas?] B.F.G. Crain. c1981. (LC)

ROGERS – Russell, Vera Rogers
My family history: 1500 to 1966. By Vera Rogers Russell. Tyler, Tex. Robert M. Rogers. 1967? (LC)

ROGERS – Skelton, Helen Rogers, 1917-
Rogers-Skelton and allied families. By Helen Rogers Skelton and Clarence C. Skelton. Baltimore: Gateway Press. Burkeville, Tex. M. & C. C. Skelton [distributors]. 1987. (LC)

ROHDE –
The family history of Gottfried & Eduard Rohde and their descendants from Aug. 1824 to September 1970, from Comal County Courthouse and family records and recollections, the heritage and tradition of freedom loving pioneers. San Antonio, Tex. Tower Litho. 1970? (LC)

ROHDE – Halm, Gilbert
Family history of Gottfried and Eduard Rohde and their descendants; from August 1824 to Sept. 1970, from Comal County Courthouse and family records... By Gilbert Halm. San Antonio, Tex. Tower Litho. 1970. (FW)

ROMERO – Seymour, Geneva Bailey
Romero, some Romero descendants. By Geneva Bailey Seymour. Lubbock, Tex. G. B. Seymour. c1981. (LC)

ROQUEMORE – Huffaker, Josephine Costello
The Roquemore report of 1967. Dallas, Tex. Huffaker. 1967. (DAR)

ROQUEMORE – Pochman, Virginia Ruth Fouts
Some early Texas families: Roquemore, Lacey, Fouts, Pochmann, Burrows, and one hundred and fifty related families; a genealogy. By Virginia Ruth Fouts Pochman. Madison, Wisc. 1942. (LC)

ROSEBROUGH – Eckhardt, Ura L.
Rosebrough family, no. 1-3, 1955-1970. By Ura L. Eckhardt. Houston, Tex. 1970. (FW)

ROSENBERG – Froelich, Reinhold
Emigration of the von Rosenbergs of Texas, 1849. By Reinhold Froelich. Austin, Tex. W. Wupperman, 1938. (NY)

ROUNTREE – Rountree, Joseph Gustave
Rowntree and Rountree family history, 1521-1953. By Joseph Gustave Rountree. Beeville? Tex. 1959. (LC)

ROUSE –
The Alexander Rouse family, 1829-1964 (135 years). Including the descendants of Alexander Rouse and Eveline Jamison of Pennsylvania... and related families of Shoop, Schmittel, Berrier, Umbrell, Shafer, Culbertson, Brumbaugh, Baxter, Zielstra, Madsen, Eaton, Grice, Johnson, Ferguson, Vaugh, Hackenberry, Bush, Willhide, Tarrant, Northcraft, Quilling, Drill, Flasher, Downin, Howell, Ridley and many others. Taylor, Tex. 1964? (PH)

ROUSH – Sheddrick, Stella Pauline Bartz, 1929-
From wild root: a history of Carl Freidrich [sic] Bartz and his wife Henrietta Charlotte Justine Raasch. By Stella Pauline Bartz Sheddrick. San Antonio, Tex. S.P.B. Sheddrick. 1986. (LC)

ROUTH – Routh, Ross H.
Stephen Routh (1797-1871) and some descendants. El Paso, Tex. Routh. 1980. (DAR)

ROUTH – Routh, Ross Holland
The Routh family in America. El Paso, Tex. Routh. 1976. (DAR)

ROUTH – Routh, Ross Holland
Routh family revisited. El Paso, Tex. Routh. 1978. (DAR)

ROUTH – Routh, Ross H.
The Routh family in America: a genealogy. By Ross H. Routh. El Paso, Tex. Routh. 1976. (FW)

ROWE – Rowe, H. A.
Christopher Rowe family of Iowa. By H. A. Rowe. Houston, Tex., 1963. (FW)

ROYAL – Ayres, Mildred Royal, 1920-
Royal-Brown heritage: with genealogical notes of related families. Mildred Royal Ayres and Frances Royal Foley. Austin, Tex. Nortex Press. c1984. (LC)

ROYALL – Pinnell, R. E.
Royall family of America. By R. E. Pinnell. Dallas, Tex? 1961. (FW)

RUCKER – Rucker, William Robert, 1917-
Rucker and Edwards heritages: a compendium of genealogical sketches and history of the families and related lines: Baird, Batte, Bostick, Bridgewater, Cunningham, Jennings, Leckey, McDougal, Shackelford. Compiled by William Robert Rucker. Dallas, Tex. W. R. Rucker. 1983. (LC)

RUDD – Youngblood, Margaret Rudd, 1912-1978-
Rudd-Pollard-Youngblood and related families: Crisp. Compiled by Margaret Rudd Youngblood; edited by Loretta Elliott Burns. Houston, Tex. Mrs. J. W. Conrad. 1980? (LC)

RUDEL – Bailey, Janet, 1940-
Ancestors and descendants of Leonard Rudel and Mary Elizabeth Lantzer. By Janet (Moore) Bailey and Gordon B. Knight. Irving, Tex. J. M. Bailey. c1987. (LC)

RUGELEY – Allen, Arda (Talbot)
Twenty-one sons of Texas. By Arda (Talbot) Allen. Limited Ed. San Antonio, Tex. Naylor Co. 1959. (LC)

RUHMANN – Ruhmann, Dorothy Beasley, 1914-
Ruhmann roots, limbs, and branches. By Dorothy Beasley Ruhmann. Arkansas Pass, Tex. Biography Press; Portland, Tex. c1983. (LC)

RUMPH – Zachry, Juanita Daniel
This man David – a Southern planter. By Juanita Daniel Zachry. Abilene, Tex. Quality Print. Co. 1971. (LC)

RUSS – Russ, Herbert M.
Russ family genealogy. Teague, Tex. Russ. 1973? (DAR)

RUSS – Russ, Herbert M.
Russ family genealogy. By Herbert M. Russ. Teague, Tex. 1973? (FW)

RUSS – Russ, Herbert M., 1919-
Russ family genealogy. Compiled by Herbert M. Russ. Teague, Tex. Russ. [1973?]. 1989. (LC)

RUSSELL – Russell, Lyman Brightman
Genealogy of the Russell family. By Lyman Brightman Russell. San Antonio, Tex. Naylor Co. 1959. (LC)

RUSSELL – Russell, Lyman B.
Genealogy of the Russell family. By Lyman B. Russell. Comanche? Tex., 1937. (NY)

RUSSELL – Spencer, Elma D. (R.)
Green Russell and gold. By Elma D. (R.) Spencer. Austin, University of Texas. 1966. (FW)

RUSSEY – Russey, George Sirrine
The Russey family in America. San Antonio, Tex. J. W. Russey. 1970. (DAR)

RUSSEY – Russey, George Sirrine
The Russey family in America; a genealogy of James Russey, 1755-1962. By George Sirrine Russey. Edited and published by John Wesley Russey, Jr. San Antonio, Tex. 1963. (LC)

- **A supplement of additions and corrections to a genealogy of James Russey.** Edited and published by John Wesley Russey, Jr. San Antonio, 1967. (LC)

RUSSEY – Russey, George Sirrine
The Russey family in America; a genealogy of James Russey, 1755-1970. By George Sirrine Russey. Rev., enl., edited, and published by John Wesley Russey, Jr. 2nd Ed. San Antonio, Tex. 1970. (LC)

RUST – Rust, Albert D.
Record of the Rust family. Waco, Tex. Rust. 1891. (DAR)

RUST – Rust, Albert D.
Record of the Rust family: embracing the descendants of Henry Rust, who came from England and settled in Hingham, Mass. 1634-1635. By Albert D. Rust. Waco, Tex. The Author. 1891. (LC)

RUST – Smith, Agnes Rust Gordon
Back when and now. San Angelo, Tex. Smith. 1976. (DAR)

RUST – Smith, Agnes R. G.
Back when and now: history of the family of Agnes Rust Gordon Smith. By Agnes R. G. Smith. San Angelo, Tex. Smith. 1976. (NY)

RUST – Smith, Agnes Rust Gordon, 1905-
Back when and now: history of the family of Agnes Rust Gordon Smith. San Angelo, Tex. Smith. c1976. (LC)

RUST – Smith, Agnes (Rust) Gordon
Back when and now; history of the family of Agnes Rust Gordon Smith. San Angelo, Tex. 1976. (NGS)

RUTH – Routh, Ross Holland, 1907-
Our Routh family: descendants of Jacob Routh (1745-1827). Compiled and published by Ross Holland Routh. El Paso, Tex. R. H. Routh. 1983. (LC)

RUTH – Routh, Ross Holland, 1907-
   The Routh family in America: a genealogy. Compiled and edited by Ross Holland Routh. El Paso, Tex. Routh. 1976. (LC)

RUTH – Routh, Ross Holland, 1907-
   Routh family revisited: a genealogy. Compiled and edited by Ross H. Routh. El Paso, Tex. Routh. 1978. (LC)

RUTH –Routh, Ross Holland, 1907-
   Stephen Routh (1797-1871) and some descendants: a genealogy. Compiled and published by Ross H. Routh. El Paso, Tex. R. H. Routh. 1980. (LC)

RUTHERFORD –
   The family Rutherford and kin. By Lizzie Finch Rutherford and Hobart Key, Jr. Marshall, Tex. Port Caddo Trading Co. 1963? (LC)

RUTHERFORD. See also:
Bard	Lewen
Bingham	Long
Clarkson	Thomas
Harkness	

RYAN – Ryan, Alexander Boggs
   A biography of Thomas Ryan and his descendants. Longview, Tex. Ryan. 1955. (DAR)

RYKER – Ryker, Kenneth W.
   Ryker family history and genealogy. By Kenneth W. Ryker. Fort Worth, Tex., 1971. (NY)

S –

SACK – Eckhardt, Ura L.
   Sack family, no. 1, 1965-1969. By Ura L. Eckhardt. Houston, Tex. 1969. (FW)

SADLER – Eckhardt, Ura L.
   Sadler family, no. 1. By Ura L. Eckhardt. Houston, Tex. 1970. (FW)

SAGER – Boehl, Beverly
   Koehler, Dreier, Sager, Rath, Thieme, and Boehl families: a genealogical delineation of German immigrants in DeWitt County, Texas. By Beverly Boehl; edited by Judith Koehler Ludvigsen. Garland, Tex. B. Boehl. c1986. (LC).

SALE – Mothershead, Harriet Godwin, 1916-
   My Sayles kith and kin. By Harriet Godwin Mothershead. Dallas, Tex. H. G. Mothershead. c1981. (LC)

SAMPLE – Franklin, Frances Sample
   The ancestry of Frances Sample Franklin. Wolfe City, Tex. Henington Pub. Co. 1972. (DAR)

SANCHEZ NAVARRO – Harris, Charles H. (Charles Houston)
   A Mexican family empire, the latifundio of the Sanchez Navarros, 1765-1867. Charles H. Harris III. Austin: University of Texas Press. 1975. (LC)

SANDIFER – Trickett, Annie Sandifer
   Sandifer: line of John D. Sandifer, c1783-1854, Johnson P. Sandifer, c1796-1866, Joseph Sandifer, 1800-1871, Joshua A. Sandifer, 1797-1882, Peter Sandifer, 1771-1844, William Nightingale Sandifer, 1760-1850, William V. Sandifer, 1792-1870 or later, and others. Compiled by (with the help of many others) Annie Sandifer Trickett. Dallas, Tex. A. S. Trickett. c1982. (LC)

SANDLIN – Sandlin, Dale S.
   The Sandlin clan. By Dale S. Sandlin. Jones Creek, Tex. 1970. (LC)

SAUNDERS – Sanders, R. S., 1921-
   Ancestors and descendants of Henry Simeon Saunders. By R. S. Sanders. [S.1.: s.n]. 1983. (McAllen, Tex: Rio Valley Pub. Co.). (LC)

SAUTER – Sartor, A. F. (Albin Francis), 1919-
   A Sartor-Shults family history. By A. F. Sartor, Jr. Pearland, Tex. A. F. Sartor, Jr. c1989. (LC)

SAWYER – Hughes, Dorothy Dillard
   Our Hughes ancestors: a story of searches and discoveries, including maternal lines of Varvel, Ewing, Huntzinger, Sawyer, Brown, Hale/Haile, Craghead, and lists of descendants. By Dorothy Dillard Hughes. Lubbock, Tex. D. D. Hughes. c1989. (LC)

SCARBOROUGH – Scarborough, Jewel Davis
   Major James Scarborough, his ancestors and descendants. Abilene, Tex. Scarborough. c1957. (DAR)

SCARBOROUGH – Scarborough, Jewel (Davis)
   Southern kith and kin; a record of my children's ancestors. By Jewel (Davis) Scarborough. Abilene, Tex. Printed by Abilene Print Co. 1951-57. (LC)

SCARBOROUGH. See also:	Davis	Ruder
	Haworth	Snyder
	Kirk	Waples
	Pearson	Wise

SCHAERDEL – Clark, Robert M. (Robert Murel), 1948-
   The Schaerdel family of Dallas County, Texas. By Robert M. Clark, Jr. Dallas, Tex. R. M. Clark. c1981. (LC)

SCHLITTLER – Steger, Mel
A Seger-Schlittler-Mahlandt history. Book prepared by Mel Steger. Houston, Tex. M. Steger. 1986. (LC)

SCHMIDT – Schmidt, Rudolph, 1913-
Genealogy of the George and Anna Schmidt family, 1843-1990. By Rudolph Schmidt. 3rd Ed. Pearland, Tex. R. Schmidt. c1990. (LC)

SCHMINCKE – Newell, Millie Snellbaker, 1937-
Millie's memo's[sic] of Schmincke, Snellbaker families. Lumberton, Tex. M. S. Newell. c1990. (LC)

SCHRAPFER – Steger, Mel
A Schrapfer-Hoch history. Houston, Tex. M. Steger, 1985. (LC)

SCHUESSLER – Bohmfalk, Johnita Schuessler
John Adam and Eva Schuessler: pioneers in Texas. By Johnita Schuessler Bohmfalk. Mason, Tex. J. S. Bohmfalk. 1984. (LC)

SCHULTZ – Durbin, Joan Schulte, 1940-
Willibald-Schulte descendants. By Joan Schulte Durbin; (June Lange collected Anthony & Paul Schulte's). Dimmitt. Tex. J. Durbin. c1981. (LC)

SCHULTZ – Sartor, A. F. (Albin Francis), 1919-
A Sartor-Shults family history. By A. F. Sartor, Jr. Pearland, Tex. A. F. Sartor, Jr. c1989. (LC)

SCHWARTZ – Fierman, Floyd S.
The Schwartz family of El Paso: the story of a pioneer Jewish family in the Southwest. By Floyd S. Fierman. El Paso, Tex. Texas Western Press. c1980. (LC)

SCHWARTZ – Guthrie, Martha Dee Schwartz, 1913-
Our kin – past and present, the Schwartz family. By Martha Dee Schwartz Guthrie. Limited Ed. Dallas, Tex. M. D. S. Guthrie. 1983. (LC)

SCHWARTZ – Guthrie, Martha Dee Schwartz
Our kin-past and present, the Schwartz family. Dallas, Tex. 1983. (NGS)

SCOGGINS – Scoggins, J. Arthur
From Saddle to pulpit. By J. Arthur Scoggins. Dallas, Tex. Wilkinson. 1952. (FW)

SCOTT – Alter, Judy, 1938-
Thistle Hill: the history and the house. By Judy Alter; forward by Lloyd "Cissy" Stewart; illustrations by Barbara Whitehead. Fort Worth: Texas Christian University Press. c1988. (LC)

SCOTT – DeVerter, Ruth Hendricks
The genealogy of the Scott and Galloway families. Baytown, Tex. DeVerter. c1959. (DAR)

SCOTT –DeVerter, Ruth H.
John Scott, Sr. family of Bourbon County, Ky., and Wayne County, Ind. By Ruth H. DeVerter. Baytown, Tex. (n.d.). (FW)

SCOTT – Scott, Mary Rebecca Dulany
A history and genealogical record of the Agrippa Scott family from 1804-1984. By Mary Rebecca (Dulaney) Scott. Tomball, Tex. M.R.D. Scott. c1985. (LC)

SCOTT –
History of the Silas H. Scott family, 1839-1956. Compiled by Olin S. Hockaday and Mrs. Pierce Johnson. Commerce? Tex. 1956. (LC)

SCOTT – Wiese, O'Levia Neil Wilson, 1928-
William Scott of Fairfield County [sic], South Carolina and his descendants. By O'Levia Neil Wilson Wiese. Waco, Tex. O'L. N. W. Wiese. c1987. (LC)

SEAL – Kuehl, Nany L. (Nancy Louise), 1947-
A Seale anthology. By Nancy L. Kuehl. [S.l.]. Twin City Pub. Co. Nacogdoches, Tex. N. L. Kuehl. 1985. (LC)

SEAL – Wilson, Stephen R. (Stephen Ray), 1938-
Our Seales. By Stephen R. Wilson. [Texas]. S. R. Wilson. 1985. (LC)

SEALE – Seale, Ida C.
Seale and allied families. By Ida C. Seale. Houston, Tex. Mrs. Irl Allen Letter Services. 1944. (LA)

SEBRING – Parsons, N. Vincent
Addendum to Sebring Collections. El Paso, Tex. Parsons and Parsons. 1976. (DAR)

SEBRING – Parsons, N. Vincent
Sebring collections. By Walter W. Sebring. Addendum by N. Vincent Parsons. El Paso, Tex. 1975. (FW)

SEBRING – Parsons, N. Vincent (Nahum Vincent), 1904-1977-
Addendum to Sebring collection. Compiled, edited by N. Vincent Parsons and Margaret P. Parsons. El Paso, Tex. Parsons. 1976.

SEBRING – Sebring, Walter Wilson
Sebring Collections. El Paso, Tex. Parsons and Parsons. 1975. (DAR)

SEELEY – Chase, Mary H.
Seeley family. By Mary H. Chase. Dallas, Tex., 1961. (FW)

SEELEY – Pinckard, Jane
Lest we forget: the Open Gates: the George Sealy residence, 2424 Broadway, Galveston, Texas. By Jane and Rebecca Pinckard; with foreward by Wayne Bell. Houston, Tex. J. and R. Pinckard. c1988. (LC)

SEITZ – Seitz, Alma Totty
Seitz and kindred families: a family history, 1753(?)-1976. Written and published by Alma Totty Seitz. Miami, Tex. Seitz. c1977. (LC)

SELL – Cell, Robert F.
Tax records, selected family names, Franklin County, Pennsylvania, 1796-1847: for selected names of the Cell family... Transcribed by Robert F. Cell. Edinburg, Tex. R. F. Cell. c1990. (LC)

SELLARDS – Sellards, Elias Howard
The Sellards through two centuries. By Elias Howard Sellards. Austin, Tex. 1949. (LC)

SELLERS – Wilson, Joy, 1939-
One Hundred and fifty years of the Sellers family. By Joy Wilson. Houston, Tex. J. Wilson. 1980? (LC)

SEWALL –
A history of the John Alexander and Laura Hilton Sowell family. By Mary Sowell Hays and Carolyn E. Sowell. Houston? Tex. 1973. (LC)

SEZONOV – Sezonov, Emmanuel, 1912-
The Sezonov Chronicle, 1880-1980 - Cronica familier Sezonov, 1880-1980. Compiled and published by Emmanuel Sezonov. Houston, Tex. E. Sezonov. 1980. (LC)

SHACKELFORD –
Shackelford clan magazine; genealogy of Shacklefords and Shackelfords. Vol. 1-12. May, 1945-Apr. 1957. Lubbock, Tex. (etc.). (MH)

SHAMBAUGH – Castleberry, Lois S.
An introduction to the Jacob and Sarah Hoobler Shambaugh line. By Lois S. Castleberry. Houston? Tex., 1950? (NY)

SHANK – Wilson, Virginia Shank
From Jacques to Jon to Jinger. Dallas, Tex. Haughton Pub. Co. c1975. (DAR)

SHARP – Hill, Euel Ray, 1934-
The Hills of Tennessee and Texas. By Euel Ray Hill; edited by Theron Lavon Smith. El Paso, Tex. E. R. Hill.. 1982. (LC)

SHARP – O'Bier, Glenda Sturges, 1953-
A Sharp family legacy. By Glenda Sturges O'Bier. Duncanville, Tex. G. S. O'Bier. c1986. (LC)

SHATTUCK – Bruce, Dorothy Odom, 1940-
Alvin Shattuck of Texas and his descendants. Compiled by Dorothy Odom Bruce & Betty A. Shattuck. Dallas? Tex. D. O. Bruce. c1981. (LC)

SHAW – Shaw, Roy L.
Shaws and related families. By Roy L. Shaw. Atlanta, Tex. Print by Bowman. 1976. (DP)

SHAW – Towell, Roy H. (Roy Harrison), 1915-
Isaac Towell & his family: including Towell, McAdams, Whitworth, Shaw, Fitzgerald & others, 1764-1990. By Roy H. Towell, Jr. Beaumont, Tex. R. H. Towell. c1990. (LC)

SHEARER – Underwood, Mary Pauline Walker, 1918-
Look backward my child; history and roster of two families whose paths merged in 1870, exactly one hundred years ago: William Dunbar Gross and Isham Shearer. Centennial Ed. Lubbock, Tex. Midwest Reproductions. 1970. (LC)

SHELBURNE – Buck, Richard W.
Shelburne: the book of Silas. By Richard W. Buck, Author. Fort Worth, Tex. Miran Pubs. c1973. (LC)

SHELLEDY – Jarboe, Mary Ritchie, 1923-
Ritchie/Shelledy family history: our people who came to Kansas Territory in 1855, John Ritchie and Mary Jane Shelledy, his wife. Richardson, Tex. M. R. Jarboe. 1984. (LC)

SHELTON – Casey, Alvin Harold, 1915-
Shelton, Wininger, and Pace families. By Harold Casey and Robert Casey. 1st Ed. Dallas, Tex. Brooks Pub. Co. Stillwater, Okla. H. Casey. c1988. (LC)

SHELTON –
A history of the Shelton family. Compiled and expanded by Keith Shelton from materials prepared by J. E. Shelton. Denton? Tex. 1972. (LC)

SHEPARD – Boyd, Margie Milner, 1925-
Rigsby relatives and related families, Shephard, Foster, Lawson: Virginia, North Carolina, Georgia, Texas, 1693-1900s: also Barclay, Bean, Burke... Margie Milner Boyd. Port Arthur, Tex. M. M. Boyd. 1986. (LC)

SHEPHERD – Shepherd, Frank C.
A genealogical history of the Shepherd family. Wewoka, Okla. Shepherd. 1935? (DAR)

SHERMAN – Trumbull, Dorthy Boyson
Continuing a special heritage: a family history, Sherman, Boyson, Trumbull. By Dorothy Boyson Trumbull. 1st Ed. Austin, Tex. Nortex Press. c1990. (LC)

SHERRILL – Kitchens, Walter Lee
The Sherrill family: 1531 members – 12 generations, 300 years in America. By Walter Lee Kitchens. Texarkanna, Tex. 1962. (LC)

SHERRILL – Sherrill, William E.
Sherrill genealogies. By William E. Sherrill. Haskell, Tex. 1912? (NY)

SHIELDS – Shields, Wm. C. Shields
Family record, Wm. C. Shields, Feb. 7, 1858, Shields and Stewart families. By Wm. C. Shields. Hunt, Tex? 1860. (FW)

SHIELDS – Wilson, R. B. (Rena Beth), 1940-
My family, Shields, Price, McKenzie, Lewis... By R. B. Wilson. Rockport, Tex. R. B. Wilson. c1990. (LC)

SHINN – Shinn, Josiah Hozen, 1849-1917-
The history of the Shinn family in Europe and America. By Josiah H. Shinn. Irving, Tex. R. S. Ferguson. c1979. (LC)

SHIPLEY – Hall, Frank Nelson-
A story of the Shiplett (Shipley) family of Muskingum County, Ohio (near Zanesville) and related families: David Roland Shiplett from Culpepper, Virginia, Charles Franklin from Maryland, Catherine Councilman (Franklin) from Baltimore, Maryland, William Perley (Caleb) Hugh from New Jersey, Amy Allen (Hughes) from New Jersey, Fred Hall of Belvidere, Illinois. The descendants of Nelson and Ephraim Shiplett. By Frank Nelson Hall. Denton, Tex. 1962. (LC)

SHIRLEY – King, Harry Tracy
John Shirley and descendant of Virginia and South Carolina. Roby, Tex. King. c1972. (DAR)

SHIRLEY – King, Harry T.
John Shirley and descendants of Virginia and South Carolina. By Harry T. King. Snyder, Tex. Feather Print., 1972. (FW)

SHIRLEY – McLin, Elva Bell, 1917-
The Bell-Shirley family: a record of antecedents and descendants of Martha Ellen (Shirley) and William Jackson Bell. By Elva Bell McLin. Austin, Tex. S.K.M. Roberts. c1988. (LC)

SHIRLEY – Moore, Augusta Letitia Shirley
A brief history and genealogy of the Shirley family. [S.l.:s..n.]. 1911. (DAR)

SHOCKLEY – Miller, Nancy, 1911-
Shockley. Compiled by Nancy Miller. Dallas, Tex. N. Miller. 1987. (LC)

SHOOK – Shook, Colonel Judson, 1925-
Bits and pieces. By Colonel Judson Shook, Jr. Dallas, Tex. J. Shook. 1989. (LC)

SHORT – Lynch, Josephine Short
Short. Houston, Tex. Lynch. 1970. (DAR)

SHUMATE –Evans, Norma Pontiff, 1937-
The ancestry and descendants of William Riley Shumate, 1777-1979. By Norma Pontiff Evans. Beaumont, Tex. Evans. c1979. (LC)

SIBLEY – Sibley, James Scarborough, 1930-
 The Sibley family in America, 1629-1972: genealogical data. Conpiled by James Scarborough Sibley. 2nd. Ed., with data added to 1982. Midlothian, Tex. J. S. Sibley. 1982. (LC)

SIC –Swantner, Robert, 1927-
 Swantner & Sic families: a Czech genealogy. By Robert and Coleen Swantner. Baltimore: Gateway Press. Kerrville, Tex. C. .M. Swantner. 1987. (LC)

SILLIMAN – Crabb, Martha L., 1928-
 Over the mountain: a narrative history of the Bean, Selman, and Germany families. By Martha L. Crabb. Baltimore: Gateway Press. Dumas, Tex. M. L. Crabb. 1990. (LC)

SILVER – Silver, Benjamin S.
 Our Silver heritage: Gershom and Millicent (Archer) Silver. By Benjamin S. Silver. Gatesville, Tex. Gatesville Print. Co., 1976. (FW)

SILVER – Silver, Benjamin Stump
 Our Silver heritage: Gershom and Millicent (Archer) Silver. By Benjamin Stump Silver and Frances Aylette (Bowen) Silver. Gatesville, Tex. Gatesville Print. Co., 1976. (LC)

SILVER – Silver, Benjamin Stump
 Our Silver Heritage: Gershom and Millicent (Archer) Silver. Also by Frances B. Silver. Gatesville, Tex. 1976. (NGS)

SIMMONS –
 Our Simmons forefathers and their descendants. Original text by George E. Crosthwaite. Original text extended by Bennett L. Smith, Editor. Fort Worth, Tex. B. L. Smith. 1974. (LC)

SIMMONS – Jenkins, Jack S., 1914-
 William Simmons of Wayne County, Tennessee and descendants. Compiled by Jack Simmons Jenkins. San Antonio, Tex. J. S. Jenkins. 1987. (LC)

SIMPSON – Perry, Max
 The descendants of Simpson-Roach families of South Carolina. Midland, Tex. Perry. c1973. (DAR)

SIMPSON – Perry, Max, 1919-
 Descendants of Mary Remer and Rev. John Simpson and the Remer and Strait families. Compiled by Max Perry. Midland, Tex. c1989. (LC)

SIMPSON – Perry, Max
 The descendants of Simpson-Roach families of South Carolina, including allied families and genealogical briefs of Berry, Bratton, Pickens, Moffett, Drennan, Boyd, Wylie, Mecklin, Sadler, Farmer, Sanders, Nelson, Springs. Compiled by Max Perry. Midland, Tex. Perry. 1974. (LC)

SIMPSON – Simpson, Blanche, 1887-1978-
Aunt Blanche's memory book. Edited by Bernice S. Dittmer. El Paso, Tex. Mangan Books. 1980. (LC)

SINCLAIR – Grigsby, Jean, 1937-
Sinkler – Sinclair – St. Clair: a family history. By Jean Grigsby. Beeville, Tex. J. Grigsby, Family Histories. c1988. (LC)

SINNOT – Morrow, Betty Moss
McGee-Cooper-Synnott. Prepared by Betty Moss Chaney-Morrow. Teaque, Tex. B. M. Chaney-Morrow. c1990. (LC)

SIROS – Burns, Betty Siros
Siros/Sirot family: including related lines, Bardin, Billig, Burns, Canivet, Casteel, Christian, (Ibsen), Cockrell, Feik, Hardin, Remmert, Sapp, Schaper and Wilke: Texas, France, Germany. Compiled by Betty Siros Burns. Limited Ed. Bismark, N.D. Burns Genealogical Services. c1979. (LC)

SISK – Sisk, Luther L. (Luther LaFayette), 1902-
The Sisk family: Virginia—North Carolina—South Carolina – Kentucky – Alabama – Tennessee – Georgia – Missouri – Texas. Escondido, Calif. L. L. Sisk. 1980? (LC)

SITTON – Sitton, Enid (W.)
Sitton and Gibson genealogy; descendants of three Revolutionary War soldiers: Joseph Sitton, North Carolina; Guyon Gibson, South Carolina; Thomas Kennedy, Virginia. By Enid (W.) Sitton. Houston, Tex., 1967? (DP)

SITTON – Sitton, Enid Wells
Sitton and Gibson genealogy, descendants of Joseph Sitton, Guyon Gibson, Thomas Kennedy. Houston, Tex. 1967. (NGS)

SIVERT – Bates, Estelle Enos
The descendants of John Frederick Sivert and Martha Curtis Sivert. Irving, Tex. Bates. 1973. (DAR)

SKELTON – Skelton, Helen Rogers, 1917-
Rogers-Skelton and allied families. By Helen Rogers Skelton and Clarence C. Skelton. Baltimore; Gateway Press. Burkeville, Tex. M. & C. C. Skelton [distributors]. 1987. (LC)

SKENE – Ball, Greg, 1962-
Family charts of the Cozby, Skeen, Walker, Rawson, Brumbelow, and Smith families. Compiled and indexed by Greg Ball. 2nd Ed. San Antonio, Tex. G. Ball. 1989. (LC)

SKINNER – Eckhardt, Ura L.
Skinner family, no. 1-8, 1959-1970. By Ura L. Eckhardt. Houston, Tex. 1970. (FW)

SLAUGHTER – Clarke, Mary Whatley
The Slaughter ranches & their makers. By Mary Whatley Clarke. Austin, Tex. Jenkins Pub. Co. c1979. (LC)

SLAUGHTER – Randolph, George Alice May
Slaughter-Cook-Beaumont. Plainview, Tex. Randolph. 1962. (DAR)

SLAUGHTER – Randolph, George Alice (M.)
Slaughter-Cook-Beaumont history and genealogy. By George Alice (M.)

SLAVENS – Slavens, Thomas H.
Descendants of John Slavin, born County Tyrone, Ireland, 1723, settled in Va., 1740, died Hiland County, Va., 1788. By Thomas H. Slavens. San Antonio, Tex. 1940. (FW)

SLAVIN – Slavens, Thomas H.
Descendants of John Slavin. San Antonio, Tex. 1940. (NGS)

SLAY – Jeffreys, J. Bradley (Jon Bradley), 1961-
A genealogy of the Slay family in America. By J. Bradley Jeffreys, coauthor, James H. Hines. Houston, Tex. J. H. Hines. c1985. (LC)

SLEETH – Roberts, Eloise M.
Four Revolutionary solders and their descendants. Avard, Okla. Roberts. 1924. (DAR)

SMALLEY – Wilson, Paul C.
A forgotten mission to the Indians. Galveston, Tex. Wilson. 1965. (DAR)

SMITH – Afton, John
Smith tales and trails. By John and Corrine Afton. {United States]. C. Afton. 1985. (LC)

SMITH – Billups, Benjamin E.
The Smith families of Texas. By Benjamin E. Billups. La Cruces, N. M. 1970.

SMITH – Gray, Faye Jones
My grandmothers: Smith's and Carter's; their ancestors and descendants. By Faye Jones Gray. Comanche? Tex., 1972. (LC) (FW)

SMITH – Herold, Virginia Lee Smith
Grandparents to remember. Austin, Tex. Felix Shuford Print. Co. 1963. (DAR)

SMITH – Larson, Jerry Laverne, 1931-
The sons of Lars: a genealogy of the Larson and Smith families of southwest Missouri. By Jerry Laverne Larson. Universal City, Tex. J. L. Larson. c1987. (LC)

SMITH –
Silas H. Smith heritage book. Independence, Iowa? Silas H. Smith Heritage Book Committee. c985. (LC)

SMITH – Smith, Ben L.
Preliminary report to some of the descendants of Samuel Smith. By Ben L. Smith. Dallas, Tex. 1971. (FW)

SMITH – Smith, C. Aubrey
A letter to my grandchildren. Austin, Tex. Von Boeckmann-Jones. c1967. (DAR)

SMITH – Smith, C. Aubrey
A letter to my grandchildren, with pictures of some recent forebears. Researched and written by C. Aubrey Smith. Austin, Tex. Printed by Von Boechmann-Jones. 1967. (LC)

SMITH – Smith, Craig W. (Craig Woods), 1913-
Be they remembered: the ancestry of Craig Woods Smith. By Craig W. Smith. {Texas?]. C. W. Smith. 1990. (LC)

SMITH – Smith, Dwight R.
Genealogy and family history, Bassett, Smith, and Brock. By Dwight R. Smith. Boerne, Tex. Paraclete Pub., 1966. (FW)

SMITH – Smith, Earl Davis
Forebears and kin of John Tyson Smith, Sr. and Nancy Melvina Skaggs. Longview, Tex. Smith. c1972. (DAR)

SMITH – Smith, Earl D.
Forebears and kin of John Tyson Smith, Sr. and Nancy Melvina Skaggs. By Earl D. Smith. Longview, Tex. 1972. (FW)

SMITH – Smith, Earl D.
Forebears and kin of John Tyson Smith, Sr. and Nancy Melvina Skaggs. By Earl D. Smith. Longview? Tex. c1972. (LC)

SMITH – Smith, Earl Davis
Forebears and kin of John Tyson Smith, Sr. and Nancy Melvina Skaggs. ?Longview, Tex. 1972. (NGS)

SMITH – Smith, Earl D.
Sgt. John McLaughlin Smith, Sr. of South Carolina (1754-1841). Longview, Tex. Smith. c1977. (DAR)

SMITH – Smith, Earl Davis, 1900-
Sgt. John McLaughlin Smith, Sr. of South Carolina, 1754-1841, his family & known grandchildren. By Earl D. Smith. Longview, Tex. Smith. 1977. (LC)

SMITH – Smith, Earl Davis, 1900-
My nine immigra[n]ts among 130 forebears. By Earl D. Smith. Longview, Tex. 1977. (LC)

SMITH – Smith, Elmer
Ellis County Smith. By Elmer Smith. Albany, Tex., 1965. (FW)

SMITH – Smith, Rev. Wesley
A family history and fifty-two years of preacher life in Mississippi and Texas... By Rev. Wesley Smith, of the Texas Conference, Methodist Episcopal Church, South. Nashville, Tenn. University Press Co. 1898. (LC)

SMITH – Williams, Letha M., 1932-
   The Smith-Womble and related families: a history. By Letha M. Williams. Big Springs, Tex. Williams. 1977. (LC)

SMITHERS – Smithers, Debra Winfield, 1952-
   Tanglewood chronicles: a pedigree of branches of the Smithers, Kelley, Winfield, Johnson, and allied families. Compiled by Debra Winfield Smithers. Baltimore; Gateway Press. Corpus Christi, Tex. D. Smithers. 1983. (LC)

SNELLLBAKER – Newell, Millie Snellbaker, 1937-
   Millie's memo's [sic] of Schmincke, Snellbaker families. Lumberton, Tex. M. S. Newell. c1990. (LC)

SNIFFEN – Sniffen, Max K., 1910-
   The Kniffen/Sniffen story: eleven generations, 1632-1989. By Max K. Sniffen. 1st Ed. Woodville, Tex. M. K. Sniffen. 1989. (LC)

SNOW – Smith, Dorothy F. H.
   The Texas Snows. By Dorothy F. H. Smith. Fort Worth? Tex. 1971. (FW)

SNOWDEN – Harrison, Sallie Stewart
   William Snowdon family, 1775-1985. Compiled by Sallie Stewart Harrison and Ethel Stewart Cole. Houston, Tex. S. S. Harrison; Brady, Tex.: E. S. Cole. 1986? (LC)

SOLBERG –
   The Solberg family from Norway to Texas. By Kathleen Solberg Sommer... [et al]. [S.l.]. Solberg Family. c1979. (LC)

SOMERVILLE – Hines, James H. (James Harvey), 1935-
   The families Somerville, Somervaill, Summerall, Summerell, Summerill, Summerlin, Sumlin, Sumrall, and Sumrill. James H. Hines; coathors, Mrs. E. L. Davidson... [et al]. Houston, Tex. J. H. Hines. c1981. (LC)

SOOBY – Sooby, Robert L.
   Sooby tribe. By Robert L. Sooby. Nacona, Tex. 1962. (FW)

SOUTH – Gee, Christine (South)
   Genealogical notes on the South family from the States of New Jersey, Pennsylvania, Maryland, Virginia, South Carolina, Kentucky, and Texas. By Christine (South) Gee. Greenville? S.C. 1963. (LC)

SOWA –Ebrom, Janet Dawson, 1949-
   The Sowa family history: six generations of Polish-Texans. By Janet Dawson Ebrom & Richard Allan Sowa. San Antonio, Tex. Sowa Books. c1981. (LC)

SOWELL – Hays, Mary Sowell
   A history of the John Alexander and Laura Hilton Sowell family. Tyler, Tex. Sowell. 1973. (DAR)

SOWELL – Hay, Mary (Sowell)
A history of the John Alexander and Laura Hilton Sowell family. Also by Carolyn E. Sowell. Houston, Tex. 1973. (NGS)

SPALDING – Spalding, William A.
Autobiography of William A. Spalding, Sr. Waxahachie, Tex. Spalding. 1952. (DAR)

SPARKS – Eckhardt, Ura L.
Sparks family, no. 1-2, 1954-1968. By Ura L. Eckhardt. Houston, Tex. 1968. (FW)

SPARKS – Taylor, Althea Copeland
Sparks, Roach, Taylor. Temple, Tex. Taylor. 1978. (DAR)

SPARKS – Taylor, Althea Copeland, 1912-
Sparks-Roach-Taylor, our ancestors and descendants. By Althea Copeland Taylor. Belton, Tex. Stillhouse Hollow Publishers, 1978. (LC)

SPEARS – Spear-Wilson, Iowa Leona, 1898-
Spear family memorial, 1620-1985: some Spear men, their ladies, and some affiliated families: a branch of the Vermont-England Spears: census records showing English roots. By Iowa Leona Spear-Wilson. Abilene, Tex. I. L. Spear-Wilson. c1985. (LC)

SPENCE – Fowler, Louise Bishop, 1927-
David and Mary (McElyea) Spence: their ancestors and descendants. By Louise Bishop Fowler. Baltimore: Gateway Press. Ore City, Tex. L. B. Fowler. 1986. (LC)

SPENCER -- Letts, Hubert W. (Hubert Winfred), 1913-
Yankee land to Dixie land: a family genealogy. By Hubert W. Letts. Corpus Christi, Tex. Home Publishers. c1986. (LC)

SPIEGELBERG – Fierman, Floyd S.
The Spiegelbergs of New Mexico, merchants and bankers, 1844-1893. By Floyd S. Fierman. El Paso, Tex. Texas Western College Press, 1964. (LC)

SPILLER – Spiller, Wayne
Meredith Spiller, his story and his descendants. By Wayne Spiller. Voca, Tex., 1964. (FW)

SPLAWN – Splawn, Jennie L. (Jennie Lillian), 1885-1960-
Genealogy of the Splawn and Collins family. Compiled by Jennie L. Splawn. Updated/by Ann Baker. Lubbock, Tex. Tex Tech Press. 1986. (LC)

SPLAWN – Splawn, Jennie L.
Genealogy of the Splawn and Collins family, also Woods family. Lubbock, Tex. 1986. (NGS)

SPOONAMORE -- Smutz, Harold Turk
Philip Spoonamore, Sr. and Jr., of Kentucky and some of their descendants in Illinois, Indiana, Missouri, and Texas. By Harold Turk Smutz. 1970. (LC)

SPRING – Perry, Max, 1919-
Descendants of John Springs (Springsteen) and Sophia Gassaway of Mecklenburg County, North Carolina: including genealogical briefs of the Springsteen and Storm families. Compiled and published by Max Perry. Midland, Tex. M. Perry. c1988. (LC)

SPRINGER – Coffey, Laura Lou White, 1919-
Springer in the South. By Laura Lou White Coffey, Lidalee Springer Mobley. Dallas, Tex. Falcon Print. Co. c1977. (LC)

SPRINGSTEEN – Perry, Max, 1919-
Descendants of John Springs (Springsteen) and Sophia Gassaway of Mecklenburg County, North Carolina: including genealogical briefs of the Springsteen and Storm families. Compiled and published by Max Perry. Midland, Tex. M. Perry. c1988. (LC)

SPROUL – Crocker, Leah (H.)
Rachel Sprouls story. By Leah (H.) Crocker. San Antonio, Tex. Fotolith Corp., 1952. (FW)

STAFFORD – Lusby, James Vernon, 1920-
Stafford – Trotter: a genealogy. By James Vernon Lusby. Houston, Tex. J. V. Lusby. 1989. (LC)

STAGER – Steger, Mel
A Steger history from Deutschland to Richland. Houston, Tex. M. Steger. 1978. (LC)

STAGER – Steger, Mel
A Steger-Schlittler-Mahlandt history. Book prepared by Mel Steger. Houston, Tex. 1986. (LC)

STANDARD – Standard, Charles Martin, 1931-
The Standard, Higgins, and related families: genealogical history of two pioneer Kentucky families and their related families. By Charles Martin Standard. Dallas, Tex. Standard. c1979. (LC)

STANFORD – Standiford, Debi, 1953-
Sudden family. Debi and Steven Standiford with Nhi and Hy Phan. Waco, Tex. Word Books. c1986. (LC)

STANFORD – Stanford, Charles M.
Descendants of Stephen Stanford, Gwinnett County, Georgia: from 1800. Austin, Tex. C. M. Stanford, 1986? (LC)

STANLEY – Flaherty, Elnora S.
Whither thou goest; a story of the Stanley family in Virginia, North Carolina, Kansas and Oklahoma. By Elnora S. Flaherty. Irving, Tex. 1973. (FW)

STANLEY – Stanley, James Savage, 1908-
Stanley ties: families related by marriage to one line of direct descendants of Sands Stanley of the Pee Dee Valley: a supplement to Sands Stanley of the Pee Dee Valley by Haywood A. Stanley (1979). By Jamers Savage Stanley, Jr. Fort Worth, Tex.? J. S. Stanley. 1982. (LC)

STANTON – Brown, Shepherd Spencer Neville, 1920-
Brown-Stanton-Evans-Sherman familes and collateral lines, 1420-1987. By Shepherd Spencer Neville Brown. Waco, Tex. S. S. N. Brown. 1987. (LC)

STANTON – Stanton, William A. (William Alonzo), b. 1854-
A record, genealogical, biographical, statistical, of Thomas Stanton, of Connecticut, and his descendants, 1635-1891. By William A. Stanton. Bethany, Okla. Richardson Reprints, 1985. (LC)

STARK – Harris, Mary Kathryn, 1933-
James Stark of Stafford County, Virginia and his descendants. Compiled by Mary Kathryn Harris and Mary Iva Jean Jorgensen. Fort Worth, Tex. M. K. Harris. c1985. (LC)

STARR – Crain, Marquerite Starr
They followed the sun. Dallas, Tex. Printed by Suburban Tribune. 1971. (DAR)

STARR –
They followed the sun; the story of James Penn Starr and Georgian Theus, their ancestors and their progenies. Compiled and edited by Marquerite Starr Crain and Janell Turner Wenzel. Dallas, Tex. Suburban Tribune. 1971. (LC)

STARR – Miller, Flora May Starr
The house of Starr. By Flora May Starr Miller. College Station, Tex. Starr Custom Binding. 1971. (LC)

STEELE – Steele, Harold E. (Harold Eugene), 1918-
A history of the Harry and Ada (Hoke) Steele families. By Harold E. Steele. Dallas, Tex. Printed by Taylor Pub. Co. (LC)

STEINBACH – DeVerter, Paul Logan
The Steinbach family. Baytown, Tex. DeVerter. 1958. (DAR)

STEINBACH – DeVerter, Paul Logan
The Steinbach or Steinbaugh family, province of lower Rhine, Alsace-Lorraine and Ohio and Indiana, U.S.A. By Paul Logan DeVerter. Baytown, Tex. 1958. (LC)

STELL – Stell, Susie (Brunson)
A tree is planted; the family tree and a bit of history of the Stells. By Susie (Brunan) Stell. Plainview? Tex. 1960? (LC)

STEPHENSON – Main, Frances Stevenson
Stephenson-Stevenson. Harlingen, Tex. Quincy A. Main Print Co. 1966. (DAR)

STEPHENSON – Martindale, Mary Jo, 1907-
Byred – Stephenson and other lineages: a genealogy. By Mary Jo Martindale, compiler. Fort Worth, Tex. Miran Publishers, c1978. (LC)

STERN – Stearns, Monyene
   The Stearns family scrapbook. Compiled by Monyene Stearns. McGregor, Tex. Stearns Enterprises, 1985. (LC)

STEVENS – McDaniel, Mabel
   Stevens family of Wilkinson County, Georgia. Dallas, Tex. Wright. 1956. (DAR)

STEVENS --
   Stevens family of Wilkinson County, Georgia. Compiled by Mable McDaniel and Elizabeth Wright. Dallas, Tex. c1956. (LC)

STEVENS –Stephens, Robert W.
   Stephens family history: ancestry and descendants of revolutionary soldier Robert Stephens and his wife, Sarah Farmer, of Virginia through their son Josiah Stephens. By Robert W. Stephens. Dallas, Tex. R. W. Stephens. c1982. (LC)

STEVENS – Wipprecht, Carl
   Notes on William Giles Stevens and his ancestors. Rusk, Tex. Wipprecht. 1974. (DAR)

STEWART – Stewart-Novak V.
   J. P. "Dick". By V. Stewart-Novak. Wolfe City, Tex. Henington Pub., 1966. (FW)

STIFF – Stiff, Judd Golladay
   My name is Stiff. Fort Worth, Tex. Miran Publishers. c1976. (DAR)

STIFF – Stiff, Judd G.
   My name is Stiff. By Judd G. Stiff. 1st Ed. Fort Worth, Tex. Miran Pub. 1976. (FW)

STIMSON – Stimson, Eula Abigail, 1896-1983-
   Our Stimson clan and kin. By Eula Abigail Stimson; documentary research by Alexander Vernelle Stimson. Hiighland Park? Tex. A. V. Stimson. c1985. (LC)

STOLL – Adams, Linda Stoll, 1947-
   John Stoll, Sr.., a Swiss immigrant and his American descendants, 1883-1987. By Linda Stoll Adams. Houston, Tex.? L. S. Adams. 1987. (LC)

STOLL – Wolf, Leonora Stoll, 1928-
   History of Andreas Stoll and his descendants: Switzerland to America, 1881-1985. By Leonora Stoll Wolf. New Braunfels, Tex. L. S. Wolf. c1985. (LC)

STONE – Stone, Dolly Mary
   Samuel Stone and his wife Mary Ann Chunn. San Antonio, Tex. The Naylor Co. c1955. (DAR)

STONE – Stone, Dolly Mary
   Samuel Stone and his wife, Mary Ann Chunn; a story of their lives, including early residence in Virginia, Tennessee, and Alabama, their migration to Missouri and later to the Republic of Texas, with data concerning their family and descendants, and also

including some genealogical history proving the ancestry of Mary Ann Chunn. By Dolly Mary Stone. San Antonio, Tex. Naylor Co. 1955. (LC)

STONE – LaGrone, Leila Stone
Such as I have, give I thee; a history of the east Texas Stones. By Leila Stone LaGrone. Carthage, Tex. c1967. (LC)

STONEHAM – Stoneham, Los L.
A history of the Stoneham family. Austin, Tex. Stoneham. 1977. (DAR)

STOREY – Smith, Robert Nelson
Storey-Price-Roscoe-Smith family history. Harlingen, Tex. Smith. 1959. (DAR)

STOREY – Smith, Robert N.
Storey-Price-Roscoe-Smith family history, 1725-1959. By Robert N. Smith. Harlingen, Tex., 1960. (LA)

STORM – Perry, Max, 1919-
Descendants of John Springs (Springsteen) and Sophia Gassaway of Mecklenburg County, North Carolina: including genealogical briefs of the Springsteen and Storm families. Compiled and published by Max Perry. Midland, Tex. M. Perry. c1988. (LC)

STOVALL –
I remember: a collection by the children of Daniel Shaw Stovall and Ida May McCook. Houston, Tex. N. H. Holman. c1986. (Houston, Tex.; D. Armstrong Co.). (LC)

STOVALL – Eckhardt, Ura L.
Stovall family, no. 1, 1966-70. By Ura L. Eckhardt. Houston, Tex. 1970. (FW)

STOVALL – Williams, Llyle Keith, 11915-
The Stovall family and related lines. By Lyle Keith Williams. Fort Worth, Tex. L. K. Williams. c1984. (LC)

STOVER – Stover, Joel A.
Brief history of the Stover family and the descendants of Joseph Martillis Stover and Sarah Cathrine Jones. By Joel A. Stover. Little Elm, Tex. 1955. (FW)

STRAIT – Perry, Max, 1919-
Descendants of Mary Remer and Rev. John Simpson and the Remer and Strait families. Compiled by Max Perry. Midland, Tex. M. Perry. c1989. (LC)

STRETCHER – Gray, Bessie Stretcher
A partial genealogy of the Stretcher family. Austin, Tex. Gray. 1967. (DAR)

STRIBLING – Heaberlin, Sam J. (Sam Joe), 1913-
The Heaberlins in East Texas: including the related family of Joe Elton Stribling. By Sam J. Heaberlin, compiler and narrator. Lufkin, Tex. Pineywoods Print. 1988. (LC)

STRIBLING – Stribling, Mary Francis
Stribling and related families. Austin, Tex. 1967. (NGS)

STRICKLAND –
The Strickland and allied families query and answer exchange. June, 1958. Fort Worth, Tex. (NY)

STRIEGLER – Striegler, Selma W.
Johan Frederick Gottlieb Striegler family history. By Selma W. Striegler. Fredericksburg, Tex.? The Radio Post? 1952? (FW)

STRONG – Johnson, Marjorie M. G.
Lineage and historical records. By Marjorie M. G. Johnson. Dallas, Tex., 1968. (FW)

STRONG – Pitts, Alice Ellison
Strong-Ellison-Henderson family history. McKinney, Tex. Pitts. c1976. (DAR)

STRONG – Strong, Rosenanda Otts
The Strong Cemetery, Rusk County, Texas. Compiled by Rosenanda Otts Strong. Longview, Tex. Kwik-Kopey Print. 1983. (LC)

STROTHER – Heard, Harold
Strother families. Amarillo, Tex. Heard. 1967? (DAR)

STROTHER – Heard, Harold
Strother families. By Harold Heard. Amarillo, Tex. 197? (FW)

STROUD – Wilson, Logan D.
No beginning, no ending. By Logan D. Wilson. Dallas, Tex. Printed by Taylor Pub. Co. 1972. (LA)

STUART – Eckhardt, Ura L.
Stewart family, no. 1-9, 1948-1970. By Ura L. Eckhardt. Houston, Tex. 1970. (FW)

STUBBS – Boswell, Jimmie John Stubbs
John Stubbs, 1718-1788 of Williamsburg, South Carolina and his descendants. Compiler, Jimmie John Stubbs Boswell. Bryan, Tex. J. R. Boswell, Sr. 1990. (LC)

STUBBS – Stubbs, William Carter
The descendants of John Stubbs of Cappahosic, Gloucester County, Birginia?, 1652. By William Carter Stubbs. Name index added, compiled by Hattie Stubbs Dickson. Corpus Christi, Tex. Professional Print. Co. 1966. (LC)

STUBBS. See also: Fairfax   Pate
                        Hardin   Sharp

STURDIVANT – Sturtevant, Robert Hunter, 1921-
Descendants of Samuel Sturtevant. Compiled by Robert Hunter Sturtevant. 1st Ed. Waco, Tex. R. H. Sturtevant. 1986. (LC)

STURTEVANT – Sturtevant, Robert Hunter
Descendants of Samuel Sturtevant. Waco, Tex. 1986. (NGS)

SUTHERLAND – Hudson, Florence Sutherland
We cousins, Volume II. San Benito, Tex. and Scottsbluff, Neb. Hudson. c1970. (DAR)

SUTHERLAND – Hudson, Florence (Sutherland)
"We cousins" (Virginia to Texas). A genealogy of several of the families comprising the Alabama settlement of Austin's Colony, 1830 and 1831, now Texas, and including the other Virginia lines of the Sutherland family. By Florence (Sutherland) Hudson. San Benito, Tex. c1957. (LC)

SWAIM – Mullane, Joseph F. (Joseph Francis), 1919-
The Swaim-Tysen family of Staten Island, New York, New Jersey, and southern states. Supplement. Joseph F. Mullane, Lloyd B. Swaim, Marjorie D. Johnson. [United States]. J. F. Mullane. 1987. (LC)

SWANTNER – Swantner, Robert, 1927-
Swantner & Sic families: A Czech genealogy. By Robert and Coleen Swantner. Baltimore: Gateway Press. Kerrville, Tex. 1987. (LC)

SWENSEN – Clarke, Mary Whatley
The Swenson saga and the SMS Ranches. Mary Whatley Clarke. Austin, Tex. Jenkins Pub. Co. c1976. (LC)

SWENSON – Clarke, Mary W.
Swenson saga and the SMS ranches. By Mary W. Clarke. Austin, Tex. Jenkins Pub. 1976. (FW)

SWING – Hayes, Florence, 1932-
My family remembered. By Florence Hayes. 1st Ed. Houston, Tex. F. M. S. Hayes. 1987. (LC)

SWOFFORD – Swofford, Minnie Ray Bachman
One man and his family; John Franklin Swofford, 1853-1921. By Minnie Ray Backman Swofford. Lubbock? Tex. 1968. (LC)

SWOFFORD – Swofford, Minnie Ray Bachman
Swofford marriage records; 1001 and then some. Compiled by Minnie Ray Backman Swofford. Lubbock, Tex. Swofford. 1974. (LC)

SYKES – Sikes, Andrew Levi, 1922-
A Sikes family history and narrative and computerized records. Researched and written by Adrew Levi Sikes. [Texas]. A. L. Sikes. 1990-. (LC)

T –

TACKETT – Eckhardt, Ura L.
Tacquet-Tackett-Tackitt family, assorted notes, no. 1-2, 1958-1968. By Ura L. Eckhardt. Houston, Tex. 1968. (FW)

TAILER –
Tailers/Taylors – lost and found. Nov. 1967-Aug. 1970. Fort Worth, Tex. (NY)

TALBOT – Abernethy, Arvord Milner, 1906-
Into the setting sun went the Abernethys, the Boltons, the Davises, the Talbots. Hamilton, Tex. A. M. Abernethy. 1986. (LC)

TALIAFERRO – Eckhardt, Ura L.
Taliaferro family, no. 1-2, 1952-1969. By Ura L. Eckhardt. Houston, Tex. 1969. (FW)

TALLY – Tally-Frost, Stephenie H.
Family Bible records. By Stephenie H. Tally-Frost. Corpus Christi, Tex. Print by Prof. Print. and Litho. (n.d.). (IG)

TANKERSLEY – Tankersley, Charles W.
Tankersley family in America. By Charles W. Tankersley. Houston, Tex., 1968. (FW)

TANSILL –
The Descendants of Edward Albert Tansil and Piety Thomas Tansil. Data compiled by Robert G. Brown III… [et al]. 1st Ed. Paris, Tex. R. G. Brown. 1983. (LC)

TAPLEY – Campbell, Kathryn Hutcherson
Hosea Tapley 1691-1981. Dallas, Tex. Campbell. 1981. (DAR)

TARBET – Tarbet, Don W. (Don Wilburn), 1932-
The "T" trail: a history of the Tarbet, Torbett, Torbet, Torbitt, and Torbit families in America. By Don Tarbet. Denison, Tex. 1985. (LC)

TARR – Hall, Ruth G. (Ruth Gaines)
De Tar & allied families, c. 1741-1992. By Ruth G. Hall & Lucille O'Brien. 1st Ed. Kerrville, Tex. R. G. Hall. 1982. (LC)

TARTER – Darter, Bertha Van Mondfrans, 1909-
The Darter, Tarter, Daughters family. By the Darter Association, International; [co-authors, Bertha Van Monfrans Darter, William Alexander Darter]. Austin, Tex. the Association. 1976. (LC)

TATE – Smith, Rachel Tate
Van Buren Tate; diary, ancestors, descendants. By Rachel Tate Smith. Albany? Tex. 1968. (LC)

TATE – Smith, Rachel Tate, 1894-
Van Buren Tate: ancestors, descendants: supplement, Ireland, 1730, United States, 1976. By Rachel Tate Smith. Austin, Tex. Smith. 1976. (LC)

TATOM – Tatom, Walter J.
Stephen Tatom and his descendants. Dallas, Tex. Tatom:Green. 1971. (DAR)

TATOM –
Stephen Tatom and his descendants. By Walter J. Tatom and John Plath Green. Dallas, Tex., 1971. (LC)

TATUM –
The name and family of Tatum or Tatham. Media Research Bureau. Yoakum, Tex. S. R. Tatum. 1973? (NY)

TAYLOR – Autry, M. Blair
The family of James Francis Taylor. Corsicana, Tex. Autry:Autry. 1967. (DAR)

TAYLOR –
The family of James Francis Taylor, with related families of Wooten, Vernon, Harrington and Pool. By M. Blair Autry (and) Mamie Taylor Autry. Corsicana, Tex. 1967. (LC)

TAYLOR. See also:

Backhouse	Haynes	Pollock
Bell	Herndon	Robertson
Bullitt	Hynes	Selden
Carew	Johnson	Shrode
Carpenter	Jones	Wallace
Carter	Kay	Watson
Castle	Kinney	Weeks
Cranmer	Kinnison	Wilbur
Crocker	Landor	Wilder
Dobyns	Lindley	Wilford
Drake	Lomax	Willis
Dwight	Maclin	Winston
Foy	May	
Glassell	Nelson	
	Perkins	

TAYLOR – Eckhardt, Ura L.
Taylor family, no. 1-8, 10-11, 1963-1969. By Ura L. Eckhardt. Houston, Tex. 1969. (FW)

TAYLOR – Ford, Ethel M. (T.)
Thomas Taylor and Benjamin Branch of Nashville, Tenn. and related families. By Ehtel M. (T.) Ford. Amarillo, Tex. 196? (FW)

TAYLOR – Ford, Ethel Taylor
Thomas Taylor and Benjamin Branch of Nashville, Tennessee, and related families. By Ethel Taylor Ford. Amarillo, Tex. 1972? (LC)

TAYLOR – Gatewood, Gorden Jefferson, 1900-
Tarlton Jones Taylor's ancestors and descendants, 1500-1986. Gorden Jefferson Gatewood. Tulia, Tex.? G. J. Gatewood. 1986? (LC)

TAYLOR – Helgeson, Betty Taylor
Some descendants of Isaac Anderson Taylor and Eleanore McFarland. Compiled by Betty Taylor Helgeson, Geneva Taylor Koons. Garland, Tex. B. T. Helgeson; Enon, Oh: G. T. Koons. 1983. (LC)

TAYLOR – Hyatt, Marjorie Burnett
The Taylors, the Tumlinsons, and the feud. By Marjorie Burnett Hyatt. Smiley, Tex. M. B. Hyatt. c1986. (LC)

TAYLOR – Neil, R. E.
Tailers/Taylors lost and found. By R. E. Neil. Fort Worth, Tex. 1967-70. (FW)

TAYLOR – Taylor, Bill N.
Historical and biographical memoirs of the Taylor and allied families. Longview, Tex. Taylor. 1967. (DAR)

TAYLOR – Taylor, L. G.
Around the fan chart; or European background and ancestry of 3 Taylor brothers... By L. G. Taylor. Houston, Tex. Universal Print. 1968. (FW)

TAYLOR – Taylor, Noel M.
Taylors at the Devil's Kitchen. By Noel M. Taylor. Houston, Tex. Taylor. c1975. (LC)

TAYLOR – Taylor, Noel M.
Taylors at the Devil's Kitchen. Houston, Tex. c1975. (NGS)

TAYLOR – Texas DAR
The John A. Taylor diary, 1826-1880. Longview, Tex.: the Chapter. 1947. (DAR)

TEAGUE – Eckhardt, Ura L.
Teague family notes. By Ura L. Eckhardt. Houston, Tex. 1970. (FW)

TEETERS – Tucker, Faye Christmas, 1907-
Doddridge and Teter: some ancestors and descendants. By Faye Christmas Tucker. Dallas, Tex. F. C. Tucker. 1986. (LC)

TEGGE – Scarbrough, Clara Stearns
The Tegge-Allen family. By Clara Stearns Scarbrough. Georgetown, Tex. Sun Publishers. 1967. (LC)

TERPENING – Terpening, Don E. (Don Everett), 1936-
Terpening workbook. Livingston, Tex. D. E. Terpening, 1984 (LC)

TERRELL – Dicken, Emma
Terrell genealogy. San Antonio, Tex. Naylor Co. 1952? (DAR)

TERRELL – Dicken, Emma
Terrell genealogy... By Emma Dicken. San Antonio, Tex. Naylor Co. 1952? (MH)

TERRELL – Doshier, Inez Christian, 1903-
Miscellaneous items on Terrill and related families. From the files of Mrs. Inez Christian Doshier. Amarillo, Tex. I. C. Doshier. 1987. (LC)

TERRELL – Eckhardt, Ura L.
Tyrell-Terrell-Terrill family, no. 1-4, 1962-1970. By Ura L. Eckhardt. Houston, Tex. 1970? (FW)

TERRY – Eckhardt, Ura L.
Terry family, no. 1-6, 1960-1970. By Ura L. Eckhardt. Houston, Tex. 1970. (FW)

TERRY – Ingmire, Frances T.
Terry and allied families of Virginia, Kentucky, Illinois, Texas. By Frances T. Ingmire. Creve Coeur, Mo. Ingmire. 1976. (FW)

TERRY – Ingmire, Frances Terry
Terry and allied families of Virginia, Kentucky, Illinois, Texas. Compiled by Frances Terry Ingmire. Creve Coeur, Mo. Ingmire. c1976. (LC)

THACKER – Sipe, Alice Erma Thacher
Thacher genealogy and Mayflower ancestors. Houston, Tex. Sipe. 1975. (DAR)

THEISS – Theiss, Edwin G.
The Theis-Theiss family history. Spring, Tex. Theiss. 1978. (DAR)

THEVENET – Thevenet, Mary Addison Woolum
Thevenet-Woolum. Dallas, Tex. Famer Genealogy Co. c1977. (DAR)

THIGPEN – Powell, George C.
Thigpen genealogy. By George C. Powell. Dallas, Tex. 1958. (FW)

THOMAS – Eckhardt, Ura L.
Thomas family, no. 1-6, 9-12, 1952-1962. By Ura L. Eckhardt. Houston, Tex. 1962. (FW)

THOMAS – Fields, Virginia B. (Virginia Butter), 1944-
Ezekiel Thomas, 1840-1917, and John Thomas, 1846-1928, of Georgia and Texas: their ancestors and descendants. Compiled, edited, and published by Virginia B. Fields. Slidell, La. V. B. Fields. C1985. (LC)

THOMAS – Horton, Louise
Some of the ancestors of Thomas Marion Thomas and Alice May Armstrong. By Louise Horton. Austin, Tex. White Cross Pr. 1974. (FW)

THOMAS – Rawlins, Richard Caldwell Mrs.
Family history of John Towson Thomas and wife, Mary Jane Gage Goodhue Thomas of Clackomas County, Oregon. Compiled by Mrs. Richard Caldwell Rawlins. Corsicana, Tex. R. C. Rawlins. 1984. (LC)

THOMAS – Thomas, Arthur E.
John Myers Thomas, ancestry and some descendants. By Athur E. Thomas. Dallas, Tex., 1961. (FW)

THOMAS – Thomas, Arthur E.
John Myers, ancestry and some descendants. Dallas, Tex., 1961. (NGS)

THOMAS – Thomas, Robert Edward
The Thomas Family in 300 years of American History. Dallas, Tex. 1978 (NGS)

THOMPSON – Eckhardt, Ura L.
Thompson family, no. 1-2, 1966-1970. By Ura L. Thompson. Houston, Tex. 1970. (FW)

THOMPSON – Emmons, C. J.
Some descendants of the Revolutionary War soldier James Thompson. Kerrville, Tex. Emmons. 1968.

THOMPSON – Garrett, Floyd, 1931-
The Thompson connection to McCaleb, McComb, Woodsides, Evans, Ponder, Gray, Lovell, MacAlpine, Arden, Thornsberry – and many related lines: the descendants of John Christopher Thompson and Sarah Elizabeth McCaleb – and how I fit in. Compiled by Floyd Farrett. Conroe, Tex. Garrett Newspapers, 1984. (LC)

THOMPSON – Jeter, Margaret McDonald, 1926-
History of the McDonald, Thomasson, Biggers, Grimes, and related families. By Margaret McDonald Jeter. Tucson, Ariz. M. M. Leter. 1989. (LC)

THOMPSON – Kelsey, Mary Wilson
James George Thompson, 1803[sic]-1879: Cherokee trader, Texian, secessionist: his papers and family history. By Mary Randolph Wilson Kelsey and her husband Mavis Parrott Kelsey, Sr. 1st Ed. College Station, Tex.: Texas A&M University, Sterling C. Evans Library. c1988. (LC)

THOMPSON – Thompson, Dale L.
Fifty years together. By Dale L. Thompson. San Benito, Tex., 1968. (FW)

THORNHILL – Thornhill, T. J.
Thornhill genealogy. Dallas, Tex. Thornhill. 1940. (DAR)

THORNHILL – Thornhill, T. J.
Thornill genealogy. Compiled and published by T. J. Thornhill. Dallas, Tex. 1940. (LC)

THORNHILL – Thornhill, Thomas James
Portions of the Book Thornhill Genealogy. Div. E-J. Dallas, Tex. 1941. (NGS)

THORNTON – Keeling, Beatrice Thornton, 1906-
Isaac Thornton, 1817-1906, his descendants and some of his forebears. Compiled by Beatrice Thornton Keeling and Wanda Willard Smith. Dallas, Tex. Smith. 1976? (LC)

THORNTON – Thornton, Walter W.
A glimpse of Thornton through the centuries. Texarkana, Tex. Thornton. 1949? (DAR)

TIBBETTS – Boodry, Bertie Holmes
Mary Tibbetts Dennison, 1877-1970, her genealogical lines. By Bertie Holmes Boodry. Beaumont, Tex. D. H. Boodry. c1982. (LC)

TILLER – Jordan, Terry G.
Deep East Texas folk. Dallas, Tex. Southern Methodist University Printing Dept. 1976. (DAR)

TILLER – Jordan, Terry G.
Deep east Texas folk: the Tillers, Crenshaws, Woodleys, Goldens, and other related families of Panola and Harrison Counties. By Terry G. Jordan. Dallas, Southern Methodist Univ. Print Dept., 1976. (FW)

TILLER – Jordan, Terry G.
Deep East Texas folk: the Tillers, Crenshaws, Woodleys, Goldens, and other related families of Panola and Harrison Counties. By Terry G. Jordan and Mary Lynn Tiller wier. Dallas, Southwwestern Methodist University Printing Dept. 1976. (LC)

TIMMONS – Scott, Janet Weir, 1929-
Tims-Weir: the ancestry of William Robert Tims of Augusta, Texas, and his wife Edytha Valette Weir of Pueblo, Colorado. Compiled by Janet Weir Scott. Maryville, Mo. J. W. Scott. 1988. (LC)

TIMS – McClellan, Aubrey L.
Tims family history (Timpson, Texas named for this family). By Aubrey L. McClellan. Shreveport, La., 1953. (FW)

TIMS – Tims, Eugene Chapel
Antecedents and descendants of Nathan Tims of Chester County, South Carolina. By Eugene Chapel Tims. Wolfe City, Tex. Henington Pub. Co. 1967. (LC)

TIPTON – Heinemann, Charles Brunk
Tipton family records in the present boundaries of the United States from Colonial times to 1950. By Charles Brunk Heinemann. Washington, 1950. (LC)

TITUS – Titus, Anson
Titus family in America; three generations. By Anson Titus. Dallas, Tex., 1937. (FW)

TOBIN – Sutton, Mack C.
Descendants of James & Esther Tobin. Typed and compiled by Mack C. Sutton. Austin, Tex. M. C. Sutton. 1984? (LC)

TODD – Murphey, Joe Earl, 1929-
Profiles: a history of the Todd and Bowden families. By Joe Earl Murphey. Arlington, Tex.? J. E. Murphey. c1985. (LC)

TOMLINSON – Hyatt, Marjorie Burnett
Fuel for a feud. By Marjorie Burnett Hyatt. Smiley, Tex. M. B. Hyatt. c1990. (LC)

TOMLINSON – Hyatt, Marjorie Burnett
The Taylors, the Tumlinsons, and the feud. By Marjorie Burnett Hyatt. Smiley, Tex. M. B. Hyatt. c1986. (LC)

TOMS – Meaney, John William, 1918-
Celtic trails to Texas: the Toms, Dunns and Meaneys. By John William Meaney. Austin, Tex. J. W. Meaney. c1984. (LC)

TORREY – Armbruster, Henry C.
The Torreys of Texas. By Henry C. Armbruster. Buda, Tex. Citizen Press. 1968. (SL)

TOTTY – Seitz, Alma Totty
Letters of interest to the Totty family, facts pertaining to early Cooke County and Wheeler County, Texas. By Alma Totty Seitz. Miami, Tex. 1968. (LC)

TOTTY – Seitz, Alma (T.)
Tottys and Totty ties: a family history, 1685-1975. By Alma (T.) Seitz. Miami? Tex. Seitz. 1975. (FW)

TOTTY – Seitz, Alma Totty
Tottys and Totty ties: a family history, 1685-1975. By Alma Totty Seitz. Miami? Tex. Seitz, 1975. (LC)

TOTTY – Seitz, Alma Totty
Tottys and Totty ties, 1685-1975. ?Miami, Tex. 1975. (NGS)

TOWLE – Towell, Roy H. (Roy Harrison), 1915-
Isaac Towell & his family: including Towell, McAdams, Whitworth, Shaw, Fitzgerald & others, 1764-1990. By Roy H. Towell, Jr. Beaumont, Tex. R. H. Towell. c1990. (LC)

TOWLES – Eckhardt, Ura L.
Towles family notes. By Ura L. Eckhardt. Houston, Tex. 1970. (FW)

TOWNLEY – Townley, Hulen Henry, 1920-
Some heirs of brother John Luther Townley. Groves, Tex.: H. H. Townley, 1987? (LC)

TOWNSEND – Eckhardt, Ura L.
Townsend family, no. 1-12, 1960-1970. By Ura L. Eckhardt. Houston, Tex. 1970. (FW)

TOOWNSEND – Wyatt, Tula Townsend
The seven Townsend brothers of Texas, 1826-1838. Austin, Tex. Aus-Tex Duplicators. 1974. (DAR)

TOWNSEND – Wyatt, Tula Townsend
The seven Townsend brothers of Texas, 1826-1838; a genealogy. By Tula Townsend Wyatt. Austin, Tex. Aus-Tex Duplicators. 1974. (LC)

TOZOUR – Chew, Pearl T.
Genealogy, paternal and maternal (Tozour, Lee, Robinson, Jennings and allied families) including Chew family. By Pearl T. Chew. Dallas, Tex. the McNaughton Pub. Co. 1972. (SP)

TRAMMELL – Cook, Clara O. (Clara Othela), 1912-
Trammel -Shelby: known ancestors and descendants of Daniel Trammel (1811-1887) and his wife Sarah (Shelby) Trammel (1815-1898), with notes on some other members of the families. Researched in part, written and/or compiled by Clara O. Cook. Brownwood, Tex. C. O. Cook. 1981. (LC)

TRAMMELL –Murff, Vaughn West
Family of Daniel, Elisha, and Francis Moore Trammell. Floydada, Tex. Murff. 1958. (DAR)

TRAVIS – Graham, Edna Earle Travis
The Travis family, 1066 thru 1976. Abilene, Tex. Graham. 1976. (DAR)

TRAYLOR – Robertson, R. T.
Ancestry and lineage of Mrs. John C. Robertson (Ruby Traylor). By R. T. Robertson. Dallas, Tex.? (n.d.). (FW)

TRENT – Trent, Ray, 1916-
Trents of Texas. By Ray Trent. Denver City, Tex. South Plains Pub. Co. c1989. (LC)

TREYBIG – Treybig, Arliss, 1934-
Descendants of William Henry Treybig and Lena Marx: a statistical history: including references to Heine, Knebel, Marx, and Treybig families in Texas. By Arliss Treybig. Rev. El Campo, Tex. A. Treybig. 1980. (LC)

TRIMBLE – Trimble, David B.
American beginnings. San Antonio, Tex. Trimble. c1974. (DAR)

TRIMBLE – Trimble, David B.
American beginnings. By David B. Trimble. San Antonio? Tex. (s.n. 1974). (LC)

TRIMBLE – Trimble, David B.
Hiestand family of Page County, Virginia. By David B. Trimble. San Antonio, Tex. Trimble. 1974. (FW)

TRIMBLE – Trimble, David B.
Hiestand family of Page County, Virginia, also Trimble and Boehun families. ?San Antonio, Tex. 1974. (NGS)

TRIMBLE – Trimble, David B.
Southwest Virginia families. By David B. Trimble. San Antonio? Tex. (s.n. 1974). (LC)

TRIMBLE – Trimble, David B.
American Beginnings, Trimble, Johnson, King, and Lewis families. San Antonio, Tex. 1974. (NGS)

TRINDLE – Trindle, Helen Margaret
   Searching for Trindles. 1968. (NGS)

TROFAST – Sherman, June Moosberg, 1948-
   The Trofast-Moosberg family: a genealogy. Compiled by June Moosberg Sherman. Lockney, Tex. J. M. Sherman. 1986. (LC)

TROTTER – Lusby, James Vernon, 1920-
   Stafford – Trotter: a genealogy. By James Vernon Lusby. Houston, Tex. J. V. Lusby. 1989. (LC)

TROW – Trow, Raymond B.
   Genealogy of Raymond Bridgman Trow. By Raymond B. Trow. Houston, Tex., 1944. (FW)

TRUBE – Trube, Mattie Ellen Brown
   Your family and Mine, Brown, Trube, Alderman, Meredith, Brodnax families. Houston, Tex. 1973. (NGS)

TRUE – Isbell, Odessa Morrow, 1922-
   Genealogy of the True & Bevers (Beavers) families: with brief data on allied families of Clack, Glasscock, Hill, Slayden, Pistole. By Odessa Morrow Isbell. Gainesville, Tex. Gainesville Print. 1983. (LC)

TRUE – True, Charles Wesley, 1916-
   The True family: some Henry True descendants in Texas: history and genealogy of ancestors [sic], descendants, and allied families of Charles and Margaret Wade True of Nueces County, Texas. By Charles Wesley True, Jr. El Paso, Tex. C. W. True. 1981. (LC)

TRUE – True, Charles Wesley, 1916-
   The True family: some Henry True descendants on the frontier: history and genealogy of ancestors, descendants, and allied families of Henry and Israel Pike True of Salem and Salisbury, Massachusetts. By Charles Wesley True, Jr. El Paso, Tex. C. W. True Enterprises. 1984. (LC)

TRUMBULL – Trumbull, Dorothy May Boyson
   Continuing a special heritage: a family history, Sherman, Boyson, Trumbull. By Dorothy May Boyson Trumbull. 1st Ed. Austin, Tex. Nortex Press. c1990. (LC)

TSCHOEPE – Waite, Annette
   German immigrants Rudolph and Augusta Tschoepe. By Annette Waite. Geronimo, Tex. Waite. 1980. (LC)

TUCKER – Archer, Jane Adams, 1942-
   Tucker cousins: descendants of Anderton Tucker, 1783-1865 and his wife Stacy Tucker, 1785-1866. [Compiled 1980 by Jane Adams Archer; original art work by Jane Adam Archer]. Lockney, Tex. J. S. Archer. c1980. (LC)

TUCKER – Tucker, D. A. (Duard Arnold), 1919-
My Tucker family: from South Carolina to Mississippi to Arkansas. Compiled by D. A. Tucker. Houston, Tex. D. A. Tucker. 1988. (LC)

TUCKER – Tucker, Reuel Walter
Memoirs and history of the Peyton Tucker family: ancestors and descendants of England, Wales, Vermont, Massachusetts, Maryland, Virginia, the Carolinas, Georgia, Tennessee, Kentucky, Illinois, Missouri, Arkansas, Louisiana, Texas, Oklahoma, and California, and genealogy. By Reuel Walter Tucker. Baltimore: Gateway Press. 1975. (LC)

TUGGLE – Owen, Doris Tuggle, 1929-
Entwinning branches, 1560-1985. Compiled by Doris Tuggle Owen. Fort Worth, Tex. Published for the author by Advanced Print. 1986. (LC)

TURKNETT – Jenkins, Frank Duane, d. 1981-
The Turknett family. By Frank Duane Jenkins. Lubbock, Tex. C. K. Wood. c1981. (LC)

TURNBULL – Kellough, Gene Ross
The ancestry of Gene Ross: including the Ross line and assorted lines of Bennett, Grimes, Llewellyn, Knighton, Turnbull and Kyle. By Gene Ross Kellough; including wills, letters, and contents of Kyle estate sale, plus "Samplings" the account of growing up in Texas 1909 through 1937. Seneca, S.C. G. R. Kellough. 1986. (LC)

TURNBULL – Turnbo, Charles Alton, 1942-
The Texas Turnbo's. Wichita Falls, Tex. C. A. Turnbo, 1977. (LC)

TURNER – Fake, Pauline Turner
Traditional ancestors of James Turner. San Antonio, Tex. Fake. c1978. (DAR)

TURNER – Fake, Pauline Turner, 1905-
Taditional ancestors of James Turner. Compiled by Pauline Turner Fake. San Antonio, Tex. Fake. c1978. (LC)

TURNER – Fake, Pauline (Turner)
James Turner (1758-1826) and his many descendants through 1978. San Antonio, Tex. c1978. (NGS)

TURNER – Ptomey, Kyser Cowart, 1915-
John Ogletree, Sr., 1740-1822: two hundred twenty five years of descendants: and the allied lines of Phillips, Turner, Sanders, French, Riggins, Martin, and McBrayer. By Kyser Cowart Ptomey. K. S. Ptomey. c1986. (LC)

TURPIN – Haack, Robert D. (Robert David), 1961-
Descendants of the Turpin and Vanston families. By Robert D. Haack. Corpus Christi, Tex. R. D. Haack. c1983. (LC)

TYNER – Tyner, Max R.
The Tyner family and some other relatives. Compiled by Max R. Tyner. George West, Tex. Tyner. c1975. (LC)

TYNER – Tyner, Max R., 1925-
The Tyner family and some other relatives. Compiled and edited by Max R. Tyner. McAllen, Tex. Tyner. c1979. (LC)

TYRRELL – Terrell, Edwin H.
Genealogical notes on the Tyrrell and Terrell family of Virginia and its English and Norman progenitors. By Edwin H. Terrell. San Antonio, Tex., 1907. (FW)

U –

UNDERWOOD – Underwood, Nancy Chambers
Fifty families. Dallas, Tex. Underwood. c1977. (DAR)

USENER – Justman, Dorothy E.
German Colonists and their descendants in Houston. Usener family. Quanah, Tex. 1974. (NGS)

V –

VADEN – Winn, Tennie Elizabeth Vaden
Genealogy of the Vaden and related families. San Antonio, Tex. Schneider Print Co. 1970. (DAR)

VADEN – Winn, Tennie Elizabeth Vaden
Genealogy of the Vaden and related families. Data collected and compiled by Tennie Elizabeth Vaden Winn. San Antonio, Tex. Schneider Print. Co., 1970. (LC)

VALLIANT – Lane, Elise D. B.
Certain descendants of Robert Spencer Valliant and his wife, Martha Hurlock Valliant through their son, William Taylor Valliant (1806-1865). By Elise D. B. Lane. San Antonio, Tex., 195-. (NY)

VAN CLEVE – Conger, William R.
Memories of Benjain Van Cleve. By William R. Conger. Fort Worth, Tex. Amer. Reference Publishers, 1968. (IG)

VANDIVER – Vandiver, Eva Mallory, 1919-
Southern genealogies of the Mallory, Vandiver, and related families, 1500-1987. Compiled by Eva Mallory Vandiver. Mineola, Tex. E. M. Vandiver.

VAN ZANDT – Carter, Sarah Elizabeth,1909-
The Van Zandt family. By Sarah Elizabeth Carter. Revision 1987. Keene, Tex.: S. E. Carter. 1987. (LC)

VAUGHAN – Stoltz, Joan V. (Joan Vaughn), 1942-
Hither, thither, and yon: a history of Vann, Vaughn, and associated families, 1823-1988. By Joan V. Stoltz. Houoston, Tex. J. V. Stoltz. 1988? (LC)

VAUGHAN – Vaughan, Jack Chaplin, 1912-
Blossom Chapline Vaughan (1877-1965) of Arkansas and Alfred Jefferson Vaughan, III (1867-1942) of Mississippi. By Jack Chapline Vaughan. Arlington, Tex. Vaughan. 1975-. (LC)

VAUGHAN – Vaughan, Jack Chapline, 1912-
Jamestowne. Little Rock, Ark. Vaughan. c1990. (LC)

VAWTER – Byler, Shirley Ellen (Vawter)
The family of Albert and Josie Vawter with Albert's ancestors. By their daughter Shirley Ellen (Vawter) Byler. Sweeney, Tex. S. E. Byler. c1985. (LC)

VENABLE – Eckhardt, Ura L.
Venable family booklet, no. 1, 1961-70. By Ura L. Eckhardt. Houston, Tex. 1970. (FW)

VERMILLION – Novak, Rynell Stiff, 1929-
Vermillion family history. Denton, Tex. R. S. Novak. 1978. (LC)

VICK – Vick, James Andrew, 1929-
Vick, Robert, son of the Virginia immigrant Joseph Vick: an account of some of his descendants. Waco, Tex. J. A. Vick. 1990. (LC)

VILLASENOR – Villasenor, Victor
Rain or gold. By Victor Villasenor. Houston, Tex. Arte Publico Press. 1991. (LC)

VINCENT – Clark, Robert M. (Robert Murel), 1948-
Hardie, Vincent, Gaines, and related families: from Virginia to Texas. By Robert M. Clark, Jr. [United States? R. M. Clark, c1989]. (LC)

VON ROEDER – Eckhardt, Ura L.
Von Roeder family, no. 1. By Ura L. Eckhardt. Houston, Tex. 1969. (FW)

VROOMAN –
Josiah B. Vrooman (Vroman) his ancestors and descendants. By Lora Vrooman Randall and Florence Vrooman Houghton. El Paso, Tex. C. Hertzog, Printer. 1946. (LC)

VROOMAN -- Wickershamn, Grace Vrooman
The Vrooman family in America. Dallas, Tex. Comstock. 1949. (DAR)

VROOMAN –
The Vrooman family in America descendants of Hendrick Meese Vrooman who came from Hollannd to America in 1664. Prepared by Grace Vrooman Wickersham and Ernest Bernard Comstock. Dallas, 1949. (LC)

W –

Wackwitz – Wackwitz, F. H. (Frederik Hendrik), 1928-
A pictorial history of the Wackwitz family 1402-1988. By F. H. Wackwitz. Van Alstyne, Tex., USA. F. H. Wackwitz. 1988? (LC)

WADE – Wade, Ophelia (R.)
Wade-Waid-Waide; a research book primarily of census, cemetery and courthouse records for the state of Ala., Ark., Ga., Ind., Ky., Mass., Miss., Mo., N.C., Okla., S.C., Tenn., Texas and Va. By Ophelia (R.) Wade. Bragg City, Mo. Author. 1975. (FW)

WADSWORTH – Wadsworth, William F. (William Franklin), 1949-
360 years of southern Wadsworths: military, probate, census, land, and genealogical records for Wadsworths from southern states between the period 1621 and 1981. By William F. Wadsworth, III. Severna Park, Md. W. F. Wadsworth, 1981? (LC)

WALKER – Ball, Greg, 1962-
Family charts of the Cozby, Skeen, Walker, Rawson, Brumbelow, and Smith families. Compiled and indexed by Greg Ball. 2nd Ed. San Antonio, Tex. G. Ball. 1989. (LC)

WALKER –
The Descendants of Elias Walker, Sr., 1762-1976 of Washington Co., Tennessee and allied families: Andes, Davis, Odom, Edgemon, Allen, Deatherage, Johnson, Pierce, King, McDaniel, Ford, Grice, Mavity, Kimball, Eastham, and others. Waco, Tex. L. Walker. 1986? (LC)

WALKER –
Genealogy of John Walker from Ireland, 1720, and some of his ancestors in England and Ireland and some of his descendants in America. Mrs. William W. (Malone) Neal... Collaborator. Compiled by Robert Walton Walker... 1900 to 1934. Fort Worth, Tex. 1934? (LC)

WALKER – Sutphin, Dorothy Lyons
The Walker family of Mississippi, Louisiana and Texas. Baytown, Tex. Sutphin. 1970. (DAR)

WALKER – Walker, Laura, 1960-
Daughter of deceit: the human drama behind the Walker spy case. By Laura Walker with Jerry Horner. Dallas. Worth Pub. c1988. (LC)

WALKER – Walker, Robert Walton
Genealogy of John Walker. Fort Worth, Tex. Walker. 1934. (DAR)

WALLACE – Phelps, James A.
The Wallace family in America. By James A. Phelps. Dallas, Tex. Clan Wallace Society. 1968. (LC)

WALLACE – Wallace, Charles B.
The Clan Wallace. By Charles B. Wallace. Dallas. Printed by Clan Wallace Society, 1967. (LC)

WALLACE – Wallace, Charles B.
The clan Wallace. By Charles B. Wallace. 3rd Ed. Dallas, Tex. C. B. Wallace. c1989. (Dallas: Printed by the Clan Wallace Society).

WALLACE – Young, Charles Hamilton
Wallace-Frierson and Allied Families. Also Bettes family. Kyle, Tex. 1982. (NGS)

WALTHER – Steger, Mel
A history of the Walther-Jessen family, 1730-1980. Houston. M. Steger, 1980? (LC)

WALTON – Eckhardt, Ura L.
Walton family, no. 1-3, 1965-1970. By Ura L. Eckhardt. Houston, Tex. 1970. (FW)

WALTON – Tinney, Joe C. (Joe Clifford), 1905-
The Walltons of Brunswick County, Virginia: descendants of George and Elizabeth (Rowe) Walton. By Joe C. Tinney. Waco, Tex. J. C. Tinney. 1983. (LC)

WAMPLER – Shouse, Genevieve M. (Genevieve May), 1919-
Wamplers in America. Compiled by Genevieve M. Shouse; indexed by John E. Shouse. Baltimore: Gateway Press. Alamo, Tex. 1981. (LC)

WARD –
The George W. Ward family: highlighting the William A. Ward family genealogy: including Biffle, Cashion, Clifton, Cox, Denman, Schell, Smith, Welsch, and other Wards. 2nd Ed. Rockport, Tex. E. D. Denman. 1989? (LC)

WARD – Douthitt, Billie
Genealogy of the Ward, Douthitt, Murphy, Heard and Cox families of Leon County, Texas. Corpus Christi, Tex. Professional Printing & Lithographing. 1968. (DAR)

WARD – Douthitt, Mrs. Billie
Genealogy of the Ward, Douthitt, Murphy, Heard and Cox families of Leon County, Texas. By Mrs. Billie Douthitt. Corpus Christi, Tex. Professional Print. 1968. (FW)

WARWICK – Letts, Hubert W. (Hubert Winfrfed), 1913-
Yankee land to Dixie land: a family genealogy. By Hubert W. Letts. Corpus Christi, Tex. Home Publishers. c1986. (LC)

WASHBURN – Dodd, Vara T.
Washburn family lineage; descendants of Cephas Washburn (1793-1860) and Abigail Woodward, pioneer missionaries to Cherokee Indians. By Vara T. Dodd. El Paso, Tex. E. H. Vowell. 1970. (FW)

WASHBURN – Vowell, Emily Holmes
   Washburn family lineage. El Paso, Tex. Vowell. 1970. (DAR)

WASHINGTON – Eckahrdt, Ura L.
   Washington family, no. 1-2, 1953-1969. By Ura L. Eckhardt. Houston, Tex. 1969. (FW)

WATERS – Eckhardt, Ura L.
   Waters family, no. 1-8, 1956-1970. By Ura L. Eckhardt. Houston, Tex. 1970. (FW)

WATERS – Newman, Harry Wright
   Waters – Turner – Wilson – Hatch families of Maryland. Fort Worth, Tex. Young Family. 1979. (DAR)

WATERS –
   William Waters: his descendants and related families. Compiled and edited by Juanita Watters, Nadine Lain (and) Quida (Watters) Nelson. Cleburne, Tex. Hallman Print & Office Supply, 1967. (LC)

WATT – Watt, Frank H.
   John Watt. Waco, Tex. Watt. c1941. (DAR)

WATTERS – Watters, Juanita
   William Watters. Cleburne, Tex. Hallman Printing & Office Supply. 1967. (DAR)

WATTERS – Watters, Juanita
   Supplement to: William Watters... By Juanita Watters. Supplement: by Juanita Watters. Cleburne, Tex. Hallman Print. 1968. (NY)

WATTERS – Watters, Juanita
   William Watters, his descendants and related families. Also by Nadine Lain and Onida W. Nelson. Cleburne, Tex. 1967. (NGS)

WATTERSON – Vest, Deed L.
   Watterson folk of Bastrop County, Texas. Waco, Tex. Texian Press. c1963. (DAR)

WATTS – Watt, Frank H.
   John Watt, pioneer; a genealogical collection. By Frank H. Watt. Waco, Tex. Lithographed by Hill Print. and Stationery Co. c1941. (LC)

WATTS – Watt, Frank Hedden
   George Watt of Xenia. The McClellans. By Frank Hedden Watt. Waco? Tex. 1947 (LC)

WATTS. See also:
   Brumbach
   De Peyster
   King
   Miller
   Reading
   Sebor
   Traill

WEATHERS – Murchison, Beatrice, 1895-
   Trees of Lineage. By Beatrice Murchison. Waco, Tex. B. Murchison. [198-?] 1960. (LC)

WEATHERWAX – Fisher, James N.
   The Weatherwax genealogy. By James N. Fisher. Houston? Tex. , 1972. (DP)

WEDMORE – Stevens, Virginia Marie Vest Seeds, 1921-
   The Wedmores of America. Compiled by Virginia Marie (Vest) Seed Stevens. Weslaco, Tex. V. M. V. S. Stevens. [1990-]. (LC)

WEIDLER – Meredith, Elizabeth V., 1926-
   Michael Weidler – his antecedents and descendants. By Elizabeth V. Meredith. Houston, Tex. E. V. Meredith. 1987. (LC)

WELCH – Welch, Jeff D.
   Welch history. Dallas, Tex. Taylor Pub. Co. 1935. (DAR)

WELCH – Welch, Jeff D.
   Welch. Also Knowles and Copeland families. Dallas, Tex. 1950. (NGS)

WELCH – Welch, June Rayfield
   A family history; the ancestry of Ransom Frank Welch and Susan Curtis Welch. By June Rayfield Welch. Dallas? Tex. 1966. (LC)

WELLS –
   Wells family research bulletin. Vol. 1-2. Grandview, Tex., 1973-4. (FW)

WELSH – Welsh, Dorothy L. G.
   Welsh family. By Dorothy L. G. Welsh. Dallas, 1964. (FW)

WELSH – Welsh, Dorothy G.
   The Welsh family. Also by Spurgeon E. Welsh, also Lau, Renoll, Hoff, Layden families. Dallas, Tex. 1964. (NGS)

WEST – Comstock, Ernest Bernard
   The West family. Dallas, Tex. Comstock. 1936. (DAR)

WEST – Comstock, E. B.
   The West family with descendants of Eleazer West, 1752-1798? Goshen, N. Y. Prepared by E. B. Comstock. Dallas, Tex., 1931. (LC)

WEST – Murff, Vaughn W.
   Some descendants of Henry West, born in 1785 in N.C. By Vaughn W. Murff. Floydada, Tex., 1961. (IG)

WEST – Wilson, Loretta West
   Claiborne Dandrige West of Buckingham County, Virginia, his ancestors and descendants. Dallas, Tex. Southern Methodist University Printing Dept. 1967. (DAR)

WETHERILL – Damon, Christine Weatherall, 1912-
Wetherall/Weatherall of the United States. By Christine Weatherall Damon. Baltimore; Gateway Press. Amarillo, Tex. 1984. (LC)

WHARTON – Alter, Judy, 1938-
Thistle Hill: the history and the house. By Judy Alter; foreword by Lloyd "Cissy" Stewart; illustrations by Barbara Whitehead. Fort Worth: Texas Christian University Press. c1988. (LC)

WHATLEY – Jones, Mary Elizabeth
Whatley grandfathers. Abilene, Tex. Jones. 1973. (DAR)

WHATLEY – Jones, Mary Elizabeth Whatley
Illustrious grandmother. Abilene, Tex. Jones. 1965. (DAR)

WHEELER –Wheeler, Edward E.
Wheeler family history, for period 1066 to 1962. By Edward E. Wheeler. San Antonio, Tex., 1962. (NY)

WHELAN – Wayland, John Terrill, 1935-
Wayland families of nineteenth century Missouri: with additions to the original Virginia line. By John Terrill Wayland. Longview, Tex. J. T. Wayland, 1982. (LC)

WHELAN – Wayland, John Walter, 1909-
Wayland family genealogy. By John Walter Wayland, Jr. 1980. (LC)

WHITAKER – Whitaker, Melvin D. (Melvin Dodson), 1932-
Whitakers of the Holme, Lancashire, England (1431) to America (1988). By Melvin D. Whitaker, Baltimore: Gateway Press. Palestine, Tex. M. D. Whitaker. c1988. (LC)

WHITE – Edlin, Billie Lou, 1921-
The Anderson White family. By Billie Lou Edlin. Odessa, Tex. B. L. Edlin, 1983. (LC)

WHITE – White, Betty Sweat, 1938-
The White family on Black and Red Rivers. By Betty Sweat White. Port Neches, Tex. B. S. White. c1990. (LC)

WHITE – White, Gifford E.
Amy White of the old 300. By Gifford White. Austin, Tex. G. White. c1986. (LC)

WHITE – White, Gifford E.
James Taylor White of Virginia and some of his descendants into Texas. By Gifford White. Austin, Tex. G. White. c1982. (LC)

WHITE – White, Gifford E.
James Taylor White of Virginia and some of his descendants into Texas. Austin, Tex. c1982. (NGS)

WHITE – White-Brann, Mildred
Our ancestors. By Mildred White-Brann. Dallas, Tex. c1940. (LC)

WHITLEY – Estes, Dorris Easley, 1920-
Joseph Whitley, Sr. and his descendants in America, 1751-1990. Compiled by Dorris Easley Estes. Baltimore: Gateway Press. Frisco, Tex. 1990. (LC)

WHITLEY – Flores, Joan Elizabeth
The John Whitley family. By Joan Elizabeth Flores. Houston, Tex. Flores. c1975. (LC)

WHITLEY –
Our wandering Whitleys; descendants of Sharp R. Whitley & John Saunders Whitley of Virginia, Kentucky, Tennessee, Illinois, Missouri, and Texas and allied families. Compiled by Helen Whitley Stroder and Routh Whitley Benbow. Clovis, N. Mex. 1974. (LC)

WHITWORTH – Towell, Roy H. (Roy Harrison), 1915-
Isaac Towell & his family: including Towell, McAdams, Whitworth, Shaw, Fitzgerald & others, 1764-1990. By Roy H. Towell, Jr. Beaumont, Tex. R. H. Towell. c1990. (LC)

WICKARD – Hilsbeck, Carter L.
Wickard-Ware-Hilsabeck family genealogy, Indiana-Ohio, 1733-1971. By Carter L. Hilsbeck. Austin, Tex., 1971. (OH)

WIKE – Wike, Monte, 1932-
The Wike family: descendants of Jacob M. Weik of North Carolina. By Monte & Noma Wike. Colorado City, Tex. M. Wike. 1978. (LC)

WILBURN – Wilburn, Samuel W.
Wilburn and Stratton history. By Samuel W. Wilburn. Texarkana, Tex., 1966. (FW)

WILEY – Eckhardt, Ura L.
Wiley family, no. 1-3, 1965-1970. By Ura L. Eckhardt. Houston, Tex. 1970. (FW)

WILKES – Johnston, Doris Ross Brock
Wilks and Young families, Texas pioneers: maternall lines, Pfeiffer, Whitesides, Mead, Newman, Marrs, Kerr. By Doris Ross Brock Johnston. Irving, Tex. D. R. B. Johnston. c1984. (LC)

WILLIAMS – Gee, William H.
Stephen Williams of Jasper County and allied families. By William H. Gee. Beaumont, Tex., 1976. (FW)

WILLIAMS – McMurry, Rhuy K. Williams
One branch of our Williams family. Weslaco, Tex. McMurry. 1974. (DAR)

WILLIAMS – O'Brien, Clara Vaughan Hatcher
Deep roots and strong branches; a chronicle of the descendants of Samuel and Pilgrim Williams including many of the families with which their descendants merged. By Clara Vaughan Hatcher O'Brien. San Antonio, Tex. Clemens Printing Co. 1972. (LC)

WILLIAMS – Sloane, Charles Albert
I remember; being the memoirs of Mrs. John Herndon (Maria Aurelia Williams) James together with contemporary historical events and sketches of her own and her husband's families. Edited and compiled by Charles Albert Sloane. San Antonio, Tex. Naylor Co., 1938. (LC)

WILLIAMS – Sowell, Carolyn E.
The P. K. Williams family. Sulphur Springs, Tex. Echo Pub. Co., 1978. (DAR)

WILLIAMS – Sowell, Carolyn E., 1939-
The P. K. Williams family: notes and photographs on the family of Paschal Klough and Joanna (Garvin) Williams of Upshur County, Texas. Compiled by Carolyn E. Sowell, Carl C. Williams, Marshall L. Williams: [drawings by Pretice A. Ables, Jr.]. Sulphur Springs, Tex. Sowell, 1978. (LC)

WILLIAMS –
Stephen Williams of Jasper County and allied families. Compiled by W. H. (Bill) Gee. Beaumont (LC)

WILLIAMS – Williamms, Lyle Keith
A genealogy of Dan Batchelor and David Neal Williams. By Lyle Keith Williams. Fort Worth, Tex., 1968? (LC)

WILLIAMS – Williams, Llyle Keith, 1915-
A page in history, a moment in eternity: an autobiography. By Lyle Keith Williams. Fort Worth, Tex. L. K. Williams. c1986. (LC)

WILLIAMS – Williams, Lyle Keith
A Genealogy of Dan Batchelor (Williams) and David Neal Williams. Fort Worth, Tex. 1958. (NGS)

WILLIAMS – Williams, Llyle Keith
A genealogy of Dan Batchelor and David Neal Williams. Fort Worth, Tex. 1968? (DAR)

WILLIAMSON – Eckhardt, Ura L.
Williamson family, no. 1-6, 1960-1970. By Ura L. Eckhardt. Houston, Tex. 1970. (FW)

WILLIS – Willis, Douglas M.
Two centuries with a Willis family and their kin. Dallas, Tex. (s.n.) 1963. (DAR)

WILLIS – Willis, Douglas M.
Two centuries with a Willis family and their kin. By Douglas M. Willis. Dallas, Tex., 1963. (FW)

WILLOUGHBY – Eckhardt, Ura L.
Willoughby family, no. 1. By Ura L. Eckhardt. Houston, Tex. 1970. (FW)

WILSON – Cunningham, T. M.
Hugh Wilson. Dallas, Tex. Wilkinson Printing Co. 1938. (DAR)

WILSON – Cunningham, T. M.
Hugh Wilson, a pioneer saint; missionary to the Chickasaw Indians and pioneer minister in Texas; with a genealogy of the Wilson family including 422 descendants of Rev. Lewis Feuilleteau Wilson, I. By T. M. Cunningham. Dallas, Tex. Wilkinson Print. Co., c1938. (LC)

Supplement of additions and corrections... Dallas, Tex. Ann Arbor, Mich. Edwards Brothers, Inc. 1944. (LC)

WILSON – Keeling, Gladys Wilson
Our Wilson ancestors. Mexia, Tex. Keeling. 1975. (DAR)

WILSON – Kelsey, Mary Wilson
Robert Wilson, 1750-1826, of Blount County, Tennessee: some of his descendants and related families including Gould, Cook, Brooks, Huson, Shearer, Stribling. Compiled from the papers of Mary Wilson Kelsey, James Cook Wilson, and Louise Kirk; illustrations from the Mavis and Mary Kelsey Collection of Art and Americans at the Sterling Evans Library, Texas A&M University. 1st Ed. Houston, Tex. M. W. Kelsey. c1987. (LC)

WILSON –Manz, Mabel Ann Anderson, 1914-
Descendants of Christopher Wil(l)son of Yorkshire, England, and New Castle County, Delaware, following the line of his seventh son John Willson. Compiled, edited, and indexed by Mabel Anderson Manz; primary research by Elinor Anderson Gaines; information gathered by Hazel Bardmess Cos; informatioin and photos contributed by Marth Wilson Kobalt. Austin, Tex. M. A. Manz. 1984. (LC)

WILSON – Maxwell, C. J.
A tentative list of the descendants of William Wilson, born 1722 – died 1801. By C. J. Maxwell. Mesquite, Tex. Printed by the Texas Mesquiter, 1937. (LC)

WILSON – Wilson, Francis W.
Advocate for Texas: Thomas Wilson. By Francis W. Wilson. Luling, Tex. F. W. Wilson. c1987. (LC)

WILSON – Wilson, John H.
The Willson (Wilson) family. By John H. Wilson. Fort Worth, Tex. 1970. (LC)

- Willson-Wilson family history, supplement (Fort Worth, 1970). (LC)

WILSON – Wilson, Leland Earl, 1925-
"Dear John": a family history of the following families: Trygstad, Benson, Wilson, Sunderhaus, Stab, Huffman, Devore, Mills, Healy. By Leland Earl Wilson. Longview, Tex. M E M Publishers. 1988, c1989. (LC)

WILSON – Wilson, Logan Drexel
No beginning, no ending. By Logan Drexel Wilson. Dallas, Tex. Taylor Pub. Co., 1972. (LC)

WILSON – Wilson, Logan Drexel
 No Begin(N)ing, No ending. Wilson and Stroud Families. Dallas, Tex. 1972. (NGS)

WIMBERLY – Debenport, Jane Clancy, 1935-
 The descendants of Joseph Ratcliff of Bienville Parish, Louisiana: including the families of Jeter, Wimberly, Davis, Dubberly, Wood, Hardy, Carmichael, Mathews, Norris, McKinney. Compiled by Jane Clancy Debenport. Midland, Tex. J. C. Debenport. c1988. (LC)

WIMBERLY – Wimberly, Vera
 Wimberly family history. Houston, Tex. D. Armstrong Co. c1979. (DAR)

WIMBERLY – Wimberly, Vera
 Wimberly family history: ancestors, relatives, and descendants of William Winberly, pioneer from Georgia to Louisiana, 1837. Compiled by Vera Meek Wimberly. Houston, Tex. D. Armstrong Co. c1979. (LC)

WINEGAR – Casey, Alvin Harold, 1915-
 Shelton, Winiger, and Pace families. By Harold Casey and Robert Casey. 1st Ed. Dallas, Tex. Brooks Pub. Co. Sillwater, Okla. c1988. (LC)

WINGFIELD – Smithers, Debra Winfield, 1952-
 Tanglewood chronicles: a pedigree of branches of the Smithers, Kelley, Winfield, Johnson, and allied families. Compiled by Debra Winfield Smithers. Baltimore: Gateway Press. Corpus Christi, Tex. 1983. (LC)

WINKLER – Myers, William S.
 Winkler history. By William S. Myers. Dallas, Tex. Author, 1909. (FW)

WIISDOM – Smith, Billy Lewis, 1925-
 Wisdom and related families. By Billy Lewis Smith. Bedord, Tex. B. L. Smith. c1986. (LC)

WISE – Wise, Jack W. (Jack Welmer), 1917-
 Wise family history from Pennsylvania to Ohio to Texas. Compiled by Jack W. Wise. New Braunfels, Tex. J. W. Wise. 1990. (LC)

WISEMAN – Parks, Louise Wiseman
 Captain Wiseman. Odessa, Tex. West Texas Printing Co. c1950. (DAR)

WITCHER –
 A Witcher fasmily history: Clabourn D. and Mary B. Austin Witcher and their descendants. Compiled by Frank Witcher and Ruth DeWitt Roach Medley. Lubbock, Tex. F. W. Medley. 1982.

WITHERSPOON – Witherspoon, Joseph Bailey
 The history and genealogy of the Witherspoon family, 1400-1972. Fort Worth, Tex. Miran Publishers. c1973. (DAR)

WITHERSPOON – Witherspoon, Joseph Bailey
The history and genealogy of the Witherspoon family (1400-1972). By Joseph Bailey Witherspoon. Fort Worth, Tex. 1973. (LC)

WITHERSPOON – Witherspoon, Joseph Bailey
The History and Genealogy of the Witherspoon Family. Fort Worth, Tex. 1973. (NGS)

WITT – Witt, Lita D.
Tribute to John and Paralee Witt: pioneers of Wheeler County in the Panhandle of Texas. By Lita D. Witt. Amarillo, Tex.? 1967. (FW)

WOMACK – Womack, Helen Ring, 1925-
The Womack trail: from Virginia to Texas. By Helen Ring Womack. Dallas, Tex. H. R. Womack. 1988. (LC)

WOOD – Allison, Edna Finney
Wood genealogy and history. By Edna Finney Allison. San Angelo? Tex. c1971. (LC)

WOOD – Wood, Christine
Wood works. Lubbock, Tex. Wood. 1971. (DAR)

WOOD – Wood, Christine Knox
Wood Works. Lubbock, Tex. 1971. (NGS)

WOOD Wood, Lester Aaron, 1915-
Rev. George F. Wood: a pictorial history of "a man and his families." Richardson, Tex.? L. A. Wood, 1985. (LC)

WOOD – Wood, William D.
Short biography of Daniel B. Wood and family; William Horn and family, Isaac F. Wood and family, W. D. Wood, his wife and her family. By William D. Wood. San Marcos, Tex., 1904. (FW)

WOODALL – Collins, Carr P.
The history of the Woodall, Dollahite, Miles, Kuykendall families in East Texas. Dallas, Tex. Collins. 1961. (DAR)

WOODALL – Collins, Carr P.
History of the Woodall, Dollahite, Miles, Kuykendall families in East Texas. By Carr P. Collins. Dallas, Tex., 1961. (DP)

WOODSON – Anderson, Joseph C., II
The Woodsum (Woodsome/Woodsom) family in America: the descendants of Joseph Woodsum of Berwick, Maine. By Joseph C. Anderson, II; Main research by Lois Ware Thurston. Baltimore, Md.: Gateway Press. Dallas, Tex. 1990. (LC)

WOODWARD – Woodward, Jewell Daphne Gerron, 1902-
Ancestors of Dr. Franklin Columbus Woodward and his descendants, 1757-1982. By Jewell Daphne Gerron Woodward, edited by George C. Woodward, Jr.; illustrated by Ed Curry, Oneida Uzzell. Fort Worth, Tex. Barr Co. c1982. (LC)

WOODWARD – Woodward, Jewell Daphne Gerron
Ancestors of Dr. Franklin Columbus Woodward and his desccendants, 1757-1982. Fort Worth, Tex. 1982. (NGS)

WOOLSEY – Rugeley, Helen Hoskins, 1911-
Cloud, Woolsey, and allied families. Data compiled by Rosa (Woolsey) Howze; produced by Amanda (Howze) Amsler; edited by Margaret (Howze) Purcell; supplementally researched and written by Helen (Hoskins) Rugeley. Austin, Tex. M. H. Purcell. c1987. (LC)

WRIGHT – Bovak, W. Stewart
J. P. 'Dick'. Wolfe City, Tex. Henington Pub. Co. c1966. (DAR)

WRIGHT –Steely, Skipper
Six months from Tennessee: a story of the many pioneers of Miller County, Arkansas... By Skipper Steely. 1st Ed. Wolfe City, Tex. Henington Pub. Co., 1982. (LC)

WROE –Routh, Ross Holland, 1907-
William Wroe, 1670-1730, and some descendants: a genealogy. Compiled and published by Ross H. Routh. El Paso, Tex. R. H. Routh, 1980. (LC)

WYNN – Buck, M. F.
Our Winn family... for 1960 reunion, Waco, Tex. By M. F. Buck. Fort Walton Beach, Fla., 1960. (FW)

Y –

YANCEY – Garrison, Lloyd R.
Descendants of Jackson M. Yancey and Elizabeth B. Goode, his wife. By Lloyd B. Garrison. Dallas, Tex. Egan Co., 1962. (FW)

YANCEY – Garrison, Lloyd R.
Notes for beginning a genealogical study of certain Yancey families... By Lloyd R. Garrison. Denton, Tex. 1960. (FW)

YANCEY – Willis, Douglas M.
Genealogy of Yancey-Medeoris and related lines... Apppendix "A"-("B"). By Douglas M. Willis. Dallas, Tex. 1959-61. (NY)

YARBOROUGH –
Yarborough family magazine, Vol. 1, No. 1. Aug. 1966. Austin, Tex. (NY)

YARBOROUGH –
In memoriumm [sic] Charles Richard Yarborough, centenarian: October 13, 1864-October 24, 1964. Austin? Tex. 1964? (LC)

YATES – Luckett, Helen Hart, 1923-
William Yates, 1850-1928: his ancestors and his descendants. Compiled by Helen H. Luckett. Fort Worth, Tex. H. H. Luckett. 1983. (LC)

YOUNG – Eckhardt, Ura L.
Young family, no. 1-4, 1966-1970. By Ura L. Eckhardt. Houston, Tex. 1970. (FW)

YOUNG – Ferguson, Chas. W.
Young family. By Chas. W. Ferguson. Dallas, Tex. Ferguson. 1973. (LC)

YOUNG – Jenkins, F. D.
Genealogy: William Young, Sr., Holland to Orangeburg, S.C., 1735. By F. D. Jenkins. Ballinger, Tex. 1975. (FW)

YOUNGBLOOD – Brown, Reba H.
The Youngblood family: some descendants of three generations: Benjamin and Susannah (Collins)... Henry and Sarah (Harvey)... John Pearl and Matilda Elias (Norwood) Youngblood of Mississippi, Louisiana and Texas.
By Reba H. Brown. Port Arthur, Tex. Brown. 1973. (FW)

YOUNGBLOOD – Eckhardt, Ura L.
Youngblood family, no. 1-5, 1961-1970. By Ura L. Eckhardt. Houston, Tex. 1970. (FW)

YOUNT – Owens, Erma Lee, 1926-
The Fraziers and the Younses: their ancestors, their descendants, and their in-laws. By Erma Lee Owens, Leha McGrew. 3rd Ed. [Texas?]. E. L. Owens. 1986-. (LC)

Z –

ZEITLER -- Zeitler, Vernon Arthur, 1917-
Upon the shoulders of giants: Zeitler, McFeaters, Hickox, Moorhead, Heckendorn... By Vernon Arthur Zeitler., Thelma Poorbaugh Zeitler. Lake Jackson, Tex. 1986. (LC)

ZUBER – Dagley, Larry G. (Larry Glenn), 1936-
A history of the Zuber family, 1680-1982. By Larry G. Dagley. Tyler, Tex. L. G. Dagley. c1983. (LC)

ZUBER – Zuber, William Physick
Ancestry and kindred of W. P. Zuber, Texas veteran. By William Physick Zuber. Iola? Tex. 1905. (LC)

ZUEHL – Blumberg, C. F.
  Carl C. and Marie Wrede Zuehl descendants. By C. F. Blumberg. Sequin, Tex., 1938. (FW)

MAJOR TEXAS LIBRARIES
WITH GENEALOGICAL BOOKS

Barker Center of American History
University of Texas
Austin, TX 78713

Corpus Christi Public Library
805 Comanche
Corpus Christi, TX 78401

DAR Museum Library
300 Alamo Plaza
San Antonio, TX 78295

Dallas Public Library
1515 Young Street
Dallas, TX 75201

El Paso Genealogical Library
3651 Douglas
El Paso, TX 79903

Ft. Worth Public Library
300 Taylor Street
Ft. worth, TX 76102

Houston Public Library
500 McKinney Street
Houston, TX 77002

Redfern Genealogical
 Research Center
301 W. Missouri
Midland, TX 79701

Scarborough Library of Genealogy,
 History and Biography of South
 and Southwest
McMurry College Library
McMurry Station
Abilene, TX 79605

Sherman Public Library
Local Hist. & Gen. Dept.
421 N. Travis
Sherman, TX 75090

Southwest Gen. Society & Library
412 W. College Street
Carthage, TX 75633

Texas State Archives Regional
 Historical Resource Depository
University Library, Angelo,
State University
San Angelo, TX 76909

Texas State Archives Regional &
 Historical Resource Depository
University Archives,
East Texas State University
Commerce, TX 75428

Texas State Archives Regional
 Historical Resource Depository
Texas A&M University
College Station, TX 77843

Texas State Library
Genealogy Collection
1201 Brazos Street
Austin, TX 78711

Walworth Harrison Public Library,
Genealogy Room
3716 Lee Street

CODES TO LIBRARY ABBREVIATIONS

DP – Denver Public Library

FW – Allen County Public Library, Fort Wayne, Indiana

GF – Genealogical Forum of Portland, Oregon

KH – Kansas State Historical Society, Topeka

LI – Long Island Historical Society, Brooklyn, N. Y.

MH – Minnesota Historical Society, St. Paul

NY – New York Public Library

OH – Ohio Historical Society, Columbus

OS – Oregon State Library, Salem

PH – the Historical Society of Pennsylvania, Philadelphia

SF – San Francisco Public Library

SP – Seattle Public Library

SL – St. Louis Public Library

SU – Sutro Branch of the California State Library, San Francisco

SW – Spokane, Washington, Public Library

GLOSSARY

sic	thus; used to indicate that the previous word has been copied directly, despite an apparent misspelling.
S. l.	Sine loco; without named place of publication.
s.n.	sine nomine; without named publisher.

TEXAS COUNTY HISTORIES AND OTHER TEXAS BOOKS USEFUL TO GENEALOGISTS

ADAIR -- Adair, A. Garland
  Under Texas skies: Travis, Bowie, Bonham and Davy Crockett. By A. Garland Adair and M. H. Crockett. Austin, Tex. Texas Heritage Foundation. 1956 (DAR)

The Alamo heroes and their Revolutionary ancestors. Alamo DAR Chapter; O'Shavano DAR Chapter; San Antonio de Bexar DAR Chapter. San Antonio, Texas: [s.n.]. 1976. (DAR)

ALDRITCH, Armistead Albert –
  The history of Houston County, Texas. By Armistead Albert Aldritch. San Antonio, Tex., [Texas]: Naylor Co. 1943. (DAR)

ALLEN, Charlotte Brawner
  Collin County, Texas ealiest marriages 1846-1858. Copied by Charlotte Brawner Allen. [S.1.]: C. B. Allen. (DAR)

ALLEN, Irene Taylor
  Saga of Anderson: the proud story of a historic Texas community. By Irene Taylor Allen. New York, N. Y. Greenwich Book Pub. 1957. (DAR)

ALLIE, Linda Brown
  Delta County, Texas marriage records 1871-1892. By Linda Brown Allie. Fort Worth, Tex. the Author. 1984. (DAR)

Ancestors of Dallas Genealogical Society Members. Edited by Helen Mason Lee and Gwen Bloomquist Newmann. Dallas, Tex. The Society. 1978. (DAR)

Angelina County, Texas marriage records 1846-1894. Copied from records in the County Court House by Anne Johnston Ford... [et al.]. 1963. (DAR)

APPLING, Arnolia
  Caldwell County, Texas, cemetery records. Comp. by Arnolia Appling, Marjorie Fairchild, Vivian Gray. 3rd Publ. Hardwood, Tex. [Appling?]. 1981. (DAR)

BAINES, May Harper
  Historic souvenir dedicated to Texas centennial, 1936. Comp. by Mrs. W. M. Baines. [Houston, Tex.]: Houston Pen Women. 1936. (DAR)

BAIRD, Delila M.
  Early Fisher County families biographical history, 1876-1910. Collected and compiled by Delila M. Baird and Josie M. Baird. Rotan, Tex. D. M. and J. M. Baird. 1976. (DAR)

BAIRD, G. H.
A brief history of Upshur County, [Texas]. By G. H. Baird. [Gilmer, Tex.]: Gilmer Mirror. 1946. (DAR)

Bandera County marriage records 1856-1891. Compiled by Mrs. Howard Graves, Mrs. Fabian Anderwald and Mrs. Ray Coffal for the Bandera County Historical Survey Committee. Bandera, Tex. A. B. Lewis. [1971?]. (DAR)

Bandera County, Texas cemetery records & index. Compiled by Mrs. Howard Denson... [et al.] for the Bandera County Historical Survey Committee. Bandera, Tex. the Society. 1928. (DAR)

BAKER, Inez
Yesterday in Hall County, Texas. By Inez Baker. Dallas, Tex. Book Craft. c1940. (DAR)

BARTHOLOMEW, Ed
The encyclopedia of Texas ghost towns. By Ed Bartholomew. Fort Davis, Tex. Ed Bartholomew. 1982. (DAR)

BARTHOLOMEW, Ed
The Houston story. By Ed Bartholomew. Houston, Tex. Frontier Press of Texas. 1951. (DAR)

BARTON, Jessie
Index to wills and administrations recorded in probate records of Gregg County, Texas. Compiled and contributed by Jessie and Sterlin Barton. Longview, Tex. J. and S. Barton. [1964]. (DAR)

BARTON, John A.
Salado, Texas cemetery records. Compiled by John A. Barton, Arthur F. McLean and Mrs. Ernest L. Allen. [S.l.: Agnes Woodsen Chapter, DAR]. 1971. (DAR)

BATES, Ed. F.
History and reminiscences of Denton County. By Ed Bates. Denton, Tex. McNitzky Printing Co. c1918. (DAR)

BATTE, Lelia M.
History of Milam County, Texas. By Lelia M. Batte. San Antonio, Tex. Naylor Co. c1956. (DAR)

Bell County cemetery records. Bell County Historical Survey Committee, Agnes Woodson Chapter (Texas) DAR, Bell County Historical Survey Society, Bell County Historical Survey Committee. [S.l.: s.n.]. 1972. (DAR)

BENDER, Lucy Rearden
Texas births, marriages and deaths, 1853-1896. Comp. by Lucy Rearden Bender. 1937. (DAR)

BENJAMIN, Gilbert Giddings
　The Germans in Texas: a study in immigration. By Gilbert Giddings Benjamin. San Francisco: R. and E Research Associates. 1970. (DAR)

BENNETT, Bob
　Kerr County, Texas 1856-1956. Bob Bennett; illustrated by Vandruff. San Antonio, Tex. Naylor Co. c1956. (DAR)

BIGGERS, Don H.
　Shackelford County, [Texas] sketches. Don H. Biggers; typed by Mary Garland Chapter (Texas), DAR. [1947]. (DAR)

BIGGERSTAFF, Inez N.
　Four thousand tombstone inscriptions from Texas, 1745-1870: along the old San Antonio Road and the trail of Austin's colonists. By Mrs. Malcolm B. Biggerstaff. [S.l.]: Biggerstaff. c1952. (DAR)

Biographical directory of the Texan conventions and Congresses. Austin Book Exchange, Inc. [1941]. (DAR)

Births, deaths, and marriages from El Paso newspapers through 1885 for Arizona, Texas, New Mexico, Oklahoma, and Indian Territory. Compiled by the El Paso Genealogical Society. Easley, S.C. Southern Historical Press. 1982. (DAR)

BLAIR, E. L.
　Early history of Grimes County. By E. L. Blair. [S.l.]: E. L. Blair. c1930. (DAR)

BLOCK, Viola
　History of Johnson County, [Texas] and surrounding areas. By Viola Block. Waco, Tex. Texian Press. c1970. (DAR)

BOATWRIGHT, Mai E.
　Tombstone inscriptions of Elm Grove Cemetery: Van Zandt County, Texas. Transcribed and annotated by Mai E. Boatwright. Mabank, Tex. Boatwright. 1973. (DAR)

BOETHEL, Paul C.
　The History of Lavaca County, [Texas]. By Paul C. Boethel. San Antonio, Tex. Naylor Company. 1936. (DAR)

BOWERS, Eugene W.
　Red River dust: true tales of an American yesterday. By Eugene W. Bowers and Evelyn Oppenheimer. Waco, Tex. Word Books. c1968. (DAR)

BRITT, Sarah Ann
　The early history of Baylor County. By Sarah Ann Britton(?). Dallas, Tex. Story Book Press. c1955. (DAR)

BROOKS, A. D.
History of Ellis County Baptist Association. By A. D. Brooks. Hillsboro, Tex. Texas Printing & Supply Co. 1907. (DAR)

BROOKS, Elizabeth
Prominent women of Texas. By Elizabeth Brooks. Akron, Ohio. Werner Co. 18896. (DAR)

BROWN, John Henry
History of Dallas County, Texas: from 1837 to 1887. By John Henry Brown. 1983. (DAR)

BROWN, John Henry
History of Texas from 1685 to 1892. By John Henry Brown. St. Louis: L. E. Daniel. 1892-1893. (DAR)

BRUCE, Leona
They came in peace to Coleman County, [Texas]. By Leona Bruce. Fort Worth, Tex. Branch-Smith. c1970. (DAR)

BULLARD, Lucille Blackburn
Marion County, Texas 1860-1870. By Lucille Blackburn Bullard. Jefferson, Tex. L. B. Bullard. 1965. (DAR)

BURK, Joel Barham
Nacogdoches County cemetery records. Collected by Joel Barham Burk; Compiled and edited by Carolyn Reeves Ericson. Nacogdoches, Tex. C. R. Ericson. c1974. (DAR)

BURK, Joel Barham
Nacogdoches County cemetery records. Collected by Joel Barham Burk; Edited by Carolyn Reeves Ericson. Nacogdoches, Tex. C. R. Ericson. c1978. (DAR)

BURKHOLDER, Nanetta Key
The 1860 census of Brazoria County, Texas. Transcribed by Nanetta Key Burkholder. [S.l.]: Brazosport Genealogical Society. c1978. (DAR)

CALHOON, Joyce
Census of 1880, Liberty County, Texas. Compiled by Joyce Calhoon & Sandra Pickett. [Liberty? Tex.]: Liberty County Historical Commission. c1979. (DAR)

CAMPBELL, Harry H.
The early history of Motley County. By Harry H. Campbell. San Antonio. Tex. Naylor. 1958. (DAR)

CARLISLE, George F. (Mrs.)
History of the Old Cemetery City, Masonic, Odd Fellow. By Mrs. George F. Carlisle (Willie Flowers). Dallas, Tex. Williams Printery. 1948. (DAR)

CARPENTER, V. K. (Mrs.)
Seventh census of the United States 1850 census, Bexar County, Texas. [Transcribed by Mrs. V. K. Carpenter]. Huntsville, Ark.: Century Enterprises Genealogical Service. c1969. (DAR)

CARROLL, H. Bailey
Texas County histories: a bibliography. By H. Bailey Carroll. Austin, Tex. State Historical Association. 1943. (DAR)

CARTER, W. A.
History of Fannin County, Texas: history, statistics and biographies, business cards and a complete directory of the county. [Compiled, written and edited by W. A. Carter]. [S.1.]: Fannon County Historical Society. 1975. (DAR)

CATES, Cliff D.
Pioneer history of Wise County, from red men to railroads: twenty years of intrepid history. By Cliff D. Cates. Decatur, [Texas]: Wise Co., Old Settler's Association. 1907. (DAR)

CAWTHON, Juanita Davis
Marriage and death notices [from] the Texas Republican, Marshall, Texas, 1849-1869. By Juanita Davis Cawthon. Shreveport, La. J. D. Cawthon. 1978. (DAR)

[Cemetery records Dallas Co., Texas] Abstracted by members of the Grand Prairie Genealogical Society. [Grand Prairie, Texas: the Society, 1970?]. (DAR)

Cemetery records of Mitchell and Nolan Counties of Texas. compiled for the Western Texas Genealogical Society by Western Texas College Students. Rotan, Tex. Anne Pettus Shelburne Chapter (Texas) DAR, 1974. (DAR)

Census of Nacogdoches, Texas 1792-1799. By Antonio Gil Ybardo... [et al.] [1978?]. (DAR)

CHABOT, Frederick C.
Alamo, altar of Texas liberty. By Frederick C. Chabot. [S.1.]: Chabot. c1931. (DAR)

CHABOT, Frederick C.
San Antonio and its beginnings. By Frederick C. Chabot. San Antonio, [Texas]: Naylor. 1931. (DAR)

CHABOT, Frederick C.
With the makers of San Antonio: genealogies of the early Latin, Anglo-American, and German families... [et al.]. By Frederick C. Chabot. [S.l.: s.n.]. c1937. (DAR)

CHANDLER, Barbara Overton
History of Texarkana and Bowie and Miller Counties, Texas – Arkansas. By Barbara Overton Chandler and J. Ed Howe. Shreveport, La. J. Ed Howe. c1939. (Dar)

Cisco Cemetery, Eastland County, Cisco, Texas. Copied and compiled by the students of Western Texas Junior College, reproduced by Anne Pettus Shelburne Chapter (Texas) DAR, G. R. C. 1977. (DAR)

The history of Clarksville and Old Red River County, [Texas]. By Pat B. Clark. Dallas, Tex. Mathis, Van Nort & Co. 1937. (DAR)

CLARK, Pat B.
North Texas 100 years ago. By Pat B. Clark. Austin, Tex. Family of Simeon E. Clark. c1947. (DAR)

CLAY, Jon H.
Kaufman County, Texas marriages. Compiled by John H. Clay. Dallas, Tex. 1980. (DAR)

Colfax, [Texas]. Edited by Jack Geddie. Fort Worth, Tex. Henry L. Geddie Co. 1963. (DAR)

A collection of memories: a history of Armstrong County, 1876-1965. Compiled by Armstrong Historical Association. Hereford, Tex. Pioneer Publishers. c1965. (DAR)

CONNOR, Seymour V.
Kentucky colonization in Texas: a history of the Peters Colony. By Seymour V. Connor. Baltimore, Md. Genealogical Publishing. 1983. (DAR)

CORNER, William
San Antonio de Bexar: a guide and history. Compiled and edited by William Corner. San Antonio, Tex. Bainbridge & Corner. 1890. (DAR)

COX, Edwin T.
History of Eastland County, Texas. By Edwin T. Cox. San Antonio, Tex. Naylor Co. 1950. (DAR)

COX, Larue
A history of First Baptist Church, Brownwood, Texas 1876-1966. By Larue Cox. Brownwood, Tex. First Baptist Church. 1968. (DAR)

COX, Mamie Wynne
    The romantic flags of Texas. By Mamie Wynne Cox. Dallas, Tex. Banks Upshaw and Co. c1936. (DAR)

COX, Mary L.
    History of Hale County, Texas. By Mary L. Cox. Plainview, Tex. M. L. Cox. c1937. (DAR)

CRANE, William Carey
    Centennial address embracing the history of Washington County, Texas. By Wm. Carey Crane. Brenham: Banner-Press. 1939. (DAR)

CRAWFORD, Helen Wooddell
    [Cemmeteries Cherokee County, Texas]. By Helen Wooddell Crawford. Jacksonville, Tex. H. W. Crawford. [1970-1974?]. (DAR)

CRAWFORD, M. J. (Mrs.)
    Cemeteries, Jacksonville, Texas and family plots. By Mrs. M. J. Crawford. c1971. (DAR)

CREIGHTON, James A.
    A narrative history of Brazoria County. By James A. Creighton; drawings by Zella McDaniel. Waco, Tex. Texan Press. 1976. (DAR)

CREWS, D'Anne McAdams
    Huntsville and Walker County, Texas: a bicentennial history. Compiled and edited by D'Anne McAdams Crews. Huntsville, Tex. Sam Houston State University Press. 1976. (DAR)

CROCKET, George Louis
    Two centuries in East Texas: a history of San Augustine County and surrounding territory from 1685 to the present time. By George Louis Crocket. Dallas, Tex. Southwest Press. 1962. (DAR)

CROFFORD-GOULD, Sharry
    Texas cemetery inscriptions: a source index. By Sharry Crofford-Gould. San Antonio, Tex. Limited Editors. c1977. (DAR)

CROSS, F. M.
    A short sketch-history from personal reminicences [sic] of early days in Central Texas. By F. M. Cross. 2nd Ed. [S.1.: Bell County Historical Society, 1969]. (DAR)

CROUCH, Carrie J.
    A history of Young County, Texas. By Carrie J. Crouch. Rev. Ed. Austin, Tex. Texas State Historical Association. 1956. (DAR)

CROUCH, Carrie J.
    Young County, [Texas] history and biography. By Carrie J. Crouch. Dallas, Tex. Dealey and Lowe. 1937. (DAR)

CURTIS, Mary Barnett
    1850 census of Tarrant County, Texas: out where the West begins. Compiled by Mary Barnett Curtis. Fort Worth, Tex. Arrow Printing. 1963. (DAR)

CUSHMAN, Evelyn D'Arcy
    Cemeteries of northeast Tarrant County, Texas. By Evelyn D'Arcy Cushman. Arlington, Tex. Chelle-Kirk Printing. 1981. (DAR)

Dallas County, Texas will books A, B, C, D; January 27, 1847-February 17, 1797.
    Abstracted by Jane Douglas Chapter (Texas) DAR, G.R.C. 1970. (DAR)

DANIELL, L. E.
    Personnel of the Texas state government: with sketches of representative men of Texas. By L. E. Daniell. San Antonio, Tex. Maverick Printing House. 1892. (DAR)

DAVIS, Ellis Arthur
    The historical encyclopedia of Texas. By Ellis Arthur Davis, Editor. Rev. Ed. [S.l.]: Texas Historical Society. [1934]. (DAR)

DAVIS, M. E. M.
    Under six flags: the story of Texas. By M. E. M. Davis. Boston: Ginn and Co. 1897. (DAR)

DAVIS, Vinita
    Marriage records index, Denton County, Texas [1875-1894]. Compiled by Vinita Davis. Fort Worth, Tex. American Reference Pub. Co. c1972. (DAR)

DE CORDOVA, J.
    Texas: her resources and her public men. By J. De Cordova. Waco, Tex. Texian Press. c1969. (DAR)

DE MAURI, Johnnie Mae
    The history of Kennedy County, [Texas]. By Johnnie Mae de Mauri. 1940. (DAR)

DESHIELDS, James T.
    They sat in high place: the presidents and governors of Texas; from the first American Chief executive, 1835-36; presidents of the Republic, 1836-46; and governors of the state, 1846-1939. By James T. DeShields. San Antonio, Tex. Naylor Co. 1940. (DAR)

Deaf County, Texas: the land and its people, 1876-1981. [The Deaf Smith County Historical Society]. [Deaf Smith Co., Tex?]. The Society. c1982. (DAR)

DESHIELDS, James T.
    Border wars of Texas: being an authentic and popular account, in chronological order of the long and bitter conflict waged between the savage Indian tribes and

the pioneer settlers of Texas. By James T. DeShields. Tioga, Tex. [s.n.], 1912. (DAR)

DIXON, Sam Houston
The heroes of San Jacinto. By Sam Houston Dixon and Louis Wiltz Kemp. Houston, Tex. Anson Jones Press. 1932. (DAR)

DIXON, Sam Houston
The men who made Texas free: the signers of the Texas Declaration of Independence – sketches of their lives and patriotic services to the Republic and State with a facsimile of the Declaration of Independence. By Sam Houston Dixon. Houston, Tex. Texas Historical Pub. Co. 1924. (DAR)

DOUGLAS, C. L.
Cattle kings of Texas. By C. L. Douglas. Dallas, Tex. Cecil Baugh. c1939. (DAR)

DUFF, Katharyn
Abilene on Catclaw Creek: a profile of a West Texas town. By Katharyn Duff. Abilene, Tex. Reporter Pub. Co. c1969. (DAR)

DUNN, Mary Franklin Deason
A history of Zion Hill Missionary Baptist Church, Rusk County, Texas 1868-1968. By Mary Franklin Deason Dunn. [Henderson, Texas: Bill Decker Printing, 1968]. (DAR)

DWORACZYK, Edward J.
The first Polish colonies of America in Texas: containing also the general history of the Polish people in Texas. Comp. by Edward J. Dworaczyk. San Antonio, Tex. Naylor Co. 1936. (DAR)

EARLE, J. P.
History of Clay County and northwest Texas. By J. P. Earle. Facsimile Ed. Austin, Tex. Brick Row Book Shop. 1963. (DAR)

Early cemetery records Abilene, Texas 1882-1960. West Texas Genealogical Society. Abilene, Tex. The Society. 1961. (DAR)

Early settlers of Terry: a history of Terry County, Texas. Sponsored by the Terry County Historical Survey Committee. Hereford, Tex. Pioneer Book Publishers. c1968. (DAR)

East Texas family records. Tyler, Tex. East Texas Genealogical Society. 1970 (DAR)

ELZER, Johnnie
    Lamplights of Lampasas County, Texas. By Johnnie Elzer. Austin, Tex. Firm Foundation Pub. House. c1951. (DAR)

The encyclopedia of the new West: containing agricultural, mercantile, commercial, manufacturing, mining... of Texas, Arkansas, Colorado, New Mexico and Indian territory; also biographical sketches... Marshall, Tex. United States Biographical Pub. Co. 1881. (DAR)

ERICSON, Carolyn Reeves
    Nacogdoches gateway to Texas: a biographical directory 1773-1849. By Carolyn Reeves Ericson. Fort Worth, Tex. Arrow, Curtis Printing Co. 1974. (DAR)

ERICSON, Carolyn R.
    First settlers of the Republic of Texas: headright land grants which were reported as genuine and legal by the Traveling Commissioners January 1840. By Carolyn R. Ericson and Frances T. Ingmire. St. Louis, Mo. Ingmire Publications. 1982. (DAR)

ERICSON, Carolyn Reeves
    Nacogdoches County marriage records 1889-1894 Book F. Indexed by Carolyn Reeves Ericson. Nacogdoches, Tex. Ericson Books. 1983. (DAR)

ERICSON, Carolyn Reeves
    Nacogdoches gateway to Texas: a biographical directory 1773-1849. By Carolyn Reeves Ericson. Fort Worth, Tex. Arrow, Curtis Printing Co. 1974. (DAR)

EWELL, Thomas T.
    A history of Hood County, Texas also a sketch of the history of Somervell County. Written by Thos. T. Ewell; [reproduced by Texas DAR, G.R.C.]. 1948. (DAR)

Family tree: quarterly of Central Texas Genealogical Society. Waco, Tex. The Society, 1968-1971. (DAR)

Fannin County folk and facts a collection of historical sketches and family histories. Written by the families and friends of Fannin County. Bonham, Tex. Bonham Public Library. c1977. (DAR)

FAULK, J. J.
    History of Henderson County, Texas. By J. J. Faulk. Athens, Tex. Athens Review Printing. c1929. (DAR)

FAY, Mary Smith
    War of 1812 veterans in Texas. By Mary Smith Fay, from notes compiled by Mae Wynne McFarland. New Orleans: Polyanthos. 1979. (DAR)

FERGUSON, Virginia G.
   Mt. Zion, Greenwood and Speegelville Methodist Churches 1878-1923. By Virginia G. Ferguson. [S.l.: s.n.] [1975?]. (DAR)

The first Presbyterian Church, Graham, Texas 1876-1951. [S.l.: s.n. 1951?]. (DAR)

FISHER, O. C.
   It occurred in Kimble. By O. C. Fisher. Houston, Tex. Anson Jones Press. c1937. (DAR)

FLEISCHMAN, Flavia
   Old river country: a history of west Chambers County. By Flavia Fleischman. Fort Worth, Tex. Miran Pub. c1976. (DAR)

FLEMING, E. B.
   Early history of Hopkins County, Texas: biographical sketches and incidents of the early settled families. By E. B. Fleming, restored by Balcones Chapter (Texas) DAR. 1983. (DAR)

Footprints. Fort Worth, Tex. Fort Worth Genealogical Society. [1957]. (DAR)

FORD, Anne Johnson [sic]
   Van Zandt County, Texas marriage record, 1855-1888. Copied from records in the County Court House by Anne Johnson [sic] Ford and Marion Day Mullins. 1958. (DAR)

FORD, Anne Johnston
   Kaufman County, Texas marriage records 1849-1881. Copied from the original records in the County Court House by Anne Johnston Ford, Marion Day Mullins and indexed by Jackie Harmonson. 1959. (DAR)

FORD, Anne Johnston
   Markers placed by the Texas Daughters of the American Revolution. Comp. by Anne Johnston Ford.. Dallas, Tex. 1936. (DAR)

FORD, Anne Johnston
   Rush County, Texas marriage record, 1843-1877. Copied from records in the County Court House by Anne Johnston Ford and Marion Day Mullins. 1960. (DAR)

FULMORE, Z. T.

   The history and geography of Texas: as told in county names. By Z. T. Fulmore. Austin, Tex. E. L. Steck. c1915. (DAR)

GARRETT, Julia Kathryn
   Green flag over Texas: a story of the last years of Spain in Texas. By Julia Kathryn Garrett. Austin: Pemberton Press. [1939?]. (DAR)

GARRISON, George P.
    Texas, a contest of civilizations. By George P. Harrison. Boston: Houghton Mifflin Co. 1903. (DAR)

GAY, Beatrice Grady
    Into the setting sun: a history of Coleman County. By Beatrice Grady Gay; drawings by Mollie Grady Kelley. Santa Anna, Tex. [s.n., 1936?]. (DAR)

Genealogical tips. Tip-O'-Texas Genealogical Society. Harlingen, Tex. The Society. 1962. (DAR)

GEUE, Ethel Hander
    New homes in a new land: German immigration to Texas, 1847-1861. By Ethel Hander Geue. Baltimore: Genealogical Pub. Co. c1982. (DAR)

GHORMLEY, Pearl
    Eastland County, Texas: a historical and biographical survey. By Pearl Ghormley. Austin, Tex. Rupegy Pub. Co. c1969. (DAR)

GILBERT, Charles E.
    Houston today: a history and guide to the South's largest city. By Charles E. Gilbert. Houston, Tex. C. E. Gilbert. c1963. (DAR)

GILPIN, John D. (Mrs).
    Genealogical records, Bibles, lineages, histories Houston Colony Society of Mayflow Descendants. Compiled by Mrs. John S. Gilpin [and] Mrs. Fred W. Lackner [for the Chapter]. [Houston, Tex.]. The Chapter. 1973-1975. (DAR)

GRACY, Alice Duggan
    Early Texas birth records. Compiled by Alice Duggan Gracy, Jane Sumner, Emma Gene Seale Gentry. Easley, S. C. Southern Historical Press. 1982. (DAR)

GRACY, Alice Duggan
    Travis County, Texas: the five schedules of the 1860 Federal census. Compiled by Alice Duggan Gracy and Emma Gene Seale Gentry. Austin, Tex. A. D. Gracy & E. G. Gentry. 1967. (DAR)

Graham centennial history: Graham, Texas 1872-1972, 100 years of progress from salt works to space age. [Young County Historical Survey Committee]. Quanah, Tex. Nortex Offset Publications. c1972. (DAR)

GRAMMER, Norma
    Smith County, Texas marriage record, 1848-1880. Copied by Norma Grammer And Marion [Day] Mullins. 1967. (DAR)

GRAMMER, Norma R.
Cooke County, Texas marriages 1849-July 1879. Copied from records in the Cooke County Court House by Norma P. Grammer and Marion Day Mullins. 1957. (DAR)

GRAMMER, Norma Rutledge
Fayette County, Texas marriage records 1838-1871. Copied from records in the County Court House and indexed by Norma Rutledge Grammer and Marion Day Mullins. 1955. (DAR)

GRAMMER, Norma Rutledge
Marriage records of early Texas, 1824-1846. Comp. by Norma Rutledge Grammer. Fort Worth, Tex. Fort Worth Genealogical Society. 1971. (DAR)

GRAMMER, Norma Rutledge
Texas marriage records, Montgomery County, 1838-1879. Comp. by Norma Rutledge Grammer. 1962. (DAR)

GRAVES, Howard (Mrs.)
History of Bandera County schools for over a century. Comp. by Mrs. Howard Graves; sponsored by the Bandera County Historical Survey Committee. Bandera, Tex. First Ed. The Committee. c1973. (DAR)

Gregg County, Texas Cemeteries. Comp. by Library Development Association. Nicholson Memorail Library, Longview, Gregg Co., Texas. Longview, Tex. The Library. [1984]. (DAR)

GREGORY, Peggy H. (Mrs.)
Record of interments of the City of Galveston, 1859-1872. Copied by Mrs. Peggy H. Gregory. Houston, Tex. P. H. Gregory. 1976. (DAR)

GRIFFIN, John Howard
Land of the high sky. By John Howard Griffin. Midland, Tex. First National Bank of Midland. 1959. (DAR)

GRIFFIN, S. C.
History of Galveston, Texas narrative and biographical. By S. C. Griffin. Galveston, Tex. A. H. Cawston. c1931. (DAR)

Hale County History. Plainview, Tex. Hale County Historical Society. 1971. (DAR)

HALEY, J. Evetts
The XIT Ranch of Texas: and the early days of the Llano Estacado. By J. Evettts Haley. Chicago: Lakeside Press. 1929. (DAR)

HAMPTON, O. V.
    Archer County, Texas cemeteries. Compiled by Mr. & Mrs. O. V. Hampton; indexed by Miss Elayne Stovall. Wichita Falls, Tex. North Texas Genealogical and Historical Association. 1970. (DAR)

HAMRICK, Alma Ward
    The call of the San Saba: a history of San Saba County. By Alma Ward Hamrick. San Antonio, Tex. Naylor. 1941. (DAR)

The Handbook of Waco and McLennan County, Texas. Dayton Kelley, Editor. Waco: Texian Press. c1972. (DAR)

HARDY, Dermot H.
    Historical review of South-East Texas: and the founders, leaders and representative men of its commerce, industry and civic affairs. Associate editors Dermot H. Hardy, Ingham S. Roberts. Chicago: Lewis Pub. Co. 1910. (DAR)

HARMONSON, Paulyne R. (Mrs.)
    Grayson County marriages 1846-1877. Copied from records in the County Court House and indexed by Mrs. A. B. [Paulyne R.] Harmonson and Marion Day Mullins. 1960. (DAR)

HARMONSON, Paulyne R.
    Harrison County, Texas marriage record 1838-1889. Copied from the original records in the County Court House by Mrs. A. B. (Paulyne R.) Harmonson and Marion Day Mullins; indexed by Jackie Harmonson. 1960. (DAR)

HARPER, Mary M.
    1860 Census Polk County, Texas. By Mary M. Harper. St. Louis, Mo. Ingmire Publications. 1984. (DAR)

HARRINGTON, Shirley Klein
    A tribute to Tomball: a pictorial history of the Tomball area. [Shirley Klein Harrington, editor]. Tomball, Tex. Tomball area Diamond Jubilee. 1982. (DAR)

HARRIS, Reed
    A history of the Tonk Valley Baptist Church, 1877-1972 Young Co., Texas. Compiled and edited by Reed Harris. [S.l.:s.n., 1972]. (DAR)

HAYNES, Emma R.
    The history of Polk County, [Texas]. By Emma R. Haynes. [S.l.]. E. Haynes. c1937. (DAR)

Hays County Historical and Genealogical Society. San Marcos, Tex. The Society. 1967. (DAR)

Heart of Texas records: quarterly of Central Texas Genealogical Society. Waco, Tex. The Society. 1972. (DAR)

Henderson County Historical Commisssion
   Old homes of Henderson County. Henderson County Historical Commission. Crockett, Tex. Publications Development Co. 1982. (DAR)

Hereford, Texas diamond jubilee: hustlin' heritage 75. [Jubilee Book Committee]. [S.l.: s.n., 1973?]. (DAR)

High Cemetery, Van Zandt County, Canton, Texas. Balch Springs, Tex. The Historical and Genealogical Society. [1976?]. (DAR)

HILL, Louis C. (Mrs.)
   Bell County, Texas records. Compiled by Mrs. Louis C. Hill and Mrs. John T. Martin. Waco, Tex. [s.n.]. 1969. (DAR)

HIPPLE, Belle Maxine Burnison
   Legacy of the Knox County prairie: a history of Gillespie-Thorp Communities. Compiled and edited by Belle Maxine Burinson Hipple. Austin, Tex. San Felipe Press. 1972. (DAR)

Historical Records Survey
   Inventory of the colonial archives of Texas: municipality of Brazoria, 1832-1837. Prepared by The Historical Records Survey, Division of Women's and Professional Projects, Works Progress [sic] Administration. San Antonio, Tex. The Survey. 1937. (DAR)

Historical Records Survey
   Inventory of the county archives of Texas: Bandera County (Bandera). Prepared by The Texas Historical Records Survey, Division of Professional and Service Projects, Work Projects Administration. San Antonio, Tex. The Survey. 1940. (DAR)

Historical Records Survey
   Inventory of the county archives of Texas: Bastrop County (Bastrop). Prepared by The Texas Historical Records Survey, Division of Community Service Programs, Work Projects Administration. San Antonio, Tex. The Survey. 1941. (DAR)

Historical Records Survey
   Inventory of the county archives of Texas: Brown County (Brownwood). Prepared by The Texas Historical Records Survey, Division of Professional and Service Projects, Work Projects Administration. San Antonio, Tex. The Survey. 1940. (DAR)

Historical Records Survey
   Inventory of the county archives of Texas: Caldwell County (Lockhart). Prepared by The Texas Historical Records Survey, Division of Community Service Programs, Work Projects Administration. [S.l.]: Caldwell Co. 1941. (DAR)

Historical Records Survey
Inventory of the county archives of Texas: Calhoun County (Port Lavaca). Prepared by The Texas Historical Records Survey, Division of Professional and Service Projects, Work Projects Administration. [S.1.]: Calhoun Co. 1941. (DAR)

Historical Records Survey
Inventory of the county archives of Texas: DeWitt County (Cuers). Prepared by The Texas Historical Records Survey, Division of Professional and Service Projects, Work Projects Administration. San Atonio, Tex. The Survey. 1940. (DAR)

Historical Records Survey
Inventory of the county archives of Texas: Denton County (Denton). Prepared by The Texas Historical Records Survey, Division of Women's and Professional Projects, Works Progress [sic] Administration. San Antonio, Tex. The Survey. 1937. (DAR)

Historical Records Survey
Inventory of the county archives of Texas: Fayette County (LaGrange). Prepared by The Texas Historical Records Survey, Division of Professional and Service Projects, Work Projects Administration. [S.1.]: Fayette Co. 1940. (DAR)

Historical Records Survey
Inventory of the county archives of Texas: Gilllespie County (Fredericksburg). Prepared by The Texas Historical Records Survey, Division of Community Service Programs, Work Projects Administration. [S.1.]: Gillespie Co. 1941. (DAR)

Historical Records Survey
Inventory of the county archives of Texas: Gregg County (Longview). Prepared by The Texas Historical Records Survey, Division of Professional and Service Projects, Work Projects Administration. San Antonio, Tex. The Survey. 1940. (DAR)

Historical Records Survey
Inventory of the county archives of Texas: Guadalupe County (Sequin) Prepared by The Texas Historical Records Survey, Division of Professional and Service Projects, Work Projects Administration. San Antonio, Tex. The Survey. 1939. (DAR)

Historical Records Survey
Inventory of the county archives of Texas: Hays County (San Marcos). Prepared by The Texas Historical Records Survey, Division of Professional and Service Projects, Work Projects Administration. San Antonio, Tex. The Survey. 1940. (DAR)

Historical Records Survey
Inventory of the county archives of Texas: Hood County (Granbury). Prepared by The Texas Historical Records Survey, Division of Professional and Service Projects, Work Projects Administration. San Antinio, Tex. The Survey. 1941. (DAR)

Historical Records Survey
    Inventory of the county archives of Texas: Jackson (Edna). Prepared by The Texas Historical Records Survey, Division of Professional and Service Projects, Work Projects Administration. [S.1.]: Jackson Co. 1940. (DAR)

Historical Records Survey
    Inventory of the county archives of Texas: Marion County (Jefferson). Prepared by The Texas Historical Records Survey, Division of Professional And Service Projects, Work Projects Administration. San Antonio, Tex. 1940. (DAR)

Historical Records Survey
    Inventory of the county archives of Texas: Milam County (Cameron). Prepared by The Texas Historical Records Survey, Division of Community Service Projects, Work Projects Administration. San Antonio, Tex. The Survey. 1941. (DAR)

Historical Records Survey
    Inventory of the county archives of Texas: Mills County (Goldwaite). Prepared by The Texas Historical Records Survey, Division of Professional and Service Projects, Work Projects Administration. San Antonio, Tex. The Survey. 1940. (DAR)

Historical Records Survey
    Inventory of the county archives of Texas: Orange County (Orange). Prepared by The Texas Historical Records Survey, Division of Community Service Programs, Work Projects Administration. San Antonio, Tex. The Survey. 1941. (DAR)

Historical Records Survey
    Inventory of the county archives of Texas: Robertson County (Franklin). Prepared by The Texas Historical Records Survey, Division of Community Service Programs, Work Projects Administration. [S.1.]: Robertson Co. 1941. (DAR)

Historical Records Survey
    Inventory of the county archives of Texas: Rockwall County (Rockwall). Prepared by The Texas Historical Records Survey, Division of Community Service Programs, Work Projects Administration. San Antonio, Tex. The Survey. 1940. (DAR)

Historical Records Survey
    Inventory of the county archives of Texas: Sabine County (Hemphill). Prepared by The Historical Records Survey, Division of Professional and Service Projects, Work Projects [sic] Administration. San Antonio, Tex. The Survey. 1939. (DAR)

Historical Records Survey
    Inventory of the county archives of Texas: Wilson County (Floresville). Prepared by The Texas Historical Records Survey, Division of Professional and Service Projects, Work Projects Administration. San Antonio, Tex. The Survey. 1939. (DAR)

Historical sketches of Chambers County, [Texas] pioneers. Book Committee, [Chambers County Bicentennial Commission]. [S.1.:s.n.]. 1976. (DAR)

History of Brazoria County. [S.1.]. Brazoria County Federation of Women's Clubs. 1940. (DAR)

The History of Duncanville, Texas. Compiled by the Duncanville Historical Commission. Dallas, Tex. Taylor Pub. Co. c1976. (DAR)

The History of Grayson County, Texas. By Grayson County Frontier Village. Winston-Salem, North Carolina. Hunter Pub. Co. c1979. (DAR)

A history of Kaufman County. Compiled by Kaufman County Historical Commisssion. Terrell, Tex. The Society. c1978. (DAR)

History of Texas, Fort Worth and the Texas Northwest Edition. Edition by B. B. Paddock. Chicago [Illinois]. Lewis Pub. Co. 1922. (DAR)

History of Texas together with a biographical history of Milam, Williamson, Bastrop, Travis, Lee, Burleson Counties. Chicago [Illinois]. Lewis Pub. Co. 1893. (DAR)

History of Texas together with biographical history of Tarrant and Parker Counties. Chicago: Lewis Publishing. 1895. (DAR)

History of Texas together with a biographical history of the cities of Houston and Galveston. Chicago: Lewis Pub. Co. 1895. (DAR)

History of the First Baptist Church, Texarkana, Texas commemorating its Semi-sequicentennial. [S.1.:s.n.]. 1952. (DAR)

A history of the Humble, Texas area. By Nina Smith, editor. [Humble, Texas]. James Tull Chapter, DAR. c1976. (DAR)

The history of the people of Live Oak County, Texas: 1856-1982. [Live Oak County History Book Committee]. [S.1.: s.n., 1982?]. (DAR)

HODGE, Floy Crandall
    A history of Fannin County featuring pioneer families. By Floy Crandall Hodge. Hereford, Tex. Pioneer Publishers. c1966. (DAR)

HOGG, Marie
> **Upshur County cemetery records of Texas.** Copied by Marie Hogg. Diana, Tex. Audie Ray, Lurline, Douglas Ray Stanley. c1974. (DAR)

HOKES, Pauline Buck
> **A centennial history of Anderson County, Texas.** By Pauline Buck Hokes. San Antonio, Tex. Naylor Company. 1936. (DAR)

HOLLAND, G. A.
> **History of Parker County, [Texas] and the double log cabin.** By G. A. Holland. Weatherford, Tex. Herald Publishing. 1937. (DAR)

HORTON, Thomas F.
> **History of Jack County...** Written and compiled by Thomas F. Horton. Jacksboro, [Texas]. Gazette Print. [1935?]. (DAR)

Houston County Historical Commission
> **History of Houston County, Texas, 1687-1979.** Comp. and edited [by] History Book Committee of Houston County Historical Commission. Tulsa, Okla. Heritage Pub. Co. c1979. (DAR)

Houston County, Texas cemeteries. Compiled by Houston County Historical Commission. 2nd Edition. Winston-Salem, N. C. Hunter Pub. Co. c1978. (DAR)

HUDSON, Weldon I.
> **Comanche County, Texas, census records: 1860 and 1870 Federal census, with index to the 1880 heads of households, and the special 1890 census of Union veterans and widows; also the 1860 slave list and the 1867 Voter's registration.** Comp. by Weldon I. Hudson and Shirley Brittain Cawyer. Fort Worth, Tex. Hudson; Stephenville, Texas: Cawyer. 1981. (DAR)

HUDSON, Weldon I
> **First settlers of Tarrant County, Texas 1841-1859, Volume 1.** Fort Worth, Tex. Weldon I. Hudson. 1983. (DAR)

HUDSON, Weldon I.
> **Johnson County, Texas marriage records 1854-1883, Volume I and II.** Fort Worth, Tex. Weldon I. Hudson. 1982. (DAR)

HUNTER, J. Marvin
> **Frontier times monthly.** By J. Marvin Hunter. Bandera, Tex. Hunter. 1926-1927. (DAR)

HUNTER, J. Marvin
    100 years in Bandera 1853-1953. By J. Marvin Hunter. [Bandera, Tex.].
    J. Marvin Hunter. c1953. (DAR)

HUTTASH, Ogreta W.
    Marriage records of Cherokee County, Texas 1846-1880. Ogreta W.
    Huttash. Jacksonville, Tex. Jayroe Graphic Arts. 1973. (DAR)

Index to probate cases 1846-1900 Dallas County, Texas. Edited by Helen Mason
    Lu, Gwen Blomquist Newmann, Margaret Gilmore Smith; compiled by Dallas
    Genealogical Society. Dallas, Tex. The Society. c1978. (DAR)

Index to the Lewis Company's 1893: biographical history of Milam, Williamson,
    Bastrop, Travis, Lee and Burleson Counties. Index compiled by Charles
    Alborn Walker family; edited by Mrs. Mary Kay Holmes Snell & Eric
    Kunze. Austin, Tex. [s.n.]. 1977. (DAR)

INGMIRE, Frances T.
    Texas Ranger service records. By Frances T. Ingmire. St. Louis, Mo. Ingmire
    Publications. 1982. (DAR)

INGMIRE, Frances Terry
    Texas frontiersman 1839-1860: minute men, militia, home guard, Indian fighter.
    Compiled by and indexed by Frances Terry Ingmire. St. Louis, Mo. The Compiler.
    1982. (DAR)

INGMIRE, Frances Terry
    Texas Ranger service records 1830-1846. Compiled and indexed by Mrs.
    Frances Terry Ingmire. St. Louis, Mo. The Compiler. 1982. (DAR)

JACKSON, George
    Sixty years in Texas. By George Jackson. 2nd Ed. Dallas: Wilkinson Pub. Co.
    c1908. (DAR)

Jacksonville, [Texas] the story of a dynamic community 1872-1972. Jacksonville,
    Tex. Jacksonville Centennial Corp. c1972. (DAR)

JAYNES, Willard
    Cass County cemeteries Texas records. [Mr. & Mrs. Willard Jaynes]. Atlanta,
    Tex. Cass County Genealogical Society. 1976. (DAR)

JENKINS, Frank Duane
    Cemetery inscriptions, Runnels County, Texas. Compiled by Frank Duane
    Jenkins. San Angelo, Tex. The Genealogical and Historical Society. 1976.
    (DAR)

JENKINS, John Holland
Recollections of early Texas: the memoirs of John Holland Jenkins. Edited By John Holmes Jenkins. Austin University of Texas Press. c1958. (DAR)

JENNINGS, Nancy Moores Watts
Texarkana pioneer family histories, Texarkana, Arkansas-Texas. Compiled by Nancy Moores Watts Jennings. Texarkana. The Pioneer Association. c1961. (DAR)

JENNINGS, Nancy Watts
A tale of two cities: a Texarkana Centennial booklet. [Compiled by Nancy Watts Jennings, Mary Lou Stuart Phillips]. [S.l.: s.n.]. 1973. (DAR)

JOHN, George O'Brien
Texas history: an outline. By George O'Brien John. New York. Henry Holt and Co. c1935. (DAR)

JOHNSON, Frank W.
A history of Texas and Texans. By Frank W. Johnson. Chicago. American Historical Society. 1914. (DAR)

JONES, Anson
Memoranda and official correspondence relating to the Republic of Texas: Its history and annexation; including a brief autobiography of the author. By Anson Jones. New York. D. Appleton and Co. 1859. (DAR)

JONES, Marie Beth
Peach Point plantation: the first 150 years. By Marie Beth Jones. Waco, Tex. Texian Press. 1982. (DAR)

JONES, Mary Wheeler
The history of West Fork Presbyterian Church, Grand Prairie, Texas 1870-1970. Compiled by Mary Wheeler Jones. [S.l.: s.n.; 1971?]. (DAR)

JONES, Mary Wheeler
Watson Cemetery inscriptions, 1846-1970 City of Arlington, Tarrant County, Texas. Compiled by Mary Wheeler Jones. [S.l.: s.n., 1970?) (DAR)

JONES, R. L.
Texas Hunt County cemetery records: Caddo Mills Cemetery. Assembled by R. L. Jones; contributed by Captain Charles Croxall (Texas) DAR, G. R. C. 1946. (DAR)

JONES, William M.
Texas testimony carved in stone. Comp. by William M. Jones. Houston, Tex. Jones. c1952. (DAR)

JURNEY, Richard Loyall
    History of Titus County, Texas 1846 to 1960. By Richard Loyall Jurney. Dallas, Tex. Royal Publishing. c1961. (DAR)

JUSTMAN, Dorothy E.
    German colonists and their descendants in Houston including Usener and allied families. By Dorothy E. Justman. 1st Ed. Quanah-Wichita Falls, Tex. Nortex Offset Pub. c1974. (DAR)

KEMP, Louis Wiltz
    The Battle of San Jacinto and the San Jacinto campaign. By L. W. Kemp and Ed Kilman. [S.l.: L. Kemp & E. Kilman]. c1947. (DAR)

KEY, Della Taylor
    Abstracts from Potter County land records, 1876-1883. By Della Taylor Key. Amarillo, Tex. D. Key. 1960. (DAR)

KEY, Della Taylor
    Early records of Potter County. By Della Taylor Key. Amarillo, Tex. Tyler-Berkley. 1961. (DAR)

KEY, Della Taylor
    In the cattle county: history of Potter County. By Della Taylor Key. Amarillo, Tex. Tyler-Berkley. 1961. (DAR)

KIRKPATRICK, A. Y.
    The early settlers life in Texas: and the organization of Hill County. By A. Y. Kirkpatrick. Waco, Tex. Texian Press. 1963. (DAR)

KITTRELL, Norman G.
    Governors who have been, and other public men of Texas. By Norman G. Kittrell. Houston. Dealy-Adey-Elgin Co. 1921. (DAR)

Land of the little angel: a history of Angelina County, Texas. Compiled by the Angelina County Historical Survey Committee; edited by Bob Bowman. Lufkin, Tex. Lufkin Printing Co. 1976. (DAR)

LANDRUM, Graham
    Grayson County: an illustrated history of Grayson County, Texas. By Graham Landrum. Fort Worth, Tex. University Supply & Equipment Co. c1960. (DAR)

LANGSTON, George (Mrs.)
    History of Eastland County, Texas. By Mrs. George Langston. Dallas, Tex. Aldridge & Co. 1904. (DAR)

LATHROP, Barnes F.
Migration into East Texas, 1835-1860: a study from the United States Census. Barnes F. Lathrop. Austin. Texas State Historical Association. 1949. (DAR)

LEDBETTER, Barbara N.
Centennial Grahamana 1872-1972. Barbara N. Ledbetter. [S.1.]: B. N. Ledbetter. 1972. (DAR)

LEFEVRE, Hazie Davis
Concho County history 1858-1958. Compiled by Hazie Davis Lefevre (Mrs. E. Walter). Eden, Tex. H. D. Lefevre. 1959. (DAR)

LEVY, Richard Butt
History of the creation and organization of Gregg County, Texas. Compiled By Richard Butt Levy; donated by Captain William Young Chapter (Texas) DAR, G. R. C. 1947. (DAR)

LINDSLEY, Philip
A history of greater Dallas and vicinity. By Philip Lindsley; Mr. L. B. Hill, Editor. Chicago [Illinois]. Lewis Pub. Co. 1909. (DAR)

LINK, J. B.
Texas historical and biographical magazine: designed to give a complete history of the Baptists of Texas from their first entrance into the state and other historical matters of interest to the denomination. J. B. Link. Austin. Link. c1891. (DAR)

A List of old Brazoria County, Texas cemeteries during or before 1900. By Cradle of Texas Chapter (Texas) DAR. West Columbia, Tex. Moder Manifold Method. c1965. (DAR)

Local History & Genealogical Society, Dallas, Texas. Dallas, Tex. The Society. 1955-1963. (DAR)

LOOSCAN, Adele B.
Harris County, 1822-1845. By Adele B. Looscan. Austin, Tex. Texas State Historical Association. [1916?]. (DAR)

LOTTO, F.
Fayette County her history and her people. By F. Lotto. Schulenburg, Tex. F. Lotto. c1902. (DAR)

LOVE, Annie Carpenter
History of Navarro County. By Annie Carpenter (Mrs. W. F.) Love. Dallas, Tex. Southwest Press. c1933. (DAR)

LU, Helen M.
>First half dozen years, Dallas County, Texas as seen through the commissioner's court minutes. Compiled by Helen M. Lu, Gwen B. Neumann. Dallas, Tex. The Compilers. 1982. (DAR)

LUCAS, Mattie Davis
>A history of Grayson County, Texas. Mattie Davis Lucas and Mita Holsapple Hall. Sherman, Tex. Scruggs Printing Co. c1936. (DAR)

Lufkin Genealogical and Historical Society (Lufkin, Texas)
>Cemetery records of Angelina County, [Texas] January, 1969-September, 1981. Compiled by Lufkin Genealogical and Historical Society. [Lufkin, Texas]. The Society. [1982?]. (DAR)

LYNCH, James D.
>The bench and bar of Texas. By James D. Lynch. St. Louis. The Author. 1885. (DAR)

MADRAY, I. C. (Mrs.)
>A history of Bee County with some brief sketches about and events in adjoining counties. [Mrs. I. C. Madray]. [Beeville, Texas: The Bee Picayune]. 1939. (DAR)

MAINER, Thomas N.
>Houston County in the Civil War. Thomas N. Mainer. Crockett, Tex. Houston Co. Historical Commission. 1981. (DAR)

Marriage records of Brazoria County, Texas 1829-1870: transcribed and indexed from Bonds, Clerk's Entries and Marriage License (Volume A), 1829-1852 and Marriage Book I, 1852-1870 (also called Book A-1/A on back of Volume). Lake Jackson, Tex. Brazosport Genealogical Society. c1982. (DAR)

Marriages, Dallas County, Texas books A-E, 1846-1877. Edited by Helen Mason Lev and Gwen Blomquist Neumann; compiled by Dallas Genealogical Society. Dallas, Tex. The Society. c1978. (DAR)

Marriages of Wichita County, Texas, 1882-1905. Edited by North Texas Genealogical and Historical Association. Wichita Falls, Tex. The Association. 1966. (DAR)

MARTIN, Madeleine
>More early Southeast Texas families. By Madeleine Martin. Quanah, Tex. Nortex Press. c1978. (DAR)

MARTIN, John T. (Mrs.)
>Milam County, Texas records. Compiled by Mrs. John T. Martin and Mrs. Louis C. Hill. Waco, Tex. [s.n.]. 1968. (DAR)

Matagorda Cemetery, Matagorda, Texas. Matagorda County, Junior Historians Chapter 310. [S.l.]: Texas DAR, G. R. C. 1974-1975. (DAR)

MATTHEWS, Sallie Reynolds
   Interwoven: a pioneer chronicle. By Sallie Reynolds Matthews. Houston, Tex. Anson Jones Press. 1936. (DAR)

MCADAMS, Ina May Ogletree
   Texas women of distinction: a biographical history. Ina May Ogletree McAdams. Austin: McAdams Publishers. 1962. (DAR)

MCCARTY, John L.
   Maverick town: the story of old Tascosa. By John L. McCarty. Norman. University of Oklahoma Press. 1946. (DAR)

MCCLESKEY, Charles S.
   A short history of the Patilo Community of Erath County, Texas. Compiled by Charles S. McCleskey. Baton Rouge, La. C. McCleskey. 1970. (DAR)

MCCONNELL, Joseph Carroll
   The West Texas frontier: or a descriptive history of early times in Western Texas. By Joseph Carroll McConnell. Jackson, Tex. Gazette Print. c1933. (DAR)

MCGINNES, Jeannette Hatter
   They found the Blacklands: a genealogical history of Moody area people 1850-1950. By Jeannette Hatter McGinnes and Hazel Alexander Potter. Waco, Tex. Texian Press. c1977. (DAR)

MCKAY, Arch (Mrs.)
   A history of Jefferson, [Texas]. Compiled by Mrs. Arch McKay; Mrs. H. A. Spellings. [S.l.: s.n.]. 1936. (DAR)

McLennan County,Texas cemetery records. Compiled by Central Texas Genealogical Society. Waco, Tex. The Society. 1965-1979. (DAR)

McLennan County, Texas marriage records. Central Texas Genealogical Society. Waco, Tex. The Society. 1961-1963. (DAR)

MCWILLIAMS, Rena Doughty
   Abstracts of laws of Texas, 1822-1846. Compiled and ed. by Rena Doughty McWilliams. [S.l.]: McWilliams. 1981. (DAR)

Memorial and biographical history of Dallas County, Texas. [S.l.]: Walsworth Pub. Co. [1976?]. (DAR)

Memorial and biographical history of Ellis County, Texas. Chicago. Lewis Pub. Co. 1892. (DAR)

A memorial and biographical history of Johnson and Hill Counties, Texas. Chicago. Lewis Pub. Co. 1892. (DAR)

Memorial and biographical history of McLennan, Falls, Bell and Coryell Counties, Texas. Chicago. Lewis Pub. Co. 1893. (DAR)

Memorial and biographical history of Navarro, Henderson, Anderson, Limestone, Freestone and Leon Counties. Chicago [Ill.]: Lewis Pub. Co. 1983. (DAR)

Menard County, [Texas] history: an anthology Menard County Historical Society. San Angelo, Tex. Anchor Publ. c1982. (DAR)

Mesquite Historical and Genealogical Society Quarterly. Mesquite, Tex. The Society. [1965?]. (DAR)

Montgomery County Genealogical Society.
Montgomery County, Texas, marriages, 1838-1894. Comp. by Montgomery County Genealogical Society. Conroe, Tex. The Society. c1977. (DAR)

Montgomery County, Texas cemeteries. Conroe, Tex. Montgomery County Genealogical Society, Inc. 1982. (DAR)

MORGAN, Jonnie R.
The History of Wichita Falls. By Jonnie R. Morgan. Wichita Falls, [Texas]. Nortex Offset. 1971. (DAR)

MORGAN, William Manning
Trinity Protestant Episcopal Church, Galveston, Texas 1841-1953: a memorial history. By William Manning Morgan. Houston, [Texas]: Anson Jones Press. c1954. (DAR)

MORRIS, Louise Elizabeth
Founders and patriots of the Republic of Texas: the lineages of the members of the Daughters of the Republic of Texas. By Mrs. Harry Joseph Morris. Dallas: Daughters of the Republic of Texas. c1963. (DAR)

MORRIS, Mrs. Harry Joseph
Citizens of the Republic of Texas. Mrs. Harry Joseph Morris. Dallas: Texas State Genealogical Society. c1977. (DAR)

Morrison & Fourmy's general directory of the city of San Antonio, 1889-90. Galveston, [Texas]: Morrison & Fourmy. 1888. (DAR)

MULLINS, Marion Day
    Anderson County, Texas marriage records 1846-1880. Copied from records in the Anderson County Court House and indexed by Marion Day Mullins. 1965. (DAR)

MULLINS, Marion Day
    Bee County, Texas marriage records 1858-1893. Copied and indexed by Marion Day Mullins. 1966. (DAR)

MULLINS, Marion Day
    Bell County, Texas marriage records 1850-1882. Copied from records on file in the County Court House by Marion Day Mullins, Vada Sutton, Leannell Sutton, indexed by Marion Day Mullins. (DAR)

MULLINS, Marion Day
    Bosque County, Texas marriage records 1860-1891. Copied and indexed by Marion Day Mullins. 1964. (DAR)

MULLINS, Marion Day
    Caldwell County, Texas marriage records 1848-1885. Copied from records in the County Court House and indexed by Marion Day Mullins. 1960. (DAR)

MULLINS, Marion Day
    Falls County, Texas marriages 1854-1881. Copied from records in the Falls County Court House and indexed by Marion Day Mullins. 1957. (DAR)

MULLINS, Marion Day
    Freestone County, Texas marriages 1851-1888. Copied from records in the County Court House and indexed by Marion Day Mullins. 1956. (DAR)

MULLINS, Marion Day
    Goliad County, Texas marriage records 1870-1891. Copied and indexed by Marion Day Mullins. 1967. (DAR)

MULLINS, Marion Day
    Grimes County, Texas marriage records 1848-1879. Copied by Marion Day Mullins. 1962. (DAR)

MULLINS, Marion Day
    Henderson County, Texas marriage record 1869-1887. Copied by Marion Day Mullins; indexed by Jackie Harmonson. 1963. (DAR)

MULLINS, Marion Day
    Hopkins County, Texas marriage records 1846-1880. Copied from the original records in the County Court House and indexed by Marion Day Mullins. 1959. (DAR)

MULLINS, Marion Day
    Hunt County, Texas marriage record 1847-1881. Copied from records in the County Court House by Marion Day Mullins; indexed made by Mrs. A. B. Harmonson. 1958. (DAR)

MULLINS, Marion Day
    Jasper County, Texas marriage record 1849-1881. Copied and indexed by Marion Day Mullins. Mullins. 1966. (DAR)

MULLINS, Marion Day
    Lamar County, Texas marriage record 1841-1875. Copied by Marion Day Mullins; indexed by Mrs. A. B. Harmonson & Jackie Harmonson. [1963?]. (DAR)

MULLINS, Marion Day
    Limestone County, Texas marriage records 1873-1883. Copied from records in the County Court House by Marion Day Mullins; indexed by Mrs. A. B. Harmonson. 1957. (DAR)

MULLINS, Marion Day
    Marriage records of Hill County, Texas 1873-1880. Copied by Marion Day Mullins. 1956. (DAR)

MULLINS, Marion Day
    Marriage records, Red River County, Texas, 1845-1877. Marion Day Mullins. 1954. (DAR)

MULLINS, Marion Day
    Marriage records 1837-1871 Nacogdoches County, [Texas]. Marion Day Mullins. 1955. (DAR)

MULLINS, Marion Day
    Parker County, Texas marriage record 1874-1886. Copied from records in the County Court House and indexed by Marion Day Mullins. 1956. (DAR)

MULLINS, Marion Day
    Refugio County, Texas marriage record, 1839-1903. Copied and indexed by Marion Day Mullins. 1966. (DAR)

MULLINS, Marion Day
    Republic of Texas: poll lists for 1846. Comp. by Marion Day Mullins. Baltimore: Geneal. Pub. Co. 1982, c1974. (DAR)

MULLINS, Marion Day
    Tyler County, Texas marriage record, 1846-1888. Copied and indexed by Marion Day Mullins. 1966. (DAR)

MULLINS, Marion Day
    Victoria County, Texas marriage record, 1838-1890. Copied and indexed by Marion Day ?. [1967]. (DAR)

MULLINS, Marion Day
Washington County, Texas marriage record, 1837-1870. Copied from the original records and indexed by Marion Day Mullins. 1953. (DAR)

MULLINS, Marion/Day
Panola County, Texas marriage records in the County Court House. By Marion Day Mullins and Mrs. A. B. (Paulyne R.) Harmonson. 1960. (DAR)

MURRIE, Pauline Shirley
Early records of Nacogdoches County, Texas. Abstracted and compiled by Pauline Shirley Murrie. Waco, Tex. P. S. Murrie. c1965. (DAR)

MURRIE, Pauline Shirley
Marriage records of Nacogdoches County, Texas 1824-1881. Abstracted and compiled by Pauline Shirley Murrie. Houston, Tex. P. S. Murrie. 1968. (DAR)

NEVILLE, A. W.
The history of Lamar County, Texas. By A. W. Neville. Paris, Tex.: North Texas Pub. Co. c1937. (DAR)

NEWHOUSE, Patricia Armstrong
Known marriages of Fannin County, Texas, 1838-1852: a reconstructed listing of lost marriage records. Compiled by Patricia Armstrong Newhouse. [S.1.]: Fannin County Historical Commisssion. [1978?]. (DAR)

NIX, John W.
A tale of two schools and Springtown, Parker County. By John W. Nix. Fort Worth, Tex. Thomaston & Morrow. 1945. (DAR)

NOLTE, Elleta
For the reason we climb mountains: Gray County, 1902-1982. Elleta Nolte. Pampa, Tex. Gray County Historical Society. 1983. (DAR)

North Runnels County pioneers. Genealogy Club, Winters High School; [ed] by Frances Bredemeyer. [Winter, Tex.: The Club]. c1976. (DAR)

NORVELL, Claudia
King's Highway: the great strategic Military highway of America, El Comino Real, the Old San Antonio Road. Mrs. Lipscomb Norvell. [S.1.]: Norvell. c1945. (DAR)

NOWLIN, W. T. (Mrs.)
Jefferson County, Texas marriage record 1837-1900. Copied by Mrs. W. T. Nowlin; indexed by Marion Day Mullins. 1969. (DAR)

NOWLIN, W. T. (Mrs.)
 Newton County, Texas marriage record 1846-1900. Copied from records in the County Court House by Mrs. W. T. Nowlin; indexed by Marion Day Mullins. 1969. (DAR)

NULLINS (Mullins?), Marion Day
 Marriage record of San Augustine County, Texas, 1837-1880. Copied from the court records and indexed by Marion Day Mullins. 1955. (DAR)

Oak leaves. Bay City, Texas: Matagorda County Genealogical Society. 1982. (DAR)

OGLE, Georgia Myers
 Elm Fork settlements: Farmers Branch and Carrolton. Compiled and written by Georgia Myers Ogle; illustrated by Sharon Marsh Cozart. [Dallas County, Texas: Peters Colony Historical Society]. 1977. (DAR)

O'KEEFE, Ruth Jones
 Archer County pioneers: a history of Archer County, Texas. By Ruth Jones O'Keefe; drawings by Col. Gaulden. Hereford, Tex. Pioneer Book Pub. Co. c1969. (DAR)

Oklahoma DAR, G. R. C.
 Fayette County, Texas justice of the peace court records beat No. 4, 1857-1869 which also includes two beat 3 cases dated May 1870; alphabetical index to the accounts receivable ledger of Edward Henkel, Merchant Round Top, Texas, Fayette County. Copied by Mrs. Josie V. Henkel Hoskinson for Black Beaver Chapter (Texas) DAR, G. R. C. 1860-1861. (DAR)

The Old three hundred in Matagorda County. McAllister Junior Historian, Chapter 241. Bay City, Tex. The Society. 1972. (DAR)

One hundreth anniversary of First Ev. Lutheran Church 1850-1950, Galveston, Texas. [S.l.: s.n.]. 1950. (DAR)

Original land holders of some Texas Counties. Pasadena, Tex. Harris County Genealogical Society. c1976. (DAR)

Our heritage: amor patriae. San Antonio, Tex. The Genealogical and Historical Society. 1959. (DAR)

Overton, Texas centennial historical book. Ora Gillispie, editor; Billie Loftis, co-editor. Overton, Tex. Overton Centennial Corporation. c1973. (DAR)

PADDOCK, B. B.
A history of Central and Western Texas. B. B. Paddock. Chicago: Lewis Pub. Co. 1911. (DAR)

PADDOCK, B. B.
A twentieth century history and biographical record of North and West Texas. B. B. Paddock. Chicago: Lewis Pub. Co. 1906. (DAR)

Panhandle-plains historical review – Canyon, Texas. Panhandle-Plains Historical Society. 1928?? (DAR)

Parade of progress, Hamilton County, [Texas] 1858-1958: Hamilton Herald-News. W. F. Billing Slea, editor. Centennial edition. [S.l.]: C. M. Hatch. 1958. (DAR)

PARKER, Richard Denny
Historical recollections of Robertson County, Texas, with biographical & genealogical notes on the pioneers & their families. By Richard Denny Parker; edited by Nona Clement Parker. Salado, Tex. Anson Jones Press. 1955. (DAR)

PARR, Grace Lee
The Justin story. By Grace Lee Parr. Quanah, Tex. Nortex Press. c1976. (DAR)

PARTLOW, Miriam
Liberty, Liberty County and the Atascosito District. By Miriam Partlow; introduction by Price Daniel. Austin, [Texas]. Atascosito Historical Society; Sam Houston Regional Library and Research Center. c1974. (DAR)

PEAVY, Ruth Riley
Cemetery records of Henderson and surrounding Texas Cos. Compiled by Ruth Riley Peavy. [S.l.: s.n., 1971?]. (DAR)

Pedigree charts of Cass people members and nonmembers. Gathered by Kathy Wicks... [et al.]. Atlanta, Tex. Bowman. 1976. (DAR)

PENNINGTON, R. E. (Mrs.)
The history of Brenham and Washington County, [Texas]. Mrs. R. E. Pennington. Houston, Tex. Standard Printing & Lithographing Co. 1915. (DAR)

PENNYBACKER, Anna J. Hardwicke
A history of Texas for schools. By Mrs. Anna J. Hardwicke Pennybacker. Rev. Ed. Austin: Pennybacker. 1908, c1895. (DAR)

The people of Nocogdoches County in 1860. Edited by Carolyn Reeves Ericson. Nacogdoches, Tex. C. R. Ericson. c1978. (DAR)

PICKETT, Arlene
    Historic Liberty County. By Arlene Pickett. [S.1.]: Tardy Pub. Co. c1936. (DAR)

PICKRELL, Annie Doom
    Pioneer women in Texas. By Annie Doom Pickrell. Austin. E. L. Steck Co. 1929. (DAR)

PIERCE, Adelaide Hall
    Deming's Bridge Cemetery, Trespalacios Baptist Church 1852-1898 and Hawley Cemetery 1898-1960, Matagorda County, Texas. Compiled by Adelaide Hall Pierce. Palacios, Tex. Palacios Beacon. 1960. (DAR)

PIERCE, Frank C.
    A brief history of the Lower Rio Grande Valley. By Frank C. Pierce. Menasha, Wisc. George Banta Pub. Co. 1917. (DAR)

Pioneer families of Anderson County, [Texas] prior to 1900. Anderson Co.; The Genealogical Society. [1983?]. (DAR)

PITTS, Alice
    Collin County, [Texas] cemetery inscriptions. Compiled by Mrs. Alice Pitts, Mrs. Wanda O'Roark, Mrs. Doris Posey. McKinney, Tex. POP Publications. c1975. (DAR)

PLUMMER, Betty
    Historic homes of Washington County, [Texas], 1821-1860. By Betty Plummer. San Marcos, Tex. Rio Fresco Books. 1971. (DAR)

POE, Charlsie
    Runnels is my county. By Charlsie Poe. San Antonio, Tex. Naylor. c1970. (DAR)

POLLARD,, Claude
    The beginnings of Texas history: address of Claude Pollard, President of the Texas Bar Association; at it annual meeting held in San Antonio, Texas, July 4, 1921. [S.1.: s.n.], 1921. (DAR)

POOLE, William C.
    Basque County, Texas. William C. Poole. San Marcos, [Texas]: San Marcos Press. 1954. (DAR)

PORTER, Roze McCoy
    Thistle Hill, the cattle baron's legacy. By Roze McCoy Porter. Fort Worth, Tex. Branch-Smith, Inc. c1980. (DAR)

POTTER, W. R. (Mrs.)
    History of Montague County, Texas. [Mrs. W. R. Potter]. [Bowie, Tex.: s.n., 1940?]. (DAR)

PRICE, Lucie Clift
Travis County, Texas, marriage records, 1840-1882. Comp. by Lucie Clift Price. Austin, Tex. Price. 1973. (DAR)

PURCELL, Mabelle
This is Texas. By Mabelle Purcell, Stuart Purcell. Austin: Lel Purcell Hawkins. c1977. (DAR)

PUTNAM, Wyvonne
Navarro Co., [Texas] history. Compiled by Wyvonne Putnam. Quanah, Tex. Nortex Press. c1975. (DAR)

The quarterly. Dallas, Tex. Dallas Genealogical Society. 1964. (DAR)

Quarterly of the Central Texas Genealogical Society. Waco, Tex. The Society. 1958-1968. (DAR)

The Quarterly of the Texas State Historical Association. Austin. The Association. 1900, 1913. (DAR)

RAHT, Carlysle Graham
The romance of Davis Mountains and Big Bend Country: a history. By Carlysle Graham Raht. El Paso: Rathbrooks Co. 1919. (DAR)

RAINES, C. W.
A bibliography of Texas: being a descriptive list of books, pamphlets and documents relating to Texas in print and manuscript since 1536, including a complete collection of laws. By C. W. Raines. Austin; Gammel Book Co. 1896. (DAR)

RAINES, C. W.
Six decades in Texas: or memoirs of Francis Richard Lubbock, governor of Texas in wartime, 1861-63. Edited by C. W. Raines. Austin: Ben C. Jones & Co., Printers. 1900. (DAR)

RAINES, C. W.
Year book for Texas. By C. W. Raines. Austin. Gammel Book Co. 1902, 1903. (DAR)

RANSLEBEN, Guido E.
A hundred years of Comfort in Texas: a centennial history. By Guido E. Ransleben. San Antonio: Naylor. c1954. (DAR)

RATHER, Ethel Zivley
    DeWitt's colony. By Ethel Zivley Rather. Austin, Tex. University of Texas. 1905. (DAR)

RAY, Thelma
    The history of Birdville, [Texas]. Compiled by Mrs. Thelma (Bailey B.) Ray. Fort Worth, Tex. T. Ray. c1965. (DAR)

RAY, Worth S.
    Austin: colony pioneers: including history of Bastrop, Fayette, Grimes, Montgomery, and Washington Counties, Texas and their earliest settlers. By Worth S. Ray. Austin:The Author. 1949. (DAR)

Records of East Texas. Lufkin, Tex. John W. Wilkins. 1969, 1970. (DAR)

RED, William Stuart
    A history of the Presbyterian Church in Texas. By William Stuart Red. [S.l.]: Steck Co. c1936. (DAR)

The Reflectory/Amarillo Genealogical Society. Amarillo, Tex. The Society. 1959. (DAR)

Reprint of biographies from the Lone Star State published by The Lewis Publishing Company, 1893: containing biographies of early settlers of Navarro, Henderson, Anderson, Limestone, Freestone and Leon Counties, Texas. [S.l.]: Stephanie H. Tally-Frost. 1966. (DAR)

Research papers on historic Matagorda, Texas (founded 1892) McAllister Junior Historians, Chapter 241. Bay City, Tex. The Chapter. 1973. (DAR)

RICHARDSON, T. C.
    East Texas: its history and its makers. Dabney White, editor; T. C. Richardson, author. N. Y. Lewis Historical Pub. Co. 1940. (DAR)

ROACH, Hattie Joplin
    A history of Cherokee County, Texas. By Hattie Joplin (Mrs. V. R.) Roach. Dallas, Tex. Southwest Press. 1934. (DAR)

The roadrunner. Tomball, Tex. Chaparral Genealogical Society. 1974. (DAR)

ROBINSON, Samuel Murray
    A brief history of the Texas Navies. Samuel Murray Robinson. Houston: Sons of the Republic of Texas. 1961. (DAR)

ROOSE, Rita Bickley
    Records of Reconstruction days in Collins County, Texas. By Rita Bickley Roose, Jeanette Bickley Bland. [S.l.]: Spring Hill Press. 1981. (DAR)

ROSE, Victor M.
    Some historical facts in regard to the settlement of Victoria [Co.], Texas: its progress and present status. By Victor M. Rose; ed. by J. W. Petty, Jr. Victoria, Tex. Book Mart. 1961. (DAR)

ROTHE, Aline
    Kalita's people: a history of the Alabama-Coushalta Indians of Texas. By Aline Rothe. [Moscow, Texas: Rothe]. c1963. (DAR)

RUFF, Nancy Blakeley
    Gregg County, Texas, marriage license index. Nancy Blakeley Ruff. [Longview, Tex.]. Ruff. 1980. (DAR)

RUFF, Nancy Blakeley
    Harrison County, Texas early marriage records 1839-1869. By Nancy Blakeley Ruff. St. Louis, Mo. Ingmire Publications. 1983. (DAR)

RUSSELL, Marie
    Marriage records, Harris County, Texas. By Marie Russell. Houston, Tex. Russell. 1980. (DAR)

SADDLER, Jerry
    History of Texas. Jerry Sadler. Austin: Sadler. 1954. (DAR)

St. Joseph's Parish (Yoakum, Texas) Historical Committee
    1869-1969 centennial St. Joseph's Parish, Yoakum, Texas/Historical Committee, [St. Joseph's Parish]. [S.l.: s.n.]. 1969. (DAR)

ST. ROMAIN, Lillian Schiller
    Western Falls County, Texas. Lillian Schiller St. Romain. Austin: Texas State Historical Association. 1951. (DAR)

SAMUELS, Nancy Timmons
    Miscelllaneous records pertaining to the Northwest Texas frontier: ca. 1855-1875; the early settlers of Palo Pinto County and nearby areas. Comp. by Nancy Timmons Samuels. Fort Worth, Tex. Mary Isham Chapter, DAR, G. R. C. 1975. (DAR)

San Jacinto County, Texas, cemeteries. Comp. by The San Jacinto County, Texas Historical Commission. Winston-Salem, N. C. Hunter Pub. Co. 1977. (DAR)

SAUL, Jennette H.
    Bandera County homes and buildings of history. Drawings by Margaret B. Focke, history by Jennette H. Saul; poem by Knowles Teel. Bandera, Tex. Bandera Bulletin. 1971. (DAR)

Schleicher County, [Texas]: or eighty years of development in southwest Texas.
Edited by R. D. Holt. Eldorado, Tex. The Eldorado Success. 1930. (DAR)

SCHMIDT, Charles F.
History of Washington County. By Charles F. Schmidt. San Antonio, Tex.
Naylor. c1949. (DAR)

SCHMIDT, C. W.
Footprints of five generations. By C. W. Schmidt. New Ulm, Tex.
New Ulm Enterprise. 1930. (DAR)

SCHUCHARD, Ernst
100th anniversary, Pioneer Flour Mills, San Antonio, Texas, 1851-1951: a scrapbook of pictures and events in San Antonio during the last 100 years.
[Ernst Schuchard, compiler]. San Antonio, Tex. Naylor. 1951. (DAR)

SCOTT, Evalyn Parrott
A history of Lamb County featuring biographies of pioneers. By Evalyn Parrott Scott. [S.l.: E. P. Scott, c1968]. (DAR)

The Shiloh pioneers 1850-1975. Shiloh Cemetery Association. Klondike, Tex.
The Association. c1975. (DAR)

SIMMONS, Frank E.
History of Coryell County. By Frank E. Simmons. [S.l.]: Coryell County News. 1936. (DAR)

SMITH, A. Morton
The first hundred years in Cooke County, [Texas]. By A. Morton Smith.
San Antonio, Tex. Naylor Company. c1955. (DAR)

SMITH, Tevis Clyde
Frontier's generation: the pioneer history of Brown County, [Texas] with sidelights on the surrounding territory. By Tevis Clyde Smith.
Brownwood, Tex. T. C. Smith. c1931. (DAR)

SMITH, Tevis Clyde, Jr.
From memories of men. By T. C. Smith, Jr. Brownwood, Tex.
T. C. Smith. c1954. (DAR)

SMITH, Tevis Clyde, Jr.
Pecan Valley days. By T. C. Smith, Jr. Brownwood, Tex. T. C. Smith.
c1956. (DAR)

SMITH, W. Broadus
Brazos County, Texas cemetery inscriptions. W. Broadus Smith. Houston, Tex. W. B. Smith. 1967. (DAR)

SMYTHE, H.
    Historical sketch of Parker County and Weatherford, Texas. By H. Smythe. St. Louis;Louis C. Lavat. 1877. (DAR)

Some history of Van Zandt County. By Wentworth Manning. Des Moines, [Iowa]. Homestead Co. 1919. (DAR)

Southern historical research magazine. Dallas: Worth S. Ray. 1936. (DAR)

SOWELL, A. J.
    History of Fort Bend County containing biographical sketches of many noted characters. By A. J. Sowell; mimeographed by the Fort Bend Chapter (Texas) DAR. 1956. (DAR)

SPEAKMAN, Mary N.
    Cemeteries of Clay County, Texas. Compiled by Mary N. Speakman and Walter F. Speakman. Wichita Falls, Tex. M. N. and W. F. Speakman. 1973. (DAR)

SPEER, John W.
    A history of Blanco County, [Texas]. By John W. Speer; edited by Henry C. Armbruster; illustrations by Connie Armbruster. Austin, [Texas]: Pemberton Press. c1965. (DAR)

SPENCER, Artemesia Lucille Brison
    The Camp County story. By Artemesia Lucille Brison Spencer. Fort Worth, Tex. Branch-Smith Inc. 1974. (DAR)

Stalkin' kin in old West Texas. San Angelo, Tex. San Angelo Genealogical and Historical Society Inc. 1973-??? (DAR)

STAMBAUGH, J. Lee
    A history of Collin County, Texas. By J. Lee Stambaugh and Lillian J. Stambaugh. Austin, [Texas]: Texas State Historical Association. 1958. (DAR)

STEELE, Hampton
    A history of Limestone County, Texas 1833-1860. By Hampton Steele. Mexia, Tex. News Pub. Co. [1935?]. (DAR)

STEGER, Charles
    Law's Chapel a history & records 1853-1976. Text compiled by Charles Steger. [S.1.: s.n.]. 1976. (DAR)

STERLING, William Warren
    Trails and trials of a Texas ranger. By William Warren Sterling. [S.1.]: Sterling. 1959. (DAR)

STEWART, Estella Burns
    Book E-Z, marriages of Huntsville, Walker County, Texas. Compiled by Estella Burns Stewart. 1970. (DAR)

STEWART, James Rush (Mrs.)
    1870 census of the United States of America, Walker County, Texas. Compiled by Mrs. James Rush Stewart. Huntsville, Tex. Walker Co., Genealogical Society. c1979. (DAR)

Stieghorst, Junann J.
    Bay City and Matagorda County: a history. By Junann J. Stieghorst: Sponsored by Junior Service League of Bay City. Austin, Tex. Pemberton Press. c1963. (DAR)

Stirpes. Lubbock, Tex. Texas Genealogical Society. 1961. (DAR)

STONE, Lucille Tillson
    Tombstone inscriptions of Runnels County, Texas. Comp. by Lucille Tillson Stone. 1978. (DAR)

STROBEL, Abner J.
    The old plantation and their owners of Brazoria County, Texas. By Abner J. Strobel. Rev. Ed. Houston, Tex. Union National Bank. 1930. (DAR)

SUMNER, Jane
    Some early Travis County, Texas records. Abstracted and compiled by Miss Jane Sumner. Easley, S. C. Southern Historical Press. 1979. (DAR)

SUTHERLAND, Mary A.
    The story of Corpus Christi. By Mary A. Sutherland. [Corpus Christi, Texas]: Corpus Christi Chapter, Daughters of the Confederacy. 1916. (DAR)

TALLY-FROST, Stephenie Hillegeist
    Cemetery records of Leon County, Texas. Recorded and indexed by Stephenie Hillegeist Tally-Frost. Corpus Christi, Tex. S. H. Tally-Frost. 1967. (DAR)

TARPLEY, Fred
    Place names of Northeast Texas. Fred Tarpley. Commerce, Tex. East State University. 1969. (DAR)

TAYLOR, Alva
    Navarro Co., history and photographs. Alva Taylor. Rev. Ed. Corsicana, Tex. A. Taylor. c1962. (DAR)

TAYLOR, Ira Thomas
    The cavalcade of Jackson County. [Ira Thomas] Taylor. San Antonio, Tex. Naylor Company. c1938. (DAR)

TAYLOR, Virginia H.
    The Spanish archives of the general land office of Texas. Virginia H. Taylor. Austin: Lone Star Press. 1955. (DAR)

Texas CAR
    Pioneer Rest Cemetery, [Fort Worth, Texas]. [Captain William Scott (Texas) CAR. 1949]. (DAR)

Texas DAR, G. R. C.
    Abstract of estate settlements, Tarrant County, Texas: Book one 1855-1859. Copied by Marion Day Mullins and [Paulyne R.] Harmonson. 1962. (DAR)

Texas DAR, G. R. C.
    Abstracts of estates and administrations Navarro County, Texas 1848-1890. compiled and typed by Mrs. Balfour H. Clark (Mabel Berry) for James Blair Chapter (Texas) DAR, G. R. C. 1952. (DAR)

Texas DAR, G. R. C.
    Abstracts of Navarro County deeds Corsicana, Texas... 1830-1855. Copied by Mrs. N. Suttle Roberts, Miss Florence Holman contributed by James Blair Chapter (Texas) DAR, G. R. C. 1960. (DAR)

Texas DAR, G. R. C.
    Abstracts of Navarro County, Texas wills 1848-1890. Contributed by James Blair Chapter (Texas) DAR, G. R. C. 1948. (DAR)

Texas DAR, G. R. C.
    Bell County cemetery records. Agnes Woodson Chapter (Texas) DAR, G. R. C.; Bell Co., Texas History Survey Committee. 1969. (DAR)

Texas DAR, G. R. C.
    [Bexar County, Texas court records & miscellaneous records]. Alamo Chapter (Texas) DAR, G. R. C. 1944. (DAR)

Texas DAR, G. R. C.
    Bible records and other genealogical material. Compiled by General Levi Casey Chapter (Texas) DAR, G. R. C. 1958-1961. (DAR)

Texas DAR, G. R. C.
Bible records. Contributed by Mary Isham Keith Chapter (Texas) DAR, G. R. C. 1958. (DAR)

Texas DAR, G. R. C.
Bible records. Contributed by the John Lewis Chapter (Texas) DAR, [G. R. C. 1976]. (DAR)

Texas DAR, G. R. C.
Bible records. From Colonel George Moffett Chapter (Texas) DAR, G. R. C. 1968. (DAR)

Texas DAR, G. R. C.
Bible records. Major Francis Grice Chapter (Texas) DAR, G. R. C. 1964-1965. (DAR)

Texas DAR, G. R. C.
Bible records [of] Texarkana, Texas-Arkansas area. Lone Star Chapter (Texas) DAR, G. R. C. 1968-1969. (DAR)

Texas DAR, G. R. C.
Bible records, will lineages. Lady Washington Chapter (Texas) DAR, G. R. C. 1973. (DAR)

Texas DAR, G. R. C.
Book A, county commrs. court minutes Angelina County, Texas 1846-1855. Anthony Smith Chapter (Texas) DAR, G. R. C. 1971-1972. (DAR)

Texas DAR, G. R. C.
Book I-A, marriage records Angelina County [sic], Texas 1846-1859 & Book I-B, 1859-1878. Anthony Smith Chapter (Texas) DAR, G. R. C. 1972-1973. (DAR)

Texas DAR, G. R. C.
Brewster, Colorado, Jeff Davis, Pecos, Reeves, Terrell & Ward Counties cemetery records with two exceptions for Far West Texas. Copied by Ollie Kate Harris and Elizabeth Wurtz Slover [for] Texas DAR, G. R. C. 1967. (DAR)

Texas DAR, G. R. C.
Cemeteries in and around Colorado County, Texas. Contributed by John Everett Chapter (Texas) DAR, G. R. C. 1962-1964. (DAR)

Texas DAR, G. R. C.
Cemeteries – Orange [County] Texas book 1. Cataloged by Mr. & Mrs. N. W. Alexander [for] William Diamond Chapter (Texas) DAR, G. R. C. 1974. (DAR)

Texas DAR, G. R. C.
  Cemetery and family records of Ball County, Texas. Betty Martin Chapter (Texas) DAR, G. R. C. 1948-1949. (DAR)

Texas DAR, G. R. C.
  Cemetery inscriptions, Parker County, Texas. Presented by Fort Worth Chapter (Texas) DAR, G. R. C. 1972. (DAR)

Texas DAR, G. R. C.
  Cemetery records, Denton County, Texas. Benjamin Lyon Chapter (Texas) DAR, G. R. C. 1947. (DAR)

Texas DAR, G. R. C.
  [Cemetery records, Galveston, Texas]. Compiled by George Washington Chapter (Texas) DAR, G. R. C. 1941. (DAR)

Texas DAR, G. R. C.
  Cemetery records of Burnet County, Texas. Ensign Thomas Huling Chapter (Texas) DAR, G. R. C. 1973. (DAR)

Texas DAR, G. R. C.
  Cemetery records of Cherokee County, Texas. Contributed by Major Thaddeus Beal Chapter (Texas) DAR, G. R. C. 1971. (DAR)

Texas DAR, G. R. C.
  Cemetery records [of Ector and Andrews Counties, Texas]. Nathaniel Davis Chapter (Texas) DAR, G. R. C. 1961-1963. (DAR)

Texas DAR, G. R. C.
  Cemetery records of Marion County, Texas. Copied by Martha McCraw Chapter (Texas) DAR, G. R. C. [S.l.] The Chapter. 1960. (DAR)

Texas DAR, G. R. C.
  Cemetery records of Smith County (1777-1956). Mary Tyler Chapter (Texas) DAR, G. R. C. 1957. (DAR)

Texas DAR, G. R. C.
  [Cemetery records of Upshur & Harrison Counties, Texas]. Submitted by Captain Thomas Black Chapter (Texas) DAR, [G. R. C.]. [1959]. (DAR)

Texas DAR, G. R. C.
  A collection of Bible and family records. Compiled by Libertad Chapter (Texas) DAR, G. R. C. 1969-1970. (DAR)

Texas DAR, G. R. C.
  A collection of Bible records. Major Jarrell Beasley Chapter (Texas) DAR, G. R. C. 1973-1974. (DAR)

Texas DAR, G. R. C.
[A collection of miscellaneous records]. Lone Star Chapter (Texas) DAR, G. R. C. 1974. (DAR)

Texas DAR, G. R. C.
A collection of miscellaneous records. Arredondo Chapter (Texas) DAR, G. R. C. 1974. (DAR)

Texas DAR, G. R. C.
[A collection of wills]. Submitted by Libertad Chapter (Texas) DAR, G. R. C. 1965. (DAR)

Texas DAR, G. R. C.
Collingsworth County, Texas cemeteries 1876-1976. La Paisana Chapter (Texas) DAR, G. R. C. [S.l.] Texas DAR, G. R. C. c1976. (DAR)

Texas DAR, G. R. C.
Concord, Liberty, Mt. Carmel, Rosemound, Sonora cemeteries in Hunt County. Collected by R. L. Jones and compiled by Mrs. S. H. Whitely [for] Captain Charles Croxall Chapter (Texas) DAR, G. R. C. 1943. (DAR)

Texas DAR, G. R. C.
Copied from Polk County, [Texas] marriage records, volume C, 1874-1893. Prepared by [members of] Robert Rankin Chapter (Texas) DAR, G. R. C. 1971. (DAR)

Texas DAR, G. R. C.
Crockett, Houston County, Texas cemetery records. Presented by Major Jarrel [sic] Beasley Chapter (Texas) DAR, G. R. C. 1972. (DAR)

Texas DAR, G. R. C.
Dallas County cemetery records. Compiled by Mrs. Geo. F. Carlisle; Copied by Mr. Edmon Lewis Crow [for] Jane Douglas Chapter (Texas) DAR, G. R. C. 1951-1952. (DAR)

Texas DAR, G. R. C.
Dallas County, Texas land surveys [and cemetery records]. By Jane Douglas Chapter (Texas) DAR, G. R. C. 1944. (DAR)

Texas DAR, G. R. C.
Dallas County, Texas marriage records, [1847-1873]. By [Willie Flowers Carlisle][for] Jane Douglas Chapter (Texas) Dar, G. R. C. 1945-1957. (DAR)

Texas DAR, G. R. C.
Dallas County, Texas marriage records 1873-1876. Texas DAR, G. R. C. 1957-1958. (DAR)

Texas DAR, G. R. C.
    [Dallas County, Texas records]. Jane Douglas Chapter (Texas) DAR, G. R. C. 1945. (DAR)

Texas DAR, G. R. C.
    Death records [from Dallas, Texas newspapers]. Compiled by Jane Douglas Chapter (Texas) DAR, G. R. C. 1948-1949. (DAR)

Texas DAR, G. R. C.
    Denton County, Texas marriage records 1875-1891. Copied from the original records in the County Court House. Copied and indexed by Mrs. A. B. Harmonson and Jackie Harmonson [for] Texas DAR, G. R. C. 1960. (DAR)

Texas DAR, G. R. C.
    Denton County, Texas record. Mary Isham Keith Chapter (Texas) DAR, G. R. C. 1978. (DAR)

Texas DAR, G. R. C.
    E. B. Black Co. funeral records, March 15, 1909 to March 19, 1923 in Deaf Smith County, Texas. Los Ciboleros Chapter (Texas) DAR, G. R. C. 1976-1979. (DAR)

Texas DAR, G. R. C.
    Early birth records of Shackelford County, Texas. Copied Dec. 11, 1946 by Eula Haskeu [for] Mary Garland Chapter (Texas) DAR, [G. R. C.]. 1946. (DAR)

Texas DAR, G. R. C.
    Early records of Potter and Oldham Counties. Copied and compiled By Della Tyler Key [for] Llano Estacado Chapter (Texas) DAR, G. R. C. 1956. (DAR)

Texas DAR, G. R. C.
    Early wills of Dallas County. Jane Douglas Chapter (Texas) DAR, G. R. C. 1955-1956. (DAR)

Texas DAR, G. R. C.
    Extracts from treasurer's book for Camden Lodge No. 135 from 1853 to Jan. 1, 1869: Extracts from secretary's minutes ... April 5, 1860 to Dec. 27, 1873, Rush County, Texas. Captain William Young Chapter (Texas) DAR, G. R. C. 1959. (DAR)

Texas DAR, G. R. C.
    [Family and genealogical records]. Jane Campbell Chapter (Texas) DAR, G. R. C. 1956-1958. (DAR)

Texas DAR, G. R. C.
Family records, Bible records and cemetery records. Corpus Christi (Texas) DAR, G. R. C. 1958-1959. (DAR)

Texas DAR, G. R. C.
Family records from Book I, St. Mark's Episcopal Church of San Antonio, Texas. Copied by Cordelia Greer Williams, San Antonio de Bexar Chapter (Texas) DAR, G. R. C. 1950. (DAR)

Texas DAR, G. R. C.
Fort Bend County deed records from the general index to Books A and B 1838 to 1851. Submitted by Fort Bend Chapter (Texas) DAR, G. R. C. 1979. (DAR)

Texas DAR, G. R. C.
Genealogical, Bible, marriage and cemetery [sic] records. Betty Martin Chapter (Texas) DAR, G. R. C. 1947. (DAR)

Texas DAR, G. R. C.
Genealogical data from real estate conveyances of Harris Co., Texas. Abstracted by Miss Katherine Reynolds; Samuel Sorrell Chapter (Texas) DAR, G. R. C. 1977. (DAR)

Texas DAR, G. R. C.
Genealogical records. Compiled by Emma Barrett and Lois Fitzhugh Foster Blount. 1972. (DAR)

Texas DAR, G. R. C.
Genealogical records. Jane Douglas Chapter (Texas) DAR, G. R. C. 1939. (DAR)

Texas DAR, G. R. C.
Genealogical records Denton County cemetery records [and] Rush County, Texas families. By Mrs. W. B. Chambers and Mrs. Mary F. Dunn for Lyon Chapter (Texas) DAR, G. R. C. 1958. (DAR)

Texas DAR, G. R. C.
Grave markers in cemeteries in and near Irving, Texas. Compiled and prepared by Mr. & Mrs. O. D. Bates [for] Elizabeth Duncan Chapter (Texas) DAR, G. R. C. 1974. (DAR)

Texas DAR, G. R. C.
Harris Co., Texas marriage records, book D, 1860-1865. [Samuel Sorrell Chapter (Texas) DAR, G. R. C.]. [1948]. (DAR)

Texas DAR, G. R. C.
History of Flower Mound Congregation of the Cumberland Presbyterian Church, Denton County, Texas. Copied by [Paulyne R.] Mrs. Harmonson [for] Texas DAR, G. R. C. [1960?]. (DAR)

Texas DAR, G. R. C.
History of Hamilton-Beeman Cemetery, Corsicana, Texas 1860-1938.
Mrs. Annie Carpenter (Texas) DAR, G. R. C. 1938. (DAR)

Texas DAR, G. R. C.
History of Temple [Texas] churches. Compiled by Gladys W. York
for Betty Martin Chapter (Texas) DAR, G. R. C. [1975]. (DAR)

Texas DAR, G. R. C.
A history of the First Baptist Church, Eldorado, Schleicher County, Texas Sept. 1, 1901-August 31, 1957. Mrs. Essa Alexander (L. M.) Hoover [for] El Dorado Chapter (Texas) DAR, G. R. C. 1958. (DAR)

Texas DAR, G. R. C.
History of Oak Ridge Baptist Church 1858-1970. By Dora Evans Johnson; indexed by Samuel Sorrell Chapter (Texas). 1979-1980. (DAR)

Texas DAR, G. R. C.
Houston County Bible records. Prepared by the Major Jarrell Beasley of Crockett, Texas DAR. 1982. (DAR)

Texas DAR, G. R. C.
Houston County, Texas marriage records. [Copied by Major Jarrell Beasley Chapter (Texas) DAR, and the Crockett Public Library]. 1982. (DAR)

Texas DAR, G. R. C.
Index to marriage records of Burnet County, Texas, book A, 1852-1865; Book B, 1865-1868. Copied and compiled by Mrs. Seth S. (Bill) Bryson [for] Ensign Thomas B. Huling Chapter (Texas) DAR, G. R. C. 1971. (DAR)

Texas DAR, G. R. C.
Index to wills of Johnson County, Texas 1854-1914. Nathaniel Winston Chapter (Texas) DAR, G. R. C. 1959. (DAR)

Texas DAR, G. R. C.
Jack County cemeteries. Compiled by Six Flags Chapter (Texas) DAR, G. R. C. 1958-1959. (DAR)

Texas DAR, G. R. C.
Jefferson County, Texas marriage records [1883-1894]. Mrs. William H. Campbell, copyist [for] George Moffatt Chapter (Texas) DAR, G. R. C. 1945-1946. (DAR)

Texas DAR, G. R. C.
Lovelady historic records, Houston County, Texas: school minutes 1889-1902; Sunday School roll 1876 & 1895. Copied by Major Jarrell Beasley Chapter (Texas) DAR, G. R. C. 1983. (DAR)

Texas DAR, G. R. C.
Marriage and probate records of Liberty, Polk and Jefferson Counties, Texas. Texas DAR, G. R. C. 1965. (DAR)

Texas DAR, G. R. C.
Marriage license record book A Galveston County, Texas. Texas DAR, G. R. C. 1941. (DAR)

Texas DAR, G. R. C.
Marriage license records of McLennan County, Texas 1850-1870. Compiled by Ruby Hall McCormick [for] Henry Downs Chapter (Texas) DAR, G. R. C. 1949. (DAR)

Texas DAR, G. R. C.
Marriage records Bexar County Courthouse [sic] San Antonio, Texas. Compiled by Mrs. Raymond R. Russell [for] Alamo Chapter (Texas) DAR, G. R. C. [1947-1948?]. (DAR)

Texas DAR, G. R. C.
Marriage records, Colorado County, Texas. Copied by Charlotte Vinson Killough, John Everett Chapter (Texas) DAR, G. R. C. 1949-1950. (DAR)

Texas DAR, G. R. C.
Marriage records, Lampasas County, Texas 1873-189? Compiled by Norma Rutledge Grammmer; presented by Fort Worth Chapter (Texas) DAR, G. R. C. 1976. (DAR)

Texas DAR, G. R. C.
Marriage records of Cherokee County, Texas 1846-1870. Copied by Marion Day Mullins; compiled by Norma Rutledge Grammer [for] Texas DAR, G. R. C. 1953. (DAR)

Texas DAR, G. R. C.
Marriage records of Cherokee County, Texas 1846-1875. Copied by Mrs. Ogreta Wilson Hutttash [for] Major Thaddeus Beall Chapter (Texas) DAR, G. R. C. 1970. (DAR)

Texas DAR, G. R. C.
Marriage records of Coleman County, Texas 1873-1890. By Mrs. E. M. (Mattiez) Jones & Miss Cleo Thompson [for] Captain William Buckner Chapter (Texas) DAR, G. R. C. 1944-1945. (DAR)

Texas DAR, G. R. C.
Marriage records of Collin County, Texas, September 10, 1846-December 31, 1875. Copied by Miss Marion Mullins, Mrs. Gus Ford [and] Mrs. R. N. Grammer [for] Texas DAR, G. R. C. 1952. (DAR)

Texas DAR, G. R. C.
Marriage records of Harris County, Texas, January 18, 1865 through June 2, 1877. Copied by Bess and Katherine Reynolds of Samuel Sorrell Chapter (Texas) DAR, G. R. C. 1952. (DAR)

Texas DAR, G. R. C.
Marriage records of Harris County, Texas [1877-1891]. Copied by Misses Bess and Katherine Reynolds of Samuel Sorrell Chapter (Texas) DAR, G. R. C. 1953-1955. (DAR)

Texas DAR, G. R. C.
Marriage records of Johnson County, Texas 1879-1883. Compiled by Anna Estes Campbell [for] Nathaniel Winston Chapter (Texas) DAR, G. R. C. 1960. (DAR)

Texas DAR, G. R. C.
Marriage records of Panola County, Texas 1846-1854 (incomplete). Copied by Marion Day Mullins [for] Mary Isham Keith Chapter (Texas) DAR, G. R. C. 1950. (DAR)

Texas DAR, G. R. C.
Marriage records of Tarrant County, Texas. Contributed by Fort Worth Chapter (Texas) DAR, Mary Isham Keith Chapter (Texas) DAR Six Flags Chapter (Texas) DAR, G. R. C. 1952. (DAR)

Texas DAR, G. R. C.
Marriages Cass County, Texas 1847-1880 books 1, 2, 3, 4 part of book 5. Copied by Norma Rutledge Grammer (Mrs. R. N.) [for] Mary Isham Keith Chapter (Texas) DAR, G. R. C. 1968. (DAR)

Texas DAR, G. R. C.
McCulloch County, Texas cemeteries. Submitted by Mary Garland Chapter (Texas) DAR, G. R. C. [1977]. (DAR)

Texas DAR, G. R. C.
Miscellaneous documents from unpublished court records. Alamo Chapter (Texas) DAR, G. R. C. [1948]. (DAR)

Texas DAR, G. R. C.
Miscellaneous genealogical records of Cherokee County, Texas. Compiled By Mrs. Ogreta W. Huttash for Major Thaddeus Beall Chapter (Texas) DAR, G. R. C. 1974. (DAR)

Texas DAR, G. R. C.
[Miscellaneous records]. Samuel Sorrell Chapter (Texas) DAR, G. R. C. 1949. (DAR)

Texas DAR, G. R. C.
>Miscellaneous records. Contributed by Six Flags Chapter (Texas) DAR, G. R. C. 1951. (DAR)

Texas DAR, G. R. C.
>[Miscellaneous records]. Joseph Ligon Chapter (Texas) DAR, G. R. C. 1947-1950. (DAR)

Texas DAR, G. R. C.
>Miscellaneous records. Records submitted by Nancy Horton Davis Chapter (Texas) DAR, G. R. C. 1960-1962. (DAR)

Texas DAR, G. R. C.
>Mortality list, adults only Corsicana, Texas, Navarro County, taken from the files of Bank Sutherland Funeral Home later McCameron Funeral Home, records now at the funeral home John Carley, Corsicana, Texas. Copied by Mrs. Balfour H. Clark, Mrs. Will Miller, Mrs. Roland Bee [for] James Blair Chapter (Texas) DAR, G. R. C. 1966-1969. (DAR)

Texas DAR, G. R. C.
>Mortality list, Travis County, Texas, years 1850, 1860, 1880. Compiled and typed by the Genealogical Chairman of Thankful Hubbard Chapter (Texas) DAR, 1945. (DAR)

Texas DAR, G. R. C.
>Nacogdoches County: Record of Wills 1865-1904. Compiled and edited by Mrs. Charles W. Morgan, Mrs. Rosalee Curtis, Mrs. Mary Muchleroy Greene. 1981. (DAR)

Texas DAR, G. R. C.
>Nacogdoches County, Texas record of Wills, 1845-1867 [and] miscellaneous Wills. Texas DAR, G. R. C. 1980. (DAR)

Texas DAR, G. R. C.
>Navarro County, Texas records: cemeteries located in Corsicana, Texas. Contributed by James Blair Chapter (Texas) DAR, G. R. C. 1945-1946. (DAR)

Texas DAR, G. R. C.
>Navarro County, Texas records. James Blair Chapter (Texas) DAR, G. R. C. 1945-1946. (DAR)

Texas DAR, G. R. C.
>North Church Community settlers their ancestors and descendants dates given from 1680-1953. Compiled by Nacogdoches Chapter (Texas) DAR, G. R. C. 1953. (DAR)

Texas DAR, G. R. C.
>Old cemeteries of Dallas, Texas. Compiled by Jane Douglas Chapter (Texas) DAR, G. R. C. 1954. (DAR)

Texas DAR, G. R. C.
Pecos and Terrell Counties, Texas cemeteries. Texas Genealogical Records Committee, DAR. 1964. (DAR)

Texas DAR, G. R. C.
Pioneer Rest Cemetery, Fort Worth, Texas. By Fort Worth Chapter (Texas) DAR, G. R. C. 1983. (DAR)

Texas DAR, G. R. C.
Probate records of Young County, Texas, 1876-1883. Compiled by Ruth M. Roebuck [for] Silas Morton Chapter (Texas) DAR, G. R. C. 1955. (DAR)

Texas DAR, G. R. C.
Record of graves in Chinn's Chapel cemetery, Denton County, Texas. Compiled and submitted by Daisy Clark Stiff [for] Texas DAR, G. R. C. 1937. (DAR)

Texas DAR, G. R. C.
Records and minutes of Liberty Baptist Church, Hunt County, Texas, later Salem Baptist Church, Fannin County, Texas 1871-1890. Compiled and copied by Paulyne Robbins Harrison for Mary Isham Keith Chapter (Texas) DAR, G. R. C. 1974. (DAR)

Texas DAR, G. R. C.
Records from James Blair Chapter (Texas) DAR, G. R. C. 1937-1957. (DAR)

Texas DAR, G. R. C.
Records from Lt. Barlow Chapter (Texas) DAR, G. R. C. 1959. (DAR)

Texas DAR, G. R. C.
Records Navarro County, Texas. By James Blair Chapter (Texas) DAR, G. R. C. 1945. (DAR)

Texas DAR, G. R. C.
Records of Collins and Denton Counties, Texas. By James Blair Chapter (Texas) DAR, G. R. C. 1945. (DAR)

Texas DAR, G. R. C.
Register of St. Matthew's Cathedral, Dallas, Texas 1852-1880. Compiled by James Campbell Chapter (Texas) DAR, G. R. C. 1958. (DAR)

Texas DAR, G. R. C.
San Saba County, Texas cemetery inscriptions. Compiled by Joyce Copps; presented by Mary Garland Chapter (Texas) DAR, G. R. C. 1977. (DAR)

Texas DAR, G. R. C.
    Selected Bible and family records. LaVillita Chapter (Texas) DAR, G. R. C. 1970. (DAR)

Texas DAR, G. R. C.
    Selected cemetery records, Coryell County, Grimes County. Mary Shirley McGuire Chapter (Texas) DAR, G. R. C. [1982?]. (DAR)

Texas DAR, G. R. C.
    Selected genealogical records. Collected by Aaron Burleson Chapter (Texas) DAR, G. R. C. 1974. (DAR)

Texas DAR, G. R. C.
    Selected Texas cemetery records Liberty, Chambers, Polk, San Jacinto and Harris Counties. Compiled by Libertad Chapter (Texas) DAR, G. R. C. 1968. (DAR)

Texas DAR, G. R. C.
    Shackelford County, [Texas] marriage records, book A, 1874-1885. Copied by Ruby McGill Dodge [for] Lee's Legion Chapter (Texas) DAR, G. R. C. 1941. (DAR)

Texas DAR, G. R. C.
    Some Grayson County, Texas, deed and probate records from the Charles Quillen Survey (township of Collinsville) and founders and early settlers of Collinsville. Compiled by Ara Dishman Morris [and] Nelle Flanery Dishman [for] Jane Douglas Chapter (Texas) DAR, G. R. C. c1962. (DAR)

Texas DAR, G. R. C.
    Some marriage records of Pecos & early Coleman and early Reagan Counties, Texas. Comanche Springs Chapter (Texas) DAR, G. R. C.. Captain William Buckner Chapter (Texas) DAR, G. R. C., Pocahontas Chapter (Texas) DAR, G. R. C. 1966. (DAR)

Texas DAR, G. R. C.
    Stickley Funeral Home, Hemphill County, Canadian, Texas. Submitted by Comancheria Chapter (Texas) DAR, G. R. C. 1977. (DAR)

Texas DAR, G. R. C.
    Texarkana pioneer family histories, Texarkana, Arkansas-Texas. Lone Star Chapter (Texas) DAR, G. R. C. 1960. (DAR)

Texas DAR, G. R. C.
    Texas, Bell County cemeteries and other records 1770-1956, Smith and Dozeer families, Austin, Texas, 1670-1956. Compiled by Betty Martin Chapter (Texas) DAR, G. R. C. [and] Thankful Hubbard (Texas) DAR, G. R. C. 1957-1958. (DAR)

Texas DAR, G. R. C.
Texas Bible records, Colorado County probate records and cemetery inscriptions 1750-1957. Compiled by John Everett Chapter (Texas) DAR, G. R. C. 1958. (DAR)

Texas DAR, G. R. C.
Texas cemetery records, Coleman County 1802-1925. Compiled by Cleo Thompson for Captain William Buckner Chapter (Texas) DAR, G. R. C. 1956. (DAR)

Texas DAR, G. R. C.
Texas [cemetery] records. Compiled by [members of] El Dorado Chapter (Texas) DAR, G. R. C. 1954-1958. (DAR)

Texas DAR, G. R. C.
Texas cemetery records of Fannin County, [1757-1954]. Compiled by Willie Allen Cravens Holman (Mrs. James L.) and Floy Crandall Hodge [for] George Blakey Chapter (Texas) DAR, G. R. C. 1956. (DAR)

Texas DAR, G. R. C.
Texas cemetery records of Lubbock and surrounding counties, 1815-1919. Compiled by Nancy Anderson Chapter (Texas) DAR, G. R. C. 1957. (DAR)

Texas DAR, G. R. C.
Texas cemetery records of Matagorda County and Calhoun County, 1788-1954. Copied by Miss Martha Louise Moore [for] Comfort Wood Chapter (Texas) Dar, G. R. C. 1958. (DAR)

Texas DAR, G. R. C.
Texas cemetery records: [San Antonio and vicinity], 1781-1955. Compiled by Mrs. Raymond R. Russell [for] Alamo Chapter (Texas) DAR, G. R. C. 1956. (DAR)

Texas DAR, G. R. C.
Texas cemetery records:; Tarrant County. Contributed by Fort Worth Chapter (Texas) DAR, Mary Isham Keith Chapter (Texas) DAR, Six Flags Chapter (Texas) DAR, Lucretia Council Cochran Chapter (Texas) DAR, G. R. C. 1953-1965. (DAR)

Texas DAR, G. R. C.
Texas Church records of Anderson County, Cemetery inscriptions of Leon County, 1807-1954. Compiled by Mrs. Newton Delone Critchfield, Mrs. Fred Hale [for] William Findley Chapter (Texas) Dar, G. R.C. 1958. (DAR)

Texas DAR, G. R. C.
Texas County court records, Caldwell County. Compiled by Alamo Chapter (Texas) DAR, G. R. C. 1974. (DAR)

Texas DAR, G. R. C.
   Texas deed records, Brazos County, 1841-1861. William Scott Chapter (Texas) DAR, G. R.C. 1956-1957. (DAR)

Texas DAR, G. R. C.
   Texas early settlers, Palo Pinto County: first one hundred years. Compiled by Grace Cunningham Perkins, Ralph Ripley Chapter (Texas) DAR, G. R. C. 1952-1958. (DAR)

Texas DAR, G. R. C.
   Texas genealogical records Committee reports. Texas DAR, G. R. C. 1934??? (DAR)

Texas DAR, G. R. C.
   Texas genealogical records, Ellis County [1680-1968]. Compiled by Rebecca Boyce Chapter (Texas) DAR, G. R. C. 1954-1970. (DAR)

Texas DAR, G. R. C.
   Texas marriage records: Austin County 1824-1849; Matagorda County 1837-1856; Wharton County 1846-1890. Compiled by Mrs. Betty M. McCrosbey, Mrs. W. F. Bradley [for] Comfort Wood Chapter (Texas) DAR, G. R. C. 1955. (DAR)

Texas DAR, G. R. C.
   Texas marriage records, Brazos County 1844-1878. Compiled by William Scott Chapter (Texas) DAR, G. R. C. 1955. (DAR)

Texas DAR, G. R. C.
   Texas marriage records, Fannin County 1838-1870. Records copied by Marion Day Mullins [for] Mary Isham Keith Chapter (Texas) DAR, G. R.C. 1955. (DAR)

Texas DAR, G. R. C.
   Texas marriage records; Grayson County collection of Bible and family records, 1704-1957. Texas DAR, G. R. C. [1957?]. (DAR)

Texas DAR, G. R. C.
   Texas marriage records, Harrison County 1838-1868. Compiled by Mrs. H. T. Lyttleton (Vivia A.) [for] Thomas Holden Chapter (Texas) DAR, G. R. C. 1956. (DAR)

Texas DAR, G. R. C.
   Texas marriage records, Johnson County, Book 1-4, 1854-1879. Record copied by Marion Day Mullins, Norma Rutledge Grammer. Contributed by Mary Isham Keith Chapter (Texas) DAR, G. R. C 1956-1957. (DAR)

Texas DAR, G. R. C.
Texas marriage records of Nueces County, wills, cemetery, church and Bible records. Compiled by Mrs. C. C. Miller, Annie Laura McFadin [for] Corpus Christi Chapter (Texas) DAR, G. R. C. 1957. (DAR)

Texas DAR, G. R. C.
Texas marriage records: Robertson County, 1838-1875. Copied by Marion Day Mullins; compiled by Norma Rutledge Grammer [for] Texas DAR, G. R. C. 1953. (DAR)

Texas DAR, G. R. C.
Texas marriage records, Rockwall County, 1876-1894. Contributed by Fort Worth Chapter (Texas) DAR, G. R. C. 1961-1962. (DAR)

Texas DAR, G. R. C.
Texas Old Priscilla Colony, Houston County, 1820-1850. Compiled by Lucille Stewart Krisch [for] Alamo Chapter (Texas) DAR, G. R. C. 1956. (DAR)

Texas DAR, G. R. C.
Texas records Brazoria County, baptismal records, Brazoria Catholic Church, 1848-1905. Asa Underwood Chapter (Texas) DAR, G. R. C. [1949?]. (DAR)

Texas DAR, G. R. C.
Texas records, Brazoria County cemetery records. Asa Underwood Chapter (Texas) DAR, G. R. C. 1948. (DAR)

Texas DAR, G. R. C.
Texas records, Brazoria County marriage records, 1829-1837. Asa Underwood Chapter (Texas) DAR, G. R. C. 1943-1946. (DAR)

Texas DAR, G. R. C.
Texas records, Brazos River Valley, 1787-1952. Compiled by Martha V. (Mrs. Richard) Callender [for] La Villita Chapter (Texas) DAR, G. R. C. 1954. (DAR)

Texas DAR, G. R. C.
Texas records, Brazos River Valley, 1821-1860. Compiled by La Villita Chapter (Texas) DAR, G. R. C. 1952. (DAR)

Texas DAR, G. R. C.
Texas records, Gonzales County marriage records, 1828 to 1890. Thomas Shelton Chapter (Texas) DAR, G. R. C. 1943-1946. (DAR)

Texas DAR, G. R. C.
Texas records, Harris County 1857-1860; wills Box "A". Copied by Mrs. Carrie S. Washburn and Miss Catherine Reynolds and Miss Bess Reynolds [for] Samuel Sorrell Chapter (Texas) DAR, G. R. C. 1943-1946. (DAR)

Texas DAR, G. R. C.
    Texas records of Harris & Jefferson Counties. Ann Page Chapter (Texas) DAR, G. R. C.; Samuel Sorrell Chapter (Texas) DAR, G. R. C.; Col. George Moffett Chapter (Texas) DAR, G. R. C. 1944. (DAR)

Texas DAR, G. R. C.
    Texas records of Navarro & Limestone Counties. Sent in by James Blair Chapter (Texas) DAR, G. R. C. and Jonathan Hardin Chapter (Texas) DAR, G. R. C. 1944. (DAR)

Texas DAR, G. R. C.
    Texas tax lists Nueces County Bible, cemetery and church records, 1610-1957. Compiled by Corpus Christi Chapter (Texas) Dar, G. R. C. 1958. (DAR)

Texas DAR, G. R. C.
    Texas wills and probate records, Wichita County, 1882-1927. Compiled by [members of] Major Francis Grice Chapter (Texas) DAR, G. R. C. 1958. (DAR)

Texas DAR, G. R.C.
    Tombstone inscriptions, family Bible records, family histories of Bowie County, Texas 1800-1957. Lone Star Chapter (Texas) DAR, G. R. C. 1957-1959. (DAR)

Texas DAR, G. R. C.
    Transcripts of early Dallas church records and lodge records and the diary of an early settler. Compiled by the James Campbell Chapter (Texas) DAR, G. R. C. 1960. (DAR)

Texas DAR, G. R. C.
    [Walker County, Texas cemetery records]. Mary Martin Elmore Scott Chapter (Texas) DAR, G. R. C. 1958-1965. (DAR)

Texas DAR, G. R. C.
    Ward County, Texas early marriage records, 1893-1945. Copied by May Robinson Eiland, Permian Sands Chapter (Texas) DAR, G. R. C. 1968. (DAR)

Texas DAR, G. R. C.
    Washington Cemetery, Houston, Harris County, Texas, 1806-1956. Copied by Mrs. Ross Brinley for Samuel Sorrell Chapter (Texas) DAR, G. R. C. 1961. (DAR)

Texas DAR, G. R. C.
    Washington Cemetery, Houston, Harrison County, Texas, 1806-1956. Copied by Mrs. Ross. 1975. (DAR)

Texas DAR, G. R. C.
    Wills, Bexar County, Texas, copied from manuscript records in Court House, San Antonio; Bexar County, Texas from Book A wills. Copied

and compiled by Mrs. Raymond Russell for Alamo Chapter (Texas) DAR, G. R. C. 1948-1949. (DAR)

Texas DAR, G. R. C.
[Young County Texas cemetery records]. Compiled by Ruth M. Roebuck [for] Silas Morton Chapter (Texas) DAR, G. R. C. 1958. (DAR)

Texas DAR, G. R. C.
1850 census of Polk County, Texas. Samuel Sorrell Chapter (Texas) DAR, G. R. C. 1978. (DAR)

Texas DAR, G. R. C.
1850 census of Navarro County, Texas 1903-1910 mortality schedules... 1836-1846 marriage records Marshall County. Compiled and typed by Mrs. Balfour H. Clark (Mabel); contributed through James Blair Chapter (Texas) DAR, G. R. C. 1955. (DAR)

Texas DAR, G. R. C.
1860 federal population census, Trinity County, Texas. Copied by Beatrice Martin Brinkley, Libertad Chapter (Texas) DAR, G. R. C. 1970. (DAR)

Texas DAR, G. R. C.
1860 Madison County, Texas. Compiled by Loretta Elliot Burns [for] Captain John McAdams Chapter (Texas) DAR, G. R. C. 1976. (DAR)

Texas DAR, G. R. C.
1867-1869 registration of voters Bexar County, Texas. Copied by Jean Holden Walker; indexed by Jane Hutsell Terral (Mrs. Kenneth) for Alamo Chapter (Texas) DAR, G. R. C. 1971-1973. (DAR)

Texas DAR, G. R. C.
1889-1900 marriage records, Bowie County. Contributed by Lone Star Chapter (Texas) DAR, G. R. C. 1949. (DAR)

The Texas Gulf Historical and Biographical Record. Beaumont, Tex. Texas Gulf Historical Society. 1975. (DAR)

Texas heritage. Fort Worth, Tex. Texas Family Heritage. 1975-1978. (DAR)

Texas land title abstracts. Paris, Tex. Wright Press. [1984]. (DAR)

The Texas spirit-of-'17: Ellis County U.S.A. Dallas, Tex. Army & Navy History Co. c1919. (DAR)

Texas State Library
Compiled index to elected and appointed officials of the Republic of Texas, 1835-1846. State Archives Division, Texas State Library. Austin, [Tex.]: the Library? 1981. (DAR)

Texas State-wide Records Project
  Index to probate cases filed in Texas: Atascosa County, September 28, 1857-March 6, 1939. Prepared by The Texas State-wide Records Project. Division of Professional and Service Projects, Works Projects Administration. San Antonio, Tex. The Project. 1940. (DAR)

Texas State-wide Records Project
  Index to probate cases filed in Texas: Bowie County, February 10, 1883-June 11, 1940. Prepared by The Texas State-wide Records Indexing and Inventory Program, Division of Community Service Program, Work Projects Administration. San Antonio, Tex. The Program. 1942. (DAR)

Texas State-wide Records Project
  Index to probate cases filed in Texas: Brazoria County, March 30, 1832-October 29, 1939. Prepared by The Texas State-wide Records Indexing and Inventory Program, Division of Community Service Programs, Work Projects Administration. San Antonio, Tex. The Program. 1942. (DAR)

Texas State-wide Records Project
  Index to probate filed in Texas: Brazos County, April 26, 1841-March 1, 1939. Prepared by The Texas State-wide Records Indexing and Inventory Program, Division of Community Service Programs, Work Projects Administration. San Antonio, Tex. The Program. 1941. (DAR)

Texas State-wide Records Project
  Index to probate cases filed in Texas: Brown County, November 19, 1878-November 7, 1938. Prepared by The Texas State-wide Records Indexing and Inventory Program, Division of Community Service Programs, Work Projects Administration. San Antonio, Tex. The Program. 1941. (DAR)

Texas State-wide Records Project
  Index to probate cases filed in Texas: Camp County, November 4, 1871-January 9, 1939. Prepared by The Texas State-wide Records Project, Division of Professional and Service Projects, Work Projects Administration. San Antonio, Tex. The Project. 1940. (DAR)

Texas State-wide Records Project
  Index to probate cases filed in Texas: Chambers County, July 31, 1876-March 6, 1939. Prepared by The Texas State-wide Records Project, Division of Community Service Programs, Work Projects Administration. San Antonio, Tex. The Project. 1941. (DAR)

Texas State-wide Records Project
  Index to probate cases filed in Texas: Coleman County, August 17, 1876-January 4, 1939. Prepared by The Texas State-wide Records Project, Division of Professional and Service Projects, Work Projects Administration. San Antonio, Tex. The Project. 1940. (DAR)

Texas State-wide Records Project
> Index to probate cases filed in Texas: Delta County, September 23, 1870-November 2, 1939. Prepared by The Texas State-wide Records Project, Division of Professional and Service Projects, Work Projects Administration. [S.1.]: Delta County. 1941. (DAR)

Texas State-wide Records Project
> Index to probate cases filed in Texas: Franklin County; August 20, 1875-August 2, 1939. Prepared by The Texas State-wide Records Project, Division of Professional and Service Projects, Work Projects Administration. San Antonio, Tex. The Project. 1940. (DAR)

Texas State-wide Records Project
> Index to probate cases filed in Texas: Gregg County; January 23, 1872-January 31, 1939. Prepared by The Texas State-wide Records Project, Division of Professional and Service Projects, Work Projects Administration. [S.1.]: Gregg County. 1940. (DAR)

Texas State-wide Records Project
> Index to probate cases filed in Texas: Guadalupe County; March 22, 1846-August 11, 1939. Prepared by The Texas State-wide Records Project, Division of Community Service Programs, Work Projects Administration. San Antonio, Tex. The Project. 1941. (DAR)

Texas State-wide Records Project
> Index to probate cases filed in Texas: Hardin County; September 9, 1867-March 18, 1939. Prepared by the Texas State-wide Records Project, Division of Community Service Programs, Work Projects Administration. San Antonio, Tex. The Project. 1941. (DAR)

Texas State-wide Records Project
> Index to probate cases filed in Texas: Hays County, November 22, 1848-December 15, 1939. Prepared by The Texas State-wide Records Indexing and Inventory Program, Division of Community Service Programs, Work Projects Administration. San Antonio, Tex. The Program. 1942. (DAR)

Texas State-wide Records Project
> Index to probate cases filed in Texas: Liberty County; December 9, 1850-July 28, 1939. Prepared by The Texas State-wide Records Project, Division of Community Service Programs, Work Projects Administration. San Antonio, Tex. The Project. 1941. (DAR)

Texas State-wide Records Project
> Index to probate cases filed in Texas: Marion County, May 15, 1860-May 2, 1939. Prepared by The Texas State-wide Records Project, Division of Professional and Service Projects, Work Projects Administration. Jefferson, Tex. The County. 1940. (DAR)

Texas State-wide Records Project
Index to probate cases filed in Texas: Morris County; January 7, 1876-March 27, 1939. Prepared by The Texas State-wide Records Project, Division of Professional and Service Projects, Work Projects Administration. San Antonio, Tex. The Project. 1940. (DAR)

Texas State-wide Records Project
Index to probate cases filed in Texas: Newton County; July 26, 1846-June 30, 1939. Prepared by The Texas State-wide Records Project, Division of Community Service Programs, Work Projects Administration. [S.1]: Newton County. 1941. (DAR)

Texas State-wide Records Project
Index to probate cases filed in Texas: Nolan County,, July 1, 1881-November 1, 1939. Prepared by The Texas State-wide Records Indexing and Inventory Program, Division of Community Service Programs, Work Projects Administration. San Antonio, Tex. The Program. 1942. (DAR)

Texas State-wide Records Project
Index to probate cases filed in Texas: Orange County, March 20, 1852-December 31, 1938. Prepared by The Texas State-wide Records Project, Division of Professional and Service Projects, Work Projects Administration. Orange County, Tex. The County. 1940. (DAR)

Texas State-wide Records Project
Index to probate cases filed in Texas: Robertson County, April 30, 1838-September 1, 1939. Prepared by The Texas State-wide Records Indexing and Inventory Program, Division of Community Service Programs, Work Projects Administration. San Antonio, Tex. The Program. 1941. (DAR)

Texas State-wide Records Project
Index to probate cases filed in Texas: Runnels County; November 30, 1880-January 16, 1939. Prepared by The Texas State-wide Records Project, Division of Professional and Service Projects, Work Projects Administration. San Antonio, Tex. The Project. 1940. (DAR)

Texas State-wide Records Project
Index to probate cases filed in Texas: Rusk County, June 18, 1843-December 29, 1939. Prepared by The Texas State-wide Records Indexing and Inventory Program, Division of Community Service Programs, Work Projects Administration. San Antonio, Tex. The Program. 1942. (DAR)

Texas State-wide Records Project
Index to probate cases filed in Texas: San Saba County; January 30, 1866-June 28, 1939. Prepared by The Texas State-wide Records Project, Division of Professional and Service Projects, Work Projects Administration. [S.1.]: San Saba Co. 1940. (DAR)

Texas State-wide Records Project
    Index to probate cases filed in Texas: Shelby County; November 1881-August 11, 1939. Prepared by The Texas State-wide Records Indexing and Inventory Program, Division of Community Service Programs, Work Projects Administration. San Antonio, Tex. The Program. 1942. (DAR)

Texas State-wide Records Project
    Index to probate cases filed in Texas: Titus County, September 18, 1893-December 15, 1938. Prepared by The Texas State-wide Records Indexing and Inventory Program, Division of Community Service Programs, Work Projects Administration. San Antonio, Tex. The Program. 1942. (DAR)

Texas State-wide Records Project
    Index to probate cases filed in Texas: Trinity County; December 12, 1872-December 13, 1939. Prepared by The Texas State-wide Records Project, Division of Community Service Programs, Work Projects Administration. San Antonio, Tex. The Project. 1941. (DAR)

Texas State-wide Records Project
    Index to probate cases filed in Texas: Waller County; October 1, 1873-May 6, 1940. Prepared by The Texas State-wide Records Project, Division of Community Service Programs, Work Projects Administration. [S.1.]: Waller. 1941. (DAR)

Texas State-wide Records Project
    Index to probate cases filed in Texas: Williamson County; October 16, 1848-December 27, 1938. Prepared by The Texas State-wide Records Porject, Division of Community Service Programs, Work Projects Administration. San Antonio, Tex. The Project. 1941. (DAR)

Texas State-wide Records Project
    Index to probate cases filed in Texas: Wood County, September 12, 1857-March 9, 1939. Prepared by The Texas State-wide Records Indexing and Inventory Program, Division of Community Service Programs, Work Projects Administration. San Antonio, Tex. The Program. 1942. (DAR)

THOMPSON, Robert Lee
    Cemetery inscriptions of Hunt County, Texas. Compiled by Robert Lee Thompson and Kathy Lynn Penson. [S.1.]: R. L. Thompson. c1977. (DAR)

THORNTON, Bobbie F.
    Cemetery records Coryell County, Texas. Typed by Mrs. Bobbie F. Thornton, presented by Mary Shirley McGuire Chapter (Texas) Dar, G. R. C. [1980?]. (DAR)

THORNTON, Bobbie F.
    1870 census and mortality schedule, Coryell County, Texas. Transcribed by Mrs. Bobbie F. Thornton. [1981?]. (DAR)

THRALL, H. S.
[History of Texas]. H. S. Thrall. [S.1.: s.n., 1878]. (DAR)

TIDWELL, Donavon Duncan
A history of the Baptists of Iredell, Texas. By Donavon Duncan Tidwell. Irving, Tex. Griffin Graphic Arts. 1970. (DAR)

A time to purpose: a chronicle of Carson County. Edited by Mrs. Ralph E. Randel and the Carson County Historical Survey Committee. [S.1.]: Pioneer Publishers. 1966. (DAR)

TOLMAN, Arlene K.
Cemeteries of Kerr County, Texas: (1859-1976). [Field notes of Arlene and Fred Tolman]. [Kerrville, Texas: Kerrville Genealogy Society, 1980]. (DAR)

Tombstone records of four cemeteries in Harris County, Texas. Compiled by San Jacinto Society, Children of the American Revolution. Houston, Tex. Houston American Bicentennial Project, 1975-1977. (DAR)

TOOLE, Blanche
Sabine County marriages. By Blanche Toole. Nacogdoches, Tex. Ericson Books. 1983. (DAR)

TOOLE, Blanche Finely
1800 population census, Sabine County, Texas. Copied by Blanche Finely Toole. Hemphill, Tex. B. Toole. [1980.]. (DAR)

Trinity County Historical Commission
Trinity County cemeteries. Comp. and edited by Trinity County Historical Commission. Burnet, Tex. Nortex Press. 1980. (DAR)

TURNER, Ida Marie
Cemeteries of Wood County, Texas. Compiled by Ida Marie Turner and Adele W. Vickery. Mineola, Tex. I. M. Turner & A. W. Vickery. 1970-1971. (DAR)

TURNER, Leo
The story of Fort Sam Houston 1876-1936. By Leo Turner. San Antonio, Tex. L. Turner. c1936. (DAR)

A Twentieth century history of Southwest Texas. Chicago: Lewis Pub. Co. 1907. (DAR)

Two hundred and fifty years: history of Alto, Texas, 1686-1936. [Alto, Texas: Alto Thursday Study Clubs]. 1976. (DAR)

TYLER, George W.
The history of Bell County. By George W. Tyler; edited by Charles W. Ramsdell. San Antonio, Tex. Naylor Company. 1936. (DAR)

ULRICH, Bebe Beasley
    Crockett newspapers 1853-1896. Bebe Beasley Ulrich. Crockett, Tex. Publications Development Company of Texas. c1984. (DAR)

UPCHURCH, Lessie
    Welcome to Tomball: a history of Tomball, Texas. By Lessie Upchurch; O. B. Lee, editor. Houston, Tex. D. Armstrong. 1976. (DAR)

USRY, John M.
    Early Waco obituaries and various related items, 1874-1908. Comp. and edited by John M. Usry. Waco, Tex. Central Texas Genealogical Society. c1980. (DAR)

VAUGHN, Michael J.
    The history of Cayuga and Cross Roads, Texas and related areas in Anderson and Henderson Counties. By Michael J. Vaughn. Waco, Tex. Texian Press. c1967. (DAR)

VERNON, Walter N.
    Methodism moves across North Texas. Walter N. Vernon. Dallas. Historical Society North Texas Conference, The Methodist Church. c1967. (DAR)

VEST, Deed L.
    Watterson folk of Bastrop County, Texas. By Deed L. Vest. Waco, Tex. Texian Press. 1963. (DAR)

VICK-RAINEY, Mary E.
    Marriage records of Walker County, [Texas] 1846-1880. Compiled by Mary E. Vick-Rainey. Huntsville, Tex. Walker Co., Genealogical Society. 1978. (DAR)

VINYARD, Lucretia Barker
    The history of the Cedar Mountains 1841-1952. By Lucretia Barker Vinyard. [Dallas, Texas]: Rhea Printing Co. 1973. (DAR)

WADE, Lelia Jeannette
    Our community organization and development of Nolan County: heritage of the great southwest. Lelia Jeannette Wade. [S.l.: s.n.]. 1960. (DAR)

WALKER, J. L.
    History of the Waco Baptist Association of Texas. By J. L. Walker and C. P. Lumpkin. Waco: Byrne-Hill Printing House. 1897. (DAR)

WARWICK, Clyde W. (Mrs.)
    The Randall County Story from 1541 to 1910. Compiled and written by Mrs. Clyde W. Warwick. Hereford, Tex. Pioneer Book Publishers. c1969. (DAR)

WEBB, Walter Prescott
    The Great Plains. By Walter Prescott Webb. Boston: Ginn and Co. c1931. (DAR)

WEDDLE, Robert S.
    Drama & Conflict: the Texas saga of 1776. By Robert S. Weddle and Robert H. Thonhoff. Austin: Madrona Press. c1976. (DAR)

Western Texas College
    Scurry County, Texas death records, 1903-1935, and Scurry County naturalization records. Comp. by Students of Dr. Tony Turk... Western Texas College. [Snyder, Texas? The College? 1970?]. (DAR)

WEYAND, Leonie Rummmel
    An early history of Fayette County. Leonie Rummel Weyand and Houston Wade. La Grange, Tex. La Grange Jounral. c1936. (DAR)

WHARTON, Clarence R.
    History of Fort Bend County. By Clarence R. Wharton. San Antonio, Tex. Naylor Company. c1939. (DAR)

WHITE, Gifford
    First settlers of Red River County, Texas. Edited by Gifford White. [Austin, Texas: White. c1981]. (DAR)

WHITE, Gifford
    The first settlers of Sabine County, Texas: from the originals in the General Land Office and the Texas State Archives. By Gifford White. St. Louis, Mo. Ingmire Publications. 1983. (DAR)

WHITE, Owen
    Out of the desert: the historical romance of El Paso. Owen White. El Paso, Tex. McMath Co. Pub. 1923. (DAR)

WILLIAMS, Annie Lee
    A history of Wharton County, 1846-1961. By Annie Lee Williams. Austin, Tex. Von Boeckmann-Jones. 1964. (DAR)

WILLIAMS, Mack
>In old Fort Worth: the story of a city and its people as published in the News-Tribune in 1976 and 1977. Mack Williams. [Fort Worth, Texas: The News-Tribune]. c1977. (DAR)

WILSON, Thomas A.
>Some early Southeast Texas families. By Thomas A. Wilson. Austin: Lone Star Press. c1965. (DAR)

Windmilling: 101 years of Swisher County, Texas history, 1876-1977. Dallas, Tex. Taylor Publ. 1978. (DAR)

WOLDERT, Albert
>A history of Tyler and Smith County, Texas. Albert Woldert. San Antonio, Tex. Naylor Co. 1948. (DAR)

WOODS, Frances
>Hood County, Texas: United States census of 1880 & marriage records 1875-1885. Transcribed by Frances Woods & Doris Lewis. Austin, Tex. Printing Craft, Inc. 1964. (DAR)

WORTHAM, Louis J.
>A history of Texas from Wilderness to Commonwealth. By Louis J. Wortham. Fort Worth: Wortham-Molyneaux Co. 1924. (DAR)

WRIGHT, Celia M.
>Heritage from the past: sketches from Hopkins County History. By Celia M. Wright. Sulphur Springs, Tex. Shining Path Press. c1959. (DAR)

WRIGHT, Mildred S.
>Hardin County, Texas cemeteries. Compiled by Mildred S. Wright. Beaumont, Tex. Southwest Genealogical Society. c1976. (DAR)

WRIGHT, Mildred S.
>Jasper County, Texas cemeteries. Compiled by Mildred S. Wright. Decorah, Iowa. Anundsen Pub. Co. c1976. (DAR)

WRIGHT, Mildred S.
>Liberty County, Texas cemeteries: part I West of the Trinity River. Compiled by Mildred S. Wright. Decorah, Iowa. Anundsen Pub. Co. c1977. (DAR)

WRIGHT, Mildred S.
>Newton County, Texas cemeteries. Compiled by Mildred Sulser Wright. Decorah, Iowa. Anundsen Pub. Co. c1975. (DAR)

YOAKUM, H.
A facsimile reproduction in one volume of history of Texas from its first settlement in 1685 to its annexation to the United States in 1846.
By H. Yoakum. Austin, Tex. Steck Co. [1954?]. (DAR)

ZIEGLER, Jesse A.
Wave of the Gulf: Ziegler's scrapbook of the Texas Gulf Coast Country.
San Antonio: Naylor Co. 1938. (DAR)

BIBLIOGRAPHY

AVERY, Carrie W.
  Genealogical Records, Volume II. Privately Printed. 1925.

CROOM, Emily Anne.
  The Genealogist's Companion & Source Book. Betterbooks. 1994. Cincinnati, Ohio.

DAUGHTERS OF THE AMERICAN REVOLUTION (DAR)
  State and Local Histories and Records. Compiled under the Supervision of Eric G. Grundset and Ana Antolin. National Society of the Daughters of the American Revolution. DAR Library, Washington, D. C. Volume Two. 1986.

EVERTON.
  Everton's Genealogical Helper. Everton Publishers, Inc. P. O. Box 368, Logan, Utah 84323 (Various Issues).

FRONTIER.
  Frontier Press Catalog, 1977. P. O. Box 3715, Galveston, TX 77552

HOFFMAN, Marian.
  Genealogical & Local History Books in Print. 5th Edition. Compiled & edited by Marian Hoffman. Genealogical Publishing Co., Inc. Baltimore, MD. (4 Volumes).

KAMINKOW, Marion J.
  Genealogies In The Library of Congress. Baltimore: Magna Carta Book Company. 1972.

KAMINKOW, Marion J.
  Genealogies In The Library of Congress. Supplement 1972-1976. Baltimore: Magna Carta Book Company. 1977.

KAMINKOW, Marion J.
Genealogies In The Library of Congress, Second Supplement 1976-1986. Baltimore: Magna Carta Book company. 1987.

KAMINKOW, Marion J.
A Complement To Genealogies In The Library of Congress. Baltimore: Magna Carta Book Company. 1981.

MICHAELS, Carolyn Leopold and Scott, Kathryn S.
Library Catalog DAR Family Histories and Genealogies. Washington: National Society Daughters of the American Revolution. 1982.

NATIONAL GENEALOGICAL SOCIETY.
The First Census of Texas, 1829-1836 TO Which Are Added Texas Citizenship Lists, 1821-1845 And Other Early Records of the Republic of Texas. National Genealogical Society, Arlington, VA. Sixth Printing, 1992.

NATIONAL GENEALOGICAL SOCIETY.
National Genealogical Society Library Book List. Marion Rollins Beasley, Librarian. 5th Edition. Arlington, VA. 1988.

SCHAEFER, Christina K.
Guide to Naturalization Records of the United States. Genealogical Publishing Co., Inc. Baltimore, Md. 1997.

TEPPER, Michael.
American Passenger Arrival Records. Genealogical Publishing Co., Inc. Baltimore, MD. 1993.

TUTTLE.
Genealogy Family History. Catalog No. 16. Tuttle Antiquarian Books, Inc., 28 South Main Street, Rutland, Vermont 05701.

TUTTLE.
Regional Genealogy. Catalog No. 17. Tuttle Antiquarian Books, Inc., 28 South Main Street, Rutland, Vermont 05701.

ALL NAME INDEX

ABBOTT -
Kenneth Dale, Jr.-1

ABERCROMBIE – 137

ABERNATHY – 1, 18, 45, 133, 173

ABLES – 1

ABSHIER – 1

ABSTON – 1

ADAMS – 1, 16, 59, 106, 109
Adam-1; Joshua-1, 16, 106; Lorenzo Dow-1, 16, 106; Robert-1

ADAMSON – 1
William-1; Wilson Esther-1

ADCOCK – 2

ADKINSON – 55

ALAWINE – 115

ALBRECHT – 30

ALDEN – 79

ALDERMAN – 2, 181

ALDRIDGE – 2
Arnold-2; Moses-2

ALEXANDER – 2, 22, 45, 64, 126, 140, 145, 158
John-158, 165; Joseph-2; Lewis-51

ALFORD – 2

ALLDREDGE – 2

ALLEE – 2

ALLEN – 2, 3, 55, 117, 128, 175, 185
Delilah Catherine Nelms-2; Ed-3; George L.-2; John Edwin-2, Kate Nelms-3; Malvina Owens-128; Moses-3, 128

ALLERTON – 3

ALLRED – 3

ALTMAN – 3

AMES – 3

AMIS – 3

AMSLER – 4

ANDERSON – 4, 8, 72
Adam-4; Alexander-4; Arthur-4; Jean-4; John Benton-4; Thomas Wesley-4

ANDES – 185

ANDREWS – 4
Ephraim-4; George-4; John-4; Varney-4

ANGLIN – 5

ANSLEY – 31, 55
Thomas-31, 55

APPLEGATE – 42

APPLING – 5

ARCHER – 5, 77, 81, 146
John McQuatty-5

ARDEN – 177

ARMISTEAD – 5, 77

ARMSTRONG – 5, 18, 176
Alice May-176

ARNING – 5
Christian-5

ARNOLD – 5, 132

ARROWSMITH – 76

ARTERBERRY – 6, 84, 104, 143

ASHLEY – 119, 133

ASHTON – 109

ASKEW – 5

ATCHISON – 51

ATCHLEY – 107

ATHEY (Athy, Athey, Atha, Athon) – 5
Captain George-5

ATKINS – 6, 55
William H.-6

ATKINSON – 6
Edward Spear-6; Renfro-6

ATTERBURY – 6

ATTERIDGE – 6

ATWATER – 14, 26

ATWOOD – 6
Thomas-6

AUSTIN – 3, 6

AUTRY – 6
Captain John-6

AVERY – 6, 70

AVERYT – 6

AXLINE – 56

AYCOCK – 6
Bill Winston-6; Frances (Bednor)-6; James-6; Jane Everline-6; Richard-6

AYERS – 73

AYLOR – 7

AYR – 90

AYRES – 50

BABCOCK – 7

BACHMAN - 112

BACKHOUSE – 174

BADER – 7
Joseph-7

BAGGARLY (de Baggerley, Baggiley, Baguley, Baggerly, Baggarly) - 7
Sadie J.-7

BAGLEY – 7

BAGWELL – 137

BAILEY – 7, 51, 93

BAIN – 7
Peter-7

BAIRD – 7, 152

BAKER – 7, 8, 20, 35, 38, 112
   Nellie B.-8; William Thatcher-8

BALDWIN – 8

BALL – 11, 42
   Nellie Castor-8

BALLARD – 8
   Cecil Raymond-8; Maurice (Bradford)-8

BALLENGER – 16, 106

BALLINGER – 1, 8, 112

BARBEE – 8

BARBER – 8, 20

BARBOUR – 8

BARCLAY – 61, 148, 159

BARCUS – 9
   Rev. Edward Rosmon-9; Mary Francis Smith-9

BARD – 154

BARDIN – 162

BARE – 9

BAREFOOT – 9

BARFIELD – 9

BARKER – 9

BARLEY – 109

BARNES – 9
   Thomas-9

BARNETT – 9, 43, 45

BARRERA – 9, 66
   Romana-9, 66

BARRETT – 10

BARRON – 10

BARRY – 127

BARTHOLOMEW – 10

BARTLETT – 136

BARTON – 8, 39
   Franklin-10; Malinda-10

BARTZ – 151
   Carl Freidrich[sic]-151

BASHAM – 10, 103

BASKERVILLE – 10

BASS – 1, 10, 83
   Lawrence-10; Peter-10

BASSETT – 10, 164

BATCHELDER – 10

BATCHELOR – 10, 115, 191
   Dan-191

BATEMAN – 11

BATES – 11

BATSON – 11

BATTE – 152

BATTLE – 11

BATTLES – 11

BAYLIES (Bayles) – 11
  James-11

BAXTER – 29, 151

BEAL (Beall) – 11, 138
  Alexander-11, 138

BEALL – 11, 92, 125
  Georgia-11, 92, 125

BEAN – 11, 42, 61, 148, 159, 161

BEAN (Mac Bean) – 11

BEARD – 12
  Richard-12

BEARDEN – 12

BEAUMONT – 12, 163

BECERRA – 12

BECK – 12
  Anton-12; Rosina Koenig-12

BECKHAM – 12

BEDDOE – 12, 59

BEDFORD – 27
  Jonas-27

BEDICHEK – 12

BEDNOR – 6
  Frances Aycock-6

BEDWELL – 13

BEEBE – 8

BEESON (Beason) – 13

BELL – 13, 75, 110, 124, 160, 174
  E. A.-13; Elzora-13; W. C.-13; William Jackson-160

BENNETT – 13, 101, 182
  Hiram-13

BENSON – 13, 192

BERGSTRESSER – 13, 14
  William Wilhelm-14

BERNARD – 14
  Ebenezer-14; Samuel-14; Timothy-14

BERRIER – 151

BERRY – 14, 78, 161
  Della Benson-14; Elija-14; Henry-14; John-14, 78, 161

BERRYHILL – 15

BERTHE – 15

BERTRAND – 40

BEST – 121

BETHEA – 77
  Hannah (Walker)-77; John-77

BETTS – 15

BEVERLEY – 15

BEVERS (Beavers) – 181

BEVILL (Beville) – 15, 78

BIARD – 15

BIBO – 15

BIERBOWER – 135

BIFFLE – 186

BIGGERS – 15, 177
  Eugene Morris-15

BIGGS – 15, 115
  John-15

BILL – 16

BILLIG – 162

BILLS – 1, 16, 106

BINGHAM – 38, 154

BIRD – 30

BIRDSONG – 26, 62, 135

BIRDWELL – 99, 122

BISHOP – 16
  Lewis Conley-16

BIXBY – 16
  Jesse-16

BLACK – 16
  William-16; William Stanley-16

BLACKBURN – 16
  William Thomas-16

BLACKMORE – 16
  Newton-16

BLACKSTOCK – 16
  Thomas Newton-16

BLACKWELL – 2, 16

BLAIR – 16, 35, 43
  John-16

BLAKENEY – 16

BLALOCK – 17

BLAND – 125

BLANDIN – 17
  Joseph L.-17

BLANKS – 17

BLANTON – 17

BLASINGAME (Blassingame, Blassingham, Blassingin, etc.) – 17
  George Washington-17

BLEDSOE – 17, 26, 62, 135

BLEWETT – 17
  William-17

BLOUNT – 42, 52, 71, 116

BLUE – 17

BLUMBERG – 17
  Carl F.-17; Catherine Ruff—17

BLUME – 18

BLUNT (Blount) – 18

BOAL – 20

BOAZ – 18
  Thomas-18

BOBB – 18

BOBST (Pabst-Bobst-Pobst-Pope) – 133, 141

BOEHL – 50, 100, 154

BOGGS – 18

BOHMFALK – 18
Friede-18

BOHUN – 18

BOIES (Boyce) – 20
James-20

BOLEN – 18

BOLLING – 18

BOLLINGER – 112

BOLTON – 1, 18, 45, 173

BONAR – 27

BOND – 18

BONEVANT – 19
James-19

BONIFACE – 57

BONIFANT – 19

BONNER – 18, 19

BONNIFIELD (Bonifield, Bonifant) – 19
Gregory-19; James-19

BOOKER – 55

BOONE – 19
Daniel-19; Edward-19; George-19; Hester Locke-19; Patty Hazelrigg-19

BOOTH – 19

BOOTHE – 19

BOROWICZ – 19

BORRER – 19
Celia-19; Elijah-19

BOSSE – 5
Wilhelmine-5

BOSTICK – 40, 152

BOSWELL – 20
Edward-20

BOUNDS – 20, 27
James C.-27; James G.-27; James H.-27

BOURET – 7

BOWDEN – 20, 133, 178

BOWDOIN – 20

BOWIE – 20

BOWLES – 20

BOWMAN – 20
George Washington—20

BOWMAR – 23

BOYCE (Boies) – 20

BOYD – 20, 161
Charles-20; Robert-20

BOYSON – 20, 159, 181

BRADBURY – 21
Laura Delcena-21

BRADEN – 81
Mary-81

BRADFIELD – 21

BRADFORD – 133

BRADLEY – 22, 30, 45, 145

BRADT – 21
Albert-21; Arent Andriessen-21

BRADY – 21
Catherine Scott—21; Robert-21

BRAMSHOTT – 26

BRANCH – 174
Benjamin-174

BRANDENBERGER – 21

BRANN – 21
Nicholas-21

BRANNAN – 8, 20

BRANNEN – 101

BRANYON – 5

BRASHEAR (Brashears) – 21

BRASWELL – 21, 63

BRATT – 21
Albert-21; Arent Andriessen (Bradt)-21

BRATTON – 161

BREAUUX – 21

BREEDING – 21

BREMER – 21

BREVARD – 22, 45, 140, 145

BREWER – 22

BRIANT (Bryant) – 23
William-23

BRICE – 22

BRIDGEWATER – 152

BRIGHAM – 122

BROCK – 164

BROCKHAUSEN – 148

BROCKETT – 61

BRODNAX – 181

BROOKS – 22, 39, 70, 192

BROOME - 22
George-22

BROUGHTON – 22

BROUILLARD – 22

BROWN – 12, 22, 23, 55, 56, 78, 90, 100, 107, 126, 130, 131, 137, 142, 148, 152, 155, 168, 181
Dorinda Alice-23, 140; Mrs. Fred Ross (Dorothy Louise Knox)-23, 100, 140; Col. Joseph-23; Margaret (Peggy Fleming)-23; Thomas Brokenberry-23; William-23

BROWNFIELD – 23, 141

BROWNING – 23
Robert-23

BROWNRIGG – 103

BRUCKNER (Brucker) – 23
Johann Adam-23

BRUMBACK – 187

BRUMBAUGH – 151

BRUMBELOW – 40, 144, 162, 185

BRUMMETT – 8, 20

BRUNDAGE – 131

BRYAN – 23, 38

BRYANT – 10, 23, 30, 103
William (Briant)-23

BRYSON – 5

BUCHALEW – 24
Mary-24

BUCHANAN – 56

BUCKLES – 24

BUCKMAN – 132

BUERGER – 50, 85

BUFFINGTON (Buffingtons) – 24

BUIE – 8, 20

BULLITT – 174

BULLOCK – 24, 39

BUMPAS – 24

BUMPASS – 24

BUNTE – 148

BURCH – 27, 45
Ary Ann-27, 45

BURGER (Buerger) – 24

BURGESS – 42, 135

BURKE – 61, 148, 159

BURKETT – 24, 135, 140
David-24, 140; John-135

BURLESON – 25

BURNETT – 25

BURNS – 25, 162

BURROWS – 98, 151

BURRUS – 112

BURT – 25
Annie Lauurie-25; Mathew-25

BURTON – 15, 25
John-25; Louise Elizabeth (Mrs. Harry Joseph Morris)-25; Richard-25

BURTSCHELL – 81

BURWELL – 25

BUSH – 26, 30, 62, 135, 151

BUSSEY – 26

BUTLER – 26

BUTTER – 26

BUTTERY – 26

BUTTON – 26

BUTTRILL – 27

BYARS – 27

BYERS – 27
James Kuykendall-27

BYLER – 27
  Jacob-27

BYRD – 27, 78

BYRED - 168

BYRNE – 28

BYRON – 28
  Ezekial-28

CABANISS – 28
  Henry-28

CAFFEY – 28

CALAME – 28

CALDWELL – 22, 28, 45, 140, 145
  David-28

CALHOUN - 29
  Archibald-29

CALLAHAN – 29
  Catharine Finian-29; Cornelius-29; Margaret Kevill-29; Peter-29

CALLENDER – 29
  Nathaniel-29

CAMAC (Cammack) – 29
  John-29; Margaret Purtle-29

CAMBERN – 29

CAMP – 29, 134

CAMPBELL – 103

CANIVET – 162

CANTRELL – 29, 30, 129
  George Washington-30;

CANTRELL (cont.)
  Martha Elizabeth Lea Carver-30

CANTRILL (Cantrell) – 29

CAPPS – 16

CARAWAY – 30, 49

CARDWELL – 30
  Robert-30

CAREW – 174

CAREY – 30

CARLEY (Kerley, Cearley, Carley) – 30, 97

CARMAN – 131

CARMICHAEL – 93, 143, 193

CARPENTER – 174

CARRELL – 99

CARRICO – 30
  Peter-30

CARROLL – 30, 35, 50, 53, 96

CARRUTH – 30

CARSON – 30
  Dr. William Cooke-30

CARTER – 31, 123, 163, 174
  Bernard-31; Elizabeth (Hill)-31; John-31; Robert A. B. (McCarter)-123

CARTHEW – 31

CARVER – 30
  Martha Elizabeth Lea-30

CASE – 131

CASEY – 31

CASHION – 186

CASSIDAY – 70
Melissa Jane-70

CASTEEL – 162

CASTLE – 174

CASTRO – 60

CATCHINGS – 31

CATES – 31
Hiram-31

CATTERTON – 31

CAYCE – 11

CEARLEY – 30, 97

CELL – 38, 43, 82

CHADWICK – 3, 31
Stokley Rowan-31

CHALK – 32, 106, 131

CHAMBERLAIN – 32

CHAMBERS – 30, 32
Charles-32

CHANCE – 26, 32

CHANCELLOR – 32
Annie Laurie Burt-32

CHANDLER – 32, 136

CHAPMAN - 14

CHASE – 32
Aquila-32

CHASTAIN – 33

CHATFIELD – 146

CHENAULT – 33

CHENEY – 42

CHEW – 180

CHILDERS – 33
Lottie (Brewer) Sr.-33; Thomas-33

CHISHOLM – 33
Jesse-33

CHOATE – 9

CHRISTIAN – 33, 162
James Terrill-33

CHRISTOPHER – 33

CHRYSLER (Kreisler, Crisler) – 33
Barbara Von Schellenberg Kreisler-33;
Matthais Kreisler-33

CHUNN – 169, 170
Mary Ann-169, 170

CHURCH – 33, 101

CLABAUGH – 33
Frederick-33

CLACK – 181

CLAIBORNE (Claybourn) – 34

CLARDY – 87

CLARK – 34, 35, 42, 59
  Amasa Gleason-34; Richard-34; William-34

CLARK(E) – 35
  Richard-35

CLARKSON – 154

CLAY – 35

CL.AYBOURN (Claiborne) – 34
  Verner Marvin-34

CLAYTON – 35
  Thomas Nelson-35

CLELAND – 35, 92

CLEM – 12, 35

CLEMEN (Clemens) – 50, 74

CLEMENT – 30, 35, 40, 53

CLEMENTS – 35

CLEPPER (Klepper) – 46, 99, 122
  Jacob-122

CLIFTON – 186

CLINK – 141

CLOPTON – 112

CLOUD – 35, 195

CLOYD – 99, 122

COALE - 92

COATES – 35

COBB – 35, 36, 40

COCKE – 36

COCKRELL – 36, 162
  Francis Marion-36; Sarah Horton-36

COKER – 36

COLBERT – 36

COLE – 36, 37, 83, 139
  "Belle Cole"-139; Mai-36, 83; William Rappleye-37

COLEMAN – 14, 37, 47, 48, 54, 64
  Robert-37

COLLADAY – 37
  Jacob Woodward-37

COLLIER – 101

COLLINS – 35, 37, 38, 92, 166
  Moses-37; Old Man Mose-37; Tolitha Eboline Valentine-38; Warren Jacob-38

COLVIN – 38

COMBEST – 38
  John-38

COMPTON – 38

COMSTOCK – 38
  Ernest Bernard-38

CONANT – 96

CONARD – 38
  John-38

CONDILL – 111

CONNOR – 38

CONRAD – 132

CONVERSE – 38
  Deacon Edward-38

COOK – 12, 13, 28, 38, 39, 70, 163, 192
  Columbis Marion-39; Mary Robertson-39

COOKE – 30, 39

COOLEY – 39

COONEY – 12

COOPER – 39, 40, 109, 162
  Hugh-39

COPEHART (Gebhardt) – 66

COPELAND – 40, 188

CORBIN – 40

CORETH – 40

COREY – 111

CORLEY – 40

CORN – 40

CORNELIUS – 8, 20

CORSE – 40

CORWIN – 84

COSBY – 40

COTHAM – 40

COTTON – 40

COTTLE – 51
  W. Z.-51; Z. P.-51

COUNCILMAN –160
  Catherine (Franklin)-160

COUNTRYMAN – 41

COVINGTON – 13, 41

COWGILL – 12

COWLING – 55

COWLISHAW – 41
  George-41

COX – 41, 42, 49, 186
  Cornelius Jackson-41; Granville H.-41; Huldah Ann Kemp-41; Huldah Wilson-41; Wesley-41

COZBY – 144, 162, 185

CRABTREE – 41

CRAGHEAD – 23, 56, 90, 155

CRAIG – 70

CRAIGHEAD – 30

CRAIN – 41
  John Malone-41

CRAMER – 42
  Nathan-42

CRANE – 42

CRANMER – 42, 174

CRANSHAW – 42, 178

CRAVEN – 12

CRAWFORD – 8, 20, 28, 42, 111
  Edward-42

CRENSHAW – 42

CRESWELL – 42

CRETIEN – 42

CRISPIN – 12

CROCKER – 174

CROCKETT – 42, 43, 51
James Robert-42

CROFT – 43

CROOK – 43
James-43; Mary Williams-43

CROSSLEY – 138

CROWE – 43
William-43

CROWELL – 43

CULBERTSON – 43, 151
John-43

CULHANE – 84, 91

CULLUM – 43
Rev. Marcus H.-43; Marcus Hiram-43

CULPEPPER – 11

CUMMINGS – 43
John-43

CUNNINGHAM – 43, 152

CURBELO (Corbello) – 44

CURRY – 44, 77
Benjamin-77; Mary-77

CURTIS – 69

CUSTARD (Castor) – 44
Henry Castor-44; Nancy Castor-44

DABBS – 44

DALBY – 44

DALE – 44

DALTON – 76

DAMRON – 44, 45, 128
Delilah Catherine (Fisher)-44, 45, 128; Delilah Fisher-128; George-44, 45, 128

DANDRIDGE – 45, 72, 73

DANIEL – 30, 45, 133
George Mayfield-45

DAPSON (Dabson) – 25

DARBY – 45

DARDEN (Dearden, Durden, Darden) – 45

DARLING – 45

DARTER (Tarter) – 45, 173

DAUGHDRILL – 11

DAVENPORT – 45

DAVIDSON – 22, 31, 45, 140, 142, 145, 148
William Mitchell-45

DAVIE – 4
Jean Anderson-4

DAVIS – 1, 8, 11, 18, 30, 42, 43, 45, 46, 75, 92, 93, 119, 143, 147, 155, 172, 185, 193
Elizabeth Jane-43; John-46, 119; Mary (Mooney)-46, 119

DAWSON – 46, 47
Thomas-46

DAY – 11, 46
Julia Halsey-11

DEAN – 46

DEARDEN (Durden, Darden) – 45

DEATHERAGE – 185

DEATON – 46, 47

DE BAGGERLY – 7

DE BERRY – 127

DE BOHUN – 18

DECKER – 47

DE JUZAN – 133

DELANEY – 47

DELOZIER – 47, 53, 54, 113

DELZELL (Dalzell) – 47
John Dalzell-47

DENHAM – 47

DENIGER – 54
Catherine-54

DENMAN – 186

DENN – 46

DENNARD – 47

DENNIS – 47

DENNISON – 178
Mary Tibbetts-178

DENNY – 47
William M.-47

DE PEYSTER – 187

DESHAY (Desha) – 47

DESHONG – 47
Louise-47

DE TAR (Tarr) – 173

DEVEREUX – 48
Julien Sydney-48

DEVERTER – 48

DEVORE – 192

DEVOUS – 46, 75

DEW – 48

DE WEES – 46

DEWEESE – 13

DIALS – 42

DICKEY – 77

DICKSON – 37, 48, 64, 125
James A.-37, 64; Michael-48

DIKEMAN – 48

DINWIDDIE – 48, 51

DISHMAN – 111

DIXON – 48
   James A.-48

DOBBS – 48, 49

DOBRITZ – 30

DOBYNS – 174

DODDRIDGE – 49, 99, 122, 175

DODDS – 149

DODGE – 49, 96

DODSON – 45, 49
   Robert-49

DOELLE – 68

DOLLAHITE – 194

DONNELL – 49

DONNELLEY – 29

DONNER – 107

DOOM – 49

DORN – 12

DOUBRAVA – 49
   Frantisha Novak-49; Vincenc-49

DOUGLAS – 49, 144

DOUGLASS – 49

DOUTHAT (Douthitt) – 49, 186

DOWDLE – 30, 49, 50, 54

DOWELL – 72

DOWNEY – 24, 50, 85

DOWNIN – 151

DOWNS – 50

DRAKE – 11, 174

DRAPER – 50

DREIER – 50, 100, 154

DRENNAN – 149, 161

DRESSER – 50

DREYER (Dreier) – 50

DRILL – 151

DRISKILL – 61

DRIVER – 30, 35, 50, 53

DUBBERLY – 93, 143, 193

DUBOSE – 16

DUCKETT – 50

DUCKWORTH – 50
   Rachel Evelyn-50, 63

DUDERSTADT – 50
   Jane Davis-50; John-50

DUGAN – 50
   Thomas Hinds-50

DUKE – 51, 112

DULANY – 47, 73, 81

DUNBAR – 51, 115
John Samuel-51; William-51

DUNCAN – 48, 51, 99, 122

DUNLAP – 51
Alexander-51; John-51; Mariah-51; Nancy Melanda-51

DUNN – 51, 52, 179
James McMurry-51; J. B. (Jewell Beatrice)-51

DURDEN (Dearden, Durden, Darden) – 45

DUTTON – 52

DUTY – 52

DWIGHT – 174

DYER – 18, 52, 71, 116
James-52

EARLE – 75

EARLY – 52
John-52

EASLEY – 52

EASTHAM – 185

EASTMAN – 52
Roger-52

EASTWOOD – 53

EATON – 151

EAVES – 53

EBERLY – 109

EBY – 53

ECHOLS – 30, 35, 50, 53, 78

ECKERT – 53
George Bernhardt-53

ECKHARD – 53
George-53; Henry-53; John-53

ECKHART (Eckhardt) – 53

ECKLUND (Ecklin) – 53
Jane-53; John R.-53

ECKMAN – 53
Hans Jacob-53

EDGEMON – 185

EDMISTON – 53

EDMONSTON – 92

EDWARDS – 47, 53, 54, 113, 149, 152

EGAN – 54
Valentine-54

EGGLESTON – 24
Horace-24

EIDT – 54
William-54

EILAND – 30

ELCHERT – 54, 96

ELDRIDGE – 142, 148

ELFERT – 54
Grand Elfert Mother-54; T. C.-54

ELGIN – 109

ELIOT – 131

ELKIN – 26, 62, 135

ELLIOTT – 50, 54, 86, 106, 127, 128
George-54; Jane Wilson-106; John-54

ELLIS – 25, 54, 121
Benjamin-121; Elizabeth (Freeman)-54; Lt. John-54; Nancy Murphree-121

ELLISON – 54, 171
John-54; Robert-54

ELTONHEAD – 40

EMBREY (Embree) – 55

EMERY – 55
Anthony-55; James-55; James Wallace-55

ENDSLEY (Ansley) – 43, 55
Thomas-55

ENGLISH – 55

EPPES – 55, 111

EPPS – 28

ERNST – 55
Friedrich-55

ERWIN – 55

ESTABROOK – 75
Mary C.-75, 90

ESTES – 54

ESTILL – 99, 122

ETHERIDGE – 142, 148

ETTER – 55

EVANS – 23, 55, 56, 93, 168, 177

EVETTS – 56

EWELL – 11

EWING – 23, 56, 90, 155
Edley-56

EXLINE – 56

FAESCH – 57

FAIL (Fales) – 56

FAIRFAX – 171

FAITH – 56

FALES (Fail) – 56

FANCHERS – 42

FANT – 57

FARMER – 76, 161, 169
Sarah-169; Willie E.-76

FARNHAM – 26

FARRAR – 111, 133

FARRIS – 57

FARROW – 111

FARWELL – 57
Henry-57; John Dennis-57; Olive (Welby)-57

FASH – 57

FAUBION – 57

FAULKENBERRY – 57

FAULKNER – 57
George-57; John-57; Martha-57

FAXON – 8

FEAZLE – 57
George L.-57

FEE – 58

FEIK – 162

FELTS – 24, 58, 140
Thomas Jefferson-24, 58, 140

FENN – 58
Andrew Jackson-58

FENNER – 58

FERGUSON – 58, 151

FERGUSON – 58

FESMIRE – 58
Martin-58

FESSENDEN – 42

FEUEBACHER – 58
Alvin Frederick-58; Emma Theresa (Hernsdorf)-58

FIELD – 58

FIKE – 59

FILLMORE – 59
John "The Mariner (1)"-59; John "The Captain (2)"-59

FINCH – 59, 134

FINE - 138

FINNEY – 59

FISER – 20

FISH – 42, 59
Alazana-42

FISHER – 31, 35, 59
Jacob-31

FITZGERALD – 122, 159, 179, 190

FITZHUGH – 59, 109

FITZPATRICK – 39

FLACK – 59

FLANDERS – 59

FLASHER – 151

FLEETWOOD – 59

FLEMING – 65, 135
Sarah-65

FLEURY – 59, 60

FLINT – 60

FLIPPIN – 120

FLORENCE (Florance) – 60

FLORES – 60

FLOURNOY – 60
Francis, Sr.-60

FLOYD – 1, 60, 83

FLURY – 129

FOHN – 60

FOLLMER (Fulmer, Folmar) – 60

FOOTE (Fouts) – 61
Luther Samuel-61

FORBES – 96

FORD – 2, 26, 61, 115, 128, 185
Ford-128; Charles Ambrose-26; Mrs. Lucia (Butler)-2, 26, 61; Lucy-128

FORDNEY – 61
Joseph Warren-61

FORE – 61

FOREHAND – 99, 122

FORMAN – 61

FORSTER – 61

FORSTON – 61

FORT – 61
Elias-61

FORTIER – 61

FOSTER – 61, 62, 135, 148, 159
George-62; John-62

FOUQUET – 64

FOUST – 62

FOUTS – 151

FOWLER – 62
John-62

FOY – 174

FOX – 62, 135

FOXWORTH – 26, 62, 135

FRANCIS – 62, 138

FRANKLIN – 155, 160
Catherine Councilman-160; Charles-160; Frances Sample-155

FRASER – 62

FRAZIERS – 196

FREAD – 63

FREE – 63
John-63

FRENCH – 14, 50, 58, 63, 132, 182
Rachel Evelyn (Duckworth)-63; Zachary Taylor-50, 63

FREYTAG – 148

FRICK – 63

FRIERSON – 63, 186

FRISBIE – 120

FROMHERTZ (Fromhart) – 63
John-63

FRONABARGER – 63
Miss Lallie-63

FROSH (Frosch) – 63
David-63; Sarah-63

FROST – 63
Benjamin-63

FRY – 69
Mary Catherine-69

FRYER – 64

FUCHS – 64
Friedericke-64; Lorez-64

FUGATT – 42

FUGITT – 42

FULBRIGHT – 37, 48, 64

FULGHAM – 30

FULLER – 64
Oliver T.-64

FULMER (Follmer, Folmar) – 60

FULMORE – 77
Agnes (Cade)-77; Andrew-77

FULTON – 144

FUNDERBURK (Funderburg) – 64
Eve (Boone)-64; Jacob-64

FUNK – 64, 75, 147

FUNSTEN – 78

FUQUA – 64

FURY – 64

FUSON – 76

FUTRELL – 115

GABLE – 78

GAINES – 64, 76, 184

GAITHER – 1, 16, 106

GALEENER – 656

GALLAGHER – 124, 125

GALLOWAY – 156

GALVEZ – 65

GAMBILL – 65

GAMBRELL – 65

GANIER – 65
Francois-65

GANTT – 65

GAR – 65

GARDNER – 65

GARRARD – 75

GARRETT – 65, 133
Stephen-65; William-65

GARRISON – 65, 66
Caleb, Sr.-65; Sarah Fleming-65; John-66

GARTMAN – 8, 20, 66

GARZA – 9, 66
Mucio-9, 66

GARZA-SADA – 66

GASSAWAY – 66, 167
Jesse-66; Sophia-167, 170

GASTON – 66
William-66

GATHRIGHT – 55

GATLIN – 27
Wright-27

GEBHARDT – 66

GEDDIE – 66

GEDNEY – 84

GEISLER – 24, 50, 85

GENTRY – 26

GEORGE – 66
Col. John-66

GERMANY – 11, 161

GERON – 67
Solomon-67

GERMAN – 67

GHORMLEY – 61

GIBSON – 67, 162
Guy-162

GIDDENS – 67

GILBERT – 55, 67
Abram-67; Elizabeth West-67

GILBREATH – 48, 49

GILES – 26, 67
Elijah-67

GILL – 67, 97
Ethel Lee (Wilkerson)-67; Levi Thomas-67

GILLELAND – 117

GILLESPIE – 28, 124, 125

GILLIAM – 24, 99, 122

GILLILAND – 67

GILMORE – 46, 68, 127
Lela Harper-68, 127

GINN – 125

GISH – 68
Christian-68

GIST – 68

GIVENS – 68
Daniel-68

GLASSCOCK – 181

GLASSELL – 138, 174

GLEN – 68
John-68

GLUECK – 81

GODBEY – 68

GOLDEN – 68, 178

GOOCH – 68

GOOD (Goode) – 69
William Mason-69

GOODE – 1995
Elizabeth B.-195

GOODELL – 116
Elizabeth-116

GOODWIN – 69

GORDON – 69
Clyde-69

GOSE – 69
Mary Frances Gerking-69; Stephen Mathus-69

GOSSELIN – 69

GOULD – 39, 70, 192

GOWDEY – 35

GRACEY – 70

GRAHAM – 70
Paralee-70

GRAMMER – 28

GRANGER – 70

GRANT – 4, 30, 70
Marshall (Mike)-70

GRAUWUNDER – 89

GRAVES – 70
Henry Lee-70; Captain Thomas-70; Wesley-70

GRAY – 18, 52, 68, 70, 71, 116, 177
Millie-71; Col. Wm. Fairfax-70

GREELEY – 71

GREEN – 71, 115
John-71

GREENE – 16, 71

GREENFIELD – 71
Colonel Thomas-71

GREENWELL – 92

GREER – 71

GREGORY – 71
Daniel-71

GREINER – 71

GRICE – 151, 185

GRIFFIN – 71, 94, 107
Lydia-94

GRIGSBY – 71
John-71; Sarah (Rosser or Prosser)-71

GRIMES – 15, 101, 177, 182

GRIMWOOD – 71
Isaac-71; Joseph C.-71; William H.-71

GROSS – 72, 159
Andrew Jackson-72; William Dunbar-72, 159

GROVES – 98

GUENTHER – 72

GUESS (Guest) – 72

GUEST (Guess) – 72

GULLETT – 72

GUNDERMAN – 72

GUNN – 72
Catherine Sherrill-72; Rev. Samuel-72

GUNTHER – 72

GURLEY – 72, 73

HAACK – 73

HACKENBERRY – 151

HADDOCK – 73

HADDOX – 47, 73, 81

HAEGELIN – 73

HAGGARD – 33, 73
Henry-33

HAGGERTY – 73

HAGLER – 73

HALE/HAILE – 23, 56, 90, 155

HALEY (Hayley) – 73

HALL – 68, 73, 74, 76, 133, 139, 160
Fred-160; L. L.-74

HALLER – 74

HALLETT – 74
John-74; Margaret-74

HALLMAN – 74

HALLMARK – 137

HALVERSON – 74

HAMILTON – 74, 142, 148

HAMMOND – 75

HAMPEL – 72

HAMPTON - 75

HAPGOOD – 90
James-90

HANBURY – 75

HAND (Hander) – 75

HANITCH – 75

HANKS – 75

HANNA – 149

HANSBOROUGH (Hansbrough) – 75

HAPGOOD – 75
James-75

HARADON – 25

HARBAUGH – 64, 75, 76

HARBOR – 76

HARDEMAN – 76

HARDIE – 64, 76, 184

HARDIN – 1, 16, 162

HARDING – 76, 97, 171

HARDISON – 76

HARDWICKE – 76

HARDY – 76, 93, 193

HARDEE - 76

HARDIE – 76, 143

HARGIS – 42, 76

HARGRAVE – 76
John W.-76

HARKEY – 37, 48, 64

HARKNESS – 154

HARLLEE – 77
Elizabeth-77; Stuart-77; Thomas-77; Virginia-77

HARMAN – 77
Lewis Givens-77

HARPER – 5, 77, 81, 146

HARRELL – 77

HARRINGTON – 77

HARRIS – 77, 93, 103, 112, 149
Rev. Robert-77

HARRISON – 75, 77, 78, 109, 135, 144
Michael Moulton-77

HARROUN – 78
Alexander-78

HARSDORFF – 30

HART – 12, 78

HARTMAN (Hartmann) – 78
Philip-78

HARTSFIELD – 78

HARVEY (Hervey) – 78

HASHIM – 78

HATCH – 187

HATTEN – 11

HATZENBUEHLER – 79

HAUSWIRTH – 148

HAVINS – 79
John-79; Mary-79

HAWKINS – 30, 79
Anna Eddy-79; John Henry-79; William Alden-79

HAWORTH – 155

HAWPRE – 79

HAYHURST – 32, 136

HAYLETT – 35

HAYNES – 79, 174
Henry-79

HAYNIE – 79

HAXTON – 79

HAYS – 61

HAZELRIGG – 51

HEABERLIN – 79, 170

HEAD – 80

HEADLEE – 80

HEALY – 192

HEARD – 39, 49, 80, 81, 91, 186
Charles-80; John, Sr.-80

HEARST – 81

HEATON – 47, 73, 81

HECHENDORN – 125, 196

HECKMANN (Hickman) – 82
Christion-82

HEFFINGTON – 77

HEGER – 148

HEINE – 180

HEINER – 81

HELLUMS – 81

HELM – 24, 50, 85

HELMS (Hellums) – 7, 81
John-81

HENDERSON – 3, 5, 30, 54, 77, 81, 84, 125, 146, 171
Mary (Barry)-81; William Barry-81

HENDRIX(CKS) - 46

HENKEL – 81
George August Edward-81

HENNECKE – 81
Jacob-81; Mary Braden-81

HENNESSEY – 59

HENNIGER – 82
Nicholaus-82

HENNING – 82
Matthew-82

HENNSLEY – 42

HENRY – 58, 82

HERBERT – 82

HERNDON – 65, 174

HERNSDORF – 58
Emma Theresa Feuerbacker-58

HERRING – 82
Baaylis E.-82; Daniel M.-82; Hines H.-82

HEUSINGER – 82

HICKMAN – 82

HICKMAN (Heckmann) – 82
Christian-82

HICKOX – 82, 125, 196

HICKS – 1, 82, 83
Captain Fabuis Haywood-82; Isaiah Luther-83; Melissa Ida-83

HICKS (Hix) – 83

HIDDLESON – 69

HIESTAND – 83, 180

HIGGINS – 26, 62, 130, 135, 167

HIGHTOWER – 36, 83
William Clayton-36, 83

HILDEBRAND – 83, 111, 122

HILL – 69, 72, 83, 84, 103, 181
Geo. A., Jr.-83

HILL (Hills) – 84

HILLMAN – 84
John M.-84

HILLS – 91

HILLSBERRY – 6, 84, 104, 143

HILLYER – 84

HILSABECK – 190

HINDMAN – 84

HINER (Heiner, Hainer, Hyner, etc.) – 84

HINKLEY – 84

HINOJOSA – 84
Lt. Diego-84

HITCHCOCK – 28

HIX (Hicks) – 83

HIXSON – 84
Naomi (Corwin)-84; Timothy-84

HOCK – 85, 156

HOCKADAY – 85
Thomas Hart Benton-85

HODDE – 24, 50, 85

HODGE – 51, 85
William Fields-85

HODGES – 85
William Fields-85

HODGES (Hodge) – 85
Robert-85

HOELSCHER – 85
Anton-85; Mary Katherine-85

HOFFMAN – 85

HOFFMEISTER (Huffmaster) – 89

HOGE – 18

HOGSETT (Hogshead) – 85
John-85

HOGSHEAD (Hogsett) – 85
John-85

HOLCOMBE – 71

HOLIDAY – 31

HOLLAND – 47, 73, 81, 85, 86, 127, 128
Thomas-86

HOLLANS – 54

HOLME – 12

HOLMES – 43, 86

HOLMSLEY – 86

HOLT – 13, 86
Michael-86

HON – 86
Jonas-86; Joseph-86; Sara E.-145

HOOD – 78

HOOK – 86

HOOPER – 87

HOOPES – 87
Daniel-87

HOPKINS – 87

HOPPER - 115

HOPPERS – 42

HOPSON – 87

HORN – 194
William-194

HORN(E) – 111

HORNBUCKLE – 93

HORNBURG – 87

HORTON – 87
S. H.-87

HOSTETTER – 87
Francis-87

HOUCHINS – 76

HOUGH – 12

HOUSE – 87

HOUSTON – 46, 87, 88, 104
Margaret Lee (wife of Gen. Sam Houston)-104; Gen. Sam-104, 88

HOUSTON (Huston) – 88

HOWARD – 16

HOWE – 88

HOWELL – 88, 151
Samuel-88

HOWZE – 88

HOYLE – 86, 148

HUDSON – 88, 89, 107

HUESKE (Huske) – 89
August-89

HUFFAKER – 89
Catherine-89; Michael-89

HUFFINGTON – 89

HUFFMAN – 192

HUFFMASTER (Hoffmeister) – 89, 90
James Hopgood-90

HUGH – 20, 160
Amy Allen (Hughes)-160; William Perley (Caleb)-160

HUGHES – 23, 56, 90, 160
Amy Allen-160

HUGHINGS – 43

HUGUELET (Huguley) – 90
Charles-90

HUGUENOTS – 33

HUIE – 74, 133, 139

HULL – 87, 90, 93

HUME – 35

HUMPHREY – 133

HUMPHREYS – 90
John-90

HUNNICUTT – 90

HUNT – 70, 90

HUNTER – 43, 90, 91, 128
Adam-90; James-91; Minerva-128; Dr. Wm.-128

HUNTINGTON – 84, 91

HUNTZINGER – 23, 56, 90, 155

HURLEY – 42

HURD – 80, 81, 91

HURDLE – 91
   A.J.-91

HURT – 91

HUSON – 39, 46, 70, 192
   John-46, 70

HUSTON – 46

HUTCHESON – 91

HUTCHINS –91

HUTCHINSON – 91

HUTSON – 77

HYNES – 174

IBSEN – 162

INSALL – 91
   Cade-91

INSKEEP – 84, 91

IRWIN – 77, 92

ISAACKS – 92

ISHAM – 111

IVES – 115

JACKSON – 77, 86, 92, 112
   William-92

JACOBS – 85, 142, 148
   James Wesley-85

JAGGERS – 97

JAMES – 34, 93, 191

JAMES (cont.)
   Mrs. John Herndon (Maria Aurelia Williams)-191

JAMESON (Jamison) – 92, 151
   David-92; Eveline-151; Mary-92

JARBOE – 92

JARRY (Jurry) – 92, 95
   W. A. F.-92, 95

JEFFRIES – 93
   Joseph Arthur-93

JENKINS – 93
   Greenberry-93

JENNINGS – 93, 107, 152, 180
   Robert B., Sr.-93, 107; Tabitha (Lockhart)-93, 107

JESSEN – 186

JETER – 78, 93, 143, 193

JEVIDEN – 12

JOHNS – 93

JOHNSON – 9, 78, 94, 96, 135, 151, 165, 174, 180, 185, 193
   Albert-135; Clyde-94; Elisha (Johnston)-94; Jared-94; John-135; Lyndon B.-94; Lyndon Baines-94; Patterson-135; Spencer-135

JOHNSTON – 26, 62, 94, 126, 135
   Lt. Benjamin-94

JOLLY – 94
   Nelson, Sr.-94

JONES – 8, 20, 29, 59, 68, 94, 97, 109, 114, 115, 132, 170, 174

JONES (cont.)
Sarah C.-114; Sarah Catherine-170

JOPLIN (Jopling) – 95

JORDAN – 95
Charles Wesley-95; Ernst-95; Lisette-95

JURRY (Jarry) – 95

KAISER (Keyser) – 95
Henry-95

KALLAM – 72

KAMPMANN – 95

KAPINOS – 95

KAPPES – 148

KATHCART – 7

KAY – 95, 141, 174

KEAGEY – 96

KEAHEY – 96

KEATING – 96

KEENER – 96, 112
Rachel-96; William-96

KEESEE – 96

KELBE – 54, 96

KELBLEY – 54, 96
Johannes-96

KELLER – 96

KELLEY – 96, 97, 165, 193
Charles-96; John-97; Virginia L.-96;

KELLEY (cont.)
Dr. William Dennis-96

KELLOGG – 29
Olive-29

KELLOUGH – 96
John Stevens-96

KELLY – 55, 137

KELSEY (Kelso) – 97
Samuel Kelso/Kelsey-97

KELSO (Kelsey) – 97
Samuel Kelso/Kelsey-97

KEMPNER – 97

KEMPS – 77
Amelia (Russell)-77; Samuel-77

KENDALL – 97

KENISELL – 97
George W.-97

KENNEDY – 2, 13, 162
Thomas-162

KENT – 97

KENTON – 92

KEPLINGER – 147

KERLEY (Cearley, Carley) – 30, 97

KERN – 97

KERR – 85, 190
Maria Elizabeth-85

KERSHNER – 97

KESSINGER – 98
  Elizabeth-98; Solomon-98

KEY – 98
  John, Sr.-98

KIDWELL – 98
  John-98

KILLEN – 98
  Daniel-98; Saluda-98

KIMBALL – 185

KIMBROUGH – 30
  Dorcas Elizabeth-30

KINCAID – 98

KING – 81, 98, 99, 115, 136, 180, 185, 187
  Juliet-136; Thomas-99; William-98

KINGSLEY – 99

KINNEY – 174

KINNISON – 174

KINSEY – 99

KINTNERS – 70

KIRK – 99, 155

KIRKPATRICK – 99

KITTRELL – 99

KLEBERG – 99

KLEPPER (Clepper) – 46, 99, 122
  Jacob-99, 122

KLINGMAN - 99
  Christine Helen-99

KLUCKHOHN – 148

KNEBEL – 180

KNIFFEN (Sniffen) – 165

KNIGHT – 100
  Henry-100; Jacob-100

KNIGHTON – 101, 182

KNOWLES – 3, 188

KNOX – 100
  Dorothy Louise (Mrs. Fred Ross Brown)-100; William Shields-100

KOEHLER – 50, 100, 154

KOEN – 100

KOLBE – 54
  Johannes-54

KOTHMANN – 100

KREGER – 84, 91

KRUEGER – 100
  Andrew-100; Auguste-100

KUCKER – 100

KUYKENDALL – 101, 194

KYLE – 101, 182

LACEY – 151

LACKEY – 84

LACY – 101
  Walter Garner-101

LA FOY – 87

LAIL (Lale) – 101

LAIN – 101, 102

LAKE – 8, 33, 101

LALE (Lail) – 101

LAMMERT – 101
F. W.-101

LANCASTER – 101

LANDERS – 101

LANDOR – 174

LANDRETH – 102
Nellie Fender-102; Zachariah—102

LANDRUM – 102

LANDRY – 102
Joseph Theolin-102

LANE – 102

LANG – 85, 143
Adam-85

LANGFORD – 49, 102
James-102; Martha-102

LANIER – 45

LANHAM – 102

LANTZER – 102, 152
Mary Elizabeth-152; Samuel-102

LARNER – 102
Wm.-102

LARSEN – 102
Lars-102

LARSON – 163

LARUE – 103

LASATER – 133

LASH – 75

LATHAM – 103, 149
William Harris-103

LATTING – 103
Richard Gano, Sr.-103

LAVENDERS – 42

LAWHON – 103
David E.-103

LAWSON – 26, 61, 103, 125, 148, 159
Anthony-103

LAYTON – 103

LEAGUE – 103

LE BARON – 103

LECKENDORN – 82

LECKEY – 152

LEDBETTER – 103

LEDFORD – 10, 103

LEE (Lea) – 33, 101, 103, 104, 180
Elizabeth Preutt-104; Isaac-104; Margaret Lea (wife of Gen. Sam Houston)-104; Moses-104

LEGNER – 111

LEHMAN (Lehmann) – 104
Ludwig-104

LEHMKUHL - 104

LEIFESTE – 104

LEIPER – 104, 109
Priscilla Jones Macon-104, 109

LEMMEN – 104

LEMONS (Lemon) – 6, 66, 84, 104, 143

LENDERMAN (Lindeman) – 105
Henry D.-105

LENOIR – 26, 62, 135

LEONARD – 104

LESLIE – 58, 104
Samuel Fenner-58

LESSENGER – 104

LEWELLEN – 1, 16

LEWEN – 154

LEWIS – 26, 77, 104, 105, 109, 142, 160, 180
Abijah-105; John-105

LLEWTER (Luter) – 108

LEHMEYER – 148

LIBBY – 111

LIDE – 105

LIGHTFOOT – 105

LIGON – 78, 105

LILLEY – 3

LINDEMAN (Lendermon) – 105
Henry D.-105

LINDLEY – 174

LINDSEY – 105, 106

LINK – 106

LINNEWEBER – 148

LINTON – 32, 106, 131

LIPPERT – 106

LIPTRAP – 106
Isaac-106

LITTLE – 106

LITTLEJOHN – 103

LITTON – 106

LIVINGSTON – 8, 20
J. M.-8, 20

LLEWELLYN – 101, 106, 182

LLOYD – 55, 106
John-55; Prudence (Emrey)-55

LOCHRIDGE - 33

LOCKE – 106
Wm. C.-106

LOCKETT – 106

LOCKHART – 107

LOCKRIDGE – 33

LOELOFF – 107

LOFLAND – 107

LOHMANN – 24, 50, 85

LOMAX – 174

LONDON – 107

LONG – 26, 107, 154

LONGBOTHAN – 28

LONGINO – 11

LONGSDORF – 18

LOOMIS – 107, 143
Judge-107; Richard Asbury-107

LOPEMAN – 107

LORANCE – 101, 102

LOSSEE – 126

LOTT – 11

LOURANCE – 101

LOUTHAN – 84
Harriet E.-84

LOVE – 33, 101, 107

LOVELAND – 131

LOVELESS – 50

LOVELL – 177

LOVETT – 43

LOVING – 107

LOWDERMILK (Loudermilk) – 107
George Washington-107

LOWERY – 43, 83

LOWRANCE – 102

LOWRY – 108

LUCKETT – 108
Thomas Hussey-108; William Rhody-108

LUDEKE-SAAK – 148

LUKER – 108

LUMPKIN – 87

LUNGER – 108
Jacob-108

LUSK – 42

LUTER (Lewter) – 108

LUTHER – 83
Isaiah-83

LYLE – 108
Judge M.-108

LYNNE – 16

LYON – 42, 108

MABERRY – 108

MACBEAN – 108

MACBEAN (Bean) – 11

MACDONALD – 77, 108

MACGHIE (McGee) – 125

MACKAY – 98

MACKELROY (McElroy) – 125
John-125

MACKENZIIE – 109

MACKEY – 26, 109

MACLIN – 174

MACOMBER – 3, 124
Edward Milton-3, 124

MACON – 109
Priscilla Jones (Leiper)-109

MACQUEEN – 28, 109

MACY – 69

MADARA – 109
William-109

MADISON – 109

MADSEN – 151

MAGEE – 109
Patrick-109; Rosanna (McCullar)-109

MAGNESS(ES) – 13

MAGRUDER – 125

MAHLANDT – 109, 156, 167

MAI (Maze) – 109

MALLORY – 110, 183
John-110

MALONEY – 110
Nancy E. (Cupp)-110; Samuel N.-110

MALTBY – 94

MANDOLA – 110

MANN – 110

MANZ (Montz) – 110

MAPLES – 107

MARKS – 9, 110

MARR – 110

MARRIOTT – 111

MARRS – 111, 190

MARSHALL – 8, 20, 111, 120

MARTIN – 5, 40, 47, 73, 81, 111, 122, 132, 182
Adam-111, 122; Thomas, Sr.-111

MARTINEZ DEL RIO – 111

MARX – 180
Lena-180

MASEAR – 111

MASON – 8, 20, 94, 111

MASSENGILL (Massengales) – 112

MASSEY – 112, 130
Frank A.-112, 130; John-112

MASSIE – 32, 106, 112, 131
John-112

MASTERS – 113
Samuel-113

MATHEWS – 143, 193

MATHIS – 47, 53, 54, 113

MATTHEWS – 9, 93, 113, 126, 136, 147
Burrell-113; Watt-113, 147

MAUDIE – 113

MAULDIN – 97

MAULE – 113
Thomas-113

MAVERICK – 113
Geo. Madison-113; Mary A.-113

MAVITY – 185

MAXEY – 4, 113

MAY – 113, 114, 174
Caleb-114; Claiborne B.-113; Margaretta (Patrick)-114

MAY (Mays) – 114

MAYFIELD – 114
Albert-114; Ann-114

MAYS – 114

MAZE (Mai) – 109

MEAD – 190

MEADOWS – 114
Daniel-114

MEANEY – 179

MECKLIN – 161

MEDEORIS – 195

MEDFORD – 93

MEDLAN – 114

MEEKS – 114
Nathan-114; Sarah C. (Jones)-114

MEELER – 114

MEGEE – 115

MEIER (Myers) – 122
Hans-122

MELTON – 115

MELUGIN – 115

MENDENHALL – 115

MENEFEE – 115
Laban-115

MENIL – 115

MERCER – 115

MEREDITH – 83, 115, 181

MERRILL – 8, 115

MERRITT – 115
Charles-115

METCALF (Metcalfe) – 116

METTS – 116

METZ – 116

MEW – 116
George William Knight-116

MEYER – 116, 148

MICKESELL – 84

MIELENZ – 24, 50, 85

MILES – 72, 116, 1994

MILLER – 18, 30, 52, 71, 94, 116, 125, 187
Elizabeth Goodell-116, 147; Jonathan-116; John G.-116; Mamie Clarice (Thompson)-116

MILLS – 26, 30, 97, 112, 192

MILNER – 116, 117

MILSAPS – 117

MILWARD – 117

MIMS – 117

MINEAR – 117
John-117

MINEAR (Menear, Myneer, Manear, Mineer) – 117

MINIER – 117
George W.-117

MINGE – 12

MINTON – 74, 133, 139

MISTROT – 117

MITCHELL – 26, 30, 62, 117, 118, 120, 135
Homer R.-118; James-118; Nancy Campbell-118

MIXON (Mixson) – 118

MOBLEY – 9

MOFFETT – 161

MOHUNDRO – 1, 16, 106

MONSON – 118
William Benjamin-118

MONTAGUE – 118
John V.-118

MONTFORT – 103

MONTGOMERY – 81, 118

MOODY – 35, 118, 119
Francis-119

MOONEY – 5, 119
John-119; Mary (Davis)-119

MOORE – 8, 17, 20, 72, 73, 97, 107, 119
John A.-119; Mary-119

MOORHEAD – 82, 125, 196

MOORMAN – 119

MOOSBERG – 119, 181

MORAN – 65

MOREHOUSE – 119

MORFORD – 126

MORGAN – 59, 119
Nellie B.-119

MORONEY – 119
Ann McCarthy-119; Joacobus-119

MORRIS – 25, 119, 120
Amos-120; Mrs. Harry Joseph (Louise Elizabeth Burton)-25; Isaac-119

MORRISS – 28

MORROW – 97

MORSE – 120

MORTER – 26, 62, 135

MOSLEY – 120

MOSS – 120
Amanda Holden-120; Crestus Howell-120; Henry-120; Howell-120; Howell C.-120; Thaddeus Augustus-120; Thaddeus A.-120; William Paul—120

MOUNT – 120

MOURNING – 42

MOUSER – 121

MOWREY – 121

MOYER – 121

MULLEN – 121

MULLENDORE – 24, 50, 85

MULLINAX (Mullineaux) - 121

MULLINEAUX – 121

MULVANEY – 121

MURCHISON – 121

MURFF – 121
Randolph S.-121

MURPHREE – 121
Benjamin-121; Daniel-121; Nancy-121

MURPHY – 49, 121, 186

MURR – 38

MURRAY – 121

MUSICK – 11, 122
Adam Martin-122; Thomas Roy-111, 122

MYERS – 8, 20, 34, 122
Hans-122

MCADAM (McAdams) – 122, 159, 179, 190

MCAFEE – 43

MCALEXANDER – 97

MCALLEY – 122

MCALLISTER – 122

MCALPINE – 99, 122, 177
Malcolm-122

MCBLAIR – 122

MCBRAYER – 132, 182

MCCABE – 122, 136

MCCALEB – 177
Sarah Elizabeth-177

MCCALL – 123

MCCANN (McCan) – 123
James-123

MCCANTS – 123

MCCARLEY – 123

MCCARTER – 123
Robert A. B. Carter-123

MCCLANAHAN – 123

MCCLELLAN – 85, 123
   Ruufus-123; Sophia Brownlow-85;
   William Brownlow-123

MCCLUE – 92

MCCLUNEY – 123

MCCLURE – 123

MCCOMB – 177

MCCONNELL – 8, 149

MCCOOK – 170
   Ida May-170

MCCORMICK – 124
   William Lee-124

MCCOWN – 124
   Simeon-124

MCCRACKEN – 55, 124

MCCRARY – 124
   Colonel Robert-124

MCCUAN (McEwan) – 125

MCCUISTON – 54, 86, 124, 128
   Noah-124

MCCULKLEY (McCulley) – 124

MCCULLEY – 124
   Sarah-124; Solomon-124

MCCULLOCH – 56, 103

MCCUMBER (Macomber) – 124
   Edward Milton-124

MCCUNE – 124
   William-124

MCCURDY – 69, 94
   John C.-69, 94

MCDANIEL – 185

MCDERMOTT – 124, 125

MCDONALD – 15, 109, 125, 177

MCDOUGAL – 152

MCDOWALL – 9

MCDOWELL – 12

MCDUFF – 125

MCEACHIN – 28

MCELROY – 125
   John-125

MCEWAN (McCuan) – 125

MCFARLAND – 175
   Eleanore-175

MCFEATTERS (McFeaters) – 82, 125, 196

MCGAFFEY – 125

MCGAVIN – 125

MCGEE (MacGhie) - 39, 55, 98, 125, 162

MCGIFFIN – 125

MCGIVERN – 124, 125

MCGREGOR – 125, 126

MCGUFFEY – 125, 149

MCILWAINE – 109

MCINERNEY – 29

MCKENZIE – 105, 109, 124, 142, 160

MCKINLEY – 126
Stephen-126

MCKINNEY – 93, 126, 143, 193
Collin-126; Daniel-126

MCKISICK – 125

MCKNIGHT – 126

MCKNIT (McKnitt) – 22, 45, 140, 145

MCLAUGHLIN – 126
James-126; Mary-126

MCLEAN – 126
John-126

MCLELLAND – 126
Rufus-126

MCMILLIEN – 20

MCMINN – 126

MCMULLEN – 30

MCNAIR – 45

MCNALL (MacNaul, McNaul) – 127

MCNEELY – 43

MCNEIL (McNeill) – 68, 127
Robert Harllee-68, 127

MCNUTT – 28

MCPHAIL – 66

MCPHERSON – 127

MCQUISTON – 127

MCWHORTER – 30, 127

MCWHORTER (McWhirter) – 127
David-127; Mary Poston (Posten)-127

MCWILLIAMS – 8

NAGGLE – 18

NALL – 37, 48, 64

NAVARRO – 127

NEAL – 127
Alfred-127; Elizabeth Polk-127

NEALE (Neale, O'Neale) – 127

NEELEY – 128
John-128

NEIGHBORS – 128

NELMS – 128
C. C.-128;; Delilah Damron-128; Rev. John A.-128; Mary Bell Crain-128

NELSON – 54, 86, 127, 128, 161, 174

NEMKEY – 128

NEVILL – 128

NEVILLE – 111, 122, 129

NEWMAN – 29, 129, 190

NEWSOM – 126

NEWTON – 60, 129

NEYSWANGER – 147

NICHOLLS – 129

NICHOLS – 129
Hannah Griffin-129; Sarah Alexander-129; Thomas-129

NICHOLSON (Nicolson) – 129
Robert-129

NIMITZ – 129

NIXON – 130
Dr. Eldred Scott Simpkins-130

NOACK (Noach?) – 130
Johann-130; Maria-130

NOBLITT – 30

NOFZIGER – 130
Christ R.-130

NOLD – 130

NOLL – 72

NORMAN – 130

NORRID – 130

NORRIS – 93, 135, 143, 193
Jane-135

NORTHCRAFT – 151

NORTHCUTT – 130

NORTHERN – 55

NORTON – 130
Martha-130; Mercer (Messer)-130

NORWOOD – 130
"General" John-130

NOVAK – 131
Joseph Robert-131; Rynell Stiff-131

NULISCH – 131

OATES – 32, 106, 131

OBERHOLTZER – 131
Samuel-131

O'BRIEN (O'Bryan) – 131
Benedict-131; Dolly-131; Henry-131; John-131; Joseph-131; Philip-131

O'BYRNE – 131

O'CONNOR – 78

ODOM – 131, 185

OERTLI – 131

OFFER – 131
Adam Hermann Joseph-131; Johann Julius August-131

OGDEN – 131

OGELTREE (Ogletree) – 132, 182
John, Sr.-132, 182

OGILVIE – 26, 62, 135

O'HARA – 132

O'HERONS – 29

OHRNDORFF – 132
Christian-132

O'KELLEY – 2

OLDHAM – 5, 132

OLIVE – 132
   James-132

OLIVER – 35

ONDERDONK – 132

O'NEALE (Neale) – 127

ONLEY – 78

O'QUINN (Quinn) – 143

ORANGE-NASSAU, HOUSE OF – 132

O'REAR – 55

O'ROARK (O'Rourke, Roark) – 132, 149
   Nathan-132, 149

ORMOND – 61
   Duke of-61

ORR – 132

OSBORNE – 101

OSMOND – 132
   Jonathan-132

OTT – 130

OUSLEY – 132, 133

OVERTON – 112

OWEN – 133
   Judge David Allen-133; Samuel Tine-133; Sarah Ward (Knight)-133

PABST (Pabst, Bobst, Pobst, Pope) – 133, 141

PACE – 74, 133, 139, 159, 193

PACKWOOD – 30

PEDIGO – 76

PAFFORD – 22

PAGAN – 97

PAGE – 13, 78, 134
   McKineth A.-134

PALMER – 3

PARK – 134
   Mary Elizabeth Teater-134; Pearson Money-134

PARKE – 134

PARKER – 126, 134
   John-134; Robert Arthur-134

PARKS – 14

PARNELL – 134

PARROTT – 112, 134
   Benjamin-134

PARSONS – 42

PARTLOW – 12

PARTRIDGE – 134

PASCHAL – 135

PASCHALL – 135
   Elisha-135

PATE – 171

PATILLO (Patillo, Pattilo, Pattulo, Pittillo) – 1, 83, 135

PATTERSON – 112, 115, 135

PATTON (Patten) – 40, 135
Isaac, Sr.-135; Jane-135

PAXTON – 135

PAYNE – 26, 62, 135

PEACOCK – 32, 136

PEARCE – 136

PEARSON (Peirson) – 8, 20, 122, 136, 155
Lawrence-136

PEARSON (Person, Persons) – 137
Johanna-137; John-137

PEAVY (Peevy, Peavy, Pevey, Puvey) – 136

PECKENPAUGH (Pechinpaughs, Pickenpaughs, Beckenbaughs, Peckinpahs, Peckenpaughs) – 136
Anna Maria Beckenbach-136; Johann Adam-136

PECKHAM – 136
Charles-136

PECORE – 24, 50, 85

PEDEN – 78

PEGUES – 136
Claudius-136; Juliet (King)-136; Samuel Butler-136

PEIRA – 111, 122

PENCE – 137

PENDLETON – 137

PENNINGTON – 137

PERES – 137

PEREZ – 137

PERKEY – 137

PERKINS – 137, 174

PERRY – 109, 137
Daniel-137

PERSON(S) (Pearson) – 137
Amos-137; Johanna—137; John-137

PESSEMIER – 137
Charles Louis-137; Marie Justine Valley-137

PETERSON – 137

PETTY – 32, 136, 138

PEYTON – 138

PFEIFFER – 138, 190

PHELPS – 138

PHILIPS – 138

PHILLIPS – 125, 132, 138, 139, 182
Wesley Ruel-139

PHIPPS - 144

PICKENS – 139, 161

PIERCE – 74, 133, 139, 185

PIERSON – 139
'Belle Cole'-139; Charlie-139

PILLSON – 76

PING – 30

PINKERTON – 139

PINNELL – 139

PIRKLE 139

PIRTLE – 140

PISTOLE – 181

PITTS – 140

PLANK – 140
David H.-140

POARCH – 87

POBST (Pabst, Bobst, Pobst, Pope) – 133, 141

POCAHONTAS – 78

POCHMANN – 151

POE – 46

POER – 112

POINDEXTER – 140

POINDEXTER (Poingdestre) – 140

POLK – 22, 24, 45, 140, 145, 149

POLLARD – 141, 152

POLLOCK – 174

PONDER – 141, 177
Hezekiah-141

PONTIFF – 141

POOLE – 55

POPE (Pabst, Bobst, Pobst, Pope) – 26, 62, 133, 135, 141

PORTER – 23, 131, 141
Wm.-141; William, Jr.-141

POSEY – 59

POTTER – 8, 141
David Magie-141

POTTS – 98

POU (Pugh) – 142
John, III-142

POWELL – 16, 130, 141

PRATT – 141

PRESTON – 142
Betty Louise Foster-142

PRICE – 11, 105, 109, 125, 142, 160, 170
Dazwell Carter-142; Martha Ann (Oliver)-142; Levi Lloyd-142

PRIMROSE – 142

PRINCE – 142
Jesse-142; Zachariah-142

PRITCHARD – 142

PRITCHETT – 142, 148

PRUSSNER – 148

PUCKETT – 142
Thomas-142

PUGH (Pou) – 142
John Pou, III-142

PULLMAN – 53

PUMMILL – 143

PURDY – 131
 Francis-131

PURIFOY – 143
 Henry Marshall-143

PUTNAM – 96
 Wilma Emery-96

PYBURN (Piborn, Pyborn, Pyburn) – 143

PYLES – 45

QUACKENBUSH – 143

QUEEN – 137

QUILLING – 151

QUINN (O'Quinn) – 143

QUINN – 143
 Esther (Martin)-143; Patrick (Peter)-143; William-143

QUIRK – 138

QUISENBERRY – 26, 62, 135

RAABE – 82
 Louisa-82

RAASCH – 151
 Henrietta Charlotte Justine-151

RADCLIFFE – 143
 Joseph-143

RAGSDALE – 6, 84, 104, 143

RAINES – 144

RALEIGH – 144

RAMSEY – 144
 Ealanor-144; Samuel-144

RANDOLPH – 144

RANNEY – 26

RANUZZI – 144

RANZAU – 144
 Ludwig-144

RATCLIFF – 93, 193
 Joseph-193

RATH – 50, 100, 154

RATLIFF – 72

RAWSON – 40, 144, 162, 185

RAY – 144, 149

RAYBURN – 145

RAYMOND – 27
 Peter-27

REA – 7, 78
 Alma Baker-7, 78

READ – 145

READING – 187

REAGAN – 52

REAMS – 77

REDFERN (Redfearn) – 145
 Francis-145; Ruth Milner-145

REED – 38, 145
Martha Burnett-145; Michael-145; Peter Hon-145; Sarah E. Hon—145

REES – 145
Rev. Isham (Reese)-145

REESE – 22, 45, 140, 145
David-22, 45, 140, 145; Rev. Isham-145; Rebecca Jean Ashley-145

REEVE – 146

REEVES – 5, 77, 81, 97, 146

REGAN – 26, 62, 135

REID – 38, 149

REINHARDT – 148

REMER – 142, 148, 161, 170
Mary-142, 148, 161, 170

REMMERT – 162

RENCHER – 146

RENEAU (Reneau, Reno) – 146

RENFREW (Renfro) – 146
William-146

RENFRO – 6, 146
William-146

RENO (Reneau) – 146

RENWICK – 146

REUTHER (Reuter, Riter) – 146

REYNOLDS – 64, 75, 76, 146, 147
Watt Matthews-147

RHEIN – 147

RHODES – 147
Myra-147

RHODES (Roads) – 147
Valentine-147

RICE – 51, 115, 147
Nordi-147

RICH – 147
William (Richee), Sr.-147

RICHARD – 27, 35, 51
George-27

RICHARDS – 27, 32, 115
George-27; Joshua-27

RICHARDSON – 13, 141, 147
Amos-141

RICHESON – 147

RICHMOND – 101

RIDDELL – 112

RIDDLE – 148
William-148

RIDLEY – 151

RIEKE – 148

RIGBY – 148

RIGBY (Rigsby) – 148
Laura Elaine-148

RIGGINS – 132, 182

RIGSBY – 30, 61, 148, 159
Laura Elaine-30, 148

RIMMER (Remer) – 142, 148
  Mary- 142, 148

RINEHART – 148

RITCHIE – 148, 159
  John-148, 159

RITER (Reuter, Reuther) – 146

RIX – 52
  Guy Scobie-52

ROACH – 137, 148, 149, 161, 166
  James-148; Luke-149; Malinda McConnell-148

ROADES – 149

ROADS (Rhodes) – 147
  Valentine-147

ROARK (O'Rourke) – 72, 132, 149
  Nathan-132, 149

ROBBINS – 144, 125, 149

ROBERTS – 26, 149

ROBERTSON – 77, 149, 174, 180
  Frances (King)-77; Mrs. John C (Ruby Traylor)-180; Sterling Clack-77; William Crockett-149

ROBINETT – 149, 150
  Allen-150

ROBINSON – 30, 46, 115, 150, 180
  Hugh-150; John-150; John Edwin-150; Stella Adolphus-150

ROCKFELLER (Rockefeller) – 63

RODDIS – 84, 91

RODEN (Rodin) – 12, 22, 147
  Jerri Gayle-12, 22, 147

RODES – 111

RODMAN – 80

ROEBUCK – 150

ROGERS – 8, 20, 138, 150, 1662

ROHDE – 150
  Eduard-150; Gottfried-150

ROMERO – 151

ROQUEMORE – 151

ROSCOE – 170

ROSEBROUGH – 151

ROSENBERG (Von Rosenberg) – 151

ROSS – 35, 76, 101, 182
  Gene-101, 182

ROUNTREE (Rowntree) – 151

ROUSE – 151
  Alexander-151; Eveline Jamison-151

ROUSH (Raasch) – 151
  Henrietta Charlotte Justine-151

ROUTH – 151, 153, 154
  Jacob-153; Stephen-151, 154

ROWE – 143, 152
  Christopher-152

ROY – 111, 122

ROYAL – 22, 152

ROYALL – 139, 152

RUCIDLO – 99
   Hazel Evalyn Kingsley-99

RUCKER – 152

RUDD – 152

RUDEL – 152
   Leonard-152; Mary Elizabeth Lantzer-152

RUDER – 155

RUGELEY – 152

RUHMANN – 152

RUMPH – 152
   David-152

RUSH – 12

RUSLER – 109

RUSS – 152

RUSSELL – 152, 153
   Green-153

RUSSEY – 153
   James-153

RUST – 153
   Agnes Rust Gordon Smith-153; Henry-153

RUTH (Routh) – 153, 154
   Jacob-153

RUTHERFORD – 154

RYAN – 154
   Thomas-154

RYKER – 154

SABIN – 13

SACK – 154

SADLER – 154, 161

SAGER – 100, 154

SALE (Sayles) – 154

SALMON – 22

SAMPLE – 109, 155

SANCHEZ NAVARRO – 155

SANDERS – 43, 70, 132, 161, 182
   Daniel-70

SANDIFER – 155
   John D.-155; Johnson P.-155; Joseph-155; Joseph A.-155; Peter-155; William Nightingale-155; William V.-155

SANDLIN – 138, 155

SANDMEYER – 148

SAPP – 146, 162

SARTOR (Sautor) – 155, 156

SAUNDERS – 155
   Henry Simeon-155

SAUTER (Sartor) – 155

SAVAGE – 12

SAWYER – 23, 56, 90, 115, 155

SAYLES (Sales) – 154

SCALES – 141

SCARBOROUGH – 155
Major James-155

SCHAERDEL – 155

SCHAPER – 162

SCHELL – 186

SCHLITTLER – 109, 156, 167

SCHMIDT – 156
Anna-156; George-156

SCHMINCKE – 156, 165

SCHMITTEL – 151

SCHOENWERK – 81

SCHRAPFER – 156

SCHUESSLER – 156
Eva-156; John Adam-156

SCHULTZ (Schulte) – 156

SCHULTZ (Shults) – 156

SCHWARTZ – 156

SCOGGIN – 107

SCOGGINS – 156

SCOTT – 59, 156, 157
Agrippa-157; John, Sr.-157; Silas H.-157; William-157

SEAL (Seale) – 157

SEALE – 157

SEALY – 97

SEAWRIGHT – 94

SEAY – 46

SEBOR – 187

SEBRING – 157

SEELEY – 32, 157
George-157

SEGER – 156

SEGURA – 117

SEITZ – 158

SELBY – 80

SELDEN – 174

SELF – 138

SELL – 158

SELLARDS – 158

SELLERS – 158

SELMAN – 11, 161

SEWALL (Sowell) – 158
John Alexander-158; Laura Hilton-158

SEZONOV – 158

SHACKELFORD (Shackleford) – 51, 152, 158

SHAFER – 63, 151

SHAMBAUGH – 158
Jacob-158; Sarah Hoobler-158

SHANK – 158
Jacques-158; Jon-158; Jinger-158

SHANNON – 27

SHAPLEY – 14
Alexander-14; David-14; John-14; Nicholas-14; Philip-14; Reuben-14

SHARP – 158, 171

SHARPE – 13

SHATTUCK – 158
Alvin-158

SHAW – 122, 159, 179, 190

SHEARER – 39, 70, 72, 159, 192
Isham-72, 159

SHELBURNE – 159
Silas-159

SHELBY – 180

SHELDON – 141
Isaac-141

SHELLEDY – 148, 159
Mary Jane-148, 159

SHELTON – 133, 159, 193

SHEPARD (Shephard) – 61, 148, 159

SHEPHERD – 159

SHERMAN – 20, 23, 55, 159, 168, 181

SHERRILL – 159

SHIELDS – 81, 105, 109, 142, 160
Wm. C.-160

SHINN – 160

SHIPLETT (Shipley) – 160
David Roland-160; Ephraim-160; Nelson-160

SHIPLEY (Shiplett) – 160

SHIRLEY – 1, 160
John-160; Martha Ellen-160; Thomas-1

SHOCKLEY – 160

SHOOK – 160

SHOOP – 151

SHORT – 160

SHRODE – 174

SHUFORD – 148

SHULTS – 155, 156

SHUMATE – 160
William Riley-160

SIBLEY – 161

SIC – 161, 172

SIKES (Sykes) – 172

SILLIMAN – 161

SILLIVAN – 115

SILVER – 161
Gershom-161; Millicent (Archer)-161

SIMMONS – 72, 73, 115, 161
William-161

SIMPSON – 43, 148, 161, 162, 170
Blanche-162; Rev. John-148, 161, 170

SIMS – 101

SINCLAIR – 12, 162

SINKLER – 162

SINNOT (Synnott) – 162

SIROS/SIROT – 162

SISK – 162

SITTON – 162
Joseph-162

SIVERT – 162
John Frederick-162; Martha Curtis-162

SKAGGS – 164
Nancy Melvina-164

SKEEN – 12, 40, 144, 162, 185

SKELTON – 150, 162

SKENE – 162

SKINNER – 162

SLAUGHTER – 12, 55, 162, 163

SLAVENS (Slavin) – 163
John-163

SLAVIN – 163
John-163

SLAY – 96, 163

SLAYDEN – 181

SLEETH – 163

SMALLEY – 163

SMALLWOOD – 109

SMART – 136

SMILEY – 43

SMITH – 11, 31, 39, 40, 42, 62, 67, 72, 78, 80, 92, 94, 96, 102, 115, 131, 142, 144, 148, 153, 162, 163, 164, 165, 170, 185, 186 Agnes Rust Gordon-153; Craig Woods-62, 164; James-67; John McLaughlin, Sr.-164; John Tyson, Sr.-164; Samuel-163; Silas H.-163; Van Elizabeth Miller-42

SMITHERS – 96, 165, 193

SNEED – 90

SNELLBAKER – 156, 165

SNIFFEN – 165

SNOW – 165

SNOWDEN – 165
William-165

SNYDER – 155

SOLES – 10

SOLBERG – 165

SOMERVILLE (Somervaill, Summerall, Summerell, Summerill, Summerlin, Sumlin, Sumrall, Sumrill) – 165

SOOBY – 165

SOUTH – 165

SOWA – 165

SOWELL – 158, 165, 166
John Alexander-158, 165, 166; Laura Hilton-158, 165, 166

SPALDING – 166
William S., Sr.-166

SPARKS – 166

SPEARS (Spear) – 14, 166

SPEIGHT – 93

SPEIR – 126

SPENCE – 87, 122, 166
David-122, 166; Mary (McElyea)-122, 166

SPENCER – 166

SPIEGELBERG – 166

SPIEGELHAUER – 59

SPILLER – 166
Meredith-166

SPLAWN – 38, 166

SPOONAMORE – 166
Philip, Jr.-166; Philip, Sr.-166

SPOTSWOOD – 72, 73

SPRING (Springs, Springsteen) – 150, 167
John Springs (Springsteen)-167

SPRINGER – 167

SPRINGS – 149, 161, 167, 170
John Springs (Springsteen)-167

SPRINGSTEEN (Springs) – 167, 170
John Springs (Springsteen)-167, 170

SPROUL (Sprouls) – 167
Rachel-167

SPURLOCK – 76

ST. ARNUEF (Arnulf?) – 131

STAB – 192

ST. CLAIR – 162

STAFFORD – 167, 181

STAGER – 167

STALEY – 24, 50, 85

STANDARD – 167

STANFORD – 167
Stephen-167

STANLEY – 167
Sands-167

STANTON – 23, 55, 168
Thomas-168

STAPPERFENNE – 148

STARK – 59, 168
James-168

STARR – 168
Geogian Theus-168; James Penn-168

STEELE – 3, 168
Ada (Hoke)-168; Harry-168

STEGER – 109, 167

STEINBACH – 168

STEINBACH (Steinbaugh) – 168

STELL – 168

STEPHENS – 169
Josiah-169; Robert-169; Sarah Farmer-169

STEPHENSON – 27, 168

STERN (Stearns) – 169

STEVENS – 96, 169
Josiah-169; Robert-169; Sarah Farmer-169; William Giles-169

STEVENSON – 97, 124, 168

STEWART – 30, 55, 160, 169
J. P. "Dick"-169

STIFF – 169

STILLIMAN – 120

STIMSON – 169

STINSON – 132

STOCKTON – 33

STOLL – 169
Andreas-169; John, Sr.-169

STONE – 70, 109, 169, 170
Mary Ann Chunn-169, 170; Mildred Richards-70; Samuel-169

STONEHAM – 170

STOOKEY – 42

STOREY – 170

STORM – 170

STOVALL – 80, 170
Daniel Shaw-170

STOVER – 115, 134, 170
Joseph Martillis-170; Lewis-134

STRAIN – 30

STRAIT – 148, 161, 170

STRANG – 131

STRATTON – 190

STRETCHER – 170

STRIBLING – 39, 70, 79, 170
Joe Elton-79, 170

STRICKLAND – 132, 171

STRIEGLER – 171
Johan Frederick Gottlieb-171

STROCK – 64, 75, 147

STRONG – 54, 138, 171

STROTHER – 171

STROUD – **171**

STROZIER – 45

STUART – 171

STUBBS – 171
John-171

STURDIVANT – 171
Samuel-171

STURGIS – 149

STURTEVANT – 171
Samuel-171

SUMMERALL – 96

SUNDERHAUS – 192

SUTHERLAND – 172

SWANSON – 115

SWAIM – 172

SWANTNER – 161, 172

SWENSEN (Swenson) – 172

SWIFT – 109

SWINFORD – 115

SWING – 172

SWOFFORD – 86, 172
John Franklin-172

SYKES (Sikes) – 172

SYNNOTT – 39, 109, 162

SYPERT – 79

TACKETT (Tacquet, Tackett, Tackitt) – 172

TAILER (Tailers, Taylors) – 173, 175

TALBOT – 1, 18, 45, 173

TALIAFERRO – 173

TALLY – 173

TALMAGE – 14

TANKERSLEY – 55, 173

TANSILL – 173
Edward Albert-173; Piety Thomas-173

TAPLEY – 173
Hosea-173

TARBET (Torbett, Torbet, Torbitt, Torbit) – 173

TARR (De Tar) – 173

TARRANCE – 78

TARRANT – 55, 151

TARTER (Darter, Tarter) – 45, 173

TATE – 80, 173
Van Buren-173

TATOM – 173, 174
Stephen-173, 174

TATTERSHALL – 92

TATUM (Tatham) – 174

TAYLOR – 92, 166, 173, 174, 175
Isaac Anderson-175; James Francis-174; John A.-175; Tarlton Jones-174; Thomas-174

TAYLOR (Tailer) – 175

TEAGUE - 78, 175

TEETERS (Teter) – 175

TEGGE – 175

TERPENING – 175

TERRELL – 11, 33, 175, 176, 183

TERRELL (Tyrell, Terrell, Terrill) – 176

TERRY – 54, 176

TETER – 49

THACKER – 43, 176
Ransom-43

THIEME – 50, 100, 154

THEISS (Theis, Theiss) – 176

THEUS – 168
Georgian-168

THEVENET – 176

THIGPEN – 176

THOMAS – 92, 132, 154, 176, 177
Ezekiel-176; John Myers-177; John Towson-176; Mary Jane Gage Goodhue-176; Thomas-176; Thomas Marion-176

THOMASSON – 15, 149, 177

THOMPSON – 3, 40, 79, 115, 116, 177
James-177; James George-177; John Christopher-177; Mamie Clarice Miller-116

THORNHILL – 177

THORNSBERRY – 177

THORNTON – 120, 177, 178
Isaac-177

THRELKELD – 34
Harriette Pinnell-34

THROCKMORTON – 8

THURBER – 90

TIBBETTS – 178

TILLER – 178

TIMMONS – 178

TIMS – 178
Nathhan-178; William Robert-178

TIPPEN – 37, 48, 64

TIPTON – 178

TITUS – 38, 178

TOBIN – 178
Esther-178; James-178

TODD – 20, 178

TOMLINSON – 179

TOMS – 179

TORBETT (Torbet, Torbitt, Torbit, Tarbet) – 173

TORRENCE – 78

TORREY – 179

TOTTY – 179

TOWELL – 122, 159, 179, 190
Isaac-122, 159, 179, 190

TOWLE – 179
Isaac-179

TOWLES – 179

TOWNLEY – 179
John Luther-179

TOWNSEND – 179

TOZOUR – 180

TRAILL – 187

TRAMMELL – 180
Daniel-180; Elisha-180; Francis-180; Sarah (Shelby)-180

TRAVIS – 180

TRAWICK – 30

TRAYLOR – 180
Ruby (Mrs. John C. Robertson)-180

TRENT – 180

TREYBIG – 180
Lena Marx-180; William Henry-180

TRIMBLE – 180

TRINDLE – 181

TROFAST – 119, 181

TROOPE – 109

TROTTER - 167, 181

TROW – 181
Raymond Bridgman-181

TRUBE – 181

TRUE – 181
Charles-181; Henry-181; Israel Pike-181; Margaret Wade-181

TRUMAN – 76

TRUMBULL – 20, 159, 181

TRUNDLE – 12

TRYGSTAD – 192

TSCHOEPE – 181
Augusta-181; Rudolph-181

TUCKER – 74, 181, 182
Anderton-181; Martha "Mat"-74; Peyton-182; Stacy-181

TUGGLE – 137, 182

TUMLINSONS – 175, 179

TURKNETT – 182

TURNBULL – 101, 182

TURNER – 6, 78, 132, 182, 187
James-182; Mary Ann-6

TURPIN – 182

TYLER – 30

TYNER – 183

TYRRELL (Terrell) – 183

TYSEN – 172

UMBRELL – 151

UNDERWOOD – 183

USENER – 183

UTTER – 14

VADEN – 183

VALLEY – 137
Marie Justine (Pessemier)-137

VALLIANT – 183
Martha Hurlock-183;

VALLIANT (cont.)
Robert Spencer-183; William Taylor-183

VANCIL – 105

VAN CLEVE – 183
Benjamin-183

VANDIVER – 110, 183

VAN HORN – 12

VANN – 184

VANSTON – 182

VAN ZANDT – 184

VARVEL – 23, 56, 90, 155

VAUGH – 151

VAUGHAN – 184
Alfred Jefferson, III-184; Blossom Chapline-184

VAWTER – 184
Albert-184; Josie-1884

VEACHE – 12

VENABLE – 184

VERMILLION – 184

VICK – 184
Joseph-184; Robert-184

VIERTEL – 22

VILLASENOR – 184

VINCENT – 64, 76, 184

VINES – 146

VINSON – 9

VISER – 123
Sarah S.-123

VON ROEDER – 99, 184

VON ROSENBERG – 151

VROOMAN (Vroman) – 38, 184, 185
Hendrick Meese-185; Josiah B.-184

WACKWITZ – 185

WADE (Waid, Waide) – 185

WADSWORTH – 185

WALDRON – 78

WALKER – 40, 72, 144, 162, 185
Elias, Sr.-185; John-185

WALL – 123

WALLACE – 126, 174, 186

WALTERS – 39

WALTHER – 186

WALTON – 112, 186
Elizabeth (Rowe)-186; George-186

WAMPLER – 186

WAPLES – 155

WARD – 49, 186
George W.-186; William A.-186

WARE – 109, 190

WARLICK – 148

WARREN – 101

WARWICK – 186

WASHBURN – 186, 187
Abigail-186; Cephas-186

WASHINGTON – 45, 109, 187

WATERS – 187
William-187

WATHEN – 75

WATKINS – 87

WATSON – 13, 174
Alex-13, 174

WATT – 187
John-187

WATTERS – 187
William-187

WATTERSON – 187

WATTS (Watt) – 187
George-187; John-187

WAUGH – 18

WAYLAND (Whelan) – 189

WEATHERS – 188

WEATHERWAX – 188

WEBB – 115

WEDMORE – 188

WEEKS – 174

WEHRMAN – 148

WEIDLER – 188
Michael-188

WEIK (Wike) – 190
Jacob M.-190

WEIR – 178
Edytha Valette-178

WELCH – 186, 188
Ransom Frank-188; Susan Curtis-188

WELLS – 35, 188

WELSH – 188

WEST – 38, 72, 73, 188
Claiborne Dandridge-188; Eleazer-188; Henry-188

WETHERILL (Wetherall, Weatherall) – 189

WHARTON – 189

WHATLEY – 30, 189

WHEELER – 18, 65, 189

WHELAN (Wayland) – 189

WHELCHEL – 28

WHITAKER – 189

WHITE – 8, 20, 22, 45, 115, 140, 145, 189
Amy-189; Anderson-189; Enoch A.-8, 20; James Taylor-189

WHITESIDES – 190

WITHROW – 9

WHITLEY – 190
John-190; John Saunders-190; Joseph, Sr.-190; Sharp R.-190

WHITTINGTON – 115

WHITWORTH – 122, 159, 179, 190

WICKARD – 190

WIKE (Weik) – 190
Jacob M.-190

WILBANKS – 87

WILBURN – 174, 190

WILDER – 174

WILEY – 190

WILFORD – 174

WILKE – 162

WILKES – 190

WILLE – 16

WILLHIDE – 151

WILLIAMS – 8, 10, 20, 30, 34, 49, 61, 118, 137, 190, 191
Dan Batchelor-191; David Neal-191; Hugh-8; Jim-8, 20; Joanna (Garvin)-191; Pilgrim-190; Maria Aurelia (Mrs. John Herndon James)-191; P. K.-191; Paschal Klough-191; Rose Marie Brown-34; Samuel-190; Stephen-190, 191

WILLIAMSON – 59, 63, 137, 191

WILLIBALD – 156

WILLINGHAM – 8, 20
Dallas P.-8, 20

WILLIS – 174, 191

WILLOUGHBY – 191

WILSON – 39, 43, 70, 78, 187, 191, 192, 193
Hugh-191, 192; Rev. Lewis Feuilleteau, I-192; Robert-39, 70, 192; William-192

WILSON (Willson) – 192
Christopher-192; John Willson-192

WIMBERLY – 93, 143, 193
William-193

WINEGAR (Wininger) – 193

WINFIELD – 96, 165

WINGFIELD – 193

WININGER – 133, 159, 193

WINKLER – 193

WINN (Wynn) – 195

WINSTON – 174

WINTHROP – 84

WISDOM – 193

WISE – 155, 193

WISEMAN – 193
Captain Wiseman-193

WITCHER – 193
Clabourn D.-193; Mary B. Austin-193

WITHERSPOON – 193, 194

WITT – 76, 194
John-194; Paralee-194

WITTY – 7
Kathryn Baker-7

WOLF – 24, 50, 85

WOMACK – 194

WOMBLE – 165

WOOD – 1, 30, 93, 143, 193, 194
Daniel B.-194; Rev. George F.-194; Isaac F.-194; W. D.-194

WOODALL – 194

WOODHEAD – 119

WOODLEY – 178

WOODS – 99, 122, 126

WOODSIDES – 177

WOODSON (Woodsum, Woodsome, Woodsom) – 194
Joseph-194

WOODWARD – 8, 20, 30, 186, 195
Abigail-186; Dr. Franklin Columbus-195

WOOLSEY – 35, 138, 195

WOOLUM – 176

WORD – 64

WORKMAN – 149

WRIGHT – 42, 195
J. P. "Dick"-195

WROE – 195
William-195

WULLENJOHN – 72

WYATT – 51

WYLIE – 97, 161

WYNN (Winn) – 195

WYNNE – 133

YANCEY – 195
Elizabeth B. (Goode)-195; Jackson M.-195

YARBOROUGH – 138, 196
Charles Richard-196

YATES – 2, 196
William-196

YODER – 12

YORSTOWN – 31
Carthew-31

YOUNG – 8, 20, 109, 125, 190, 196
William, Sr.-196

YOUNGBLOOD – 152, 196
Benjamin-196; Henry-196; John Pearl-196; Matilda Elias (Norwood)-196; Sarah (Harvey)-196; Susannah (Collins)-196

YOUNSE – 62, 196

YOUNT (Younses) – 196

YURATICH – 16

ZAHN – 30

ZIELSTRA – 151

ZEITLER – 82, 125, 196

ZUBER – 196
   W. P.-196

ZUEHL – 197
   Carl C.-197; Marie Wrede-197

Other Heritage Books by Lu Verne V. Hall:

Delaware Bible Records, Volume 6

New England Family Histories and Genealogies: State of Massachusetts

Other Heritage Books by Lu Verne V. Hall and Donald O. Virdin:

Delaware Bible Records, Volume 5

New England Family Histories and Genealogies: Miscellaneous New England States

New England Family Histories and Genealogies: States of Maine and Rhode Island

New England Family Histories and Genealogies: States of New Hampshire and Vermont

New England Family Histories: State of Connecticut

Texas Family Histories and Genealogies

Other Heritage Books by Donald O. Virdin:

Civil War Correspondence of Judge Thomas Goldsborough Odell

Colonial Delaware Wills and Estates to 1800: An Index

Delaware Bible Records, Volume 2

Delaware Bible Records, Volume 3

Major General Alfred Thomas Archimedes Torbert: Delaware's Most Famous Civil War Hero

Maryland and Delaware Genealogies and Family Histories

Pennsylvania Genealogies and Family Histories: A Bibliography of Books about Pennsylvania Families

Some Pioneer Delaware Families

The Virdins of Delaware and Related Families

Virginia Genealogies and Family Histories: A Bibliography of Books about Virginia Families

Other Heritage Books by Donald O. Virdin and Donald M. Hehir:

CD: Delaware Bible Records, Volumes 1-4

www.ingramcontent.com/pod-product-compliance
Lightning Source LLC
Chambersburg PA
CBHW070935230426
43666CB00011B/2443